It's Time For the Truth!

The JFK Cover-up:
The *Real* Crime of the Century

Charles E. Hurlburt

Copyright 2012 Charles E. Hurlburt

All rights reserved

ISBN 978-1480107267

To Ruth; my wonderful, faithful and understanding wife, who put up with all those hours devoted to researching, writing, editing and formatting. I could not have done it without you.

Table of Contents

Chapter	Page
Introduction	7
1. November 22, 1963: The Basic Facts	19
2. The Autopsy	33
3. The Non-Investigation	53
4. A Fork In The Road	73
5. Cuba—Rosetta Stone to the Assassination	97
6. Who Was Lee Harvey Oswald?	113
7. Jack Ruby—Screwball Or Mob Pawn?	137
8. The Case Against Oswald	159
9. The Enigma of Dealey Plaza	171
10. Conclusions	209
11. The Cover-Up: Villains and Heroes	251
12. Keeping the Lid On	275
Epilog	283
Bibliography	309
…….Sources	315
…….Index	351

Sources by Chapter

Introduction Source List	315
Chapter One Source List	315
Chapter Two Source List	318
Chapter Three Source List	319
Chapter Four Source :List	321
Chapter Five Source List	321
Chapter Six Source List	325
Chapter Seven Source List	328
Chapter Eight Source List	333
Chapter Nine Source List	334
Chapter Ten Source List	336
Chapter Eleven Source List	345
Chapter Twelve Source List	347
Epilog Source List	350

Illustrations

Figure		Page
1	Autopsy "Stare-of-Death" photo	36
2	Kilduff at press conference	41
3	Autopsy X-ray, side view	44
4	Autopsy photo, back of head	45
5	Low head entrance "explained"	46
6	FBI's location of entrance wounds	47
7	Zapruder frames 312-313	48
8	Autopsy photo, back of head side view	49
9	Backyard photos of Oswald	124
10	Oswald Faces	130
11	Bullet hole in jacket	174
12	Bullet hole in shirt	175
13	Autopsy photo, back wound	176
14	Autopsy "face sheet"	177
15	Drawings of wound locations	178
16	CE 399 and other comparison bullets	179
17	View from street to TSBD window	184
18	View from the "sniper's nest"	186
19	Overview of 7-shot-trajectory theory	192
20	Stretcher Bullet?	194
21	Front view of shirt, slits	203
22	The base of CE 399	207

23	Path of bullet/s through two men	213
24	Zapruder frame 230	215
25	Overview, TSBD lunchroom/staircase	219
26	Overview of Tippit shooting area	224
27	Triple Underpass from the west	235
28	Drawings of head wound	240
29	Mary Moorman photo	244
30	Connally's jacket	287

INTRODUCTION
Innocence Lost

I was in the computer room starting up a program when one of my fellow programmers burst through the door to announce; "The President's just been shot in Texas! They think he may be dead!" At first I thought he must be trying to pull one of his famous pranks, but then I noticed the stunned expression on his face and the moisture in his eyes and I knew he was serious. A lump formed in my throat and I thought, "Oh no! Here we go again; another international crisis."

Like most people who were born in the first half of the 20th century, I vividly remember where I was and what I was doing when I heard the shocking news that President Kennedy had been shot. At that time, I was a thirty-one-year-old computer programmer working at Itek Corporation in Bedford, Massachusetts. Itek is located just a mile or so from Hanscom Air Force Base, which at that time was considered one of the most important military bases on the east coast, if not in the entire nation. Barely a year before, we had all lived through the most terrifying confrontation in the history of the world, the Cuban missile crisis, which came within an eye blink of erupting into nuclear war. It was an especially tense few days for us at Itek, working so close to one of the most strategically important targets in the event of a nuclear missile exchange. I was not the only employee who had worked through those nerve-wracking hours with an ear glued to the radio and ready to make a mad dash for the car at the first indication that hostilities were imminent. But just when war seemed to be inevitable, Kennedy and Khrushchev struck a back-channel deal; the removal of the missiles from Cuba in exchange for Kennedy's promise never to allow a repeat of the previous year's abortive Bay of Pigs attempt to invade Castro's island fortress, just ninety miles off our shore. Many of those who knew about the deal thought it was an act of appeasement by Kennedy, but America and the world breathed a huge sigh of relief that nuclear war had been averted and we went back to concentrating on our work. Now, only thirteen months later, we became alarmed again over the news that the President had been killed while riding in a motorcade through Dallas. Many thought that Cuba or the Soviet Union must have been behind the assassination and, if so, it could bring us once again to the brink of war. It would not occur to many at that time that Kennedy's promise never to allow another invasion attempt, rather than his stand against Khrushchev, may have been a major factor in his death.

Early Acceptance

Like most Americans, I accepted the official findings of the prestigious President's Commission, chaired by Supreme Court Chief Justice Earl Warren. The Warren Report was published in September, 1964. It confirmed the conclusions of the Dallas Police and the FBI that Lee Harvey Oswald was the assassin of JFK and that he had acted alone. Although I shared the prevailing skepticism about the way Oswald was himself killed by Jack Ruby (having been one of millions who watched it happen live on television), there seemed to be no compelling reason to disbelieve what the authorities were telling us. The evidence seemed conclusive.

A rifle had been found on the sixth floor of the Texas School Book Depository Building where Oswald worked, which was soon established by the police to have been obtained by him through a mail-order catalog. Three cartridge casings had been found near the easternmost sixth floor window from which several witnesses said shots were fired, and these casings were connected to Oswald's rifle. When Dallas Police Officer J. D. Tippit was shot to death in the Oak Cliff suburb of Dallas less than forty-five minutes after the President was killed, police converged on that area and were soon tipped off that a suspicious looking person had been seen sneaking into the Texas Theater without buying a ticket.

When Oswald was apprehended in the theater he was carrying a revolver with which he briefly tried to resist arrest. This revolver was mail-ordered by Oswald, apparently around the same time as the rifle found on the sixth floor. The cartridge casings found on the scene of the Tippit shooting were said to have been fired from Oswald's revolver. Several eyewitnesses identified Oswald in police lineups as the man they saw fleeing the scene of the policeman's shooting. All the evidence seemed to point in only one direction; that Oswald was the killer of both Officer Tippit and President Kennedy.

The Awakening

But some were unconvinced by the highly publicized evidence and did their own investigating. Books critical of the official verdict soon began appearing. In 1966, out of mild curiosity, I read *Rush to Judgment* by Mark Lane. From that moment on, I became a serious student of what came to be known as "the crime of the century" and I joined the ranks of what the "establishment" likes to refer to as "conspiracy buffs".

One did not have to accept every word that Lane wrote to see that there was a lot more to this case than the public had been told. By then I had left Itek and was working at MIT in Cambridge, Massachusetts and had access to their libraries. It was in one of these libraries that I discovered Edward J. Epstein's book, *Inquest*. This book not only reinforced points made by Lane, but also examined in great depth the inner workings of the Warren Commission. Epstein had originally intended his work to be a master's thesis on the operation of a governmental investigatory body. He did not start out to write an exposé. Therefore, the Commission's lawyers were quite cooperative with him, granting him frank interviews that they never would have granted to a conspiracy theorist like Lane. Epstein's revelations into the mind-set and approach of the commissioners and their staff convinced me beyond all doubt of one startling fact: that the conclusions as to Oswald's lone guilt were reached without proper and adequate investigation, and that the authorities, from the Dallas Police to the White House, were more interested in wrapping up the case of JFK's death in a neatly completed package than they were in discovering the facts.

I soon discovered that the Warren Report and the accompanying twenty-six volumes of "supporting" evidence and testimony were also in the MIT library. Following *Inquest* I started in on the Warren

Report itself. As I read the Report I constantly referenced the appropriate volume to see how the "supporting" testimony matched what was being said in the Report. I also checked what Lane and Epstein had claimed about the testimony in their analysis. Although I found a few cases of what might be considered biased selectivity in their quotes from the Report, I never found a case of outright misquoting. On the other hand, I did find *numerous* cases, many of them pointed out in Lane's and Epstein's books, where the Report completely misrepresented or misinterpreted the testimony and/or evidence detailed in the twenty-six volumes. Some of the most shocking examples were found in the testimony of the doctors who attended President Kennedy and Governor Connally (who was also wounded during the assassination) at Parkland Hospital as they described the wounds, and in the findings of the Bethesda doctors during and immediately after the President's autopsy.

What was equally as disturbing as the many discrepancies between the content of the Report and the content of the "supporting" volumes, was the *omission* of so many facts from the Report that, had they been included, would have shed a lot more doubt on the official verdict. For example, Commander Humes, the senior of the three autopsy doctors and supposedly in charge of the proceedings, testified to the commission as follows:

In the privacy of my own home, early in the morning of November 24th [two days after the autopsy] I made a draft of this report which I later revised. *That draft I personally burned in the fireplace of my recreation room.* The report which we have submitted represents our thinking within 24-48 hours of the death of the President, all facts taken into account of the situation. [Emphasis added]

This startling testimony was never mentioned in the report itself, but was buried among the twenty-six volumes of testimony and exhibits.[1] Humes later explained his action by saying there were blood stains on his note papers, making them too gory to keep on file.

The Quest

Always intrigued by mysteries and puzzles, I found that the more I read about the JFK assassination, the more puzzling and intriguing it became. A great deal of physical evidence seemed to contradict other evidence and didn't fit into the official version of events, nor did all the evidence fit into any alternative scenarios offered by the critics of the Warren Report. From 1966 until 1980, I read every book and magazine article that I could find on the subject of the JFK assassination, eventually compiling three large scrapbooks and an extensive library in the process.

In 1976, after both Robert Kennedy and Martin Luther King had been gunned down by assassins' bullets, the Senate Select Committee on Intelligence Activities uncovered the fact that there had been plots against Cuban dictator Fidel Castro conducted by certain US intelligence (CIA) agents working with high-ranking members of organized crime. This information was not made available to the Warren Commission during its investigation, in spite of the presence on that commission of former CIA Director Allen Dulles, who was well aware of these plots against Castro. This new information, together with pressure from the family and friends of Dr. King, helped to persuade Congress to appoint the House Select Committee on Assassinations (HSCA) to reopen the Kennedy and King assassination cases. Like all the critics of the Warren Report, I was elated that perhaps we would finally learn the truth, although it was the opinion of most critics that they should have also included the Robert Kennedy case in their new investigation.

A long and frustrating two years later, the HSCA reached the conclusion that there had *indeed* been a conspiracy involved in the deaths of *both* Kennedy and King. In the case of the JFK killing, this conclusion was reached only at the very end of their investigation and only because of the discovery of a tape recording of the shots being fired in Dealey Plaza. This recording was through a police dictabelt tape made via the microphone of one of the motorcycle officers riding to the rear of Kennedy's limousine. The mike was stuck in the ON position for several minutes through the crucial time period. It was examined by acoustical experts at Bolt, Beranek and Newman in Cambridge, Massachusetts, the same firm who analyzed the famous "gap" in one of the Nixon tapes during the Watergate investigation. Their work was then expanded through further analysis by Professor Mark Weiss of Queens College of New York after a detailed reconstruction of the shots in Dallas. They testified to the HSCA that there was a 95+ percent chance that *at least* four shots were fired rather than three, and that the third shot came from the area of the so-called "grassy knoll."[2] This tape will be discussed in more detail in later chapters. After appearing to be heading toward the same conclusions as the Warren Commission, the House Select Committee, at the eleventh hour, was convinced by the Dallas Police tape that there had indeed been, in all likelihood, a conspiracy in the JFK case. They still insisted that there was no evidence that anyone other than Oswald had scored hits in Dealey Plaza that day, but at least they had taken a major step in the right direction.

During this period, I was able to obtain my own "bootleg" copy of the now famous Zapruder home movie film and a set of slides showing various pieces of evidence, such as Warren Commission exhibit 399, the famous "magic bullet." After the HSCA's report was published, *Gallery Magazine* produced and distributed a plastic recording of the Dallas police tape that contained the enhanced sounds of the four shots that convinced the members of the HSCA that there had indeed been a second gunman. I copied this recording onto a cassette tape and used it, synchronized with the Zapruder film, as the centerpiece for several lectures on the topic that I gave to high school students, teachers and people where I worked.

It was on this same plastic record that another "buff", a rock drummer named Steve Barber, noticed voices and the sound of a bell. He pointed out these sounds to the authorities, who had the sounds analyzed by the National Academy of Sciences in 1982. They used the time-frame of the sounds on the tape to assert that it could not have been recorded at the time of the assassination and thereby disputed the validity of the HSCA's conclusion that the tape revealed shots at all, let alone one from the knoll, thus putting the HSCA conclusion of conspiracy in dispute.

By then it had become clear that the HSCA's recommendation, that the US Justice Department should follow leads that the committee had provided, was never going to be acted upon.[3] The subject was fading from everyone's mind, except for a few die-hard researchers who had both the determination and the financial resources to continue their pursuit of the truth. Not being in the position to join their ranks, I moved the issue to the back burner for the next ten years.

The Re-awakening

When Oliver Stone's movie *JFK* came out in December of 1991, I assumed it would be received about as well as its predecessor, *Executive Action* (a box-office dud). I was afraid it would do nothing more than provide ammunition to the Warren Report supporters, who were still prevalent and prominent in the main-stream media. I was elated to find that I was wrong. Stone's movie was not only much better in every way than *Executive Action*, it was a smash hit, nominated for the Academy Award for Best Picture with Stone nominated for Best Director; this in spite of the tidal wave of indignant panning of the movie by the major media, which began even before it was released. Suddenly the controversy surrounding the Kennedy assassination was alive and well again. Demands began to grow for the release of all governmental files on the case, most of which had been "sealed" until well into the 21st century. Meanwhile, the establishment media continued to ridicule Stone and the rest of the "conspiracy buffs" and to prop up the Warren Report.[4] By the term "establishment media", I mean the Columbia Broadcasting System (CBS), newspapers like the *New York Times* and the *Washington Post*, and the *Time/Life* conglomerate, operated until 1964 by Henry and Claire Booth Luce and their many followers. The Luces were active in supporting efforts to overthrow Fidel Castro, and Mrs. Luce did her best to promote the idea that Oswald had been recruited by Castro to kill Kennedy. She told investigators employed by the HSCA about a call from her friend William Pawley shortly after the Bay of Pigs invasion failed. Pawley had been one of the founders of the Flying Tigers in pre-WW2 days and later became a CIA operative active in the anti-Castro movement in Miami. He told Luce that he was involved in a plan to use a small fleet of boats to launch raids against Cuba. Luce claimed she also received a call on the evening of the assassination from one of the Cubans who went on anti-Castro boat raids with Pawley. Mrs. Luce said she "was given the impression by both callers that Oswald had been hired by Castro to kill JFK." Her story could not be confirmed, however, because Pawley died in a highly suspicious "suicide" in January of 1977 and the Cuban was never located.[5]

Critics of the Warren Report's version of the events in Dallas have long suspected that the Luces were responsible for suppressing for several years the Zapruder movie film of the assassination after it was purchased by *LIFE Magazine*, and that they did so because they knew this film, by itself, destroys the "lone-assassin" theory.[6]

My dormant fascination with this case was revived when I viewed Stone's movie the first day that it was released. In spite of taking a few artistic liberties with the facts, it was quite well done. The main area in which criticism of this movie may be justly leveled is in Stone's and Kevin Costner's portrayal of New Orleans District Attorney Jim Garrison, who was not the selfless crusader portrayed in the movie. It also sometimes presented too blurry a distinction between fact and supposition. It did, however, accurately portray most of the indications of conspiracy that the authorities overlooked or ignored and the critics had been pointing out for years.

Throughout 1992 and 1993 there was a resurgence of interest in the assassination of President Kennedy, caused first by the popularity of Stone's *JFK* and followed by the thirtieth anniversary of the historic event. Yet, a disturbingly large percentage of the American public still did not appreciate what all the controversy was about or the seriousness of the implications. Even for those whose interest was piqued by Stone's movie, the degree of that interest was generally at the level one might hold for any other famous murder case. This was especially true for those too young to remember much, if anything, of that era. It is important to understand, however, *why* a handful of researchers became immersed in this case almost to the point of obsession; one reason for this book. Stone's *JFK* inspired me to do what I had been thinking about for years and start writing a book of my own. It has been a work in progress ever since. With President Kennedy's death now a half-century behind us, why do we need another book about it? Because there are a dwindling few who watched the events surrounding JFK's death unfold and who have studied the case in depth, because most Americans today were too young to know or remember anything about it unless they have studied the case, and because nearly all of the previous books on the subject focused on one or two aspects of the case, such as the photographic or medical or testimonial evidence. My goal is to provide an overview of all aspects of this very epochal and controversial event in our history, and to summarize previously uncovered facts brought to light by many independent researches over the years since 1963. With the fiftieth anniversary approaching it seems like a good time to introduce it, especially for those young enough to regard this case as "ancient history." Not only does the JFK assassination have all the elements of the most cleverly contrived murder mystery (with the added punch of being fact, not fiction), it is also an event that changed the history of the world and is felt by many to have been the day that America lost its innocence. For sheer magnitude of historical impact, it ranks with the assassinations of Abraham Lincoln and Julius Caesar. The events that took place in Dallas on that weekend in November of 1963 left behind some of the most baffling and intriguing mysteries in the history of crime. But what also compels the continued determination of so many independent researchers is the fact that scores of people who were witnesses to, or in some way involved with, one or more of the aspects in this historical trilogy of murders (President Kennedy, Tippit, Oswald) have themselves met with suspicious deaths (see chapter titled "Keeping the Lid On"). Coupled with the destruction, distortion or suppression of the most crucial evidence in the case, much of which could prove whether or not the official verdict against Oswald as the "lone assassin" was correct, we have what is obviously a systematic attempt to cover up the truth of what happened that day in Dallas.

Much of the public was justifiably incensed over our government's having locked up almost all relevant files and evidence for either 75 years (Warren Commission) or 50 years (HSCA), but few were aware that the US Navy ordered everyone who was present at the autopsy of the President to keep silent about what they saw or heard that evening, under penalty of court martial. This, added to the evidence contained in the small number of autopsy photos and X-rays that have come to light after long governmental suppression, evidence showing strong indications of having been doctored, cannot help but point to a case of fraud and deception at the highest levels of our governmental agencies. Many people involved are now dead, some by natural causes, many by violence, so we will probably never unravel the details nor know the names of the conspirators. For years I had faith that researchers would some day discover the names of those behind Kennedy's death. After all this time, that faith has all but vanished. But we may yet learn the major players in the cover-up that followed and their motives.

Progress?

As things stood when I began this book in mid-1992, I would have had to live to be one hundred and seven years old to see any of the files on the case released. Without Stone's movie and the resulting public pressure to convince the U.S. Congress to pass a resolution to open the classified Warren Commission, House Committee, CIA and FBI files on the assassination, these files were destined to remain sealed from researchers until the year 2029 (HSCA) or 2039 (Warren Report). By that time everyone responsible for the murder of John F. Kennedy and everyone who played a role in the original investigation will be dead (most already are). But, thanks in large part to Stone's *JFK*, legislation was passed by the U.S. Congress that prompted the release of most of these files, once they were reviewed and screened by a specially selected panel. On October 27th, 1992, exactly one week before the national election, President H. W. Bush signed the Assassinations Records Collection Act into law. Notably exempt from this release, however, were the all-important autopsy photos and X-rays. Throughout 1993 researchers waited anxiously for President Clinton to appoint a committee to screen and approve the release of the various groups of files. In spite of his delay in naming this panel, in late August of 1993 the first of these files began to escape from the locked rooms of the National Archives. With no review panel yet in place, the CIA released about *ten percent* of what it had on Lee Harvey Oswald and other related assassination materials. Periodically, additional releases were made, but much of the text had been heavily censored.

Finally, in April of 1994, the Assassination Records Review Board was completed and allocated a meager budget with which to hire the staff that was to collect and review files. Two years later, Warren Report critics were still waiting for the "smoking gun" to appear. There were a few very interesting tidbits of minor embarrassment to the FBI and CIA, but it was not surprising, in view of all the redactions, that no highly significant information could be found.

Meanwhile, the government's apologists branded (and continue to brand) everyone who has the audacity to question the official version of things, or the way in which those conclusions were reached, as "nuts", "scavengers", or "weirdoes". How can any US citizen remain blasé about the possibility that elements within our own government helped replace our President, and then perpetrated the most blatant cover-up to hide the truth? And even more importantly, how can the US press and other news media, whose job it is to expose wrong-doing at all levels (as they did so admirably in the Watergate affair), continue year after year to assist in that cover-up by being nothing more than apologists for a government that continues, administration after administration, to foist its grand deception on the American People?

Wild, baseless accusations you say? I challenge the reader to peruse this work with an open mind and then ask himself how wild and baseless they are. If nothing else, I promise you will at least come away with a better understanding of what the furor has been about over the past several decades.

It is important as you read my work, that you have a clear understanding of how much is fact and how much is conjecture on the part of the author or other writers. So let me point out from the outset the following: **A**–The motive for JFK's murder described in chapter five, though based on the multitude of facts presented in the chapter, is a theoretical conclusion reached by the author and many of the serious and knowledgeable critics of the official findings; **B**–The author's version of the shot sequence in chapter nine is obviously conjecture based on interpretation of the available evidence; **C**–The conclusions and names mentioned in chapter ten are educated guesses based on probability and are not outright accusations; **D**–Unproven theories of other authors and researchers will be identified as such; **E**–The occasional deduction of the author from the previously stated facts will be indicated in italics. Other than these areas, the information provided in this book is factual.

I have also made the individual chapters each focus on their own aspect of the case, meaning that they can be read out of sequence if you wish without losing much of the overall view. For this reason you may notice some key points repeated occasionally.

I am often asked what is new in my book that hasn't been brought out yet. I want to state up front that there are no new revelations in this book. My purpose has been to gather together most of the important evidence, testimony, theories and counter-theories that have been building for the past five decades of which most of the general public are not aware. In doing so, I have attempted to present this information in a more organized and understandable way than has been done before, while making a last-ditch attempt to arouse enough interest to prompt a new look at the case. I welcome any comments, pro or con about my work. My email address is: charliehcg@gmail.com.

There have been at least a hundred books written on the subject of President Kennedy's assassination, many of them still available. But if you want a book that was written by someone who has lived through the entire event and its aftermath, and one that provides you with the essential facts of each major aspect of the case without overwhelming you with minutiae, this book is for you. I would not have had the courage to write this book during the first couple of decades following JFK's murder when only a very few brave souls were willing to point an accusing finger at their own government. It is to those intrepid truth-seekers that this book is dedicated.

Chapter 1

NOVEMBER 22, 1963: THE BASIC FACTS
Another "Date That Will Live in Infamy"

Jack Kennedy had barely eked out a win in the conservative state of Texas in the Presidential election of 1960, even with the popular Texas Senator, Lyndon B. Johnson, running with him. Kennedy had selected Johnson as his running mate to help secure that state, knowing that Texas would be vital to winning the election over then Vice-President Richard Nixon. It would be no less vital to his re-election in 1964, but political in-fighting between Texas Senator Ralph Yarborough on one side and Governor John Connally and Vice-President Johnson on the other was creating potentially serious dissension in the ranks of the Texas Democratic Party, which the Kennedy/Johnson ticket could ill-afford. The President was persuaded that a "fence-mending" trip to Texas was necessary to pull the party back together and ensure carrying the state in 1964.[1]

Texas at that time was rife with ultra-right-wing groups, such as the John Birch Society, the Ku Klux Klan and the Minutemen, who despised the policies of the comparatively liberal President. Many members of the various police forces in the state, including several in the Dallas Police Department, belonged to one or more of these radical groups.[2] An atmosphere of hate and intolerance pervaded the region, as evidenced by an incident in which UN Ambassador Adlai Stevenson had been spat upon and struck with a placard by demonstrators just a month prior to JFK's visit.[3] On the morning of the President's arrival in Dallas, a virulently anti-Kennedy ad was printed in the *Dallas Morning News* and a handbill in the form of a "wanted" poster was distributed along the parade route, claiming that Kennedy was "Wanted For Treason."[4]

Some of the President's closest advisors urged him not to make the trip, especially after the FBI learned of a plot to kill him in Miami just four days earlier. Police informant William Somersett managed to secretly record right-wing extremist Joseph Milteer as Milteer described how a plot was in the works to kill JFK from an office building using a high-powered rifle, and that a patsy would be arrested to "throw the public off." This caused the planned motorcade through that city to be cancelled.[5]

There had also been a scheduled visit to Chicago by the President on November second, which was cancelled at the last minute because of two separate threats that were discovered in the days immediately preceding that date. One of the Secret Service agents who knew about these threats complained to his superiors that the service's reaction to these threats was shoddy and incomplete. He was Abraham Bolden, the first African American to be assigned the White House protective detail. Soon after his unwelcome criticism he was falsely accused of accepting bribes and served thirty-nine months in jail before being released when his accuser recanted. He has since received several awards for his achievements since that black period of his life.

But Kennedy was determined not to allow threats to control his movements. The Texas plans remained in place. Before reaching Dallas, the Presidential party made a brief stop-over in Fort Worth on November 21st. They spent the night there and JFK gave a breakfast address before boarding Air Force One for the short hop to Love Field in Dallas. The plane arrived at 11:37 AM. President and Mrs. Kennedy spent a few minutes greeting a crowd of admirers, who were being held in check by a chain-link fence. This type of spontaneity was fairly commonplace with President Kennedy, and always caused apprehension among the Secret Servicemen assigned to protect him.

The motorcade finally got under way between 11:45 and 11:50 AM.[6] It had been estimated that the trip to the Trade Mart in the Dallas Market Center, where the President was to give his next address, would take thirty-eight minutes. The Trade Mart was on the outskirts and on the other side of town. A map of the route through the city, published in the morning's newspaper, showed the entourage following a nearly straight path along Lemmon Avenue, Turtle Creek Boulevard, Cedarspring Avenue, Harwood Street, and then turning right onto Main at the City Hall. It would then, according to the map, continue on Main all the way to the freeway entrance, which would lead it to The Trade Mart.[7]

The ride through the city took longer than expected because of the large and enthusiastic crowds that greeted the President along the route. At 12:30 PM, five minutes behind schedule, the lead car carrying Police Chief Jesse Curry, Sheriff Bill Decker and two Secret Service agents reached the intersection of Houston and Main Streets at the end of the downtown area. Here, instead of continuing down Main, as indicated on the map, where it could have proceeded at an increased pace and been farther away from any buildings with open windows, it turned right onto Houston Street for about fifty yards, passing on its right the Criminal Courts Building, situated on the southeast corner of Houston and Elm. It then took a sharp left onto Elm Street, directly in front of a seven story brick edifice known as the Texas School Book Depository (TSBD). Elm, Main and Commerce Streets begin to converge at this point as they all approach a triple underpass beneath a railroad bridge located about two hundred yards west of Houston Street. The area between the bridge and Houston Street had been made into a little grassy, park-like triangle and was locally known as Dealey Plaza, after George Bannerman Dealey, a Dallas civic leader and founder of the *Dallas Morning News*.[8]

On the northeast corner of Houston and Elm sat the eight-story Dal-Tex building which housed several manufacturing firms. On the fourth floor, one of these firms produced ladies garments and was owned by Dallas businessman Abraham Zapruder. Mr. Zapruder had purchased a new Bell & Howell 8mm movie camera only the day before but had decided to leave it home that morning because the weather looked too rainy for a good photo opportunity when the motorcade came by. But when the skies cleared by mid-morning, he decided to go home and get his camera. By 12:25 he and his secretary, Marilyn Sitzman were standing atop a concrete pedestal that was part of a decorative structure known locally as the pergola, located just beyond the book depository building on the north side of Elm. Marilyn steadied her boss as they waited for the presidential motorcade to pass before them.

To negotiate the 120 degree turn from Houston onto Elm, the motorcade, particularly the oversized Presidential limousine, had to slow down to about ten to twelve miles per hour. As it passed the Book Depository and approached the pergola, situated atop a slight grassy rise to the vehicle's right, and before the President's vehicle began to pick up speed, a series of gunshots rang out. Kennedy, who was seated in the back to the right of his wife Jackie, was hit at least twice. Governor Connally, who was sitting directly in front of him, was also hit. A bystander named James Tague, standing beside the bridge support near Commerce Street, was struck on the cheek by a fragment of curbstone thrown up by a bullet or fragment thereof. Secret Service agent Greer, who was behind the wheel of the limo, almost came to a stop at the sound of the first shot, perhaps fearing that the shooter might be up ahead and they were riding into an ambush.[9] The brake lights can be seen lit up in some of the movies taken by bystanders. Then a final burst of gunfire struck the President in the head, showering the occupants of the vehicle and motorcycle officer Bobby Hargis riding directly behind and to the left of the limo with blood and brain tissue. The officer thought, from the amount and direction of the debris, that the shot came from the top of the knoll to the right front of the automobile.[10] Kennedy was thrown backward and to his left into his wife's arms. Mrs. Kennedy immediately climbed over the back of her seat onto the rear of the car, apparently in an attempt to retrieve a piece of her husband's skull that was now perched precariously on the trunk.[11] As she did so, Secret Service agent Clint Hill ran up from the follow-up car and climbed aboard the back of the limo. As Mrs. Kennedy slid back into the seat, Hill grabbed onto a rail just as Greer finally accelerated and sped through the underpass and onto the Freeway, with Hill spread-eagled over the trunk and holding on for his life. But now they were on their way to Parkland Hospital instead of the Trade Mart. The trip took six minutes.

Reactions

Abraham Zapruder, though shocked and stunned by the gunfire and the sight of Kennedy's head exploding, somehow managed to continue filming throughout the sequence until the limo disappeared under the triple underpass. He then dismounted from the pedestal and went to find someone to whom to turn his film over. The history of that film has been confused and hazy, but it was somehow turned over to the Secret Service who made copies. Within twenty-four hours of the assassination, *LIFE Magazine*, a subdivision of Time, Inc., had purchased the original from Zapruder for a total, paid over several years, of $150,000. A copy was given to the FBI with which to conduct its investigation, but *LIFE* would refuse to allow the film to be seen by any except a select few (such as Dan Rather, a prominent TV commentator who was in Dallas covering the presidential visit for CBS) for years to come.

Although it was obvious at a glance that the head wound was fatal, several doctors and nurses at Parkland Hospital worked feverishly to sustain the President's life. A tracheotomy was performed by Dr. Malcolm Perry, who made the incision horizontally through the center of a very small wound in the victim's throat, just below the Adam's Apple.[12] But all efforts failed and John Fitzgerald Kennedy was pronounced dead at 1:00 PM, Dallas time. There was an impromptu news conference held at the hospital in which Presidential Press Secretary Malcolm Kilduff told reporters that the President was dead as a result of a "gunshot to the right temple."[13] Dr. Perry who, in performing the tracheotomy had the best look at the small wound in the throat, said that the bullet had entered the front of the neck and had come out the back of the head. He was later persuaded to say that it could have been either an entrance or an exit.[14] *None* of the Parkland doctors had observed any evidence that Kennedy had been shot from behind. They saw a large exit wound where the entrance wound was later reported found by the Bethesda doctors.[15] Governor Connally had been hit in the back by a bullet that passed through his chest, breaking a rib in the process. He had also suffered a fractured wrist bone, caused by a missile that passed through the wrist from back to front, and a small puncture wound in his left thigh. His vital organs had been spared by the bullet as it passed through his torso and the doctors were able to treat him successfully. In time, he would fully recover.

As soon as the President was declared dead, a heated argument arose between the local authorities, led by Dallas County Medical Examiner, Dr. Earl Rose, and the Secret Service agents who insisted that the body, along with Mrs. Kennedy and Vice-President Johnson, be flown immediately back to Washington. This was contrary to Texas law, which specifies that in any homicide occurring in that state, an autopsy is to be performed in the district in which it occurred. Dr. Rose was forcibly overruled[16] and as soon as a casket was delivered by a local funeral home, the body was placed inside, wrapped in sheets and towels and a plastic bed liner to protect the inside of the casket.[17] It was then driven to Love Field and loaded onto Air Force One for the sad journey back to Washington. Around the time the casket was leaving Parkland, a hospital orderly named Darrell Tomlinson moved a gurney (wheeled stretcher) from in front of a men's room door. When the gurney bumped the wall a whole bullet rolled out from under the edge of the mat. Tomlinson turned the missile over to the director of hospital security, O. P. Wright, who gave it to Secret Service agent Richard Johnsen. This bullet would later become the source of immense controversy. Whether this bullet was actually the one later known as Commission Exhibit 399 is open to question. [18]

Meanwhile, back in Dealey Plaza, there was mass confusion in the first few minutes after the shots as to their source. Many bystanders and police officers had the impression that at least one of the shots had come from a tree-lined wooden fence atop the rise that was just down the street from the Book Depository.[19] Several people ran in that direction and Police Officer Joseph Smith encountered a man behind the fence who showed him Secret Service identification. It was later discovered that all SS men had gone with the motorcade to the hospital. Constable Weitzman also claimed to have encountered SS men.[20] Some witnesses said they thought the shots had come from an upper floor of the Book Depository building. The police soon concentrated their efforts on that building, and in a few minutes found three empty cartridge casings on the floor under the partially open easternmost window on the sixth floor. One of the three shells had a mysterious dent in the lip. It could not have held a bullet in that condition.[21] A long, brown paper bag was also found near that area, which was the right size to have contained a disassembled rifle. A more thorough search was conducted among the many stacks of book cartons on the floor and turned up a rifle with a telescopic sight. It was found near the northwest staircase, diagonally opposite the apparent sniper's nest, and had been wedged between two stacks of cartons in such a way as to be barely visible without moving some of the boxes. It was obviously hidden with time consuming care, not tossed quickly into a pile of boxes.[22]

At 12:44 PM the following broadcast went out over police radio channel 1:

Attention all squads. The suspect in the shooting at Elm and Houston is reported to be an unknown white male, approximately thirty, slender build, height five feet six, weight one hundred sixty five pounds, reported to be armed with a thirty caliber rifle; no further description or information at this time.

No definitive source or explanation for this description was ever produced. One suggested source was TSBD superintendent Truly (when he noticed employee Lee Oswald missing). But if that were true, the description would have included his name. The other source suggested is eyewitness Howard Brennan, but he gave his description quite a bit later than 12:44. It only vaguely matches that of Oswald, who was twenty-four, not thirty, five feet nine or eleven inches tall—not five feet six (see Chapter 6 for a discussion of some mysterious height variances), and weighed 150 pounds—not 165[23]

The Tippit Shooting

Sometime between 1:05 and 1:15 PM, Officer J. D. Tippit was patrolling a suburban area of Dallas called Oak Cliff, south of the center of town, when he spotted a young white male walking along 10th Street. According to the authorities' star witness to the shooting, Helen Markham, the officer pulled up alongside the walker, a few feet past the corner of Patton Street, and the young man stopped and spoke with the officer briefly through the passenger side window. Then Tippit got out of the car and started to walk around to the front, as though to confront the suspect. As he reached the left front fender, the man pulled a gun out of his belt and fired four shots into the officer, killing him instantly. The assailant then hurried across the front yard of the house on the corner and fled down Patton Street. Several eyewitnesses were in the area. Three or four saw the actual shooting and several others saw a man walking rapidly away with a gun in his hand. The Commission's main witnesses were Helen Markham and William Scoggins. Other witnesses, such as Acquilla Clemons and Mr. and Mrs. F. Wright, saw it quite differently.[24] One of the witnesses, Domingo Benavides, attempted to use the police radio in Tippit's car to inform the dispatcher of the shooting. However, Benavides didn't know how to operate the radio, so T. F. Bowley, who happened on the scene a few seconds too late to see the shooting or anyone fleeing, took the radio and alerted the station to what had occurred. This call was placed at 1:16 PM. The exact time of this call is of utmost importance in determining if Oswald could have been the killer.[25] Soon, additional police arrived on the scene and, after questioning some of the witnesses, a description of the suspect was broadcast. The height was changed to five feet eleven inches, the weight remained at 165 and the characteristics, "black wavy hair and fair complexion", were added; still not a very accurate description of Oswald. At least two witnesses later described Tippit's assailant as "short, stocky with bushy hair" (included Helen Markham, the Commission's star witness).[26] At 1:40 PM someone made the following statement over police radio channel 2:

Shells at the scene indicate the suspect is armed with an automatic .38 rather than a pistol.

There were numerous problems with the shells, including loss of the chain of evidence[27] At 1:45, the radio log shows the following:

Have information the suspect just went into the Texas Theater on West Jefferson, supposed to be hiding in the balcony.[28]

Oswald's Arrest

A nearby shoe store employee named Brewer had spotted a suspicious looking man outside his store and observed him enter the theater without paying. He alerted the ticket salesgirl who phoned the police. The origin of "hiding in the balcony" remains unexplained. Several squads of police converged on the theater, which contained only a dozen or so patrons watching an old war movie. Police Officer M. N. McDonald said that he entered the darkened theater through a side or back door and stopped to question a man sitting near the front. This man told him that the one he wanted was seated in the third row from the back.[29] McDonald then approached a man sitting alone in that row. As he got close, Lee Oswald rose and, allegedly, took a punch at McDonald, pulling a revolver from under his shirt as he did so. A scuffle ensued in which both Oswald and McDonald suffered some facial scratches as McDonald grabbed the gun and prevented it from firing, although the hammer allegedly struck the cartridge in the chamber hard enough to leave a slight impression in it. Other officers quickly came to McDonald's assistance and Oswald was disarmed, handcuffed and rushed out past a screaming crowd, which had mysteriously materialized outside the theater, to a waiting squad car that brought him downtown to the police station. Then began a long, confused afternoon and evening of intense interrogation of the prisoner. The police were joined by representatives from the Secret Service and the Federal Bureau of Investigation. Identification cards were found in Oswald's wallet, some of which gave his real name and some of which bore the name Alek James Hidell. This was later determined to be an alias under which he ordered both a Mannlicher Carcano rifle (allegedly the one found on the sixth floor of the building where he worked) and the revolver he was carrying when he was arrested.[30]

It was soon established that Oswald's wife was living in the Dallas suburb of Irving with a woman named Ruth Paine. The Paine household and garage were searched and yielded a wide assortment of politically oriented literature, pamphlets, photographs and photographic equipment. A diary describing Oswald's sojourn to Russia was also found.

Around 7:00 PM that evening the Dallas Police felt that they had sufficient evidence to charge Oswald with the slaying of Officer Tippit, and he was arraigned for that crime. By 1:30 AM on Saturday morning he had also been arraigned for the murder of John F. Kennedy.[31] Meanwhile, he was exposed several times to the questions of a multitude of reporters, and calmly denied knowing anything about the reasons for his arrest.

On Friday evening an autopsy was performed on the body of the late President at Bethesda Naval Hospital in Maryland. The autopsy report would state that Kennedy had been struck by two bullets fired from above and behind him—contrary to the conclusions of everyone in Dallas who had observed the shots or had seen the wounds.

Throughout the day on Saturday, the 23rd, the grilling of Oswald continued. The police allowed him to make a couple of phone calls but he failed to reach the lawyer he had hoped to obtain to represent him. In one of the frenetic "press conferences" in the hallway of the police station, conducted as Oswald was led from one room to another, he asked for "...someone to come forward and give me legal assistance." He continued to refuse to answer questions while protesting his innocence in both crimes. In response to a reporter's question he shouted, "I'm just a patsy."[32]

At the insistence of the FBI, much of the evidence was surrendered to their agents by the police, and a mammoth investigation by the Bureau was launched. On several occasions between Friday evening and Saturday evening, witnesses to the Tippit shooting and to Oswald's alleged movements right after the assassination were shown police line-ups containing Oswald. A few made a "positive identification", but there have been many questions raised as to the propriety of the line-ups and the interpretation of the witnesses' responses. There was no effort made by the police to see that Oswald was among others of similar general appearance. He would have stood out like a "sore thumb."[33] Only one eyewitness at the assassination scene claimed to have actually seen a man fire from the sixth floor window of the Texas School Book Depository. Howard Brennan, a steamfitter who had taken a few minutes off from his job to watch the motorcade from a point directly across from the TSBD, was asked to view a line-up on Friday evening but, to the deep disappointment of the police, he could not make a positive ID of Oswald as the man he saw in the sixth floor window, about 120 feet away.

The hope that anyone could have positively identified a particular person from that distance, even with good eyesight (which Brennan admitted he did not have), indicates the desperation of the police to get an ID.[34]

Oswald's Murder

As a shocked nation watched the funeral arrangements for their fallen leader, the police prepared to transfer Oswald to the County Jail on Sunday morning. At 2:15 AM, Sheriff's Officer Perry McCoy received an anonymous phone call from a man who warned that if the transfer took place as planned, Oswald would be killed.[35] Earlier on Saturday evening, Dallas Police Officer Billy Grammer claims to have received a similar phone call. But the plan was not changed and, in spite of supposedly intensified security in and around the building, a local night-club owner, police buff and small-time hoodlum named Jack Ruby somehow managed to enter the basement a few moments before Oswald was brought downstairs to be placed into the transfer vehicle. As the prisoner was being led from the elevator to the waiting car, Ruby stepped out from behind Officer William Harrison and fired one bullet, point blank, into Oswald's abdomen.[36] Ruby was immediately subdued, disarmed and locked up. Officer Grammer, who had received one of the threatening phone calls, seeing the familiar face of Jack Ruby being led away, suddenly realized that the voice he had heard on the phone the previous evening was in all likelihood that of Mr. Ruby.[37] Oswald was given artificial respiration, which only served to aggravate his stomach wound and ensure his demise, before he was rushed to Parkland Hospital where he soon died of internal injuries. Thus did Lee Harvey Oswald achieve the dubious distinction of becoming the first person in history to be murdered on nation-wide television.

The Warren Commission is Born

Ruby's murder of Oswald in the basement of the police station aroused everyone's suspicions that it was done to silence Oswald and prevent him from naming fellow conspirators. The whole country was in a turmoil of both grief and anger. Rumors began to fly that the Russians or the Cubans were involved, especially after it became public knowledge that Oswald was a former defector to the USSR. In response, Waggoner Carr, the Attorney General of the state of Texas, set out to form a Texas Court of Inquiry to look into the matter.[38] Several congressmen and senators began demanding a congressional investigation. President Lyndon B. Johnson, however, decided that what was needed was a special "blue-ribbon" panel, composed of some of the country's most esteemed personages, who could convince the public that their inquiry was beyond reproach. His choice to head up this panel was the then Chief Justice of the Supreme Court, Earl Warren. Warren was regarded as a progressive whose court decisions were much too liberal for conservative groups like the John Birch Society. They had billboards scattered across the nation calling for Warren's impeachment[39], but the majority of Americans held him in high esteem. Warren was reluctant at first to accept this unenviable task, perhaps sensing what lay ahead, but LBJ was a master arm-twister and Warren could find no way to refuse the assignment. Six other men from various areas of government were selected to serve with Warren on the new President's Commission on the Assassination of John F. Kennedy. The Warren Commission began its meetings in December of 1963. It hired a staff of lawyers to examine evidence and interview witnesses. It relied heavily upon evidence supplied to it by the FBI, including a second level copy of the FBI's copy of the Zapruder movie, which now had become the single most controversial if not the most important piece of evidence in the case. The commission published its report in September of 1964, after what was characterized as "one of the most complete and extensive investigations in history." It concluded that Lee Harvey Oswald was the lone assassin of President Kennedy. It found "no evidence" of any conspiracy involved in his death, or in the shooting of Oswald by Jack Ruby. Marina Oswald, who had married Lee during a period when he had defected to Russia in 1959-1962, became a "guest" of the authorities, particularly the FBI, immediately after the assassination. She remained so for the next several months as they continually grilled her about her husband's background, habits and activities leading up to the assassination. Lee's mother, Marguerite, was also placed in protective custody[40] The Warren Commission relied heavily upon the testimony of Marina in reaching their conclusions about her husband's personality, movements and political philosophies. Marina at first protested that her husband was innocent and had, in fact, greatly admired Kennedy, but later gradually began to change her story in several important respects as repeated threats of deportation back to Russia took their toll. One of the best illustrations of this can be found in two quotes attributed to Marina on the subject of her husband's opportunities to practice with his rifle. Quoted in an interview with the FBI on 12/3/63:

Marina said she had never seen Oswald practice with his rifle or any other firearm and he had never told her that he was going to practice.

Testifying before the Warren Commission on 2/3/64:

Rankin: Did you learn at any time that he had been practicing with the rifle?

Marina: I think he went once or twice. I didn't actually see him take the rifle, but I knew he was practicing.

Rankin: Could you give us a little help on how you knew?

Marina: Lee told me. And he would mention it in passing he would say, 'Well, today I will take the rifle along for practice.'[41]

The Warren Commission Report was accepted with high praise, especially by the news media, who were greatly impressed with the sheer volume of it (the report was well over 800 pages and some of the 26 accompanying volumes were even larger). Tensions eased and fears of a new confrontation with our communist adversaries abated. But there was a small nucleus of die-hard skeptics who were not satisfied that all the nagging questions had been answered by the Warren Report. Books and magazine articles began to appear, which pointed out discrepancies between the conclusions reached by the Commission and the published testimony and evidence. Gradually, public confidence in the official verdict eroded, fueled, at least for a time, by the investigation of New Orleans District Attorney Jim Garrison, who prosecuted prominent New Orleans businessman Clay Shaw as a conspirator in the assassination in 1969. When Garrison's case against Shaw failed miserably, it was a major set-back for all critics of the Warren Report.

The Second Look

On April 4th, 1968, Dr. Martin Luther King was shot and killed in Memphis, Tenn. The authorities tracked down and arrested James Earl Ray, who was coerced by his lawyer into pleading guilty to the crime and sentenced to life in prison. In spite of Ray's subsequent claim of innocence, the official judgment was that he acted alone in killing Dr. King.

On June 5th, 1968, Robert Kennedy was also gunned down and killed in a hotel pantry in California, having just made a victory speech in celebration of winning the California presidential primary in his bid for the White House. The official verdict was that Sirhan Sirhan was the lone assassin, in spite of numerous questions about the number of shots fired exceeding the capacity of Sirhan's gun, and about the angle and close proximity of the entrance wounds in RFK's head and body. The "lone nut", "no conspiracy" war cry of the governmental agencies was starting to wear a little thin.

These events, followed a few years later by the Watergate scandal and the first resignation of a US President, exacerbated the old questions and doubts about the assassination of President Kennedy. When a Senate committee headed by Senator Frank Church, was established in 1976 to look into alleged abuses of power among our intelligence agencies, it uncovered the startling story of CIA/Mafia collusion in plots to assassinate Cuban leader Fidel Castro. This information was not provided to the Warren Commission, even though one of its members, Allen Dulles, had been the Director of the CIA at the time these anti-Castro plots were hatched. Mr. Dulles chose not to share this important fact with his fellow commissioners. This revelation, along with pressure by Martin Luther King's widow and the Congressional Black Caucus to reopen the case of the King murder, persuaded the US Congress to launch a new investigation into both the MLK and JFK assassinations.

In 1977, The House Select Committee on Assassinations was formed. Over the next year and a half (most of which was wasted with political in-fighting) the HSCA re-examined the evidence, re-interviewed many of the witnesses, and interviewed some for the first time. Then, in 1979 it issued its report, which found that both Reverend King and President Kennedy had probably been victims of conspiracies. In the Kennedy case, they concluded that the most likely responsible parties were certain Mafia chieftains, i.e. Carlos Marcello of Louisiana and/or Santos Trafficante Jr. of Florida. As the Committee disbanded, it made detailed recommendations for further investigation of both cases to the US Department of Justice, but no action on those recommendations was ever taken.

Chapter 2
THE AUTOPSY
Three Blind Mice

While the Dallas Police and the FBI were in the initial stages of their investigation of the suspect apprehended in the Texas Theater on the afternoon of November 22, another crucial stage in the inquiry into the assassination of the President was taking place that evening as his autopsy was conducted at Bethesda Naval Hospital in Maryland. From start to finish (and beyond), the autopsy of our thirty-fifth President was literally riddled with controversy, contradiction, unconventional procedure, deception and falsification. It has been criticized by experts in forensics as one of the sloppiest, most incomplete and most inconclusive autopsies in medical history. The very fact that there was an autopsy performed was kept from the press and the public for days. As the years went by, more and more startling information about what took place was brought forth as people who participated in it, or were on hand in some capacity, spoke out about what they observed. Ironically, the autopsy that would be performed in Texas on Oswald, the accused assassin, was professionally and competently executed and recorded, in marked and obvious contrast to that of the President he was alleged to have slain.

For openers, according to law, the President's autopsy should *also* have been done in Texas where the death occurred. In the face of strong protests by Dallas County officials, the body was removed at virtual gunpoint by Secret Service agents, taken to Love Field and flown back to Washington.[1] Given the choice of Walter Reed Army Hospital or Bethesda Naval Hospital, it made perfect sense to bring the body to Bethesda, since Kennedy was a former Navy man. What did *not* make sense was the choice of surgeons to perform the most important autopsy of the twentieth century. Commander James Humes, Doctor J. Thornton Boswell and Colonel Pierre Finck may have been competent doctors, but of the three only Finck had any appreciable experience with gunshot wound cases, which is why he was a late addition to the team requested by Humes.² By the time Finck arrived, the autopsy team had already taken X-rays of all parts of the body except the extremities. At his insistence they then proceeded to X-ray those areas as well.³ Ironically, it is these very additional X-rays that were among the missing five years later when Attorney General Ramsey Clark convened a panel of forensic experts to examine the X-rays and photographs in an effort to quell the rising tide of criticism of the Warren Report and to undermine the Garrison investigation.⁴

The choice of non-forensic people who happened to be military men seemed highly suspicious from the beginning, and became immeasurably more so when the Clay Shaw trial elicited the revelation by Colonel Finck that the three doctors were under severe limitations as to what they could and could not do in examining the body. Col. Finck, testifying during the trial of Clay Shaw:

Question: Why did you not dissect the track of the bullet wound which you have described today and you saw at the time of the autopsy at the time you examined the body? Why?

Col. Finck: As I recall I was told not to, but I don't remember by whom.

At least some of these limitations were apparently imposed by Dr. George Burkley (Admiral, US Navy and Kennedy's personal physician) and other unidentified top-ranking military people watching the proceedings.⁵ In Burkley's case, he was probably trying to keep the public from learning about Kennedy's Addison's disease, a handicap that had, up to that time, been successfully suppressed. But one wonders about the motives of the other "brass" in that room.

One of the most important results of the restrictions upon the three surgeons was the failure to dissect tissues to detect any possible path through the body (or even into the chest cavity) for the bullet that entered the back. The back wound seemed to mystify the three doctors as they tried unsuccessfully to probe it. This is made quite clear by the FBI Summary Report dated 12/9/63, which states: "Medical examination of the President's body revealed that one of the bullets entered just below his shoulder to the right of the spinal column at an angle of 45 to 60 degrees downward, there was no point of exit, and that the bullet was not in the body."[6]

The report later goes on to quote Col. Finck during performance of the autopsy: "There are no lanes for an outlet of this entry in this man's shoulder."

The now famous "single bullet theory" is based on the assumption, made *after* the autopsy was completed and the body was in Washington, that the bullet that entered JFK's back transited the neck and came out through the tiny wound the Dallas doctors had noted in the front of the throat. No forensic expert would have given serious consideration to the throat exit idea after being told the dimensions of the throat wound (two thirds the size of the entrance wound in the back). It is common knowledge, especially among doctors, that missiles traversing a body make larger holes on the way out than on the way in.

It is of great significance that this throat transit assumption was not reached *during* the autopsy, because the doctors who were performing it did not even know about the wound in the front of JFK's throat. It had been obscured by the tracheotomy incision made by Dr. Perry at Parkland Hospital that afternoon while performing his tracheostomy. (The word "tracheostomy" refers to the procedure designed to insert a long-term breathing tube, while "tracheotomy" refers to the temporary, emergency incision in the throat and trachea.) A tracheotomy incision made by any competent doctor is a small, neat, often vertical slit at the windpipe, not the large, gaping, ragged, horizontal wound shown in one of the autopsy photos (See Figure 1, below)

Figure 1

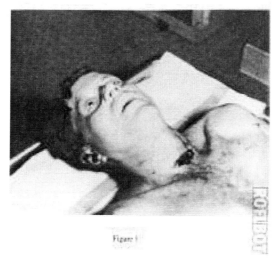

Figure 1

It was not until the following morning, after the body was no longer available for examination, that Dr. Humes spoke on the phone with Dr. Perry and learned of this small "puncture" wound in the throat. After learning belatedly of this throat wound, Humes then referred to it in his report as the "wound presumably of exit."[7] In spite of it's small size, Humes seized upon this wound as a means of explaining why no bullet had been found for the back wound; it must have gone through and exited the throat.

It has struck several researchers as quite strange that Humes and the others were not made aware of the wound in the throat by the President's personal physician, Dr. George Burkley, who was present at Parkland in Dallas and who must have known of its presence.

The "no bullet found" story is contradicted by X-ray technician Jerrol Custer, who described to researchers Harrison Livingstone and William Law the discovery of a whole though mutilated bullet that rolled out of the sheet wrappings when Kennedy's back was lifted off the autopsy table. Custer described this as a bullet that had "mushroomed" at one end from striking something hard. He is supported by James Jenkins, assistant to Dr. J. Boswell.[8] This may be the missile that caused the shallow back wound after being deformed and slowed down by passing first through Kennedy's back brace (see shot-by-shot analysis in Chapter 9). In addition to the "mutilated bullet", Admiral David Osborne stated that there was a completely intact bullet that he claims fell out of the President's wrappings when he was removed from the casket. Osborne told author David Lifton that he held the "reasonably clean, unmarred" bullet in his hand.[9] He is supported by the existence of an FBI receipt for "...a missle [sic] removed by Commander James J. Humes", which has been discovered among the files in the archives. It was dated 11/22/63 and addressed to Capt. J. H. Stover, Jr., Commanding Officer, US Naval Medical School[10] Neither of these missiles were even mentioned in the Warren Report, much less given an exhibit number.

The neck transit assumption, lacking any physical evidence to support it and contradicted both by the relative size and the relative location of the wounds, was later expanded by Arlen Specter, Warren Commission staffer (who later became a U.S. Senator), into the conclusion that this same bullet went on to inflict all of Governor Connally's wounds. Connally, who was riding in the jump seat directly in front of the President, was struck in the back by a bullet that transited his chest, cracking a rib. According to Specter's theory, it exited the chest, went on through his right wrist, and ended up in his left thigh, where it was later (supposedly) found on a stretcher by a Parkland Hospital orderly and became Warren Commission Exhibit 399. This conclusion became one of the most controversial elements of the government's findings in this case. Even the commissioners themselves had trouble with it, as evidenced by this exchange during one of their earliest meetings:

Lee Rankin, Chief Council for the Warren Commission, on 1/27/64:

We have an explanation there in the autopsy that probably a fragment came out the front of the neck, but with the elevation the shot must have come from, and the angle, it seems quite apparent now, since we have the picture of where the bullet entered in the back, that the bullet entered below the shoulder blade to the right of the backbone, which is below the place where the picture shows the bullet came out in the neckband of the shirt in front, and the bullet, according to the autopsy, didn't strike any bone at all...so how could it turn and...

Rep. Boggs: I thought I read that the bullet just went in a finger's length.

Rankin: That's what they first said. They reached in and they could feel where it came, it didn't go any further than that, about part of a finger or something, we have to go into considerable items and try to find out how they could reconstruct that when they first said that they couldn't even feel the path beyond the part of a finger. And then how could it become elevated; even so it raised rather than coming out at a sharp angle that it entered. So the basic problem, what kind of a wound is it in the front of the neck is of great importance to the investigation.

Could there be any more devastating blow to the "single bullet theory" than this admission by the very commission that invented it?

The Pre-autopsy Autopsy

The Warren Commission's above described dilemma was far from the only controversy to be produced by the autopsy. Of utmost interest and importance is the question, raised by David Lifton in his book, *Best Evidence*, of whether JFK's body was surgically "doctored" at some point, such as Walter Reed Army Hospital, before the official autopsy began. Lifton discovered that documents had been found in the LBJ library that contain transcripts of communications between Air Force One and Walter Reed discussing arrangements to have the body taken there after arrival at Andrews.[11] As bizarre as this may sound there are several strong indications that something along these lines may indeed have taken place at Bethesda, if not Walter Reed.

Lifton is a physics engineer who once worked on the Apollo space program. He first became aware of the body alteration possibility when he discovered a hitherto unnoticed section in the report submitted by FBI agents James Sibert and Francis O'Neill, who were observing the autopsy proceedings and taking notes. In their report the agents stated that Humes vocally observed, as he began to examine the body, that there appeared to have been "surgery of the head area, namely in the top of the head." In interviews, the agents said that their use of this phrase was a direct quote from Commander Humes as he examined the body.[12] Since none of the Dallas doctors had touched the head, where did this "surgery" come from, Lifton wondered? He spent years pursuing this question, interviewing many of the people who were involved in the autopsy or the transport of the body from Parkland to Bethesda. During the course of his investigation he found many disturbing allegations made by those who were assisting in some way in the morgue during the autopsy. Lifton finally concluded that the evidence indicates that Kennedy's body was either secretly removed from the unobserved far side of the plane after it landed at Andrew's Air Force Base, or was somehow transferred to Air Force 2 before returning to Washington. This would mean an empty casket was being off-loaded in public view at Andrews. The body was then secretly flown by helicopter to Walter Reed Hospital, so the theory goes, where a pre-autopsy exam was performed to locate and remove bullets. In this process the brain was removed, examined and replaced in the skull before the body was transported by a black "decoy" ambulance, to the back entrance.

Lending support to this outlandish sounding theory are some of the aides at Bethesda, who have told interviewers (Lifton and others) that the brain stem was already surgically severed when the body was received, and that the brain literally fell out into Dr. Humes hands when he went to remove it. Humes conjectured that the "rupture" had been caused by the bullet, but the morgue technicians said it looked like it had been surgically cut.[13] James Jenkins, Dr. Boswell's assistant, said that there were small serrated saw cuts in the skull bone, which served to enlarge the massive defect in the right rear of the head, and that no craniotomy was required to remove the brain.[14]

One of the most disturbing mysteries surrounding the president's brain is the official autopsy weight, which was recorded as 1500 grams. An average adult brain weighs 1300-1400 grams.

When you consider that the least brain tissue reported missing from JFK's head, by the various people who saw it, was about one third of the total brain, one wonders what brain they were weighing to arrive at a figure of 1500.[15]

Some of the morgue aides said that the body arrived in a zippered body bag inside a plain, cheap shipping casket, which came in via the rear entrance, several minutes *before* the Navy ambulance bearing the ornate casket and Mrs. Kennedy arrived at the front. Paul

O'Connor, James Jenkins, Dennis David and Floyd Reibe all told researchers David Lifton and William Law (in widely separate interviews) about both the casket and the body bag. A funeral home document states, "Body removed from metal shipping casket."[16] X-ray technician Jerrol Custer, swears that he saw Jackie arriving at the front entrance as he was on his way to get the first batch of Kennedy's autopsy X-rays developed. Chief-of-the-Day Dennis David told author William Law that he witnessed much the same sequence.[17] However, the autopsy doctors themselves and other aides dispute these claims. In fact, there are so many conflicting statements, opinions and recollections that one begins to wonder if all these people witnessed the same event.

Adding to this mystery is the fact that there was another body in another casket in the anteroom just outside the main morgue during these proceedings. The corpse of an Air Force Major had arrived about an hour before Kennedy's body. What is most intriguing about this body is that the two enlisted men whose duties included logging and tagging new arrivals at the morgue both claim that they were told by their superiors, in no uncertain terms, *not* to log, tag or store this body in the locker (contrary to usual procedure). James Jenkins and Paul O'Connor were normally in charge of logging all newly arriving bodies but were told to ignore this casket. It remained in the anti-room throughout the autopsy on JFK.[18]

Destruction of Evidence

According to the X-ray technicians and photographers who took pictures during the autopsy, there were dozens of photos and X-rays taken through every stage of the procedure. Unfortunately, only a handful seems to have survived. According to one source involved in the autopsy, the Secret Service has since burned most of the photos and X-rays taken that night. According to Mark Crouch, his close friend in the Secret Service, James K. Fox, told him about the removal from SS Chief Bouck's safe and burning of many of the photos and X rays on the night of Dec. 6 or 7, 1963, two weeks after the autopsy.[19] Apparently, they didn't do a thorough job because in 1978, during the House Select Committee's investigation, Secret Service agent Regis Blahut snuck into his chief's office and opened the safe containing the remaining photos and X-rays. He started to remove at least one of the controversial photos before someone approaching scared him off. The hastily dropped photo was noticed and Blahut's fingerprints were found on it. He later admitted to the act, but said it was done out of innocent curiosity. The safe had apparently been left closed but unlocked by Chief Bouck.[20] Combine this with the fact that Humes burned his "rough draft notes" in his fireplace the morning after the autopsy, and then add the fact that the brain itself, along with a package of tissue slides, are *still* among the missing exhibits, and a pattern begins to emerge that should be obvious to even the casual observer. This startling mystery of the missing brain came to light when a forensic expert was granted permission to view the autopsy materials and asked to examine the brain. The foot locker containing the brain and tissue slides was last known to be in the possession of Robert Kennedy.[21]

One of the several motives for withholding the photos may be that they could show an entrance wound in the right temporal region, which could not have come from a bullet fired from the TSBD building. The fatal head shot (or one of them) striking this general area was indicated, even before the autopsy by several eyewitnesses both inside and outside the motorcade, who made statements to that effect immediately after the assassination. This included white house press secretary Malcolm Kilduff at Parkland Hospital as he announced that the president was dead, "from a shot to the right temple." (Figure 2.)

Malcolm Kilduff at Parkland press conference

Figure 2

Years later, autopsy technicians Dennis David, James Jenkins and Jerrol Custer all told researcher William Law that they observed an entrance wound in that area.[22]

The autopsy photos and X-rays have been provided a special status unique in the annals of crime investigation. Rather than the usual strict chain-of-evidence rules being followed there was a bizarre and suspicious series of transfers of possession. They seem to have been passed from the Navy (whose personnel performed the autopsy) to the Secret Service and from there to the FBI. Then somehow they were deemed the property of the Kennedy family, although they never actually entered the hands of any family member or representative. This purely paper transfer allowed the family then to issue a "Deed of Gift" of these materials to the National Archives in October of 1966, with an attached proviso of limited access granted only through the family representative Burke Marshall. This, our government claims, exempts these materials from both the Freedom of Information Act and the Assassination Records Collection Act.

In spite of all efforts to contain them, some of the photos and X-rays have leaked out to the public. One such leak was through a former Secret Service agent named James Fox. He retired not long after the assassination but not before his boss had "allowed him" to make a copy of several of the photos. Fox later turned his copies over to a friend, Mark Crouch, who has since allowed selected researchers to reproduce them in their books. Another leak came when photographic expert and long-time Warren Report critic Robert Groden was hired by the House Select Committee on Assassinations to analyze all the film involved in the JFK case. Groden claims that he was allowed to make copies and thus acquired the X-rays and colored autopsy photos (the Fox set was in black and white). These too have now been published in at least two books authored or co-authored by Groden.

A few government-selected forensic pathologists who have been allowed to review the photos and X-rays held by the archives have "confirmed the authenticity" of both the published and unpublished photos, in spite of the fact that those photos and X-rays that have surfaced contain the most blatant contradictions imaginable. For example, the X-ray of the side view of the head, which was examined by the House Committee in 1978 and published in several books since then, shows the entire bone structure in the right front of the face, including the right eye-socket, to be *missing*. This condition is completely contradicted by all the photos which show the face to be intact and undamaged, and by all the medical personnel in both hospitals (See Figure 3 below). *As outrageous as this fact is, no explanation for it has yet been offered!*

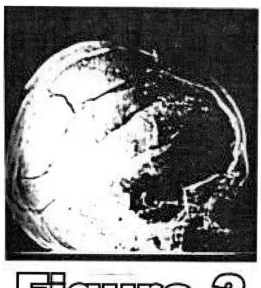

Figure 3

Roaming Wounds

Further evidence of doctoring can be found in the photos of the back of the head. In 1968, a special panel of forensic experts was convened by then Attorney General Ramsey Clark to examine these photos and X-rays. This panel was made up of forensic experts who all had ties to the CIA and were motivated to conform to the official autopsy report. Never-the-less, they concluded that the photos show that the entrance wound was near the top of the skull, four inches higher than the autopsy doctors had placed it. (See Figure 4 below)

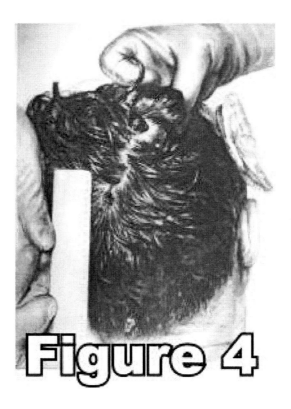

Figure 4

The Clark panel discovered that the autopsy doctors had made a mistake and located the hole four inches lower than it actually was. The doctors have never agreed with this finding.[23] How is it possible for experienced doctors (even if not forensic experts) to make a mistake of this magnitude? To make that wound consistent with a downward angle it was moved up, in spite of the doctors' placement (See Figure 5-top below),

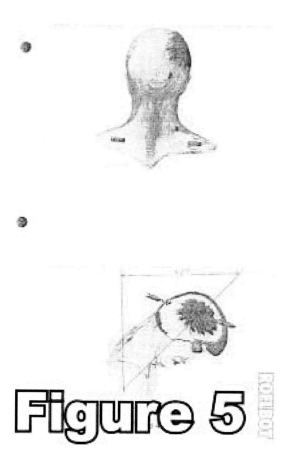

The FBI re-enacted the position of the two victims in the limo with white dots indicating where the doctors said the bullets entered (See Figure 6 below).

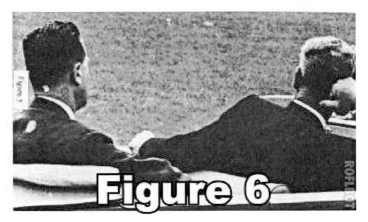

Figure 6

They realized that, given the angle of declination from "Oswald's" window, the low back wound would *not* have exited from the throat and the low head wound *would* have exited from the throat–not the top of the head. Their first explanation for the low head entry to a top-of-the-head exit was to depict the President's head tipped forward at a forty-five degree angle (Figure 5 bottom). But Zapruder frames 312-313 show JFK's head inclined forward no more than about 12-15 degrees (Figure 7 below), thus necessitating the relocation of the head entry wound up to the cowlick area.

It's Time For the Truth!

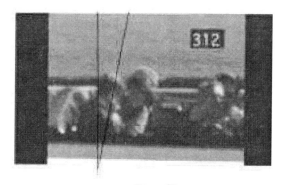

Figure 7

But the most alarming problem here is that these photos show no large defect whatever in the rear of the head, where every doctor at Parkland Hospital and every morgue assistant who saw the body said there was one. They all described the large gaping wound in the back of the head as a wound of exit.[24] This defect should appear in the very spot where the photo now displays the small "entry wound" (See Figure 4 on page 45). For a more detailed discussion of the differing descriptions of the location of the head wounds Google *Doug Horne JFK autopsy*, where Horne, a key member of the Assassination Records Review Board, presents his very interesting findings.

David Lifton's theory of body and casket shuffling as described in Best Evidence *would require the skill and planning of Houdini, plus a lot of luck, to avoid detection. It is difficult to conceive of how it actually happened, but somehow something had to have been done to the President's body before Humes and company got their hands on it. How else can one explain the brain stem being severed and no craniotomy required to remove it?*

The photographs of the back of the head that hide the large exit wound in the occiput can be explained by a reconstruction of the skull done by the Gawler's Funeral Home morticians after the autopsy was over. This is readily apparent when one compares Figure 4, page 45, with the gory side view shown in Figure 8 below, which bears no resemblance to the view of the neatly combed back of the head.

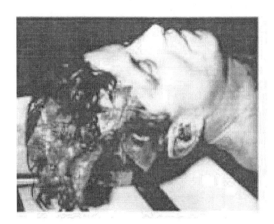

This could have been done between midnight and 5:00 AM to "make the body ready for viewing."²⁵ Skull fragments were pieced together like a jigsaw puzzle, Plaster-of-Paris was used, and the scalp, with hair washed and combed, was pulled over the devastated area. If touching up of the photos was done, it was to show an entrance wound in the cowlick area that may or may not have existed.

It is infuriating that evidence can be so obviously and blatantly tampered with, manufactured, destroyed or withheld, and still fail to raise more than the protestations of a handful of dedicated researchers, whom the news media still refuse to take seriously.

The Ensuing Controversy

In 1992, in response to the furor raised by Oliver Stone's *JFK*, Drs. Humes and Boswell, backed up a couple of months later by Finck, came out semi-publicly via two very unscientific articles published in the prestigious *Journal of the American Medical Association* (JAMA) with their reaffirmation of the essential findings of the Warren Commission–that JFK was struck by only two bullets from above and behind.²⁶ One of these bullets, they claim, hit him in the back of the head and the other was the one that entered the upper back, came out his throat and went on to cause all of Connally's wounds. So there we were, being asked once again to swallow the "single bullet" or "magic bullet" theory! This closed interview conducted by a concurring interviewer instead of in a give-and-take news conference, did nothing to inspire confidence in the doctors and their objectivity or motivation. It seemed to be more an attempt to defend their performance at the President's autopsy, than any real defense of the findings of the Warren Commission.

The media ignored the fact that, even if what the doctors said could be proven beyond doubt, it would in no way erase the multitude of other evidence pointing to more than one gunman. The one-sided and unprofessional presentation did not escape the notice of quite a few fellow doctors, however. Several MD's and PHD's wrote very scholarly letters to the editor of JAMA voicing rather indignant criticism, not only for Humes and company's specious arguments, but for the *Journal*'s having tarnished its reputation as a scientific publication by printing what amounted to a lawyer's brief.²⁷

The overall conduct of the autopsy, together with the suppression of and falsification of the photos, X-rays, Zapruder film frames, etc., is a clear indication that only high ranking conspirators could perpetrate a cover-up of this magnitude.

Is it any wonder that the Justice Department ignored the recommendations of the House Select Committee on Assassinations and made every effort to forestall passage of the bill to release all the files on this case?

The controversy over the Presidential post-mortem can best be summarized through the following list of contradictory statements by those who were on the scene.

1. The brain **was/was not** severed from the brain stem when the body arrived at the morgue at Bethesda

2. The cerebellum (in the lower rear part of the brain) **was/was not** severely damaged.

3. The body **did/did not** arrive in a plain, cheap shipping casket.

4. The body arrived in a: **plain black ambulance at the back entrance/grey navy ambulance at the front entrance**.

5. The body was enclosed in **sheets/a body bag**.

6. There **were/were not** terry cloth towels wrapped around the head

7. There **was/was not** previous "surgery of the head area at the top of the head".

8. The spinal cord **was/was not** removed.[28]

9. A mutilated bullet **did/did not** fall out when the back was raised.

10. The incision in the throat **was/was not** enlarged between Dallas and Bethesda.

11. The bullet entry wound in the back of the head was: **at the edge of the hair-line/four inches higher in the cowlick/not there at all**.

12. Their **was/was not** a small entrance wound in the right temple or just back of the right eye.

It's Time For the Truth!

Add to this list the fact that the photos are not consistent with the X-rays, or even with each other. Neither agrees with the medical personnel's observations. Major portions of several books on this case have been devoted to covering the many discrepancies and contradictions in the medical evidence (the little we have been allowed to see). One such book, titled *JFK: Conspiracy of Silence*, was written by Parkland surgeon Dr. Charles Crenshaw, with JFK researchers Lens Hansen and Gary Shaw. Dr. Crenshaw, supported by Dr. Robert McClelland, two of the several doctors who tried in vain to save the dying president at Parkland, decided (after years of imposed conformity) to publicly dispute the autopsy finding that shots only struck JFK from the rear. Those in attendance in Trauma One that fateful Friday afternoon were made to feel they were under an implied order not to make waves by saying anything that would directly contradict the official autopsy report, and they went along with it to protect their careers. This is merely a milder version of the official gag order that everyone in the Bethesda morgue during the autopsy that night was forced to sign. They were all individually ordered by their superiors not to discuss what they saw or heard, under threat of court martial.[29] Only much later were some of the technicians and one of the doctors (Boswell) willing to talk with researchers. The conflicting statements from those who witnessed the same event only add to the many questions that need to be answered about this most baffling of all autopsies.

Chapter 3

THE NON-INVESTIGATION

"...The Truth Isn't What You Want to See"

Over the years, one of the most frequently asked questions put to those who disbelieve the official verdict of the events in Dallas has been: "What motivation could all the various investigatory groups have to deliberately avoid an honest and thorough pursuit of the truth in this case?" In today's world, this question may sound naive to many, but back in the 1960's it seemed like a valid point. Naive or not, I will attempt to provide an answer in regard to each individual group who worked on the case. The short answer, which can apply in varying degrees to each of these groups, is *vested interest*.

First let us look at the Dallas police. Although the responsibility for protecting the President was borne by the Secret Service up until the time he was shot, thereafter the primary responsibility for apprehending the killer or killers fell on the shoulders of the local law enforcement agencies. In the first thirty minutes or so after the shots were fired, it is difficult to imagine how the Dallas authorities could have done a *worse* job. They failed to formally arrest a single person at the scene, although they did detain momentarily and then release over a dozen people, of whom at least two may have been part of the assassination team. These included Eugene Brading, a California gangster. Brading, who had recently changed his name to Jim Braden, was on parole from a mail fraud conviction. He had long term connections to organized crime. He was questioned by the Dallas Police on the afternoon of the shooting because he was reported seen in the Dal-Tex building moments after the assassination under "suspicious circumstances."[1] Then we have a man who may have been Charles Harrelson, a hit man for the Mob, who bore a striking resemblance to one of three "tramps" rousted from a railroad car behind the TSBD parking lot and brought to the police station for questioning immediately after the assassination. Later he was in prison for the slaying of a judge. At the time of his arrest for that crime he admitted to having taken part in the JFK assassination, but now denies it. He is a dead ringer for the youngest of the three tramps brought in for questioning on 11/22/63.[2]

Except for Brading, the police did not even record the names of these "suspects" before releasing them. They also failed to adequately seal off either the Depository building *or* the parking lot behind the wooden fence that separated the lot from the grassy knoll. According to researcher Harold Weisberg, it was *never* completely sealed off. Newsmen and others were seen coming and going for hours.[3]

They "misidentified" the rifle found on the sixth floor of the TSBD as a 7.65 Mauser, which is quite different from a 6.5 Italian Mannlicher Carcano. These were not off-hand verbal comments to that effect but a sworn affidavit from Deputy Sheriff Seymour Weitzman to the FBI.[4] Later, they failed to preserve the "chain of evidence" on the cartridge cases found on the scene of both the TSBD and the Tippit shooting, and the rifle found on the sixth floor, which should have made them inadmissible in any trial against Oswald for that crime. Not one piece of evidence in either the assassination or Tippit slaying was preserved in a way which would have allowed it to be used in any courtroom trial of Oswald, had he lived.[5] Meanwhile, they failed to retain or even take any notes during the many interrogation sessions with Oswald that weekend. Captain Will Fritz cited the "lack of office space" as the excuse for not recording any of the several sessions with the alleged assassin.[6]

In spite of what seems to be gross incompetence, they were fortunate enough to have had an ideal suspect handed to them through a set of circumstances that appeared to be incredibly "dumb luck", but which may have had a more sinister explanation. The source of the suspect's description, which was broadcast within fourteen minutes of the shooting of the President, was never satisfactorily identified. The Warren Commission pointed to the description provided by eyewitness Howard Brennan, a man who was sitting across the street from the TSBD and the only one to have seen a shooter in the sixth floor window. But there are two problems with the assumption that Brennan was the source of the description broadcast at 12:44 PM. First, it is extremely doubtful that Brennan, who had very questionable eyesight, could have provided such details of a man who was kneeling behind a carton gun rest or standing behind a very dirty window. The window was open only about a foot at the bottom and a standing man would only have been seen clearly from about the hips down to the knees. Second, Brennan claimed he gave his description of the sixth floor assassin to Secret Service Agent Forest Sorrells about ten minutes after the shots. But Sorrells did not return from Parkland Hospital until twenty to twenty-five minutes after the motorcade sped away from Dealey Plaza at 12:30, too late to account for the 12:44 broadcast. The story that Oswald was an immediate suspect because he was the only TSBD employee missing after the shots were fired, has been proven false. Nor does it explain why his name was not then broadcast along with the description.[7]

Is it any wonder that with so much egg on their collective face, the Dallas police would do what many other police departments in the country would have done under such circumstances; make sure that their case against the "bird in the hand" would stick? Especially after both Police Chief Jesse Curry and District Attorney Henry Wade were so quick to proclaim to the TV cameras, on the evening of the assassination, that they had all the evidence they needed to prove that Oswald killed both Officer Tippit and President Kennedy. In a TV interview on that Friday evening, Wade was recorded saying:

–there's no one else but him. I figure we have enough evidence to convict him

Homicide Captain Will Fritz, Chief Curry, and DA Wade all made definitive statements to the press within thirty-six hours of the crime.[8]

The FBI

As to the next level of the investigation, the FBI, it is difficult to know just how much of their single-minded approach was due to the same type of eagerness to wrap up the case against Oswald as that exhibited by the police, but certainly there seemed to be a large amount of that element involved. The impetus behind that attitude was Director J. Edgar Hoover's well-known feelings towards JFK. Hoover was a confirmed Kennedy hater. His obvious disdain for his boss, Attorney General Robert Kennedy, was common knowledge among insiders in Washington. He viewed JFK's amorous meanderings with poorly disguised disgust. But most of all, he had feared that the President would allow Hoover's automatic retirement, due on January 1, 1965 when the director would turn 70, to occur without the desired waiver to override it.

Mark North, in *Act of Treason,* does an exhaustive job of detailing Hoover's attitudes and actions before and after 11/22/63.9 With Kennedy gone, he knew that his close friend LBJ would grant that waiver. Hoover was also an avowed "commie" hater. An opportunity to pin JFK's death on an apparent communist sympathizer would have been very hard for Hoover to pass up. Given the evidence against Oswald already compiled by the local authorities, all Hoover had to do was tell his agents to make sure that the case was as air-tight as possible, and what J. Edgar wanted, J. Edgar got.

He must have felt this would breathe new life into the waning flames of the Cold War and keep the pressure on Cuba, the USSR and those "commies" in SE Asia. As it turns out, he was more right than wrong.

Moreover, the FBI had failed miserably to keep tabs on Oswald after his return from the USSR. There is even the possibility that Oswald was working for them. If it turned out that Oswald was anything other than a "lone nut", Hoover's bureau would take a large share of the blame for the assassination. Embarrassment to the bureau was to be avoided at any cost. In fact, Hoover did not confine his efforts at keeping the investigation focused on Oswald to his own bureau. In a phone conversation with Walter Jenkins (special assistant to LBJ) on the day Oswald was killed by Ruby, Hoover said:

The thing I am most concerned about, and so is Mr. Katzenbach (Deputy Attorney General), is having something issued so that we can convince the public that Oswald is the real assassin. (Senate Intelligence Committee Report on the Kennedy Assassination, p. 33)

The Warren Commission

Then we come to the Warren Commission, who depended far too heavily on the Dallas Police, the FBI and the CIA to provide the evidence that they were to re-examine and expand upon. As explored in other sections of this book, the primary purpose of this body was never meant to be a search for the answer to the question, "Who killed President Kennedy?" The purpose, as it was put to Earl Warren by President Johnson, was to quell the rumors that might lead this country into war. In this regard, the Warren Commission was a brilliant success. Warren's reluctance to accept the assignment comes through clearly in the following quote on how his meeting with Johnson went.

Warren: I saw McGeorge Bundy first. He took me in, and the President told me how serious the situation was. He said there had been wild rumors, and that there was the international situation to think of. He said the head of the Atomic Energy Commission had told him how many millions of people would be killed in an atomic war. The only way to dispel these rumors, he said, was to have an independent and responsible commission, and that there was no one to head it except the highest judicial officer in the country. He said that if the public became aroused against Castro and Khrushchev there might be a war. If you're putting it like that, I said, I can't say no.[10]

Basically, all the Commission did in their "investigation" was to verify, clarify and confirm what the police and the FBI had already concluded. There was virtually no independent examination of the evidence. They lacked both the means and the mind-set to conduct any meaningful independent investigation.

Far from being of common mind in their interests and goals, the members of the commission were a diverse lot. Commissioners Dulles, Ford and Russell were very conservative in their political views and had very little admiration for Chairman Earl Warren, who was seen by many as the most liberal Chief Justice ever to sit on the Supreme Court. FBI Director Hoover despised Warren for his "left-wing" views and decisions. This fact, combined with Hoover's fear of having the case against Oswald examined too closely lest any embarrassing cans of worms be opened, prompted a noticeable lack of cooperation between the FBI and the commission, particularly whenever the commissioners showed any sign of exploring new territory. This greatly disturbed the commissioners and the staff, as will be made apparent in the next chapter.

Although the FBI and the Warren Commission did share the common goal of avoiding disrupting revelations and pinning the guilt for JFK's death on Lee Harvey Oswald and him alone, the FBI has never agreed with the Commission's theory that one bullet passed through both Kennedy and Connally. Perhaps that was because two of their agents who attended the autopsy filed a report, as mentioned in chapter 2, even before the Warren Commission held their first meeting, in which they stated that the bullet wound in JFK's back only penetrated about two inches, and that the doctors expressed puzzlement as to where the bullet went. The FBI is not known for admitting that it is wrong, even when it is, and in this case they seem to have been quite correct.

The WC Staff

The seven commissioners spent surprisingly little time attending sessions or listening to testimony. The bulk of the work was done by their staff of lawyers. Like the commissioners, the staff was made up of people with varying degrees of skepticism about the claim that Oswald was the lone assassin, ranging from quite a bit to none. The most adamant supporters of the lone assassin theory were, not surprisingly, the most closed-minded, rejecting any effort to explore evidence or question witnesses who might cast doubt on the "no conspiracy" conclusion. In this group were commissioners: Allen Dulles, Gerald Ford, John McCloy and Chairman Earl Warren. They were joined in their tunnel-vision by staffers David Belin, Joseph Ball, Albert Jenner, Arlen Specter, Norman Redlich and General Council J. Lee Rankin.

On the side of at least some degree of objectivity were commissioners: Hale Boggs, Richard Russell and John Cooper, and staff members Burt Griffen, Leon Hubert and Wesley Liebeler. Unfortunately, they were in the decided minority and their expressions of doubt were simply ignored. Senator Russell in particular expressed many doubts that Oswald was alone in the crime, both during the Commission's discussions and later, right up to the time of his death. Russell was the only Commissioner who ever referred to Oswald as the *"alleged* assassin." Russell tried to get a footnote added to the Warren Report that he disagreed with the conclusion that JFK and Connally were struck by the same bullet and that there was no evidence of a conspiracy, but Warren insisted on unanimity and his footnote was never included. In 1968, researcher Harold Weisberg met with former Warren Commissioner Russell to discuss the Commission's findings. Russell had often expressed doubts about the Report and, according to Weisberg, had "urged me to disprove the Report he had been tricked into agreeing to sign".[11]

The Warren Commission was reputed to have conducted "one of the most exhaustive inquiries in the history of crime", according to President Johnson, the news media and, of course, the Commission itself. But Edward Epstein, in his early book *Inquest*, provided us with a revealing overview of just how thorough this "exhaustive" investigation was. He did an analysis of the types of witnesses interviewed, the amount of time devoted to each, and the amount of time each commissioner devoted to attending the hearings. His results were startling. Attendance records of these hearings show that, on average, each commissioner heard only forty-five percent of the testimony! The attendance varied widely, with Senator Russell hearing the least (about six percent) and Allen Dulles hearing the most (about seventy-one percent). Forty-three percent of the hearings was devoted to testimony by Oswald's family or acquaintances in pursuit of his life history. Twelve percent was devoted to testimony related to the conduct of various government agencies. Less than one third of the hearings was devoted to the facts of the assassination itself. The allocation of testimony is perhaps the best indication of the presumption of guilt against Oswald.[12]

Meanwhile, several dozen witnesses who were at the scene and who might have provided vital information about possible other gunmen *were not even called*. The following is a listing of many (but probably not all) of these potentially valuable witnesses.

Most of the **motorcycle officers** accompanying the motorcade, including **Officer James Chaney**, riding just to the right of the President's limo.

Bill Newman and his wife...witnesses closest to JFK on the grassy knoll side when the fatal shot struck.

Arnold Rowland and his wife...witnesses who reported to police that they saw two men in the sixth floor windows of the TSBD just prior to the assassination.

Carolyn Walther...witness who also reported seeing two men with rifles in a window on the 6th floor a few minutes before the shooting.

Carolyn Arnold...a secretary in the TSBD who reported she saw Oswald in the second floor lunchroom at 12:15 or later, about the time that Rowland and Walther saw two men in the sixth floor windows.

Orville Nix...who was on the SW corner of Elm & Houston taking movies of the motorcade. His film was later analyzed by Itek Corp. in 1966 because it seemed to show an assassin at the top of the knoll. Itek, who did a lot of work for the government, including the CIA, said "no assassin". The original Nix film has since disappeared while in the custody of the House Select Committee headed by Robert Blakey. Mr. Blakey has apologized to the Nix family for losing the film.[13]

Norman Similas...on the south side of Elm St. He had taken some photos that showed the front of the TSBD, including the sixth floor window just before the shots. He lent these to a Toronto newspaper and they were never returned.

Ed Hoffman...on the overpass that crosses over Elm Street, only a few yards west of the parking lot behind the picket fence. Right after the shots, he saw a man behind the fence pass a rifle to a second man, who then quickly disassembled it and put it in a tool bag. This man was dressed like a railroad worker and quickly left the area. Hoffman, a deaf mute, was unable to get anyone in authority to pay heed to his story.[14]

Adm. George Burkley...present at both Parkland and Bethesda Hospitals.

ALL 22 of the other military personnel who were present at the autopsy (not counting the autopsy doctors).

FBI agents Sibert and O'Neill, who attended the autopsy and filed a report on it, which described the wound in JFK's back (not neck).[15]

Jean Hill...in Dealey Plaza across from the grassy knoll from the limo when the last shot was fired.

Mary Moorman...another witness next to Jean Hill.

Beverly Oliver...a few feet away from Hill and Moorman.

Charles Brehm...on the grassy triangle south of Elm St.

Marie Muchmore...on the grassy triangle behind Brehm.

John Chism...on the north side of Elm in front of the Stemmons Freeway sign.

Mary Chism...standing next to her husband John.

A. J. Millican...also near the Stemmons sign.

Mary Woodward, Maggie Brown, Aurelia Lorenzo, and Ann Donaldson..also on the north side of Elm near the sign.

L. C. Smith...at the corner of Main and Houston Streets.

W. W. Mabra...standing near Mr. Smith.

Robert West...across Main from Smith and Mabra.

Virgie Baker....standing in front of the TSBD.

Hugh Betzner, Jr....at the intersection of Elm and Houston.

Any of these witnesses might have been able to provide important and revealing information, had they been called to testify.

Scope of the Warren Report

Another interesting statistic was supplied by Mark Lane in *Rush to Judgment.* Out of the 552 people who testified as Warren Commission witnesses, only 94 testified in the presence of one or more of the commissioners (and *none* in the presence of all seven). The remaining 458 submitted sworn statements or were questioned by a staff lawyer. Of the 94 that the commissioners questioned, only a few were among the really important ones in determining the basic facts of the shooting.[16]

When the Report was presented to Lyndon Johnson by Earl Warren in September of 1964, LBJ's first response was, "It's heavy!" The size and apparent scope of the Report so impressed the members of the news media that they immediately embraced it as "gospel" before anyone had a chance to read it, let alone analyze it. Later, thanks to the patient and determined efforts of a few "doubting Thomas's," we learned that this report and its "supporting" twenty-six volumes of testimony and evidence, were padded with such trivial and useless gems as Marguerite Oswald's dental charts and Lee Oswald's elementary school grades. But this Commission could find no room in its Report for one of the most essential pieces of evidence of all; evidence that would have shed some light on the single-bullet-theory—the results of the spectrographic and neutron-activation analysis tests conducted by the FBI on the nearly unscathed bullet supposedly found on a stretcher in Parkland Hospital (CE 399), the unfired bullet in the rifle, the fragments found on the limo floor, the scrapings from the dent in the windshield chrome, the bullet holes in JFK's clothing and the curbstone that was struck by a stray fragment. These results were not only excluded from the report, they have been among the highly classified and closely guarded documents pertaining to the case. One can only assume that the reason for this is that these tests would have provided incontrovertible and unambiguous answers to two crucial questions:

A. Were the material in the fragments taken from Connally and the metallic traces around the bullet hole in the back of Kennedy's jacket identical in composition to the metal in bullet 399?

B. Were the materials in the mutilated fragments found on the floor of the limo, the fragments removed from Kennedy's head, and the material from the smear taken from the windshield chrome dent, ALL from one and only one bullet?

If the answer to either of these questions was NO, then the one-assassin theory is destroyed, since that would have meant more than three shots must have been fired. It is a reasonable assumption that if these tests proved the case against Oswald to have been plausible, they would not only have been included in the Warren Report, they would have been proudly displayed in every publication in the country instead of being one of this Government's most closely guarded secrets.

The case of Captain Alfred Dreyfus, a French Army officer accused in 1894 of attempting to sell information to the Germans, bears some interesting similarities to the case of the JFK assassination. Dreyfus was convicted as a spy on questionable evidence and sentenced to Devil's Island. There was one officer who defended Dreyfus and sought to reveal the truth of the matter (that Dreyfus was innocent), but he was systematically thwarted by the military establishment. His superiors knew the truth, but also knew that the Army would have been embarrassed by it, so they were determined to let an innocent man take the blame "for the greater good."

One cannot help but be struck by the parallels between the Dreyfus case and the assassination of President Kennedy. The Warren Commission's single-mindedness can best be demonstrated by presenting the following samples of dialog from members of the commission's staff.

Commission attorney Wesley Liebeler, in a memo to chief council Lee Rankin:

The best evidence that Oswald could fire as fast as he did and hit the target was the fact that he did so.

Commission attorney David Belin, in a memo to Lee Rankin on 1/30/64, when the commission had hardly even begun its investigation and before the invention of the single-bullet-theory:

In determining the accuracy of Oswald, we have three major possibilities: Oswald was shooting at Connally and missed two out of three shots, two misses striking Kennedy; Oswald was shooting at both Kennedy and Connally and all three shots hit their intended targets; Oswald was shooting at Kennedy and the second bullet missed its intended target and hit Connally instead.

The overall approach and attitude of the Warren Commission members and the majority of the Commission's staff of young, ambitious lawyers are nicely summarized in a couple of lines from an Andrew Lloyd Webber classic:

Close your eyes, for your eyes will only tell the truth, and the truth isn't what you want to see. In the dark it is easy to pretend, that the truth is what it ought to be.

The News Media and the Garrison Investigation

Tragically this same seductive theme was enthusiastically adopted by the majority of the American news media, and to a large extent, remains their philosophy today. Without doubt, one of the principal reasons for the continued reluctance of the news media to admit that there might be some truth to the critics' allegations of a plot behind the death of JFK is the fiasco of the Garrison case. Jim Garrison was the District Attorney of New Orleans during the years following the assassination. Since New Orleans was once Lee Harvey Oswald's home town and the scene of much of his strange political activity in the summer of 1963, Garrison was more interested in the Kennedy murder than most, right from the beginning. His interest was greatly magnified by a conversation with Senator Russell Long in late 1966 in which Long expressed total disbelief in the findings of the Warren Commission. This launched Garrison on a crusade to "solve the assassination."[17] He conducted a clandestine unofficial investigation of his own, in which his primary suspects were David Ferrie, who Garrison knew had worked for prominent right-winger Guy Bannister (who died in June of 1964), and the mysterious Clem Bertrand, who had prodded New Orleans attorney Dean Andrews to contact Oswald while he was in the Dallas jail and offer him legal assistance

During his two-year investigation Garrison uncovered what he considered proof that Bertrand was really Clay Shaw, a prominent New Orleans businessman with multi-national connections that Garrison felt were very likely CIA connections. Once the word of this inquiry leaked to the press, however, Garrison's job made Don Quixote's task seem like child's play. Suddenly, he had the full weight of the Federal Government behind a campaign to ruin both his reputation and his investigation. His potential witnesses began dying under mysterious circumstances or were denied extradition by state governors who refused to cooperate with Garrison in any way. Then he discovered that his new volunteer staff was infiltrated with FBI and CIA informants.

It was during this period that the "Clark panel" got into the act. Both to undermine Garrison's efforts and to attempt to stem the rising tide of criticism of the Warren Report, Attorney General Ramsey Clark convened a panel of four "forensic experts" in February of 1968. They were supposedly the first to get an opportunity to examine and study the photos and X-rays of the President taken during his autopsy. The panel took all of *two days* to complete their study and to write their report, in which they voiced complete support for the essential findings of the Warren Commission. Aside from the fact that an honest evaluation of the evidence could not begin to scratch the surface in just two days, the panel, in spite of its efforts to support the government's case, nonetheless issued statements in their report that inadvertently further demolished it. For example, in one statement found near the end of their report in reference to the X-ray of the neck area, where the "single bullet" was supposed to have traversed from back to front through Kennedy's neck, the panel reported that there were "several metallic fragments, present in this region." According to the Warren Commission, bullet CE 399 passed through the President's neck without striking any bone, so how could it have left lead fragments behind? The only lead missing from 399 was from the butt.[18] There was already more lead removed from and still inside Governor Connally's body than was missing from CE 399, the "magic bullet". Now the panel is telling us of *more* fragments that apparently came from this most unusual bullet.

And what did the Attorney General, the highest law-enforcement officer in the land, do with this new report? He *sat on it for eleven months*, waiting for what he considered to be the most opportune moment to spring it on an unsuspecting public and press. This moment turned out to be the eve of a critical court hearing, on January 17, 1969, in which Garrison's subpoena for access to the autopsy films was to be argued. The publicity attending the release of Clark's "bombshell" effectively sabotaged the hearing and Garrison was denied access to the films. This was only one part of a concerted effort by government officials to sabotage DA Garrison's investigation.[19]

By the time the trial of Clay Shaw actually got under way in Jan. of 1969, Dave Ferrie, upon whom Garrison felt his whole case hinged, had died a very mysterious death (which Ferrie himself had predicted as soon as news of Garrison's investigation became public). It was ruled a suicide by drug overdose on the strength of two un-Ferrie-like notes that were found in his apartment, but Garrison suspected that the drug had been forced down his throat.

At that point, Garrison must have realized that his prosecution of Shaw was a hopeless case. Any other prosecuting attorney would have dropped the charges, knowing that whatever case he might have had was now gone. Garrison, however, was so convinced that the world needed to hear and see the evidence of a conspiracy behind Kennedy's death that he decided to proceed with the prosecution of Shaw, knowing full well that he would lose. He had bragged so loudly to the press that he had the proof to "break the case of the Kennedy assassination wide open", that he could not back down now.

During the trial of Shaw, Garrison subpoenaed and obtained the Zapruder movie film from LIFE Magazine. The Shaw jury members were the first ordinary Americans to see this film (five years after the Warren Commission used a copy of it to help "solve" the assassination). The sight of JFK's head being driven violently back and to the left when struck by the fatal shot was enough to convince the jurors that he had been shot from the front and, therefore, there must have indeed been a conspiracy involved. However, Garrison was unable to convince them that Clay Shaw was Clay/Clem Bertrand or was in any way involved with the CIA or with people like Bannister and Ferrie, much less that he had anything to do with the death of Kennedy. It took the jurors less than an hour to return a verdict of "not guilty." After all his premature claims of proof, Garrison became the laughing stock of the country, especially to those who were prone to sneer at all suggestions of conspiracy in the assassination. The "critical community," those who had been dedicating a large portion of their lives to uncovering the truth of the case and to showing that the

Warren Commission had been grossly mistaken, was devastated and discredited.

The news media, ignoring the fact that Garrison had at least convinced this jury that there had to have been more than one gunman, had a field-day blasting not only Garrison but all "conspiracy nuts." The damage to the cause of truth in this crime was so great that several Warren critics went so far as to wonder out loud if Mr. Garrison had been an agent of the US government who was put up to that fiasco of a trial for the express purpose of discrediting the critics. But Garrison's continued opposition to the official verdict from then until his death indicates that he was sincere in his quest for the truth. His inept handling of the Shaw prosecution was the result of a combination of several factors, including his cracking under the immense weight of the magnitude of the case and the intensity of the pressure brought by the Government and the media as they made every effort to turn the investigation into a farce and to discredit Garrison and his staff. No matter, the result could not have been more damaging to the cause of the critics if he *had* set out to deliberately sabotage it. Those few pillars of the news media who might have been starting to exhibit some doubt about the official verdict felt that Garrison had duped them and they became even more determined not to be led astray again. This determination remains intact for most of the media today.

The Second Look

Then we had the House Select Committee to Investigate Assassinations (HSCA) in 1976-79. It was empowered to re-investigate the assassinations of President Kennedy and Dr. Martin Luther King. Although this committee conducted its investigation with a slightly more open-minded approach than its predecessors, it was hampered by several obstacles. First, the HSCA went through several changes of leadership before the investigation even got off the ground. The first Committee Chairman, Congressman Thomas Downing, was convinced there *was* a conspiracy involved in the JFK case. Richard Sprague, a prosecutor from Philadelphia, was appointed Chief Council. Sprague admitted to having read nothing about the case, but at least seemed to approach the task with an open mind and a determination to conduct a thorough investigation.

Unfortunately, no sooner had the HSCA established itself when that congressional year ended and Chairman Downing retired. After a tough fight, the Congress voted to re-establish the Committee for another year and Congressman Henry Gonzalez took over the chairmanship. Gonzalez was *also* convinced there had been a conspiracy behind the assassination of Kennedy. He had been in the motorcade when it happened and was determined to get to the truth. Then a clash of egos erupted between Gonzalez and Sprague. At the same time, the *New York Times* and other papers began putting out a barrage of articles critical of Sprague. Gonzalez attempted to fire Sprague but was voted down by the other eleven committee members. This infuriated Gonzalez, who promptly resigned as chairman. Congressman Louis Stokes took over and tried to keep Sprague on as Chief Council. But by now Sprague's credibility was too damaged and demands mounted for his resignation. He fought long and hard to stay on (which further delayed the actual investigation work) but was eventually forced out.[20]

His replacement, Robert Blakey, came to his job with a totally different viewpoint than his predecessor. Blakey held the firm opinion that the Warren Commission had been right and that his committee would only serve to verify that fact. As an experienced Washington insider, he was much more concerned with producing an acceptable report within the allotted time than with uncovering new leads. (See Gaeton Fonzi's *The Last Investigation,* Thunder's Mouth Press, Nov. 1993, for an excellent analysis of why this investigation failed.) But because of the new information that had been discovered by the Senate Committee on Intelligence just a year or so earlier (the CIA/Mafia efforts to assassinate Castro), and because of the results of analyzing the Dallas Police tape, Blakey was forced to change his thinking a great deal. He continued to believe that Oswald fired all the shots that actually struck Kennedy, but he and the rest of the HSCA were at last willing to come out publicly and admit that the critics of the Warren Commission had been essentially correct all along; there had been conspiracies behind the assassinations of both Kennedy and King.

This conclusion was not met with enthusiasm by the media, who had long committed themselves to full support of the Warren Commission's "lone-assassin theory". At first forced to accept the new scientific evidence that the Warren Commission had been wrong about the existence of a second gunman, some nevertheless went so far as to suggest that the existence of a fourth shot from the knoll area did not necessarily mean there was a conspiracy. They advanced the notion that it might have been another "lone nut" who just happened to have picked the same general area in which to commit his crime.

That anyone could seriously make such a statement is a classic illustration of how far the people who refuse to admit a conspiracy are willing to go in the suppression of logic.

But the House Select Committee's conclusion that Kennedy was "probably killed as a result of a conspiracy" was only a partial victory for the Warren Report critics. The HSCA's conclusion pointed the finger of guilt *only* at certain organized crime figures, namely Carlos Marcello of New Orleans and Santos Trafficante Jr. of Tampa.

In fairness, it must be pointed out that Blakey's Committee was severely restricted, like the Warren Commission before it, by the continued "stone-walling" of the CIA, who refused to release many of the relevant files on the grounds of "national security". In particular, anything related to the surveillance of the Mexico City embassy, which Oswald was alleged to have visited in the summer of 1963, was suppressed.[21] They were also hampered by a severe time restriction, since by the time they got through all the haggling over leadership and procedural issues, there were only a few months left to complete their investigation. But there also seems to have been a pronounced reluctance to look hard enough for the truth, similar to that displayed by the Warren Commission. One telling indication of this comes from none other than Commander Humes of the autopsy team. Dr. Humes, after testifying before the committee in 1978, told George Lardner, Jr. of the *Washington Post*: "They had their chance and they blew it. They didn't ask the right questions."

Many Americans still believe the HSCA's theory that "the Mafia did it." While there is strong evidence that certain Mafia bosses and hit-men were part of the conspiracy, there are major problems with the conclusion that the Mob was the only organization involved. To many researchers, including this writer, the most important problem with that conclusion is simply this: if the Mob were the only culprit behind JFK's murder, then why have all the authorities—the FBI, the CIA and the Justice Department—been so reluctant to follow up the leads presented by the House Select Committee and to continue the pursuit of the guilty parties, and how was crucial evidence suppressed and falsified at such high levels?

The ARRB

Finally, we had the Assassinations Records Review Board, appointed in 1999. The ARRB was charged only with screening for national security issues and then releasing most of the long-withheld files related to the assassination of the President. In spite of its limited mandate, it ironically added a great deal of information, through interviews with the medical personnel involved at both Parkland Hospital and Bethesda Medical Center, that further demolished the Warren Commission's report. Douglas Horne in particular, who was the ARRB's chief analyst for military records, has stated that, not only was there something seriously wrong with the autopsy photographs, but that the photographs currently in the National Archives, supposedly of Kennedy's brain, are not of his brain at all. He says that there were *two* brain examinations done a week or so after the autopsy and that the first one, of the president's actual brain, has never been entered into the official record. He goes on to say that the damage displayed in the "official" brain photos in no way represents the damage seen by the medical staffs in both hospitals. (Google Doug Horne)

This brings to mind the mysterious presence of the body of the Air Force Major mentioned in Chapter Two. Could this have been there to supply a substitute brain?

Thanks to the ARRB there is now a web site named *The Assassination Archives & Research Center* (aarclibrary.org) where anyone can access the Warren Report and its twenty-six volumes of testimony and exhibits, the House Select Committee on Assassinations' report and its twelve accompanying volumes, and a host of other assassination related documents.

It is now obvious that the only type of investigation that would have some chance of success in getting to the truth of the JFK assassination is one that is led by a person who has never been committed to the official verdict and who has no vested interest in protecting any agency, organization or individual who might be involved. Such an investigation would also need to have complete access to any and all files held by any governmental agency, including the CIA and other intelligence agencies, and subpoena power to compel anyone, up to and including the current occupant of the White House, to testify under oath. Any new investigation that lacks even one of these requirements would, in all probability, be doomed to the same failures as its predecessors.

One development that would virtually assure that a new investigation would be totally thorough and honest would be for the main-stream media to abandon their long-standing commitment to the findings of the Warren Report, admit that they had been deceived by their respect for Chief Justice Warren and his illustrious panel, and get behind the effort to uncover the truth of this case with the same zeal they displayed during the Watergate affair.

Anyone who doubts the perpetual bias of the news media in this case need only consider their reaction to the developments in May, 1992, described in the previous chapter (The Autopsy). In mid-month, Drs. Humes and Boswell gave an interview to a friendly fellow doctor, that was then published in the *Journal of the American Medical Association* (JAMA), in which they defended their performance and findings in the autopsy, and reiterated that the evidence shows that JFK was struck by two bullets fired from behind. This news was given extensive and highly favorable coverage by all elements of the news media, many of whom claimed that this "should put an end to all that scurrilous conspiracy talk". Two weeks later, when three autopsy technicians (including Jerrol Custer who took the X-rays and Floyd Riebe who took the photographs) held a press conference in New York to refute the doctors' claims and to state that the photos and X-rays had been doctored to hide a front entrance wound and a rear exit wound in the head, this event was virtually ignored by the media! There were a couple of very brief radio reports and 3/4 of an inch given the story by *USA Today*. Most major newspapers and TV stations failed to report it. As long as the major publications and TV networks continue to facilitate the cover-up through their periodic airing of documentaries designed to dispel conspiracy theories and through such one-sided reporting of news pertaining to the assassination, they will continue to be viewed in the same light as the "stonewalling" agencies, as accessories after the fact, by those of us who feel that the truth must ultimately be faced.

Chapter 4
A FORK IN THE ROAD
"...the Saddest Are These: It Might Have Been"

Among the many formerly "TOP-SECRET" documents uncovered after years of repeated petitions by researcher par excellence Harold Weisberg are the transcripts of two of the earliest executive sessions of the Warren Commission.[1] It is easy to see why the government was so reluctant to expose these documents to the light of day, because what is said in these meetings totally undermines any image of the commission as a "truth-seeking" investigatory body.

It was during these meetings and the days surrounding them that the course of the investigation was determined. It may not have been a conscious and mutual decision to follow the path of least resistance and avoid any real challenge to the pat solution presented by the FBI, but such a decision was made none-the-less. Once embarked upon, there was no turning back, no allowance made for the possibility of having chosen the wrong path.

The first transcript, of the Warren Commission's meeting on January 22, 1964, was first exposed in Harold Weisberg's *Post Mortem*. The second one, of the commission's session on January 27, 1964, comprised the bulk of Weisberg's *Whitewash IV*. In reading over the transcripts of these meetings I was intrigued by the question of whether or not there was an obvious "fork in the road," a point at which a different response by Chairman Earl Warren would have sent them down another path; one that might have led to the truth. I feel I discovered such a critical point in each of these two discussions. The first meeting discussed the problem of the FBI's "pat" and immediate solution to the assassination, a clear indication that they were aware of this uncharacteristic rush to judgment. And yet they continued to rely almost exclusively on the evidence and interpretation of that evidence fed to them by Hoover's bureau. In the second meeting they are faced with the dilemma of how to follow up on the "dirty rumor" that Oswald was a paid agent of the FBI without stepping too heavily on Hoover's toes in the process. Toward the end of this lengthy discussion (which I have shrunk quite a bit for the reader's sake) I have identified what I feel is a very important fork in the road, where Earl Warren had to choose between a real investigation and a rubber stamp. As you will see, the wrong path was taken. Following the actual text, at this crucial point I have presented a hypothetical alternative response by Chairman Warren, which might well have steered the investigation onto the path that could have led to the truth in this case, and thereby affected the course of our history over the ensuing years. In reproducing this conversation verbatim, replete with a surprising number of ungrammatical and difficult-to-follow sentence structures, I will occasionally skip over sections that are of minimal relevance. These skips will be indicated by a vertical ellipsis. Along the way, I have inserted a few parenthetical [bracketed] clarifications and editorial comments of my own.

Executive Session–January 27, 1964

I will skip the early part of the meeting where the subject in the previous (January 22) meeting of the FBI's "open and shut case" was continued, and pick it up at a point where the main topic was the "dirty rumor" that Oswald had been a paid informant for the FBI and what should be done about it. General Counsel J. Lee Rankin and all the commissioners except Gerald Ford were in attendance. As you read the transcript of their conversation, it will become apparent that opinion is about equally divided between two avenues of approach. Arguing in favor of performing their own independent investigation of the sources of the "rumor" were Senator Richard Russell, Senator John Cooper, and Congressman Hale Boggs. Arguing in favor of relying primarily on FBI Director Hoover's word were Lee Rankin, and Allen Dulles. John McCloy and Chairman Warren seem to be undecided as to the best approach. Warren vacillates from leaning toward doing their own work, to wanting to avoid angering Hoover at all costs. In the end, a compromise seems to have been reached wherein they will employ a combination of both approaches. However, the subsequent record shows that *no* independent examination of the sources of this story was ever conducted, and they simply accepted Hoover's word that the "rumor" was false.

Warren: Well, gentlemen, since we met last week, Mr. Rankin and I have explored this situation we discussed considerably. We talked to the Texas people, and we have given considerable thought to it since, and I am going to ask Mr. Rankin to start at the beginning and just tell you the story as we got it.

Rankin: I received a call from Waggoner Carr, the Attorney General of Texas, and in that call he was quite excited. He was on his way to Texarkana from Austin.

Dulles: This is after our meeting the other night?

Rankin: This was before.

Dulles: Going Back?

Rankin: Yes. He said he thought he had some information that he thought should get to me immediately and it was to the effect that the FBI had an undercover agent who was Oswald, and he said it came up this way, that the matter was developed at a meeting in chambers with the judge, Brown, of the court, and it was in relation to the production of evidence where Ruby's attorney asked that part of the evidence that the FBI developed be furnished to them. And during that time the District Attorney had responded or opposed the motion for the evidence by saying that the various usual grounds, and that the FBI never did this before, and in addition to that he thought he knew the reason why they were willing to do it this time, and that it was *that Oswald was an undercover agent for the FBI.* [emphasis added]

Russell: Was that in open court, Mr. Rankin?

Rankin: That is what I understood.

Dulles: In chambers?

Rankin: In chambers. That he also knew the number that was assigned by the FBI to Oswald, which was 179, and he knew that he was on the payroll or employed, I think that is the way he put it, employed by the FBI at $200 per month from September of 1962 up to the time of the assassination. That was all that he knew about it. He didn't get the information from District Attorney Wade, but he had gotten it from someone else and he didn't tell me who that was, but he said it was a person in whom he had complete faith and could rely upon. I called the Chief Justice immediately and went over and saw him and told him the story, and he thought it was material of such importance to the commission that the entire commission should be called and advised with regard to it. We had a meeting, then, and told the information, and it was the consensus of the meeting that we should try to get those people up here, including the District Attorney, [Wade], the Attorney General [Carr], Special Council with the Attorney General, Leon Jaworski, and Bob Storey [former dean of Southern Methodist University Law School], and Mr. Alexander, the Assistant Attorney General at Dallas. We asked them all to come up, and they did on Friday. At that time they were–they said that the rumors were constant there, that Oswald was an undercover agent, but *they extended it also to the CIA,* for him, assigned to him in connection with the CIA [emphasis added] and gave that to him, and none of them had any original information of their own. They said that the source of their information was a man name of Hudkins who was a reporter for the *Houston Post*, and that it had been circulated by a greater portion of all the reporters in the Dallas area who had been working on this matter in various forms.

Russell: Did he explain why this hadn't been published? This would have gone across the country like wild fire.

Rankin: Well, they said part of it had been published. The fact that it was claimed that Oswald was an undercover agent, and I noticed *The Nation,* [a non-establishment magazine] although I hadn't seen it before, refers to an article in January, the first of January, by Hudkins from which he referred to the undercover agent story. But he does not give the number or the $200 a month at that time. We asked if they asked Hudkins of where he had got his story and they said they had not...We did discover amongst the papers that we received from the Secret Service, a report which the Chief Justice received from Mr. Moore, I believe it was Mr. Moore, which referred to a Mr. Sweatt, who was the Deputy Sheriff in Dallas County, in which he said that Oswald was an undercover agent and was being paid so much a month for some time back to September, and that it had a number which he gave in that report as No. 172. This report by the Secret Service agent was of a conference or inquiry that he made in the area to Sweatt back on December 17th. The report was dated January 3 and we didn't get it until January

23..We didn't know what to expect from this, because that was 20 days after the date of the report, and we wondered whether the Secret Service was withholding something from us, since they had this in their hands clear back on January 3, the date of the report. The explanation since has been that they were trying to check it out, that there was no purpose to withhold from us even though it seemed like a long period, since they hadn't gotten any further report from Mr. Sweatt at all.

Dulles: What was the origin? Who was Sweatt?

Rankin: He was the Deputy Sheriff of Dallas County.

Dulles: He was the one who gave it to the Secret Service?

Rankin: Yes.

Dulles: He didn't say where he got it?

Rankin: No. They have since then, the Secret Service, has investigated, we asked them to, and they have gone to Sweatt and Sweatt has said he got it from Hudkins—back to the same source.

Dulles: Back to the same source?

Rankin: And there is nothing that we have received from any investigative agency checking out Hudkins in this report. You probably saw the *New York Times* story, saying that the FBI, Sunday, that the FBI denied that he was acting as an undercover...

Russell: That is from Mr. Hoover. Somewhere in this material I read in which he denied this report. It apparently was current at some earlier date, that he wrote a letter specifically stating that Oswald was never connected with the FBI in any capacity, secret or otherwise.

Rankin: ...But they had never made any effort to go to Sweatt and see what his story was, although apparently it was common talk there, too, because there are some references to a public official saying that Oswald was acting as an undercover agent, and there is also some statements in the press that some police officers made such statements after the assassination. But there is nothing to show that there was any effort to try to check it out. These stories we generally discount as possibly an effort to blame the FBI for some of the matters involved.

Russell: Has Hudkins claimed his journalistic immunity? Have they gone back to him?

Rankin: They haven't even asked him, or at least indicated they had ever taken his statement or anything like that.

[There followed a discussion of whether it was possible that District Attorney Henry Wade, who was a former FBI man, might have had a reason to spread such a story to embarrass his old agency, but found no reason to suspect that.]

.

.

.

Russell: What steps, if any, have we taken to clear up this matter, Mr. Rankin, if it can be cleared up, to determine whether there is anything to it or not?

Rankin: Well, we have discussed various possibilities, that is, the Chief Justice and myself have, and I want to tell you about them, and I think you will have to instruct us what you want us to do. We thought about approaching the Department [of Justice] with a request that the Attorney General [Robert Kennedy] inform us as to the situation, not only as to what he would say about whether Oswald was or was not an undercover agent, but also with the supporting data that the commission could rely upon, and there is some difficulty with doing that. As the head of the Department, the FBI, of course, is under the Attorney General, but I think we must frankly recognize amongst ourselves that there is a daily relationship there involved in the handling of the problems of the Department and the work of the FBI for the Department, and that we wouldn't want to make that more difficult. [There had always been a serious strain between Hoover and Bobby Kennedy.] We were informed by Mr. Willens, the liaison with the Department, who has worked with us and has done very fine work here, that it is the feeling of the Department, not the Attorney General because he is not here, but Mr. Katzenbach [Deputy Attorney General], and Mr. Miller, Assistant Attorney General in charge of the Criminal Division, that such a request might be embarrassing, and at least would be difficult for the Attorney General, and might, if urged, while he would get the information we desired, make very much more difficult for him to carry on the work of the Department for the balance of his term.

Russell: If he would transmit to us what they told him, the FBI has a very large measure of autonomy in their operations.

Rankin: In light of that, I suggested the possibility for the commission to consider that I should go over and see Mr. Hoover myself, and tell him this problem and that he should have as much interest as the commission in trying to *put an end to* any such speculations, [emphasis added. Note, "put an end to", not "get to the bottom of"] not only by his statement, which I would be frank to tell him I would think would not be sufficient, but also if it was possible to demonstrate by whatever records and materials they have that it just couldn't be true, and see if we couldn't get his cooperation to present that with the understanding that the commission, and stated understanding, at the time, the commission would have to feel free to make such other investigation and take testimony if it were found necessary, in order to satisfy the American People that this question of an undercover agent was out of the picture.

Boggs: What other alternatives are there?

Rankin: Well, the other alternative would be to examine Hudkins, the reporter, to examine Sweatt, who says now that he...

Dulles: Where is Hudkins now, do you know, down in Dallas?

Rankin: In Houston, yes, I assume.

Dulles: What paper is he with?

Rankin: *The Houston Post*.

.

.

.

Rankin: ...To examine Hosty, the FBI agent who was working in that area, and to examine the Special Agent in Charge of the area, and to examine Mr. Hoover, under oath, right up the line. [Completing an outline of the obvious minimum the commission should do!] I felt, however, as I told the Chief Justice, that I thought this commission was entitled to have the full cooperation of another Government Agency, and that we don't have what I would consider any substantial proof of this rumor. *We do have a dirty rumor here that is very bad for the commission, the problem, and it is very damaging to the agencies that are involved in it, and it must be wiped but insofar as it is possible to do so by this commission.* [Emphasis added]. Here we have "smoking gun" proof of the primary goal of the commission's Chief Counsel, and no doubt one of the main reasons it took so long to get the US Government to release this document!] So it seemed to me, in light of that, the way I would treat it if I were in their position would be to have someone approach me, tell me the problem, and see what I frankly could do to clear my skirts if there was a way to do it, and as long as the commission didn't agree not to go further, if they felt that would not satisfy them, I don't see how the commission would be prejudiced.

Boggs: Mr. Wade, what significance did Wade attach to this?

Rankin: I don't think he—you could say he believed. I don't think you could say he disbelieved it. He had just thought there was too much there to disregard, but he just thought, he seemed to indicate, in his statements, that he couldn't believe it would be possible. But he didn't indicate by any statements that he didn't believe it couldn't happen. He just couldn't believe that the FBI would ever let that happen, to get to that position. [The gist of all these negatives seems to indicate that Wade was trying to keep an open mind on the question, but could not accept that the FBI would employ an assassin, as if the FBI would have known in advance that they were employing a future accused assassin.]

Warren: Well, Lee [Rankin] and I both agreed that we shouldn't leave this thing in this present posture, that we should go ahead and try to clear the matter up as best we can. We did argue a little about the approach, whether we should go first to the FBI and ask them for an explanation or whether we should first go and try to see if there is any substance to the claim by interrogating the newspaperman who claims that he has knowledge of the situation, or whether we should go first to the Bureau. Now, my own suggestion was to Lee that we find out first from these people as far as we can if there is any substance to it or whether it is just plain rumor. We were told that Sweatt says he got his information from one fellow, Alexander claims he got it from Sweatt, and somebody else claims he got it from the newspaper man. Now, I thought that if it were necessary we could get these three people in one room at the same time, and find out if anybody claims or has claimed in the past to have had actual knowledge of it, and if they don't claim to have it, we will find out why they spread the rumor.

·

·

·

Warren: Lee, on the other hand, felt it would be the better part of cooperation to go over and see Mr. Hoover and tell him frankly what the rumor was, state that it is pure rumor, we haven't evaluated the facts, but ask him, first, if it is true, and secondly if he can supply us with information to establish that these facts are not true, and they are inconsistent with what would be the way of operation of their Bureau. Now, I don't know, *whatever you agree to would be all right with me* [emphasis added]. Lee thought that if he went down and asked those people to come up here and testify, that they might use the fact that we had asked them to testify as the springboard for an article which would blow this thing out into the public domain, and that we might do a disservice in that way. But I am not sure of that. I rather dislike going to the FBI and just ask them to establish to us that a rumor can't be true until we have at least looked into it.

Russell: There are two reasons for that Mr. Chairman. One would be if you went down there in the first instance to the FBI and got a statement and when you start pursuing it you would look like you are impeaching.

Warren: That is my point.

Boggs: Exactly.

Russell: I think the best way to handle it would be to try to exhaust it at the other hand before you go to the FBI. That would be my judgment. [Bravo, Senator!]

·

·

Russell: If Oswald had never assassinated the President or, at least been charged with assassinating the President, and had been in the employ of the FBI and somebody had gone to the FBI they would have denied he was an agent.

Dulles: Oh, yes.

Russell: They would be the first to deny it. Your agents [in the CIA] would have done exactly the same thing.

Dulles: Exactly.

Russell: Say, 'I never heard about the man' who may have been on the payroll for five years.

Cooper: Yes.

Cooper: ...I was thinking about another alternative, and that is that you advise them about these rumors and that you have to look into them before you ask them, to prevent any evidence to the contrary. But I think I would maintain a kind of relationship with them where they would not feel you were around investigating the FBI. Is that possible?

Rankin: Well, I think that is possible. I would think that if it is definitely untrue, if it were my agency, I would be all over saying "let me prove it. Let me show you anything you can to satisfy you that it isn't true."

Cooper: We have a duty which is outside the FBI's position, which is, if you believe there is something which should be looked into, and we wouldn't believe that if we weren't talking about it. My only point is whether or not it would be reasonable to inform the FBI that you have had these statements, therefore you have to ask these people where they got their information. Before you asked Mr. Hoover, you present us with all the proof to the contrary, because as you say, if he presents all this proof to the contrary, then the situation changes a little bit. It would appear to him that you are trying to impeach his testimony. In the other way, it seems to me that we are just telling him that it was brought to us and we ought to inquire into it.

McCloy: Do we have a statement from Mr. Hoover that this man was not an agent? Was that communicated in the record?

Rankin: Yes.

Warren: It was? A letter?

Russell: I know there was a letter. I don't know who it was written to, a very short letter.

Warren: It was one of those letters we responded to last week. It was in that letter.

Boggs: I think that was a letter that had to do with a request directed to us on what degree of cooperation we should give the defense counsel in the Ruby trial, isn't that right?

Rankin: Yes.

McCloy: I would like to explore again this relationship between the Department of Justice and the FBI. Just why would it be embarrassing for the Attorney General of the United States to inquire of one of his agencies whether or not this man, who was alleged to have killed the President of the United States, was an agent? Does the embarrassment supersede the importance of getting the best evidence in such a situation as this? [A very good question, from an unlikely source, since McCloy was among the least open-minded throughout the investigation.]

Rankin: Well, I think it is a question of whether we have to put him into that position in order to get the job done, because there is, in my opinion, not any question but what there will be more friction, [between Robert Kennedy and Hoover] more difficulty with his carrying out his responsibilities, but I think we have a very real problem in this commission in that we have meetings all the time and they know what it is about, that they know these people are up here, and they know this has come out in the paper now, it is in *The Nation* article, and we are meeting rather rapidly here in the last few days, and they can guess probably what it is about, certainly after the meeting with the Texas people.

Cooper: I would like to suggest something else. In view of all the rumors and statements that have been made, not only here but abroad, I think to ask the President's brother, the dead President, to do this, it wouldn't have any backing in it. It would have no substance in his purpose but some crazy people would translate it from his official position to a personal position. It may sound far fetched but he would be implying as a person that something was wrong. You can't overlook any implications.

McCloy: I think that would perhaps be an element in the thing, but it still wouldn't divert me from asking this man who happens to be the Attorney General whose sworn duty it is to enforce justice, to ask him just what is within his knowledge in regard to such a serious thing as this. It is an awkward affair, but as you said the other day, truth is our only client. [If only it were true!]

Boggs: Yes.

McCloy: I think we may have to take this first step, that the Senator [Cooper] speaks about, but I don't think we could recognize that any door is closed to us, unless the President closes it to us, and in the search for the truth.

Rankin: I was asking the question and talking to the Chief Justice, and say we ran this out with Hudkins and these other people, and found that they said that they would not give us the source of their information, they wouldn't say it was a fabrication, but they wouldn't – so it isn't washed out, and then are we going to be able to leave it there or don't we always have to go back to our Federal agency and try to establish the truth?

Warren: We do.

Rankin: I don't see how the country is ever going to be willing to accept it if we don't satisfy them on this particular issue, not only with them [the FBI] but the CIA and every other agency.

[There followed a lengthy discussion of whether the reporter, Alonzo Hudkins, whose article in the *Houston Post* caused this whole ruckus, would claim "journalistic privilege" and protect his source of the story. The commissioners were not sure of what the law was in Texas pertaining to their ability to force him to reveal his sources. Finally:]

Russell: We can't afford not to ask him, whatever the law in Texas is, we can't afford not to ask him a question.

Warren: That is right. [So far, still leaning in the right direction.]

.

.

.

Dulles: There is a terribly hard thing to disprove, you know. How do you disprove a fellow is not your agent? How do you disprove it?

Boggs: You could disprove it couldn't you?

Dulles: No.

Boggs: I know, ask questions about something.

Dulles: I never knew how to disprove it.

Boggs: So I will ask you. Did you have agents about whom you had no knowledge whatsoever?

Dulles: The record may not be on paper. But on paper you would have hieroglyphics that only two people knew what they meant, and nobody outside of the agency would know and you could say this meant the agent and somebody else could say it meant another agent.

Boggs: Let's take a specific case. That fellow Powers [Francis Gary Powers, shot down over Russia in his U-2 plane while Oswald was in Russia] was one of your men.

Dulles: Oh, yes, he was not an agent. He was an employee.

Boggs: There was no problem proving he was employed by the CIA?

Dulles: No. He had a signed contract.

Boggs: Let's assume that Powers did not have a signed contract but he was recruited by someone in CIA. The man who recruited him would know, wouldn't he?

Dulles: Yes, but he wouldn't tell.

Warren: Wouldn't tell it under oath?

Dulles: I wouldn't think he would tell it under oath, no.

Warren: Why?

Dulles: He ought not tell it under oath. Maybe not tell it to his own government, but wouldn't tell it any other way.

McCloy: Wouldn't he tell it to his own chief?

Dulles: He might or might not. If he was a bad one then he wouldn't.

Boggs: What you do is you make out a problem if this be true, make our problem utterly impossible because you say this rumor can't be dissipated under any circumstances.

Dulles: I don't think it can, unless you believe Mr. Hoover, and so forth and so on, which probably most people will.

[There follows several more minutes of covering the same ground over again. Then:]

McCloy: Have you talked to Katzenbach [Deputy Atty. General, in charge while Robert Kennedy was in mourning for his brother], Lee?

Rankin: No.

McCloy: Willens [Howard Willens, staff director for the commission] has indicated that Katzenbach says they will be embarrassed.

Rankin: Greatly embarrassed.

McCloy: Greatly embarrassed.

Russell: If what?

Rankin: If the Attorney General were asked to check this out and then report to us.

Warren: But they seemed to think there would be no embarrassment for us to check it out ourselves. They think that is all right. They think it is all right for us to do that. Now, my own thought is this: I am not going to be thin-skinned about what Mr. Hoover might think [Really?] but I am sure if we indicated to Mr. Hoover that we were investigating him, he would be just as angry at us as he was, or would be, at the Attorney General for investigating him. [*Obviously, their primary concern.*]

-
-
-

Warren: ...We must go into this thing from both ends, from the end of the rumormongers and from the end of the FBI, and if we come into a cul-de-sac, why we are there, but we can report on it. Now that is the way it would appeal to me. These are things where people can reasonably disagree. Whatever you want to do I am willing to approach it in that manner. [Pretty wishy-washy for a Supreme Court Chief Justice]

-
-
-

Rankin: Would it be acceptable to go to Mr. Hoover and tell him about the situation and that we would like to go ahead and find out what we could about these…

McCloy: Hudkins' sources.

Rankin: Then if he reacts and says, "I want to show you that it couldn't be", or something like that, beforehand, what about that kind of approach?

Warren: Well, Lee I wouldn't be in favor of going to any agency and saying, "We would like to do this". I think we ought to know what we are going to do, and do it, and take our chances one way or the other. I don't think we should apologize or make it look that we are in any way reticent about making any investigation that comes to this commission. [Sounds good, but...] But on the other hand, I don't want to be unfriendly or unfair to him. [Right back to the old fear of Hoover, the all-pervasive shroud that hung over this commission.] My own judgment was that the most fair thing to do would be to try to find out if this is fact or fiction.

Rankin: What I was fearful of was the mere process will cause him to think, in light of these people being here and all, and the meetings of the commission, that we are really investigating *him*.

Warren: If you tell him we are going down there to do it, we *are* investigating him, aren't we?

Rankin: I think it is inherent.

-
-
-

McCloy: This is going to loom up in all probability to be one of the major issues in our investigation, I think. That, and whether there is a relationship between Ruby and Oswald. It explains a good bit. This starts off, *The Nation* article starts off, "Well, why wasn't the Secret Service notified that there was this defector in this building?" If he was on the payroll of the FBI they would think he was all right. They would not think of his being a defector. [Makes you think, doesn't it?]

[There follows a digression into some of the actual facts of the assassination that are in conflict, and how they are going to approach any attempt to resolve these issues. This discussion leads to this interesting exchange.]

-
-
-

Rankin: Part of the difficulty in regard to it is that they [the FBI] have no problem. They have decided that it is Oswald who committed the assassination, they have decided that no one else was involved, they have decided…

It's Time For the Truth!

Russell: They have tried the case and reached a verdict on every aspect.

Boggs: You have put your finger on it.

•

•

•

Rankin: ...And I think their reaction probably would be, "Why do you want that. It is clear."

Russell: "You have our statement, what else do you need?"

McCloy: Yes, "We know who killed Cock Robin." That is the point. It isn't only who killed Cock Robin. Under the terms of reference, we have to go beyond that. [But, in spite of their obvious awareness of the FBI's prejudice, they never did examine that question, let alone go beyond it, with the shadow of Hoover looming over their heads. There followed a brief diversion by Boggs into the question of Ruby's connections to Cuba, then Warren attempts to wrap things up.]

•

•

•

Warren: Well, Lee, as I understand your approach would be this: You would go to Mr. Hoover and say, "Now, Mr. Hoover, as you know, there are rumors that persist in and around Dallas and are getting into the national press, to the effect that Oswald was an undercover FBI agent. The rumor has gone to the extent of stating the date on which he was employed, the number under which he was employed, and the amount of money that he received for his services, and that continued right up until the time of the assassination. Now we are going to have to try to run that rumor down to see if anyone claims positive knowledge or whether it is plain rumor. Can you, and will you, give us all the information that you have which will enable us to ferret this thing out, to the very limit?"

Rankin: That is what I would like to do. Reserving at the same time the right to go to these other people and take their testimony.

Warren: That would be implicit in it.

•

•

•

Russell: It seems to me that we have two alternatives. One is we can just accept the FBI's report and go on and write the report based on their findings and supported by the raw materials they have given us, or else we can go and try to run down some of these collateral rumors that have just not been dealt with directly in this raw material that we have.

Boggs: I think we must do the latter. [Else, why are they even in business?]

Russell: So do I.

Warren: I think there is no question about it.

Russell: Of course the other is much easier.

McCloy: We wouldn't be doing the FBI a service and doing the commission a service.

Russell: The FBI would like to see us very much do it.

•

•

•

Boggs: What we have to do is tell our counsel what to do.

Warren: Yes. What do the rest of you think of the approach of Mr. Rankin, the way we have laid it out here in the last few minutes?

Dulles: Doesn't that combine your idea, too, Mr. Chairman? It seems to me it is a marriage of the two.

Warren: It is just a question of whether you have the cart or the horse first. We disagreed a little on which approach to take, but if you think his approach is reasonable, is a reasonable approach to it, it is perfectly all right with me. I would be glad to go along with it. [Here, Warren for the third time relinquishes his authority as Chairman and caves in to the desires of his General Counsel to rely primarily on Hoover's word—a crucial fork in the road.]

[A couple of minutes later...]

.

.

.

Russell: Well, Mr. Chairman, I was not primarily responsible for Mr. Rankin's employment by the commission [for which I bet the Senator was eternally grateful] but he is our counsel and if that is the way he wants to do it, I will make a motion that we proceed as he thinks is best in respect to this matter.

Warren: Is there a second?

McCloy: I think it is all right.

Dulles: Along the lines we have discussed here.

Warren: All those in favor say aye.

Chorus of "aye"

Warren: Unanimously adopted.

And so, after all the great sounding rhetoric about what they ought to do, the commission grants official permission to its General Counsel, Mr. Rankin, to proceed as he sees fit. Obviously, this is to ask FBI Director Hoover if Oswald was one of his men, when he has already gone on record that he was not. What followed in the subsequent months was a series of memos back and forth between Rankin and Hoover in which Hoover went so far as to supply written affidavits from a few of his agents to the effect that they never employed Oswald in any way. The commission never called Alonzo Hudkins or Allen Sweatt or William Alexander to testify about the source of the "dirty rumor", in spite of the fact that several commissioners repeatedly stated during the course of the above meeting that this is what ought to be done. Let's go back a page and pick up the conversation again at the point that I labeled a "fork in the road", and see what might have happened if Chairman Warren had possessed any real desire to uncover the truth.

Boggs: What we have to do is tell our counsel what to do.

Warren: Yes. I don't know what the rest of you think of Mr. Rankin's approach, but I have been sitting here pondering this dilemma we are faced with, and it is a really tough one. I know we are all concerned about what Mr. Hoover's reaction would be if we give any indication that we are investigating his agency or questioning whatever information he supplies us. But what concerns me more than that is what the future is going to think of this commission if we fail to do everything possible to get to the facts in this case. What if some day, in some way, it turns up that Oswald was indeed an undercover agent of some kind and it becomes clear that we did not thoroughly follow up all possible leads to that fact? Do you gentlemen want your name attached to a report that could be discredited in that fashion? I certainly don't want my name on it as Chairman, I can tell you that! Now what I would strongly urge this commission to do is to subpoena the three men who were involved in the broadcast of this rumor and get them here for some intensive questioning. Lee, you may inform Mr. Hoover that we are proceeding along these lines and why we feel it is our solemn duty to do so, and ask for his full cooperation in doing whatever he can from his end to supply any relevant data on this question. However, we are not going to depend solely on the FBI for our information in investigating this case. If we do that, then we have accomplished nothing more than rubber stamping their case for them. Do you all agree?

What could they have said to an argument like that? Perhaps this book and all the countless other books that have been written about the assassination of JFK and about the investigation thereof would have been unnecessary had Chief Justice Warren made a statement along those lines at any one of these early meetings. But he did not. And because he did not, his name and the names of the others on this commission are forever tainted with the ignominy that is now attached to that piece of fiction called the Warren Report.

One last interesting sidelight to this January 27th meeting is the fact that Gerald Ford, one of the commissioners and now an ex-President, summarized the contents of this meeting in a book he co-authored in 1965 with John Stiles, titled *Portrait of the Assassin*. Ford's objectives with this were twofold: first, to paint a convincing picture of Lee Harvey Oswald as the type of person who would kill a president; second, to try to show the commission as having done a thorough and honest job of investigation. He raised some official eyebrows in quoting from the transcript, since it was still classified Top Secret at the time. Also interesting is his synopsis of what this conversation said about the work of the commission. I have quoted his synopsis below for your evaluation of his honesty on this subject.

It was the consensus of all seven men that the only way to proceed was to conduct extensive and thorough hearings of as many witnesses as was necessary to exhaust not just this rumor but dozens of other rumors. Where doubts were cast on any United States agency, independent experts would be hired [none were] and the investigation conducted in such a way as to avoid reliance on a questioned authority. No matter what the cost in time or money, every facet of the events in Dallas had to be explored. The commission drew up an exhaustive list of witnesses and collected for analysis all pertinent books and magazines and newspaper articles. The staff compiled a directory of names of all persons said to have had any part in the matter. Then began months of hearings, hours of taking sworn testimony, which led from one skein of facts to another. Seldom has a crime appeared to be more complicated and mysterious. Never has a crime been so thoroughly investigated.[2]

Ironically, only *six* of the commissioners were actually present, and Ford was the one who was not. He is commenting on the conduct and the decisions made in a meeting that he did not even attend (see attendance page of transcript below).[3] He alludes to "an exhaustive list of witnesses," but somehow they managed to avoid the dozens itemized in the previous chapter. They also declined to examine the autopsy photos and x-rays, relying instead on rough, inaccurate sketches when considering the President's wounds and their significance. (See Figure 13 in Chapter 9).

I will leave it to the reader to judge how accurate and honest Mr. Ford was in the above assessment of the commission that he so steadfastly defends.

As one reads the above transcripts it is obvious that the commissioners did not sit and conspire to participate in the cover-up of the truth in this case. But it is also obvious that they lacked the will to follow up on leads that tended to point to anything or anyone other than Oswald as the "lone assassin."

TOP SECRET

12.

PRESIDENT'S COMMISSION

ON THE

ASSASSINATION OF PRESIDENT KENNEDY

- - -

Washington, D. C.

Monday, January 27, 1964.

The President's Commission met, pursuant to call, at 2:30 p.m., in the Hearing Room, Fourth Floor, 200 Maryland Avenue, Northeast, Washington, D. C., Chief Justice Earl Warren presiding.

PRESENT:

Chief Justice Earl Warren, Chairman
Senator Richard B. Russell, Member
Senator John Sherman Cooper, Member
Representative Hale Boggs, Member
John J. McCloy, Member
Allen W. Dulles, Member

- - -

J. Lee Rankin, General Counsel

TOP SECRET

Chapter 5
CUBA - ROSETTA STONE TO THE ASSASSINATION
Executive Action Turns Inward

There are two favorite motives attributed to the plotters by those who believe that John F. Kennedy's death was the result of a right-wing conspiracy. One, which was provided wide publicity by Oliver Stone's movie, *JFK*, proposes that Kennedy was murdered because he intended to withdraw from Southeast Asia once the 1964 reelection was won, and had in fact already begun going in that direction. Kennedy had signed National Security Action Memo 263, which called for the removal of 1000 troops by Christmas of 1963.[1] The argument for this being the plotters' primary motive was skillfully and exhaustively detailed in James Douglass' magnum opus, *JFK and the Unspeakable*. But to the three factions who supplied the personnel to carry out the crime, the more compelling motive was his policy toward Cuba, combined with his brother Robert's crusade against the kingpins of organized crime. Mafia leaders like Sam Giancana of Chicago had not only contributed substantial funds toward Jack Kennedy's campaign for the White House, they had also used considerable muscle and voter fraud to ensure that he took the state of Illinois. When Bobby was appointed Attorney General and began the most intensive campaign in history against the mob, they naturally felt betrayed. The depth of this feeling is made quite evident in the book, *Double Cross*, by Sam Giancana's younger brother, Chuck, and his godson, Samual M. Giancana.

Warren Commission staffer David Belin has often referred to the murder of Dallas Police Officer J. D. Tippit as "the Rosetta stone to the assassination". Belin's view, that Oswald's alleged murder of Tippit is the key to the crime and is convincing evidence that he was on the run from his assassination of the President, was representative of the view held by the Warren Commission as a whole. However, not only is there considerable doubt as to Oswald's guilt in the Tippit killing, this event is by no means the major key to unlocking the mystery of why JFK was killed and who

It's Time For the Truth!

was behind it. To find the real key, we must go back to a point almost five years before the assassination.

Castro Takes Over

With the help of his fellow revolutionary, Che Guevara, and the active assistance of the U.S. Central Intelligence Agency, Fidel Castro succeeded in overthrowing Cuba's dictator Fulgencio Batista on January 1, 1959. He immediately began instituting broad social reforms, including the nationalization of the island's sugar industry. If this weren't enough to shock his U.S. backers, Castro then proceeded to set up a "socialistic society" and struck an alliance with the Soviet Union, all the while denying he was a communist. This produced deep concern at all levels of the U.S. government. It also prompted a mass exodus of Cubans who were either Batista supporters or had supported Castro but felt betrayed by his turn toward communism. The vast majority of them migrated to the Miami area where they established a community now known as "Little Havana".

The real Havana had for many years been the "capital" of organized crime. There was not a gambling casino in Cuba that was not owned and operated by the mob. We used to think of Latin night clubs in terms of Carmen Miranda and Ricky Ricardo, but these were really the bastions and money making machines of the crime syndicate. Within a few months of Castro's takeover, the casinos were closed down and the crime bosses who owned them were expelled from the country. A few, most notably Miami crime boss Santos Trafficante, Jr., were imprisoned in Cuba until they managed to buy their release. It would seem more than a coincidence that Trafficante was released just as Ruby made one of his trips to Havana.[2]

Suddenly, there were three interwoven groups who had a deep desire to get rid of Fidel Castro: the American government, spearheaded by the CIA, who wanted to remove a communist threat only ninety miles off our shores; the Cuban exiles, who wanted their homeland back; the gambling syndicate, who wanted their casinos and base of operations back. To say that these groups were "interwoven" is to understate the situation. In some cases it was difficult to tell in which group a particular individual belonged. The Cuban exile community began to organize itself and to plan for the eventual return to a Castro-less homeland.

The Exiles Splinter

The problem was that the community subdivided itself into far too many factions for its own good. Some of the major ones were: The Christian Democratic Movement (MDC), headed by Augustin Batista, who had ties to Santos Trafficante; The Cuban Student Directorate (DRE), backed by former Cuban President Carlos Prio Socarras; Friends of Democratic Cuba, founded by Sergio Arcacha Smith; Junta of the Government of Cuba in Exile (JURE), led by Manuel Ray; Insurrectional Movement for the Recovery of the Revolution (MIRR), headed by Dr. Orlando Bosch; Alpha 66, founded by Antonio Veciana. From the latter half of 1959 until April of 1961, the leaders of the various exile groups were assisted by the U.S. to establish bases in Florida, Panama and Guatemala, from which they planned to invade their homeland and overthrow Castro. With President Eisenhower's approval, an incursion force was put together toward the end of 1960, under the sponsorship of CIA Director Allen Dulles and Vice-President Richard Nixon, who expected to be elected to the Presidency in November. He was Eisenhower's "Action Officer" on Cuba while Vice-President.[3] When Kennedy pulled off a stunning upset and won one of the closest elections in American history, he inherited the Dulles/Nixon plan to invade Cuba. Dulles assured Kennedy that all was in readiness for the invasion, which was supposed to trigger an internal uprising that would lead to Castro's ouster from power. What Dulles failed to tell the President was that the CIA had plans in place to try to assassinate the Cuban leader in conjunction with the invasion. Only a small handful of surplus World War 2 B26 bombers, flown ostensibly by Cuban pilots, was said to be needed to destroy Castro's air force on the ground before it could be used against the invasion force. Kennedy gave the go-ahead for the invasion plan, with the proviso that U.S. involvement would be well concealed.

The Invasion

On April 17, 1961, 1600 Cuban guerrillas calling themselves "Brigade 2506" led by this country's version of James Bond, E. Howard Hunt (a name made famous after the Watergate break -in)[4], his fellow CIA crony Frank Sturgis, one of the more prominent of the Cubans who were arrested in the Watergate,[5] and a few of the more prominent Cuban exiles, left their base in Guatemala City and landed at the Bay of Pigs on the southern shore of the island. Everything went wrong, from start to finish. There was *one* air strike, which did succeed in catching some of Castro's planes on the ground, but failed to destroy all of them. Additional strikes were needed to finish off the remaining planes, but by then Kennedy had begun to have second thoughts about the whole plan. He feared that the world would condemn this obviously U.S.-backed invasion of a foreign country. He was determined that it should look like a purely Cuban undertaking, but a second air strike would remove all doubt of American involvement. He refused to approve another strike, or to provide any air cover over the beachhead. His aides say that he never committed to providing US air support but the CIA assured the exiles that he would do so when the time came.[6]

The remaining planes in Castro's air force were enough, lacking opposition, to pin down the invading forces until his army could be mobilized and rout the guerrillas. The predicted uprising of the Cuban people did not take place, nor did the plot to eliminate Castro succeed. Of the 1600 men who had waded ashore, over a hundred were killed, and almost three quarters of Brigade 2506 were captured. Only a few managed to escape. Both those who did manage to get off the beach and those who were captured felt betrayed by Kennedy's lack of support and began to have serious doubts about his commitment to their cause.

The President and the CIA

Kennedy, on the other hand, felt betrayed by his own Central Intelligence Agency. He had been, at best, inadequately informed as to the goals, expectations and chances of success of the invasion. At worst, he had been systematically and intentionally lied to by CIA Director Allen Dulles, Deputy Director Richard Bissell and the rest of the CIA high command. In the weeks that followed, Dulles, Bissell and General Charles Cabell were all fired (or forced to resign) by the President, who threatened to "splinter the CIA into a thousand pieces and scatter it to the winds." He never actually went that far, but he did drastically reorganize the agency and shifted responsibility for clandestine operations to the Pentagon. He fired the three top officers and was turning intelligence responsibilities over to the Joint Chiefs of Staff.[7]

Further down the CIA's chain of command were cold-warriors such as Tracy Barnes, second in command under Bissell in arranging the Bay of Pigs invasion. Afterward, he became head of the new and illegal "Domestic Operations Division." According to contract agent Robert Morrow in his book *Betrayal*, Barnes received information from Oswald while he was in Minsk, and was involved in a secret plan which included the purchase of four Mannlicher Carcano rifles.[8] Then there was Richard Helms, who replaced Bissell after the Bay of Pigs failure as the CIA's Deputy Director of Plans. He failed to inform his new Director John McCone, of the plots to eliminate Castro. It was Helms who, in 1953, had first urged the creation of the MKULTRA mind control program.[9] They were joined by William Harvey, chief of the CIA's Cuban task force in 1960-62, one of the organizers of the CIA-Mafia plots against Castro.[10] Desmond Fitzgerald was Harvey's replacement as chief of Task Force W, a division of Operation Mongoose. He assured Rolando Cubela (AM/LASH) that he had the full support of Robert Kennedy for the plans to assassinate Castro. He was meeting with Cubela in Paris when JFK died.[11] General Edward Lansdale was given the task of coordinating Operation Mongoose, the plan to assassinate Castro.[12] Colonel Sheffield Edwards was Director of the Office of Security for the CIA.[13]

All these upper echelon intelligence and military people, along with operatives E. Howard Hunt and Frank Sturgis were not ready to concede Cuba to their bearded enemy. Harvey was in charge of the agency's "Executive Action" program (code-named ZR/RIFLE), whose mandate was to draw up assassination plans against foreign rulers who were considered to be a threat to a "democratic" western hemisphere and who could not be dealt with through "normal" methods. This program had been in effect since before the invasion and, according to insiders like CIA/Pentagon liaison Fletcher Prouty (who's views were represented by Mr. X in Stone's movie *JFK*), it had claimed some successful coups, most notably, the Congo's Patrice Lamumba in 1960, and the Dominican Republic's Rafael Trujillo in 1961. It employed hired assassins from the French Corsican Mafia as well as from U.S. based crime families.[14] Mr. X in Stone's movie gives a good, though brief, rundown of the accomplishments of this "Executive Action" program. Its existence is what prompted President Johnson to remark a few years later that "we were running a damned 'Murder Incorporated' in the Caribbean." In spite of Kennedy's reorganization, Harvey and his CIA operatives decided to accelerate their plots against Castro. One of the super-secret CIA programs that may have been utilized in these anti-Castro plans was a mind-control project started back in 1953 during the height of the Korean War at the urging of Richard Helms. This project was code-named MKULTRA and had at least four sub-programs. One of these sub-programs, called ARTICHOKE, was charged with the task of developing a feasible way to produce a dependable "Manchurian Candidate," a hypnotically controlled assassin. Its project leader was Sheffield Edwards. The existence of this program did not come to light until the Senate Intelligence Committee discovered it in 1975.[15] While this program may not have played a role in the JFK assassination, its nature indicates the lengths to which the cold-warriors were willing to go to achieve their goals. This program is covered in detail in John Marks *The Search for the Manchurian Candidate*

In spite of his disillusionment with the CIA, President Kennedy approved the establishment of a new anti-Castro project based in Miami and named JM/WAVE. It was supposed to keep a low profile, confined to propaganda activities and the occasional hit-and-run commando raid. Based on the University of Miami campus, it controlled hundreds of CIA officers and contract agents.[16] But Harvey and JM/WAVE Operations Chief David Morales had other ideas. In defiance of the President's orders and seemingly encouraged by Attorney General Bobby Kennedy, Harvey, Morales and Lansdale continued to enlist the aid of the more violent and adventurous of the Cuban exiles, plus elements of organized crime, in formulating their plans to assassinate the Cuban premier. They merely renamed the program from ZR/RIFLE to Mongoose. This was the best known of the several anti-Castro programs. As approved by Kennedy, it was not supposed to include attempts to kill Castro, but the officers in charge had a different view.[17]

In one of the earliest attempts to get Castro, Frank Sturgis (nee Fiorini), who had been part of the Bay of Pigs invasion brigade, and Alexander Rorke, another CIA contract agent and close friend of both Sturgis and E. Howard Hunt, persuaded eighteen-year-old Marita Lorenz to use her feminine charms to get close enough to Castro to poison him. She succeeded in becoming his mistress for a time, but her poison plans went awry when the capsules she planned to use disintegrated while hidden in a jar of cold-cream. The poison capsules were supplied by Frank Sturgis. This story came out during the Senate Intelligence Committee hearings in 1976.[18] After that, several other far-fetched schemes were devised, most of them like something out of a third-rate spy movie, but all of them failed.

The CIA/Mafia Connection

The main link between the CIA and the Mafia was established between the CIA's William Harvey and the dapper mobster, John Roselli, who was the Chicago Mob's West coast representative and one of Chicago crime boss Sam Giancana's closest lieutenants. Roselli began his syndicate career working for Al Capone and Frank Nitti. He later was sent to Hollywood to pressure the movie studio magnates into allowing more mob influence into the movie industry.[19] There, he became acquainted with Howard Hughes and his close advisor and aide, ex-FBI agent Robert Maheu. Later, in the early 70's, Roselli would tell syndicated columnist Jack Anderson about his role in bringing the CIA and the mob together for the common goal of killing Fidel Castro, using Maheu as the go-between. Maheu served as Hughes right-hand and retained close ties to the CIA, FBI and key Mob figures.[20] This tendency to talk, it is widely believed, is what led to his being found floating in a barrel in

Biscayne Bay, Florida about the time that the Senate Intelligence Committee was planning to question him for the third time. [21]

Maheu, who had known Harvey from back in their days in the FBI together, had since Castro's takeover been working closely with the CIA on all projects involving Cuba. He not only was friendly with Roselli and other Giancana henchmen like Richard Cain, aide to Mob boss Sam Giancana, but also had ties with Florida crime boss Santos Trafficante, Jr. He helped to train Cubans for the Bay of Pigs invasion.[22]

The CIA/Exiles Connection

A high-level connection between the CIA and the third leg in the anti-Castro triangle, the Cuban exiles, was established via a ranking agent whose code name was Maurice Bishop. Researcher and HSCA investigator Gaeton Fonzi is convinced that Bishop was actually David Atlee Phillips, who was Chief of Cuban Operations in Mexico City in November of 1963.[23] He worked with Antonio Veciana, a co-founder of the anti-Castro organization known as Alpha 66, one of the most violent of the exile groups. This group launched several raids on Soviet ships in Cuban ports, to the embarrassment of the Kennedy administration.[24] Veciana was the source of one of the most intriguing pre-assassination "Oswald sightings." He testified, in 1976 before the Schweiker subcommittee of the Senate Select Committee on Intelligence Activities, and in 1977 before the House Select Committee on Assassinations, that in August of 1963 he had met with his CIA "case officer" Maurice Bishop in a Dallas office building. Accompanying Bishop at that meeting was a young man who uttered not a word during the fifteen or so minutes he was with them before Bishop dismissed him. Veciana claimed to have recognized that man later, after the assassination of JFK, as Lee Harvey Oswald. The HSCA was skeptical of the authenticity of his story, but Fonzi, the staff investigator, was convinced of Veciana's truthfullness.[25] Oswald was still living in New Orleans at that time, leaving us to wonder whether this was the real Oswald or the impersonator who began making appearances shortly after this meeting took place. (See next chapter for more on these "false Oswald" sightings.)

At the lower levels of the CIA chain of command, connections between the agency and the Cuban exiles were too numerous to count. Contract agent E. Howard Hunt organized an anti-Castro group named the Revolutionary Democratic Front (FRD), which claimed among its most prominent members Manuel Artime, who was one of the leaders of the Bay of Pigs brigade and the CIA's "Golden Boy" among the Cuban exiles. He and Hunt were "best friends." He worked closely with Dominican Republic President Anastasio Somoza in their common efforts against Castro.[26]

These connections also included: Antonio deVarona, VP of the Cuban Revolutionary Council, who was a former prime minister of Cuba under Carlos Prio Socarras (president of Cuba before Batista took power in 1952);[27] Sergio Arcacha Smith, who was an organizer and leader of several anti-Castro groups;[28] and former Cuban President Socarras himself, who had long-term ties with Santos Trafficante, Jr. and had been a Castro supporter before the revolution succeeded in ousting Batista. After Castro turned to communism, Socarras worked with CIA employees like Frank Sturgis and Bernard Barker (of Watergate break-in fame) and other fellow Cubans like Jose Aleman, Sr., one of his former cabinet ministers and investment partners.

The fact that Aleman was married to the daughter of "Lucky" Luciano's attorney was only one of many connections between Socarras and the Luciano/Lansky/Trafficante crime family. Aleman built Miami Stadium and left it to his son.[29] That son, Jose Aleman, Jr., was a former FBI agent and a close associate of Santos Trafficante, Jr. Aleman Jr. testified before the HSCA where he elaborated upon a quote by Trafficante, first revealed by the *Washington Post* on 5/16/76. Aleman explained to the investigating committee that he had met with Trafficante in a Miami hotel room in September of 1962 to discuss arrangements for a sizable loan to Aleman that would be "coming from the teamsters union with the blessing of Jimmy Hoffa." The conversation then turned to what Robert Kennedy had been "doing to Hoffa." Aleman claims that Trafficante said, "It is not right what they are doing to Hoffa...mark my word, this man Kennedy [meaning JFK] is in trouble, and he will get what is coming to him...Kennedy's not going to make it to the election, he is going to be hit."³⁰ He later tried to explain that Trafficante meant JFK would be "hit by a lot of votes."

E. Howard Hunt was also instrumental in helping set up a blanket organization named the "Cuban Revolutionary Council", which encompassed all the smaller anti-Castro groups. The New Orleans chapter of the CRC was led by Arcacha-Smith (until he was fired for misappropriating funds) and Carlos Bringuier. It was Bringuier who had started a well-publicized scuffle with Oswald in New Orleans as he was passing out his pro-Castro Fair Play for Cuba leaflets in September of 1963, and who subsequently debated Oswald on the radio (more on this in the next chapter).

Oswald and Bannister

The New Orleans CRC people operated out of ex-FBI agent Guy Banister's offices on the second floor of a building on the corner of Camp Street and Lafayette Place. Banister was listed as a private detective but was much more involved in the anti-Castro crusade than in any detective work. He listed his office as being at 531 Lafayette Place,³¹ but the entrance at that address led upstairs to the same office area as the entrance at 544 Camp Street, which address was printed on some of the Fair Play for Cuba leaflets that Oswald was handing out on the streets of New Orleans that summer of 1963. This address was found on FPCC leaflets confiscated at the Paine home and from Banister's office after the assassination.³² The intriguing question here is, what was the "left-wing" Oswald with his pro-Castro leaflets doing hanging around in the same offices as the right-wing, violently anti-Castro Banister and company?

Another Oswald-Banister connection is provided in the person of David Ferrie. Ferrie is one of the first people questioned (besides Oswald) in regard to the assassination of the President. Within a day or two of the shooting, Ferrie was interviewed, first by New Orleans District Attorney Jim Garrison, and then by the FBI. This was prompted by the fact that when Oswald was arrested in Dallas on November 22nd, he was carrying Ferrie's library card. The FBI gave Ferrie a "clean bill", but Garrison became convinced that Ferrie,

Banister and others involved in the anti-Castro movement had been somehow involved in the assassination. The FBI's report on their questioning of Ferrie was classified "Top Secret".[33]

Ferrie was a multi-talented individual, although he was afflicted with a rare disease that rendered him hairless, and was an overt homosexual who had been barred from the priesthood and fired from his pilot job with a major airline because of it. With his often askew red wig and painted-on eyebrows, Dave Ferrie was a strange sight. Although Joe Pesci did a great job of portraying Ferrie in Stone's *JFK*, he could not come close to the truly bizarre appearance of the man. In spite of his weirdness, Ferrie was a crack pilot, a soldier-of-fortune and a jack-of-all-trades who worked for and with several people at the same time. In addition to being a military trainer of the Cuban exiles for Banister and Bringuier, he was an aide-de-camp for New Orleans crime boss Carlos Marcello.[34] At the time JFK was killed Ferrie was in a New Orleans court awaiting the decision on RFK's latest attempt to deport Marcello. Once DA Garrison decided to open his investigation into the plot to kill the President, he considered Ferrie to be the key to unraveling the tangled web of CIA/Mafia/Cuban exile intrigue that he felt certain had led to John F. Kennedy's fate in Dallas, although he tended to downplay or even ignore the Mafia leg of the triangle.

The Supporting Cast

The names mentioned in the preceding paragraphs are just the tip of the iceberg that was the CIA/Mafia/Cuban triumvirate. There are literally dozens of people who played important roles in one or more of these organizations whose common goal was the elimination of Fidel Castro, and who gradually came to see Jack Kennedy as the number one obstacle in attaining that goal. Below is a brief summation of a few more of the key cogs in this most complex machine.

Norman Rothman

A former New York City bookmaker who became operator of one of the casinos in Havana and a gun-runner for Castro during the revolution. He became a prominent member of the Lansky/Trafficante crime family, operating out of Miami. He plotted with Frank Sturgis and associates to murder Castro after the expulsion of the Mob from Cuba.[35]

Rolando Cubela (code name, AMLASH)

An anti-Castro Cuban activist supplied by E. Howard Hunt through Manuel Artime. One of the principals in the various CIA/Mafia plots to kill Castro.[36]

John Martino

An associate of Trafficanti, Marcello and Rosselli who was heavily involved in the anti-Castro plots and later claimed to have been part of the plot to kill JFK.[37]

David Morales

Miami CIA station chief (JMWAVE), associate of Johnny Rosselli, John Martino and David Atlee Phillips. Was heavily involved in CIA/Mob attempts to get Castro. Shortly before his death he bragged to friends about his role in the assassination of his bitter enemy, JFK.[38]

Rolando Masferrer

A former Batista senator and henchman known as "El Tigre" because of his brutal private army that fought against Castro's rebels before the overthrow. He became one of the leaders of the Miami-based exile groups and developed close relations with underworld leader Santos Trafficante Jr. and other anti-Castro leaders such as Carlos Bringuier, Orlando Bosch and Loren Hall.[39]

Orlando Bosch

A Cuban exile terrorist and assassin trained by Frank Sturgis. He was a close associate of Carlos Bringuier and a prominent member of "Operation 40", a CIA sponsored internal "police force" whose purpose was to keep the other exiles in line and eliminate traitors to the cause. This terrorist was charged, but not convicted, in the bombing of a Cuban airliner in 1975 which killed 73 people.[40]

Manuel Orcarberro Rodriguez

Leader of the Dallas unit of Alpha 66. Reputed to be vehemently anti-Kennedy as well as anti-Castro, he is known to have purchased arms from Dallas gunsmith John Thomas Masen (an Oswald look-alike and possible impersonator), who was associated, like many others in the anti-Castro community, with the ultra-right-wing Minutemen.[41]

Pedro Diaz Lanz

A pilot who assisted Castro to overthrow Batista and was made chief of Castro's air force, until he and his close friend, Frank Sturgis, turned against Castro when he "turned communist." Lanz was employed by Hunt in several anti-Castro activities.[42]

Loren Eugene Hall

A mercenary with ties to both the CIA and the Mob. He was claimed by J. Edgar Hoover to have been one of the men who visited Sylvia Odio on the night she claims to have been introduced to "Leon Oswald" by "Angelo" and "Leopoldo", as discussed in the next chapter. Hall first admitted, then denied, ever having visited the Odios. The other two men named by Hoover as having accompanied Hall have steadfastly denied being there and seem to have corroboration for their stories.[43] Hall *was*, however, associated with Frank Sturgis and his fellow CIA operative Gerry Patrick Hemming, as well as with Santos Trafficante Jr., with whom he was imprisoned for a time by Castro after the overthrow of Batista. He became, in the years following 1963, a prolific source of "disinformation" on pro-Castro Cuban threads to the assassination.

Hall later told DA Jim Garrison he was offered $50,000 to kill JFK but turned it down.⁴⁴

Gerry Patrick Hemming

Lee Harvey Oswald's Sergeant during their Marine stint at the Atsugi base in Japan. Hemming became another soldier-of-fortune and CIA operative working with Frank Sturgis and various anti-Castro groups. He and Lanz were said by Marita Lorenz to have been in a two car caravan with her and Sturgis on a trip from Miami to Dallas on November 21, 1963; a trip that she realized later was a prelude to the assassination.⁴⁵

Charles Nicoletti

A hit-man for Santos Trafficante involved in the drug trade who worked with John Rosselli in the plots to kill Castro. Alleged to have been in Dallas with Rosselli on November 22, 1963.⁴⁶

The Final Straw

Between the Bay of Pigs invasion and the Cuban missile crisis a year and a half later, Kennedy managed to partially placate the exiles by buying back the captured survivors of Brigade 2506, and continuing to hold out hope that another invasion attempt might be in their future.⁴⁷ But when JFK persuaded Khrushchev to remove his missiles from the island by promising that no further invasions would be sponsored or allowed by the United States, that hope was dashed.⁴⁸ The exiles and their CIA sponsors became more furious with Kennedy, but they refused to believe that he really planned to uphold his bargain with Khrushchev, and Kennedy continued for a time to encourage that faith. However, when the CIA-backed commandos, hell-bent on creating an international incident that would force JFK's hand, began attacking Russian ships in Cuban harbors and trying to kidnap Russian officers, Kennedy called a halt to all exile activity. He sent the FBI to raid their training camps, confiscating their caches of arms and explosives, and reined in their CIA sponsors. This was "strike three"–the last straw–the act of ultimate betrayal. Kennedy had to go. Even his brilliant tactic to avoid nuclear war in the missile crisis was considered an act of appeasement by these right-wing extremists.

To millions of Americans, the Kennedy administration may have been "Camelot," but to the more fanatic of the cold-warriors, it represented the most dangerous threat to our national security since the Axis powers launched World War Two. JM/WAVE Operations Chief, David Morales, became a vocal Kennedy hater and proclaimed on his death bed, "Well, we got that SOB didn't we."

I know of very few critics of the official assassination story who believe that "The CIA killed Kennedy," although this is often the way it is expressed, especially by those who would demonize our views. To blame the entire agency is as absurd as saying that the entire organized crime syndicate or the entire Cuban exile community was responsible. But *elements* from these three groups, who were working so closely together toward the goal of ridding Cuba of Fidel Castro, came to see President Kennedy as a traitor, not only to their Cuban cause, but to the country's cold war against communism in general.

However, revenge for his "traitorous actions" was not the only motive for the cold-warriors' desire to kill Kennedy; for some, not even the major motive. The more calculating among them conceived of an even better reason to assassinate a U.S. President. If it could be made to appear that he had been killed by a leftist Castro-supporter, perhaps acting under Castro's orders, the country would demand retaliation and Cuba would then be invaded in earnest. Enter Lee Harvey Oswald.

Chapter 6
WHO WAS LEE HARVEY OSWALD?
A Man of Many Faces

Researching the death of JFK has proven to be one of the most frustrating experiences imaginable for all who become mired in the morass of its mystery. One of the many reasons for this is the aura of intrigue that surrounds the young man accused of the crime. Lee Harvey Oswald was the epitome of contradiction. In spite of decades of intense investigation by both government and independent researchers, Oswald remains almost as much a mystery today as he was on the day he was shot by Jack Ruby.

Oswald was born in New Orleans, Louisiana in October of 1939, two months after the death of his father. He had an older brother named Robert, born in 1934. His mother, Marguerite, had been married previously and had given birth to a son, Lee's half-brother, John Pic, in 1932. Marguerite had several difficult periods during her life as a single parent, and in December of 1942, at the age of three, Lee was placed in an orphanage for a short time. But a year later his mother withdrew him to move to Dallas, Texas. In May of 1945, Marguerite was married for a third time, to a man named Edwin Ekdahl. Robert and John were sent off to a military school, but Lee stayed at home where he became very attached to Ekdahl, the only father he was to know. However, this marriage lasted but three years before ending in divorce.

In 1952 when Lee was thirteen, he and his mother moved to New York City. Robert had just joined the Marines and for a short time Lee and Marguerite lived with John Pic, who was then in the Coast Guard and stationed in the area. Soon Lee and his mother found their own apartment in the Bronx, but Lee refused to attend school there and was soon remanded to the area Youth House for his truancy. He was psychologically evaluated and found to be "emotionally disturbed due to inadequate attention and affection from his mother." Marguerite, in turn, evaluated Youth House and found it wanting. She decided she had had enough of the big city so she and Lee, now fourteen, moved back to New Orleans in early January, 1954.[1]

Lee had an uncle in New Orleans named Charles F. Murret, known as "Dutz" to his friends, several of whom were associates of crime boss Carlos Marcello. Murret was a bookmaker, which connected him to the illegal gambling operations of Marcello. Although he denied being close to Lee, especially after Lee's defection to Russia, Murret was nevertheless close enough to his nephew to put Marguerite and Lee up in the Murret home for a few days until they found their own apartment, then to help Lee and his mother move into their new home. Oswald is said by those who knew him as a youth to have expressed "leftist" sentiments as early as age sixteen. His reading included the works of Karl Marx and he expressed an admiration for the socialist philosophy.[2] Yet, this admirer of socialism could not wait to join the United States Marines. In fact, he dropped out of High School at the start of his tenth grade when he was not yet sixteen and tried to enlist by submitting a false statement of his age. He was disappointed when the recruiter saw through his ruse and told him to come back in a year. At age 16, Oswald even persuaded his mother to sign an affidavit that he was 17, but the recruiting officer didn't believe it.

It was during that year that Oswald began to show an interest not only in Communist literature but in the field of counter-intelligence. One of his favorite TV programs was *I Led Three Lives;* the story of a secret double agent who had infiltrated the Communist Party, and probably the earliest television program portraying the counter-intelligence world. A few days after his seventeenth birthday, in the fall of 1956, Oswald went back to his Marine recruiter and this time he was accepted.[3]

Oswald as a "Jarhead"

There were a lot of young people with liberal or left-wing politics around that time. Many of them later became "flower-children," "hippies" or draft-dodgers as the war in Vietnam escalated. They had a strong aversion to the "military-industrial complex" and everything for which militarism stood. The last thing one would expect someone of that persuasion to do would be to volunteer for service in the military, much less a branch as "gung-ho" as the Marine Corps. Perhaps for no other reason than to follow in his older brother's footsteps, Lee Harvey Oswald became a Marine and soon was sent to one of our most sensitive bases in the world at that time, Atsugi, Japan. It was from Atsugi that the top-secret U-2 spy plane took off for its high-altitude surveillance missions over China and the USSR. It was reputed to be the home of the mind-control program code-named MKULTRA. For that reason and others Atsugi was referred to as a "CIA base."[4] Atsugi was the home of the Joint Technical Advisory Group, the CIA's main base of operations in the Far East.

Although Oswald espoused a fondness for the Russian language and political system so openly that he was given the name "Oswaldskovich" by his fellow Marines, he was assigned duties that allowed him access to "top-secret" areas and data.[5] Atsugi was not far from Tokyo, and Oswald often went into town, like most of the American servicemen, to visit the many nightclubs and meet girls. One such club, named the Queen Bee, was too expensive for low-paid enlisted men like Oswald (one date there could exceed what Oswald was netting per month). Nevertheless, he was seen there on several occasions in the company of one of the hostesses who, according to another Marine buddy, was questioning Oswald about his work at Atsugi. Some researchers hypothesize that Oswald was being funded by his superiors to frequent this over-his-head establishment and feed false information to this "KGB spy." Fueling suspicion that Oswald was more than he appeared to be was a Marine medical report showing that he was treated for a venereal disease that he contracted "in the line of duty, not due to his own misconduct."[6] His "dates" with the "KGB spy" may be the explanation for his being treated for gonorrhea contracted "in the line of duty." He did, however, display some propensity for misconduct during his career in the Marines. In April of 1958 he was given a summary court-martial for possession of a privately owned, unregistered weapon. Two months later, he received another court-martial, this time for dumping a drink on an officer in a bar.[7]

Oswald spent time in the Philippines as well as Japan before returning to his point of embarkation, El Toro, California just prior to his discharge. While in the Marines, Oswald barely managed to keep himself qualified on the rifle range. His buddies often kidded him about his lack of marksmanship. But what he lacked in physical coordination and talent he seemed to make up for in intellectual ways. Somehow he managed to "teach himself" to speak and understand the Russian language so well that when he defected to Russia shortly after receiving an early "hardship" discharge from the service, (he submitted an application on August 17th, 1959, and it was approved within two weeks).[8] his soon-to-be-wife, Marina, thought he was a native Russian.[9] According to Kerry Thornley, one of Oswald's Marine buddies, this high-school dropout, who averaged two or more spelling errors per written English sentence, was extremely intelligent and well-read. His reading interests covered a wide range of subjects and included the Russian newspaper *Pravda* and books written in Russian.[10] Thornley later wrote a book about his buddy titled *Oswald*, but it was a flop. Some of his Marine friends said, after the events of November 22, 1963, that they always thought that Oswald must have been receiving intensive training in Russian while in Japan. This opinion was given some weight by Lieutenant Colonel A. G. Folsom's testimony to the Warren Commission about a poor score Oswald received on a test in Russian, given while he was based in California. His "poor score" came in February of 1959. By that summer he was conversing fluently with the aunt of a Marine buddy.[11] This was just before he got his discharge four weeks early, in September of 1959, supposedly to care for his mother. She had been injured in a minor accident that had occurred nearly a year earlier and from which she had by then fully recovered.

Intelligence Training?

Another indication that Oswald did not pick up the Russian language completely on his own came out of the Warren Commission's executive session of January 27, 1964. A little later in the conversation excerpted in Chapter 4, General Council Lee Rankin made the following intriguing and unexplained comment to the attending commissioners as part of a general discussion of Marina Oswald's testimony about her husband.

Rankin: ...In addition to that, there is this Spanish dictionary, and the books about Spanish...although he had known some Spanish before going to Russia, and we are trying to run that down and find out what he studied at the Monterey School of the Army in the way of languages.[12]

The Monterey School specializes in teaching foreign languages to the military, usually as part of intelligence or counter-intelligence training. We have no other indication of what prompted Rankin to make this remark, but there could be no clearer indication that Oswald was being groomed for some sort of intelligence work. One week before being granted his discharge Oswald applied for a passport, ostensibly to attend Albert Schweitzer College in Finland. His passport was approved in just six days. Having obtained his early discharge, Oswald spent only three days with his mother, who by then was living in Houston Texas, before leaving for New Orleans and from there to Russia. He went by steamship to England and by plane from there to Helsinki, Finland. His passport showed that he arrived in Helsinki a day earlier than any commercial flight could have gotten him there, indicating a chartered or military plane was used. He arrived in Southampton, England on October ninth and in Helsinki later the same day, at a time suggesting other than commercial air travel. He then boarded a train for the last leg of his journey to Moscow.[13]

A few days after his arrival in Moscow on October sixteenth, 1959, Oswald applied for Soviet citizenship, but the Russians appeared to be disinterested in what he had to offer and refused his request. Having been ordered to leave the country, Oswald, out of despair, desperation or perhaps clever stratagem, slashed his left wrist in his hotel room. His "Intourist guide", who was due for a meeting with him at about that time, came along and found him in time to prevent his bleeding to death. After a short stay in a local hospital, he again pleaded with the Russian officials to allow him to stay. This time they said they would consider his request.

Oswald as "Traitor"

After vainly awaiting further word for three days, Oswald appeared at the American Embassy in Moscow, where he turned over his passport and stated in writing that he was declaring his future allegiance to the Soviet Union. He bragged that he had highly sensitive radar secrets to offer the Russians, almost as if he assumed that the Russians had the embassy bugged and would hear his offer of help. Oswald displayed an unusual knowledge of the legal niceties involved in renouncing citizenship.[14] Perhaps he was right about the bug because after letting him stew for over two months, on January fourth, 1960, the Russians granted Oswald an "identity document for stateless persons" and he was sent to Minsk, Byelorussia, (now Belarus) to work in an electronics factory making radio parts. He was set up in a "luxury" apartment, unattainable to most workers at his level, and boasted of living more lavishly than his factory foreman.

Six months later, Francis Gary Powers' U-2 spy plane was shot down over Russian territory. Although the Russians were aware of these over-flights, they had never been able to shoot down a U-2 before because of the extremely high altitudes at which these planes flew. Oswald, thanks to his work at the Atsugi base, may have known for what altitudes the Russian missiles needed to be calibrated. Many have suspected that it was his knowledge that enabled Powers' plane to be shot down. This incident scuttled the planned summit meeting between President Eisenhower and Premier Khrushchev, which might have succeeded in producing the world's first limited nuclear test ban treaty. Some skeptics have advanced the theory that Oswald was sent to Russia by the Office of Naval Intelligence (ONI) for the express purpose of providing enough information to the Russians to *allow* them to shoot down a U-2 and thus ward off what they considered to be a dangerous thaw in East-West relations. Even more extreme is the school of thought, led by researcher Michael Eddowes, author of *Khrushchev Killed Kennedy* (later re-titled as *The Oswald File*), that the Russians assumed from the outset that Oswald was a spy and turned the tables on us by substituting their own look-alike agent and sending him back home to spy for them and, some think, with the goal of killing

Kennedy. After the assassination the Soviets were so afraid that they would be accused of hiring Oswald to kill JFK that they sent "defector" Yuri Nosenko here two months after the assassination with inside information about the USSR's total disinterest in Oswald.[15]

Oswald's movements and actions during his stay in Russia remain clouded to this day. The Warren Commission relied heavily upon his "historic diary", which was found in his affects after his death. This was a rambling account of his stay in the USSR that experts determined was written in Oswald's own hand. However, other experts have expressed the opinion that the entire diary was written in one or two sittings, rather than day by day. Several of the entries and references contain chronological inaccuracies. This lends more weight to the suspicion that his purpose in Russia was other than he claimed.

A "Change of Heart"

Whatever his goal, after fifteen months in the USSR, living more luxuriously than he ever had in the United States and having married a Russian woman whose uncle was a high-ranking officer in the Soviet Ministry of Internal Affairs (roughly equivalent to our FBI), Oswald once again appeared at the American Embassy in Moscow on July eighth, 1961, and declared his desire to return home to America. His passport was promptly returned to him by the Americans, no questions asked, but the Russians were not so quick and it wasn't until May of 1962 that the Oswalds were notified by the embassy that everything was in order for their return to the U.S. In the meantime, Marina had given birth to their first daughter, whom they named June. On June first, 1962, the three Oswalds were given a loan of $435 by the American Embassy to cover their travel expenses, and they boarded a train for the start of their trip. The Oswalds met little resistance from either the Russian or the American government in leaving the USSR for the US.[16]

There are several intriguing discrepancies in the story of their journey to the United States. The first leg of the journey was from Moscow to Amsterdam, Holland, via East Germany. However, differences in passport stamps indicate that Marina and Lee did not take the same route to Amsterdam. There is some evidence that Oswald stopped briefly in West Berlin before going on to Holland on his own. A page in Oswald's address book contained a hand drawn map with a primary East-West access-station prominently marked.[17] Marina later testified that they stayed in Holland for *three* nights before resuming their journey, but records indicate that they were only there for *one* night. She also said at first that they *flew* from Holland to New York City and then took a train from New York to Texas. But she later concurred with the Warren Commission's findings that they had crossed the Atlantic by *ship* and had docked in Hoboken, New Jersey. Here, they were met by Spas Raikin of the Traveler's Aid Society. He brought them to New York City where they boarded a plane for Dallas. Raikin was Secretary General of American Friends of the Anti-Bolshevik Bloc of Nations, with ties to many CIA-backed groups, including Guy Banister's.[18]

Strangely, there was no *known* attempt by either the CIA or the FBI to "debrief" Oswald about his stay in Russia, nor was there any action taken against him in regard to his defection. The Marine Corps could have prosecuted him for treason but didn't, in spite of having had to change a lot of secret codes when he defected.[19] In an era when even tourists returning from the USSR were being extensively questioned in an effort to glean any scrap of potentially useful intelligence data, it is incomprehensible that a returning defector would be thus ignored. But was he?

Back in the USA

During the period in Lee Oswald's life between his return from the Soviet Union with a Russian wife and November twenty-second, 1963, his activities were no less mysterious. Upon the arrival of the Oswald family in Texas, they settled down in Fort Worth where they were welcomed and embraced by the anti-communist White Russian community. These people took a shine to Marina and her baby but Lee still appeared to harbor pro-communist leanings so he did not mix well with this anti-communist group. Yet, it was during this period and among these people that he met a most intriguing exception to the rule. He was befriended by a man named George DeMohrenschildt, a petroleum engineer and secretly a member of the "intelligence community." Many researchers believe that DeMohrenschildt was assigned by the CIA to perform an "unwitting debriefing" of Oswald. This inexplicable relationship between the highly educated man-of-the-world and the reclusive high school drop-out was one of the most puzzling parts of Oswald's life, and one that the House Select Committee wanted to explore with DeMohrenschildt in 1977. Unfortunately, DeMohrenschildt's life had taken a serious turn for the worse since the assassination. He had suffered mental problems for which he had spent a short time in the hospital. On the very day that committee investigator Gaeton Fonzi finally located him and was about to meet with him to invite him to testify, he (apparently) committed suicide by shotgun in his own bedroom. Jay Epstein, author of *Inquest*, was seeking DeMohrenschildt in connection with the book he was writing at that time (*Legend*) in which he espouses the theory that Oswald may have been a Soviet agent.[20]

During the months following Oswald's return to the States, he seemed to have trouble holding down a job for any length of time. After working for a short while at a Fort Worth metal factory, Oswald took the advice of his friend DeMohrenschildt and abruptly quit that job to move to Dallas where the Oswalds were invited to share the home of Ruth and Michael Paine. Here, with DeMohrenschildt's help, he soon found work at the graphic-arts company of Jaggers-Chiles-Stovall where he had the opportunity to enhance his photographic skills. Since JCS did a lot of government contract work, including maps made from classified pictures obtained from the U-2 spy plane, it seemed a strange place for a former defector to the USSR and an overt Marxist to find work; another in a long list of strangely lax security precautions involving Oswald.[21]

The Mysterious Gun Purchases

In March of 1963, according to the official records, Oswald ordered and received through the mail, from Klein's Sporting Goods of Chicago, the Mannlicher-Carcano rifle with which he was accused of killing the President. He had already acquired via mail-order in January the .38 revolver with which he would allegedly shoot Officer Tippit. These were both ordered using the Alek Hidell alias. *For a Texan to mail-order weapons from outside the state is about as sensible as a*

Floridian obtaining his oranges that way. During his two days in captivity, Oswald admitted that he owned the revolver but steadfastly denied ever owning a rifle. Yet, according to Marina's Warren Commission testimony, Lee told her he used his rifle in an attempt to kill retired right-winger General Edwin Walker on April tenth, 1963, but missed, even though Walker was sitting only about thirty yards away in his living room at the time the bullet came crashing through the window. *If this shooter was indeed Oswald, his marksmanship took a dramatic turn for the better between then and 11/22/63.* The bullet dug out of the wall was too mutilated to be identified as to caliber. It was first described by police as a steel-jacketed 30.06 slug, quite different from Oswald's copper-jacketed 6.5mm ammo.²²

When the Dallas Police confiscated Oswald's belongings from the Paine house and garage after the assassination, they found a photograph of the back of the Walker house. In the driveway, there was a car that apparently did not belong to the General. When this photo was submitted to the Warren Commission, it had a small hole in it, right where the license plate on that car should have been, although the hole had not been there when the photo was found by the police.

Those Strange Photos

The Oswald family moved from one Dallas apartment to another and were living on Neely Street when, in the early Spring, the three famous backyard photographs, allegedly taken by Marina, showed Lee brandishing a rifle, with a pistol on his hip, holding two Russian language newspapers of opposing political views. *LIFE Magazine* featured one of these pictures on the cover of its February twenty-one, 1964 issue, and it served to solidify Oswald's guilt in the minds of the American people. When Oswald was confronted with these photos while in the custody of the Dallas Police, he steadfastly denied that they were of him, claiming that someone had superimposed his face on someone else's body. As far-fetched as this may sound, it is precisely what many researchers believe to be the case, in spite of the fact that the official investigative bodies in 1964 and 1977-78 found that the photos were authentic. The HSCA concluded that the photos were genuine on the basis of guide marks on the edges of the negatives which matched the marks made by Oswald's camera, and on Marina's testimony.[23]

There are several aspects to these photos that critics have pointed out in their efforts to support the idea of falsification. First, the chin of the man in the pictures seems squarer than Oswald's chin, and there is an obvious horizontal line between the chin and the lower lip, which could be the separation between two parts of a montage. Second, the shadow of his nose is at a straight vertical angle while the shadow of the rest of his body is not. Furthermore, this shadow seems to keep its position relative to the rest of the face in all three pictures, even though the tilt of the head differs. Third, according to some, the face and head in each of the three pictures seem exactly the same, including size, while the rest of the body size varies slightly with the distance from the camera. However, a close examination of full-sized prints of these photos reveals that there are slight but discernible differences in both size and expression (See Figure 9 below). Moreover, there is one indication that these photographs were indeed authentic, which I find quite convincing. It was discovered in 1977 that Oswald had given a signed copy of one of these photos to his friend George DeMohrenschildt. On the back of it someone had written in Russian, "Hunter of Fascists. Ha Ha!" Marina, who is now convinced that her husband was innocent of the assassination, says that she wrote those words in reference to Lee's claim that he had taken a pot-shot at General Walker. The dedication "To my friend George from Lee Oswald," was determined by experts to have been in Oswald's handwriting.[24]

Figure 9

Although she was not always truthful with the authorities in the months following the assassination, she would have no reason to lie about the incident after she became convinced, and was trying to convince the public, that her husband was not Kennedy's killer.

Back to New Orleans

In April of 1963, after ten months in the Dallas-Fort Worth area with his marriage growing progressively rockier, Oswald again decided that they needed a change of scene. Once more, he uprooted his family and returned to the place of his birth, New Orleans. Again settled in his old home-town, Oswald went public with his pro-Marxist, pro-Castro support, passing out leaflets, appearing on radio talk-shows and attempting to establish his own one-man cell of the Fair Play for Cuba Committee. But his base of operations for printing and storing his pro-Castro leaflets was in the same office building (544 Camp St.) as the anti-Castro, right-wing, ex-FBI agent Guy Banister. In fact, Banister's secretary, Delphine Roberts, says she saw Oswald in the company of Banister, Dave Ferrie and several Cuban exiles on numerous occasions. She told author Anthony Summers that Banister knew about and accepted Oswald's use of the 544 Camp St. address as a base for his FPCC operations and had indicated to her that "He's with us".[25] This group was frantically engaged at the time in supplying arms and training to Cuban guerrillas who were still, in spite of the Bay of Pigs failure, hoping to overthrow Fidel Castro.

At that time, this same office building was the headquarters for the anti-Castro Cuban Revolutionary Council's New Orleans unit (New Orleans was second only to Miami as a hotbed of anti-Castro activities). One of the leaders of this group was a shop owner named Carlos Bringuier. Oswald walked into his store and offered to use his Marine experience to help train the Cuban exiles in their preparations to fight Castro.[26] When he was seen a few days later, passing out *pro*-Castro Fair Play For Cuba Committee leaflets, Bringuier and a few of his fellow exiles sought Oswald out and confronted him on the street. There was a brief scuffle in which one punch was thrown, by Bringuier, but *Oswald* was the one arrested. While he was in jail for disturbing the peace, Oswald asked for and was granted a private interview with FBI Special Agent John Quigley (who kept no notes). Shortly afterward he was bailed out by a friend of his uncle "Dutz" Murret.[27] After the street fracas with Bringuier, he and Oswald accepted an invitation to debate politics on a local station, where Oswald openly declared that he was a "Marxist."[28]

During this period, Oswald obtained work as a machine oiler at the New Orleans coffee firm of W. B. Reily Co., Inc. The company's owner, Mr. Reily, happened to be a financial backer and prominent member of the Crusade to Free Cuba, a front group for the Cuban Revolutionary Council.[29] While he was so employed, Oswald spent quite a bit of his time scanning sporting goods magazines at the Crescent City Garage right next to the coffee company. This establishment was run by Adrian Alba, who told the Warren Commission not only of Oswald's magazine browsing but of once seeing Oswald handed an envelope through the window of one of the "government cars" that Alba's garage routinely serviced.[30] But the Commission was much more interested in the possibility that Oswald may have ordered his guns through ads found in Alba's magazines. Oswald spent too little time on the job at Reily's, and was eventually fired.

It's Time For the Truth!

One can only wonder if Oswald was really the leftist he portrayed himself to be and was attempting to infiltrate the right-wing group run by Banister (and Banister was stringing him along) or was not a leftist at all but creating that image of himself for some reason. Either alternative would indicate that he was *some* sort of undercover agent or agent provocateur. Many researchers believe that he was being controlled by some agency of the U.S. government, but to what purpose is anything but clear. It does seem quite apparent that he *was* being manipulated both by an intelligence agency and by those who were planning to assassinate the President. Some researchers have concluded that he was actually being programmed through hypnotism.[31]

The Impersonations

The appearances of an Oswald impersonator in the two months prior to the assassination are well documented by many critics. Richard Popkin based his early book, *The Second Oswald*, on these events. The bulk of these "false Oswald" sightings took place in the period between the end of September and November 22, 1963. Some of them involved encounters at; a car dealership, a used furniture store, a gun-shop, and (several times) at the Dallas Sports Drome Rifle Range, where on at least one occasion "Oswald" drew obvious attention to himself by firing at his neighbor's target. For a brief but excellent summary of these events, see Anthony Summers' *Conspiracy*.[32]

The two most heavily discussed incidents occurred during a common time period, September 25 to October 1, 1963. Oswald had sent his pregnant wife back to Dallas where their second child could be born among friends. It was then that, according to the FBI, the CIA and the Warren Commission, he took a trip by bus to Mexico City where he allegedly visited both the Cuban and the Russian embassies, ostensibly to obtain a passport to Cuba with the intention of ultimately returning to the USSR.

Although someone who represented himself to be Lee Harvey Oswald spoke with employees of both of these embassies, there were several problems with the efforts to prove that it was actually Oswald. The descriptions given by the people who talked to the visitor did not match Oswald. They described their vociferous visitor as speaking crude and halting Russian, hardly the kind of ability Oswald had with the language. The CIA took pictures of the visitor entering and leaving the embassies who was supposed to have been Oswald but obviously was not. The CIA said these pictures (of an older, heavy set man) were submitted through "clerical error", and later said that their surveillance camera was not working on the day of Oswald's visit.[33] The CIA had both embassies bugged. Tape recordings of conversations were produced, but the agents who listened to the tapes (before they were "routinely destroyed") said the voice was not that of Lee Harvey Oswald.[34] Finally, the CIA had to admit to the investigators on the HSCA that they had no idea who this person calling himself Oswald really was. But the agency still maintained that the real Oswald did indeed go to Mexico City and visit both embassies at that time, and the Warren Commission accepted the story and used it as evidence of his instability and leftist politics.

During the same period, three people unexpectedly visited the home of Sylvia Odio in Dallas between September 25th and 27th (she was unable to pin down the exact date). Two of her visitors were "Latin Americans or Mexicans" who called themselves "Leopoldo" and "Angelo" and said they were members of the left-wing Cuban exile organization named JURE. They convinced Miss Odio that they knew her father, who was in prison in Cuba, and said they were looking for financial help from the Odios. The third person was an unkempt and sulky young man who remained outside during the meeting. He was referred to as "Leon Oswald," whom the other two described as a rather "loco" American ex-Marine who was chiding his Cuban friends for not "killing Kennedy after the Bay of Pigs." She never heard "Leon" speak but was told on the phone the next day what he supposedly said.[35]

Miss Odio's experience became a problem for the Warren Commission when she notified the local FBI office that she recognized the man arrested in the Texas Theater on the afternoon of the assassination, whose face she saw displayed on television, as the "loco" American who came to her door, in the period in which he was supposedly in Mexico City. Unfortunately, the commission did not get around to interviewing her until late July, when they were trying to wrap up their investigation, and then it was in the form of a deposition taken by commission staff lawyer Wesley Liebeler. In fact, she was one of the last witnesses to testify, even though the FBI had taken her potentially enlightening statement as early as December. Since Mrs. Odio's story was confirmed by her sister, who had answered the door when the three men visited their apartment, the commission believed that the visit occurred, but concluded that the Odios were mistaken in their identification of "Leon" as Lee Harvey Oswald. True to Warren Commission form, no follow-up investigation was performed on this or any of the other "false Oswald" incidents. The HSCA also failed in its feeble probe to give proper attention to this glaring indication of conspiracy.

One interesting thing that most of these sightings of "Oswald", including the Odio incident, have in common is the description of this "Oswald" as being unkempt and in need of a shave. Researchers point out that the "historical Oswald" was always clean-shaven and neatly, though often casually, dressed. Richard C. Nagell was a former CIA operative who became *The Man Who Knew Too Much*, and has a most interesting story to tell. He told author and journalist Dick Russell (not to be confused with Senator Richard Russell) that he had met both Lee Harvey Oswald and Leon Oswald and that they were of similar size, build, hair color and facial structure. But Leon was less articulate and intelligent than Lee Harvey and was an avowed member of the radical right. It is significant that none of Oswald's relatives or friends referred to him as "Leon". It was always "Lee".[36] This could account for some of the "second Oswald" encounters by people who later could not firmly identify the man they saw as Lee H. Oswald. Another right-winger from the Dallas area who bore a striking resemblance to Oswald was gunsmith and expert marksman John Thomas Masen. Masen was a member of the ultra-right and ultra-militant Minutemen, and had sold firearms and ammunition to the Dallas unit of Alpha 66, one of the most aggressive of the anti-Castro exile organizations. This man may have been the "Oswald" double seen by Deputy Sheriff Craig running from the TSBD a few minutes after the assassination.[37]

The real Oswald, who apparently did visit Mexico City, if not the two embassies, at the end of September of 1963, arrived back in Dallas in early October. Marina was now living with Ruth Paine, one of the friends they had made through George DeMohrenschildt, at her home in Irving, Texas, just a few miles outside Dallas. By mid-October, Mrs. Paine had helped Oswald obtain a job as an order-filler at the Texas School Book Depository in downtown Dallas. He rented a room in a boarding-house in the suburb of Oak Cliff and visited his wife in Irving on weekends, hitching a ride with co-worker Buell Wesley Frazier, who lived near Mrs. Paine. On October 20, Marina gave birth to their second daughter, named Audrey. Lee was a proud father who seemed to enjoy his children. Meanwhile, the "false Oswald" sightings continued. These incidents may have been one reason why FBI Special Agent James Hosty was keeping an eye on Oswald and attempting to question him on a few occasions during this period. According to the Warren Report, this prompted Oswald to deliver a belligerent note to the local FBI office, addressed to Hosty—a note which Hosty was ordered by his superior to destroy immediately after the President was killed.[38]

Which "Oswald" Was the Real One?

In addition to the several impersonations that took place in and around Dallas and in Mexico City, it seems very likely that other identity games had been played out while he was in Russia, and perhaps even after his death. Several researchers have pointed out some puzzling disparities in Oswald's physical appearance during the different time periods of his short adult life.

First, there is the matter of his height, which was recorded as 5' 11" on all documents but one before he left for Russia. The only exception was his enlistment application for the Marines at age 17 when he was still growing, where he listed his height as 5' 9". The problem is that *every document*, such as his several employment applications, that he filled out *after* returning from Russia gave his height as 5' 9". In photos of Lee and Marina in Minsk, he appears only slightly taller than Maria, who was 5'5" or 5'6".[39] Did he shrink while in Russia?

Then there are the photographs of Oswald in Russia, which do not really look like the same man who was arrested in Dallas (see Figure 10 below).

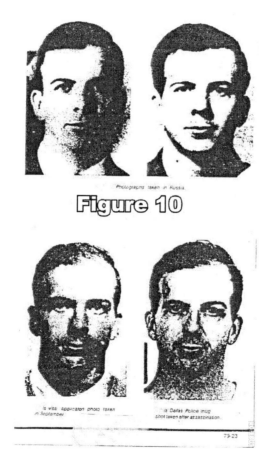

Figure 10

Add to that the fact that his mother and his brother commented on how he looked, acted and talked differently upon his return home from the Soviet Union. His half brother, John Pic, found him to look *very* different and to speak with a strange accent.[40]

When actor Gary Oldman was preparing for his role as Lee Harvey Oswald in Oliver Stone's movie he studied tapes of Oswald's voice to be able to better imitate him (and did an outstanding job). Oldman commented on the lack of any trace of southern accent for a man born and brought up in New Orleans and who lived much of his life in Texas. He further commented that the man he studied did not even seem to speak like a native American. He is not the first to get this impression of Oswald's speech idiosyncrasies. Even FBI Director Hoover issued a memo while Oswald was in Russia, in which he voiced his suspicion that someone else was using Oswald's birth certificate. The memo was issued in June, 1960, to the Office of Security, Department of State. No reason was given for the suspicion.[41] All of this lends support to the theory that it was not the real Oswald who came back from Russia.

The Last Weekend

On November 21st, Oswald deviated from his usual routine and asked his co-worker Buell Frazier to drive him out to Irving after work that Thursday afternoon instead of waiting until Friday. When Frazier inquired as to why the special trip, Oswald said he needed to get some curtain rods for his room in Oak Cliff. That evening he spent some time playing with June and trying to make up with Marina, as they had argued the last time they were together. However, relations were still a bit strained between them and Oswald went to bed early. The next morning he left $170 on the dresser for Marina and exited the house before she was awake. The Warren Commission reported that Oswald also left his wedding ring behind in a tea cup for Marina to find. If true, this would seem to indicate that he knew there was a good chance he would not be seeing her again because of what he intended to do that day. However, as one researcher has pointed out, in Volume III of the commission's Hearings, Ruth Paine testified that FBI agent Odum came to her home after Oswald's death to ask Paine on behalf of Marina (who was now being held in a motel for interrogation) if she could find Lee's ring for her. It was with Odum's "help" that the ring was found in the bedroom in the tea cup. This would indicate that the ring was *not* found by Marina on Friday morning.

As Oswald approached Frazier's house to get his ride to work, Buell's sister, Linnie Mae Randle, looked out the kitchen window and observed Lee walking into the driveway carrying a brown paper package, which she later described as about two feet long. When Frazier came out and got into the car, he looked into the back and saw the package lying on the seat. He asked Oswald what it was and Lee reminded him that he had come home to pick up some curtain rods. Frazier later testified that the bag was about 24-27 inches long, about the right length for curtain rods and much too short to have been the disassembled rifle, which measured 34.8 inches. The FBI and the Warren Commission believed he and his sister must have been wrong in their estimate of length. They even gave Frazier a polygraph test, which he passed. The most convincing evidence of his accuracy, however, was the way he described Oswald carrying the package as he walked on ahead of Frazier on their way from the parking lot to the Book Depository. He said that Lee cupped one end of the package in his right palm and had the other end tucked under his armpit, almost as if he was trying to conceal it. There is no way that the 38 inch bag later found on the sixth floor and assumed to have carried the disassembled rifle could have been held in such a manner. When he entered the building, several steps ahead of Frazier, no one saw anything in his hands.[42]

During the course of the morning, several fellow workers remembered seeing Lee at his usual duties. The last person to remember seeing him before the shots were fired was secretary Carolyn Arnold. According to an FBI report she testified that she caught a glimpse of Oswald in the first floor hallway as she was standing in front of the building. But researcher Anthony Summers located her in 1978 and interviewed her about this FBI report. She was shocked at what that report said about her testimony. She told Summers that what she had really told the FBI was that she saw Oswald in the second floor lunchroom, sitting at a table eating his lunch at 12:15 or shortly thereafter.[43]

The President was scheduled to come by that spot at 12:25 and no one knew that they were running five minutes behind schedule. If Oswald was planning to shoot him, he was certainly waiting until the last minute to get set up for it.

About ninety seconds *after* the shots, Oswald was encountered in the same second floor lunchroom by Officer Marion Baker, who had rushed into the building moments after the last shot was fired. He collared superintendent Roy Truly on the way in and told him he wanted to get up to the roof. They paused for a few moments to try for a freight elevator but it wasn't at their floor and someone had left the door open so that it could not be called. They went to the stairway in the back left-hand (northwest) corner and Truly led the way up the stairs. As Baker reached the second floor landing, he happened to spot someone through a small window in the door to the vestibule leading to the lunchroom. He entered the lunchroom and challenged Oswald. Just then Truly came in and told the officer that the man worked in the building. With that, Baker and Truly continued their trek up the stairs, and Oswald, Coke in hand, calmly walked through the office area and out the front door.[44] A little over an hour later, Oswald was apprehended in the Texas Theater as a suspect in the shooting of Officer Tippit. He was hauled off to the downtown station where he would spend the next forty-four hours or so, until his fateful encounter with Mr. Ruby.

More Questions

In later years, as researchers dug up more and more information, doubts rose as to the identity of the man buried in the grave marked "Oswald." Researcher and author of *Khrushchev Killed Kennedy*, Michael Eddowes, persuaded Marina to push for exhumation. After a great deal of haggling with the Texas authorities, Oswald's body was exhumed in October of 1981 and tests were performed to determine if the body was indeed that of Lee Harvey Oswald. Although the authorities confirmed that it was Oswald in that grave, the two morticians who had prepared him for burial back in 1963 and who were present during these tests, swear that this is not the person they embalmed! One indication they pointed to was that a craniotomy had been performed on Oswald during his autopsy, but the body they disinterred showed no sign of a craniotomy.[45] It is also interesting to note that when the disinterment took place, they found the seal on the burial vault broken and the body much more decomposed that it should have been, indicating that the coffin had been previously opened.[46]

Since there seem to have been at least *two* Lee Oswalds in action during the period leading up to the assassination of John Kennedy, it is very difficult to know for sure which one was where and doing what at any point in time. Having the same man apparently leading two lives is confusing enough, but we also have to contend with at least one imposter as well. If *all* of the CIA, FBI, Warren Commission and HSCA files pertaining to Oswald are eventually opened in uncensored form, we may finally find out just what role Oswald was playing, and his enigmatic actions may begin to make some sense. One thing is quite clear, however. He seems to have been a much more likely candidate for the role of "patsy" than to have been one of the assassins of President Kennedy.

If Oswald was not a Marxist but actually a right-winger like those with whom he was associating in the summer of 1963, or at least sympathetic to their cause, he may very well have been involved in some way in the plot to kill JFK. At least with those political leanings, he would have had a motive. But if Oswald was really the Marxist idealist he claimed to be—the type of man who may well have wanted to kill the right-wing extremist General Walker—why would he train his rifle on a President whose personality and policies, for the most part, he greatly admired and who was one of Walker's most hated enemies?

Oswald's motive for killing the President was one of the questions the Warren Commission found the most troublesome. For lack of anything more specific, they finally settled on the assumption that he was simply a bitter, deranged man seeking a place in history—trying to accomplish something noteworthy for the first time in his life. Certainly this has been the motive for some major crimes in the past, but very seldom does the notoriety-seeker steadfastly deny his guilt, as Oswald did during the two days he was a prisoner of the Dallas police. Assassins seeking notoriety proudly proclaim their deed.

Weigh this supposed motive, assumed by the Warren Commission, against the motive of the right-wing military-intelligence-industrialist zealots who despised Jack Kennedy for his relatively soft anti-communism stance, his "betrayal" at the Bay of Pigs, and his deal with Khrushchev over Cuba. There has been a lot of conjecture, pro and con, over whether the hypothesis in Oliver Stone's *JFK* was correct when he heralded Garrison's theory that Kennedy was killed because he intended to scale down our involvement in Vietnam. This was the real Jim Garrison's belief, and there are indications that a withdrawal may have been in Kennedy's plans for after his re-election in 1964. The evidence for this argument is best put forth in John Newman's *JFK and Vietnam*. But even without this additional incentive, there were ample reasons why the cold warriors wanted him out of the way.

To those who adhere to the theory that it was the *pro*-Castro Cubans (or Castro himself) who engineered the assassination of JFK in retaliation for the efforts of the U.S. Government to murder the Cuban leader, I would ask these questions: Would they have relied upon someone like Lee Harvey Oswald, a seemingly unstable ex-Marine who couldn't shoot worth a damn, to carry out that assignment? Or, alternatively, would they have set up as a patsy a man with such a pro-Castro, pro-Russian reputation? Oswald makes a perfect patsy *only* for those who would wish to point the finger of blame directly at Cuba and its communist premier.

Defector or Agent?

The enigma of Lee Harvey Oswald has baffled and frustrated all students of the Kennedy assassination for several decades. While we may never have a definitive answer to just who and what Oswald was, the fuzziness of his portrait is perhaps made a bit clearer by a passage from Robert Sam Anson's work, *They've Killed the President* (Bantam, 1975).

Maybe the problem with understanding Oswald is that we think we know him so well. So ignore his name and consider the facts: a man who works at a CIA base; has his records altered by the military; defects to Russia with no money; takes a plane when no planes are available; marries the niece of a high-ranking Soviet official; slips across the iron curtain without leaving a trace; threatens espionage and is not arrested; lives in a community infiltrated by intelligence agents; befriends a former spy; is seen in close contact with two intelligence agents; makes travel arrangements in the company of an employee of the CIA; uses an alias; keeps an office in a building with other agents; eludes detection by surveillance devices; gets a passport when one should be denied; and is finally shot down in a room crowded with police by a former informer for the nation's chief investigative agency. Absorb these things, and then imagine that the man happened to be named John Smith. Who do *you* think he was?[47]

One additional bit of fascinating information that may indicate who or what Oswald was has been provided by author Dick Russell in *The Man Who Knew Too Much* and later by author Lamar Waldron in *Legacy of Secrecy*. They point out that CIA files reveal that several other young Americans had "defected" to Russia and then "re-defected" during that time period. One of them was an ex-Navy man named Robert Webster, who went to Russia two weeks before Oswald did and returned to the US two weeks before Oswald. Webster shared several other similarities to Oswald, including returning with a Russian wife. This has all the earmarks of a US intelligence program designed to send ex-servicemen to the Soviet Union on spy missions.[48]

Obviously, there are a myriad of unanswered questions surrounding the accused assassin of JFK, many of which will probably always remain a mystery. If I had to select the most important questions to have the answers to, they would be these:

1. What or who was behind his learning of the Russian language, his early discharge, his ease in getting into and out of the Soviet Union and the lack of any official debriefing when he returned?

2. What was the meaning of his association with right-wing, anti-Castro activists in New Orleans (544 Camp St.) in Sept. of 1963?

3. Why did he go to Mexico City later that same month, and what is the CIA hiding pertaining to his supposed visits to the Cuban and Soviet embassies?

4. Who were the Oswald imposters and at which of the questionable sightings was it the real Oswald and which an imposter?

5. What was in the package that he brought to work on the day JFK died?

6. What did he *really* do between the time he left the boarding house at 1:00 PM on 11/22/63 and when he entered the Texas Theater?

I still believe that it is possible, even at this late date, to find the answers to at least some of these questions. But it will take the combined power of the American public and the news media to force our government to cooperate in getting those answers.

Chapter 7
JACK RUBY: SCREWBALL OR MOB PAWN?
An Expendable Asset

According to the Warren Commission, Jack Ruby was a frustrated, neurotic night-club operator who was paranoid about his Jewishness, so he decided to show the world that "Jews have guts" by performing the "patriotic act" of killing the President's accused assassin and saving Mrs. Kennedy the necessity of coming back to Dallas for the trial of her husband's killer.[1] After their "exhaustive investigation," the Warren Commission also concluded that Ruby had no ties to any significant organized crime figures. The absurdity of these two conclusions was being documented even before the Commission's report was presented to President Johnson.

Jack Ruby was born Jacob Rubenstein, the fifth of eight children of Joseph and Fannie Rubenstein, in March of 1911 on Chicago's West Side. The West Side was one of the roughest sections of a very tough city, and life for young Jack was anything but easy. His father was an inveterate wife-beater, which no doubt contributed to his mother's eventual commitment to a mental institution when she was sixty-one.[2]

Jack was an habitual truant from school and a problem child at home. By the age of eleven he was referred to the Institute for Juvenile Research, where a psychiatric evaluation was performed. In an effort to provide a more wholesome environment for the troubled youth and his siblings, they were placed in foster homes.[3] Ruby lived in his foster home for about five years, but by the time he was fifteen he was spending most of his time running the streets with his buddies. At age sixteen he dropped out of school completely after finishing the fifth grade. By that time, Jack and his friend Barney Ross had begun running errands for Chicago's famous gangster, Al Capone.[4]

Ruby's temper and willingness to scrap soon earned him the nickname "Sparky," which stuck with him for the better part of his life. He dabbled at a wide variety of odd jobs, which included scalper of tickets for sporting events, seller of bootleg music sheets, bagman for union racketeers and bouncer at various night-clubs. In his spare time he helped break up meetings of the German-American Bund (Nazi fund raisers and propagandists) who were seen in Chicago frequently in the 1930's.[5]

When President Franklin D. Roosevelt ended Prohibition in 1933, Ruby and several of his cronies left Chicago and moved out to California for about four years. There he tried his hand as a tipster at the Bay Meadows racetrack and sold newspaper subscriptions.[6]

In 1937 Ruby returned to Chicago and went to work as an "organizer" for the newly formed Scrap Iron and Junk Handler's Union. The founder of this union was Leon Cooke, who was soon relegated to the position of Financial Secretary when the mob-connected Jack Martin took over the presidency. By late 1939, Martin was under investigation for racketeering. He and Cooke had a serious falling out that culminated in a violent argument on December 8, 1939, in which Martin finally pulled a gun and fatally shot Cooke in the back. Ruby was in the building at the time. He and Martin were arrested but Ruby was soon released and Martin somehow convinced the authorities that he had fired in "self-defense," a plea that doesn't often work in cases where the victim is shot in the *back*.[7]

In spite of Ruby's close friendship with Cooke, he stayed on under Martin as a "bagman" for the union until several months after it was reorganized as the Waste Material Handler's Union, at which time the presidency was taken over by Paul Dorfman. Dorfman was a man with close ties to Jimmy Hoffa, which were to become even closer in later years as they both rose in the ranks of the Teamsters Union.[8]

In mid-1940, Ruby suddenly left the union, and from then until mid-1943, when he was inducted into the Army Air Force, he went back to selling various novelties and games of chance, operating out of a series of cheap hotel rooms. At thirty-two, he was drafted and served as an aircraft mechanic until his discharge in February, 1946, as a Private First Class.

Jack and his three brothers (Hyman, Earl and Sam) then formed a novelty company that they named Earl Products Co. They made and distributed miniature cedar chests, punch boards, key chains, bottle openers, etc. The brothers argued constantly about business issues, and soon Hyman, the oldest, left the company. At this point, the other brothers decided that they needed a more American-sounding name to succeed in business, so all three legally changed their surname from Rubenstein to Ruby.[9] But the business still faltered and bickering among the brothers continued, so in 1947 Jack split off from Earl and Sam and for years to come they were not on speaking terms.

The Last Relocation

It was in 1947 that Jack Ruby suddenly relocated to Dallas, Texas, supposedly to help his sister Eva manage the Singapore supper-club. Later, Ruby was to claim that he was "sent" to Dallas by the Chicago mob, when he would have preferred to go back to California.[10] While we can't prove or disprove his claim, it is true that at this time the syndicate was expanding its operations into the Southwest.

After Ruby killed Oswald in 1963, an informant gave the FBI another version of why Ruby left Chicago for Dallas. According to this story, bookie Ben Zuckerman had been holding out on his partner Lennie Patrick (a very close friend of Ruby for many years) and had been shot to death by the mob as a result. Patrick advised Ruby to leave town because he (Ruby) had been operating a "book" without mob approval.[11]

Whatever the motivation for Ruby's move to Dallas, the evidence is ample that he had associations with mobsters both in Chicago and after he arrived in Dallas. Arriving at about the same time was Paul Roland Jones, who had previous convictions for drug smuggling and murder. Jones had been introduced to Ruby in Chicago by mobsters Paul "Needle Nose" Labriola and Jimmy Weinberg (who were later found dead by garroting in the trunk of a car in 1957).[12]

Thanks to a tip from a crime reporter on the *Chicago Daily News* named Jack Wilner, the FBI learned as early as the very day that Ruby shot Oswald that Ruby had played a role in the Chicago mob's attempt to take over the rackets in Dallas. According to Wilner's sources, a newly elected Dallas sheriff, Steve Guthrie, was offered a bribe by Chicago mobsters. The FBI questioned Guthrie on December 7, 1963, and Guthrie confirmed that he had been approached in late 1946 by Paul Roland Jones, who said that he represented the Chicago syndicate. Guthrie also said that Ruby's name came up several times over the course of their "negotiations" –a series of meetings with Jones and his mob friends that Guthrie managed to have secretly recorded, after the initial contact was made through Dallas Police Lieutenant George Butler. According to Guthrie, Ruby was to have come down from Chicago to operate a new, plush night-club that would be a "front" for mob operations.[13]

When the Warren Commission looked into Ruby's background, they chose to reject Guthrie's testimony about Ruby's involvement and to believe Lieutenant Butler, who at this point was saying that Ruby's name was never mentioned in any of the meetings that he attended with Guthrie. However, that is not the story he had told Chicago newsman Mort Newman a few months earlier. According to Newman, Butler had said that Ruby was "very much involved" in the syndicate plans laid out and recorded by the Dallas authorities.[14]

One would think that the recordings would prove which version was the truth, but unfortunately, like so much of the evidence related to JFK's death, some of these recordings could not be found by the time the Commission did its investigation. The ones that were available contained no mention of Ruby. According to Seth Kantor, author of *The Ruby Cover-up,* only twenty-two out of forty-two recordings were found.[15] It is interesting to note, however, that between the 1946 meetings with Guthrie and Butler, and the day in November of 1963 when Ruby managed to somehow elude the "watchful eyes" of the police and enter the basement to shoot Oswald, Ruby and Lieutenant Butler became good friends. More on this later.

The Nightclub Owner

Shortly after arriving in Dallas, Ruby paid off his sister, Eva Grant, and took over sole ownership of the Singapore Club, which he promptly renamed the Silver Spur. In October of 1947 his friend Paul Roland Jones was arrested on bribery and narcotics charges.

He was convicted, but while out on bail and appealing the case over the next two years, he could often be found at Ruby's club.[16]

Ruby managed the Silver Spur until he sold it in 1955. Meanwhile, another pair of night-club entrepreneurs arrived on the scene shortly after Ruby renamed his club. They were Ralph Paul, a forty-eight-year-old unmarried Polish immigrant, and Joe Bonds (real name, Joseph Locurto), who came in from New York City and took over the Sky-Vu Club. Then in 1948 they bought the Blue Bonnet Club, a local hangout for much of Dallas's criminal element. Bonds and Ruby soon began "running together" and associating with a Dallas safe-cracker named Jack Todd. In 1953, Ruby and Bonds opened the Vegas Club together. Bonds was eventually convicted of running a white slavery racket and of sodomizing a fifteen-year-old girl. He was sent away for eight years.[17]

Ruby's relationship with Ralph Paul was not that of a "buddy," but of a business partner. Over the years between 1947 and 1963 Ruby would borrow over $5000 from Paul, none of which was ever repaid, according to Paul.[18] Ruby's business ventures took him from club to club, all of them "strip joints." He continued running the Vegas Club for a while after Bonds went to prison, but eventually turned its operation over to his sister, although he still kept a hand in it right up to the day he shot Oswald. Every success in this business seemed to lead to another failure, one of which, in 1953, brought him close to suicide. He left Dallas and returned briefly to Chicago to try and get a grip on himself. This apparently worked and soon he was back in Dallas and back in business.[19]

In 1959 he and a friend opened up a relatively high class private club named the Sovereign Club, but Ruby did not relate well to this class of clientele and the club was failing. His friend Ralph Paul financed the conversion of this club into a strip joint and it was renamed the Carousel Club, the club he was still operating in November of 1963.

The Wheeler Dealer

During the late 1950's and early 60's Ruby tried his hand at a number of intriguing activities. The FBI tried to use him as an informant for a while, because of his known connections with drug traffickers, but they apparently never obtained any useful information from him. He seemed more interested in using them to harass his competitors. After a few months, the FBI gave up on him.[20]

Early in 1959, not long after Castro's takeover of Cuba, Ruby managed to arrange a sale of surplus jeeps, located in Shreveport, Louisiana, to Castro, through a gun-runner named Robert McKeown. McKeown remembered that Ruby wanted to tie the deal in with an attempt to gain the release of three men being held in prison by Castro. The deal never came off, according to McKeown, but not long afterward Loren Hall, Santos Trafficante Jr. and another associate were released from Castro's prison and exiled to Miami.[21] Many think this was no coincidence.

Around this same time, Ruby became involved in a gun running operation headed by Norman "Roughhouse" Rothman, one of Trafficante's chief lieutenants, and Thomas Davis III, a convicted bank robber who seemed to have ties to the CIA. Originally, the guns were smuggled into Cuba to assist Castro and his rebels in their overthrow of the Batista dictatorship (the syndicate was playing both sides in anticipation of a victory by Castro). But after Castro took over and started casting the mobsters out, the guns were brought in to be used against *him*.[22]

One of the strongest indications that Ruby continued to be involved in Cuban intrigue as late as 1962 is the story told to the Warren Commission by Nancy Perrin Rich, (none of which the commission chose to include in its final report). Mrs. Rich, during the summer of 1962, was married to Robert Perrin. They had just separated, so Nancy moved to Dallas where she found work as a bartender at Jack Ruby's Carousel Club, with the help of members of the Dallas Police Department. When Ruby began to push her around, as he did with most of his female employees, she tried to file charges against him. But she was dissuaded from doing so by the police, who told her it would not only be a waste of time but would merely land her in more trouble. At that point, she quit her job at the Carousel.[23]

Later that summer, while Nancy and her husband Robert were temporarily reconciled, they attended a series of meetings at an apartment in Dallas where the subject of smuggling guns into Cuba was discussed. The principal player at these meetings was a U.S. Army Colonel from Virginia named (it was later learned) L. Robert Castorr. Perrin had been helping to bring refugees out of Cuba. The Colonel wanted to pay him to bring arms *in* as well. They were shown a shack in the back of the apartment that Nancy described as full of all kinds of military armaments, including land-mines, hand grenades and a Browning Automatic Rifle.

The Perrins did not like the smell of the scheme and tried to avoid it by asking what they thought was an exorbitant fee, but the Colonel didn't bat an eye at their price of $10,000 per run. At their second meeting, the Colonel made a phone call and soon a large sum of money was delivered to the apartment. To Mrs. Perrin's amazement, the "bagman" turned out to be her old employer, Jack Ruby. At the third meeting, the couple declined the offer and left. A few weeks later, Robert Perrin died from a fatal dose of arsenic. His wife scoffed at the pronouncement that it was a suicide.[24]

The New Orleans Connection

In May and June of 1963, while Oswald was engaged in his bizarre, two-faced behavior in New Orleans, Jack Ruby suddenly decided to visit "The Big Easy" looking for fresh strippers for his club acts. He contacted Harold Tannenbaum, who ran a place called the Old French Opera House on Bourbon Street. Tannenbaum worked for associates of mob boss Carlos Marcello. He introduced Ruby to a new "hot" dancer named Janet Adams, stage name Jada. Soon, Jada was dancing in Ruby's club in Dallas. Tannenbaum and Ruby remained in close contact throughout that highly significant summer of 1963. Researchers suspect that there was more to Ruby's interest in New Orleans than merely procuring fresh talent for his club. One reason for this suspicion has been Ruby's comment to one of his former employees while sitting in a jail cell after his conviction for murdering Oswald. Wally Weston, comedian and MC at the Carousel before the Dallas tragedies, told the HSCA that Ruby "...was shook –he said, 'geez, they're going to find out about Cuba, they're going to find out about the guns, find out about New Orleans, find out about everything'."[25]

Strip clubs of the type Ruby operated had replaced the cheap dance halls and saloons of the past in "open" towns like Dallas. The liquor and girls were under the control of organized crime. The exotic dancers had to belong to the American Guild of Variety Artists (AGVA), which was controlled by the mob.[26] This fact alone makes it difficult to understand how the Warren Commission could reach the conclusion that Ruby had no ties to organized crime. But if that were not enough, consider some of his other known associates in the period leading up to November of 1963.

More Mob Ties

Joseph Campisi was one of Ruby's closest friends, according to both his sister Eva Grant and his roommate George Senator. Campisi ran several Dallas businesses, including a restaurant known as a gathering place for gangsters. He was an associate of known Mafioso Joseph Civello.[27]

Joseph Civello was high enough in the Mafia to have attended the famous 1957 Apalachin New York syndicate meeting at which many mobsters were arrested. Civello reported to Louisiana crime boss Carlos Marcello. He admitted to the FBI after the assassination that he had known Jack Ruby "for about ten years."[28]

Lewis McWillie, Ruby's long-time friend and idol, had run the Tropicana Casino in Havana for Mafia chieftains Santos Trafficante Jr. and Meyer and Jake Lansky before Castro expelled them all from the island. In the August-September time-frame of 1959, prior to that expulsion, Ruby had paid two visits to his old friend in Havana. The full purpose of these trips has never been made clear, but there are indications that while in Cuba he visited Santos Trafficante Jr. in prison (where Castro had put him while deciding what to do with him). It was shortly thereafter that Trafficante was released and exiled to Miami. By 1963, McWillie was back in Chicago. It has been of great interest to researchers, including the HSCA, that Ruby made at least six phone calls to his old pal McWillie in September of 1963, ostensibly to seek his help in solving problems Ruby was having with the AGVA.[29]

Lennie (Leonard Levine) Patrick was one of Ruby's close friends from the old Chicago days. He was a Capone mobster who was a convicted bank robber and had been accused of several gangland murders but was never prosecuted because the witnesses suddenly died or were scared off. By 1963, Patrick was still in Chicago and now a close associate of Chicago's latest crime boss, Sam Giancana. Ruby is known to have placed telephone calls to Patrick during November of 1963.[30]

David Yaras had been a close buddy of both Lennie Patrick and Jack Ruby in the early days in Chicago. Patrick and Yaras were strongly suspected of killing bookmakers Ben Zuckerman in 1944 and James M. Ragen in 1946, and were considered to be "syndicate hit-men". An intriguing phone call was placed by Barney Baker to Dave Yaras on the evening of November 21, 1963.[31]

Barney Baker was a liaison man between Teamsters boss Jimmy Hoffa and several Mafia leaders, including Jake Lansky and "Bugsy" Siegel. Baker was a huge (370 pounds) muscle-man for Hoffa who had been convicted of extortion and had only been out of prison four months when Ruby phoned him on November 11th. Interestingly, that same day Ruby obtained a doctor's prescription for a drug to calm his nerves, which he then had refilled only four days later.[32]

There is also considerable evidence of phone calls or meetings between Ruby and several other known crime figures in the weeks just prior to the assassination: John Roselli, Sam Giancana's right-hand man; Frank Caracci, a Marcello henchman; Al Gruber, a former roommate of Ruby's in the old Chicago days and an associate of top Teamster officials; Murray "Dusty" Miller, a former Teamster official with ties to several underworld figures; Nofio Pecora, one of Carlos Marcello's most trusted lieutenants; Irwin Wiener, a close Hoffa associate with ties to Trafficante and Giancana.[33]

The evidence pointing to the above-described links between Ruby and organized crime was largely ignored by the Warren Commission, even though most of it was available to them in 1964. It was taken much more seriously, however, by the HSCA fourteen years later. Unfortunately, even then the leads were not fully followed or explored and the recommendations for further investigation, which the committee made to the US Department of Justice, were ignored.

The Dallas Police's "Buddy"

In cities like Dallas, the excesses of clubs like Ruby's Carousel were largely condoned by local law enforcement. Most strip club owners catered to the police to get them to overlook their many infractions of local ordinances, supplying them with free or reduced-rate drinks and "dates" with the entertainers, but Ruby raised his cultivation of the police to new heights. He often served as a police informant against customers or employees who had angered him in some way. He acted as his own bouncer and frequently used his fists, a blackjack or a pistol on the heads of unruly or uncooperative people, usually women or drunks who could offer no effective resistance.[34] In the sixteen years between 1947 and 1963, Ruby's police record showed at least nine arrests, but the charges almost never stuck. The greatest penalty he served was a $35 fine for ignoring a traffic citation.[35]

Ruby seemed to be fascinated by the police and was described by several who knew him as a "police buff." He often hung around the station house shooting the breeze with the officers and developed at least a passing acquaintanceship with almost everyone from District Attorney Henry Wade on down. After the assassination, Police Chief Jesse Curry told the Warren Commission that he estimated that Ruby was personally acquainted with between 25 and 50 men on the force. There is evidence that the actual number was several times that.[36]

One member of the Dallas Police who had known Ruby for at least twelve years was Officer William (Blackie) Harrison. It was Harrison whom Ruby stepped out from behind as he lunged forward that November morning in the basement of the station house to shoot and kill Oswald.[37]

Journalist and author Seth Kantor, who has perhaps explored the Ruby aspects of the JFK assassination more thoroughly than anyone, finds that Officer Harrison had the best opportunity to phone Ruby on the morning of November 24th and keep him apprised of exactly when Oswald was about to be brought to the basement to be placed in the transfer vehicle.[38]

Another of Ruby's pals on the force was George Butler, the man who was contacted by Paul R. Jones in 1946 and who helped Sheriff Guthrie set up Jones and his friends in a bribery "sting." In November of 1963, Butler and Harrison were both members of the Juvenile Bureau of the Dallas Police Department. They both were also part of the security team charged with the responsibility of protecting Oswald as he was being transferred from the police station on the morning of November 24, 1963. One of the many newsmen waiting in the basement for this transfer to begin, Thayer Waldo of the *Fort Worth Star Telegram*, knew Officer Butler very well. He described him later to the Warren Commission as a person with "this almost stolid poise...through even the most hectic times." But when Waldo encountered Butler a few minutes before Oswald was brought down to the basement, he seemed "an extremely nervous man...I noticed that his lips were trembling...It struck me as something totally out of character."[39]

The Oswald Assignment

Of all the perplexing aspects of the life of Jack Ruby that lend mystery to the all-important and fundamental question of why Ruby killed Oswald, none is more significant than his movements and actions between noon of November 22 and 11:21 AM of November 24, 1963. One of the principal reasons the Warren Commission was able to convince most of the public and the press in 1964 that Ruby's act was spontaneous and unpremeditated, and therefore the irrational act of a lone psychotic, was the fact that Ruby had sent a money-order to one of his dancers from a Western Union office just minutes before the shooting of Oswald. The Western Union records confirmed the time of this transaction to be 11:17 AM. It took approximately seventy-five seconds to walk from the Western Union office to the police station, so Ruby was in position to fire his shot less than three minutes before Oswald arrived on the scene. The official argument, therefore, is that if Ruby had planned or been put up to this murder, he would not have wanted to cut it this close. However, the commission never really considered the possibility that those in charge of the transfer were waiting for Ruby to arrive on the scene or that Ruby had been stalking Oswald all weekend, looking for the right opportunity, which finally arrived on Sunday morning.

Let's look at Ruby's actions and whereabouts during the time of the assassination itself. The Warren Commission found that he had been in the *Dallas Morning News* offices from 11:30 to 1:30 on Friday, the 22nd, placing ads for his club. Ruby himself said that as soon as he heard that the President was dead, he left the newspaper office and went directly to the Carousel. But at least one reporter told the FBI that Ruby was "missed for a period of about twenty to twenty-five minutes" before reappearing at the paper shortly after the shots were fired. Some witnesses in Dealey Plaza told of seeing a man they thought was Ruby in the area at the time of the shots. On the other hand, advertising salesman John W. Newnam claims that he was with Ruby when news of the shooting was brought in at about 12:40, and that Ruby seemed quietly stunned by the news. But if Ruby was indeed at the newspaper office the entire time, why did he not walk the four blocks to see his "beloved President" pass by?[40]

Ruby's story of going directly from the newspaper office to his club seems to have been a lie. He was seen at Parkland Hospital by at least one witness who knew him well, moments after the President was brought into trauma room A. This was newsman Seth Kantor, who spoke briefly with Ruby and was asked if he thought Ruby should close his club for a night or two because of the tragedy. The Warren Commission chose, of course, to believe that Kantor was mistaken, even though his claim was corroborated by another witness, a housewife named Wilma Tice, who also claimed to have seen a man addressed as "Jack," who Tice said looked just like Oswald's killer, around the same time that Kantor saw him.[41] Some researchers have wondered if Ruby might have planted CE 399, the "magic bullet," on the stretcher while he was mingling amongst the mass confusion of those few minutes. Ruby did eventually go to his club that afternoon where he placed several phone calls. From there he went to the home of his sister Eva, where he stayed until about 7:00 PM, according to her. He may have actually left earlier, because a reporter from the *Dallas Morning News* said he saw Ruby on the third floor of the Police and Courts Building, where Oswald was now a prisoner, as early as 6:00 PM. Detective A. M. Eberhardt saw him on the same floor around 7:00 PM. Between 7 and 8 PM a reporter from WFAA, a Dallas radio and TV station, said he saw Ruby start to enter Captain Fritz's office where Oswald was being questioned, but was stopped by two officers who said, "You can't go in there, Jack."[42]

By 9:00 PM on Friday, Ruby was again at his apartment, telephoning his older brother Hyman and two of his sisters back in Chicago. From there he went to catch the end of an 8-10 PM service at his temple. After partaking of the after-service refreshments, he brought sandwiches to police headquarters, even though he was told on the phone that they were not needed. Later, he would admit, then deny, that he had carried his revolver in his trousers pocket all through the weekend. Once again, he easily gained access to the third floor where Oswald was being questioned. He then heard that there would be a news conference featuring Oswald in the basement around midnight. Ruby was in the basement for this gathering, but was forced to observe the proceedings from atop a table in the back of the room, as the mob of reporters and photographers blocked him from getting any closer.[43] In his pro-Warren Commission book - *Case Closed*, Gerald Posner contends that if Ruby had been stalking Oswald he would have killed him at this point. However, it is obvious that Oswald was too far away and that the crowd shielded Oswald from any possible attempt at a clear shot. It was at this conference that District Attorney Henry Wade, answering more questions after Oswald was removed from the hectic scene because of concerns for his safety, described the prisoner as a member of the Free Cuba Committee, a right-wing, anti-Castro group. This error was immediately corrected by a voice from the back of the room that called out, "That's Fair Play for Cuba, Henry." Newsreel footage clearly shows that the voice belonged to none other than Jack Ruby.[44] One wonders where Ruby got such detailed information about Oswald at such an early point.

From police headquarters, Ruby delivered his sandwiches to radio station KLIF, arriving at about 1:45 AM. Sometime between then and the time he returned to his apartment between 4:30 and 6:00 AM on Saturday morning, Ruby headed toward the *Dallas Times Herald*. On the way, he chanced upon a couple of acquaintances, sitting in a parked car. He spent the next hour or so talking with police officer Harry Olsen and his girlfriend, Kay Helen Coleman, who was a stripper called Kathy Kay at Ruby's Carousel Club. The three of them discussed the assassination and all expressed the opinion that the "dirty cop-killer, Oswald" did not deserve a fair trial but "should be cut to ribbons."[45]

It was some time after 3:30 AM when Ruby left his two friends and continued on to the *Times Herald*. Here he made sure that his ads for the next day, announcing that his club was closed in memory of the President, would be bordered in black. After chatting for a while with the employees, he drove back to his apartment and woke up his roommate, George Senator. Senator had known Ruby for years. He had been running in bad luck lately, so Ruby had let him use his spare bedroom rent-free in exchange for occasional work at the club. Ruby demanded that George get dressed while he phoned Larry Crafard, a young drifter who was currently working and sleeping at the Carousel. Crafard had a Polaroid camera that was often used during evenings at the club to photograph celebrities with the entertainers. Ruby and Senator picked up Crafard and his camera, and the three drove to the edge of the downtown area where Ruby wanted to examine a billboard he had noticed previously. The sign called for the impeachment of Supreme Court Chief Justice Earl Warren. Although Ruby did not seem to know who Earl Warren was, he took pictures of the sign and seemed upset about the probability that the ultra-conservative John Birch Society was behind the placement of this billboard.[46] Then Ruby brought Crafard back to the club and he and Senator went home to get a few hours sleep. It was then 6:00 AM on Saturday morning.

On Saturday afternoon, Ruby made several calls to various people during which he exhibited great interest in the exact time that Oswald was going to be transferred to the county jail (where he would have been beyond easy access to Ruby). He learned that the transfer was planned for 4:00 PM that afternoon, and was overheard to say, "You know I'll be there."[47] But the transfer was postponed when Chief Curry was informed of the traffic jam being created by the hundreds of mourners who were slowly filing through nearby Dealey Plaza. They began to consider an after-dark move of the prisoner. During the course of that afternoon, newsmen and TV crewmen would encounter Jack Ruby at their vans outside the police station and on the third floor, once again handing out sandwiches and acting like he belonged there.[48] Sometime between 4:30 and 7:00 PM, Chief Curry and Captain Fritz made a decision to wait until the next morning and transfer Oswald in the daylight hours. Ruby was probably around the station when the announcement was made to the press, sometime between 7:30 and 8:00 that evening, that Oswald would not be moved before 10:00 in the morning.

During the early hours of Sunday morning, both the local FBI office and the sheriff's office received anonymous phone calls warning that certain armed groups were determined to execute their prisoner if he were moved as planned.[49] Later, Dallas Police Officer Billy Grammer would claim to have received a similar phone call and to have subsequently recognized the voice on the other end of the line as that of Jack Ruby. The logic of Ruby's issuing such a warning may seem obscure, but he may have been trying to avoid carrying out his assignment to silence Oswald by encouraging the police to make it impossible. But they did not cooperate, so Ruby was then obliged to carry out that assignment. According to Grammer, after the shooting of Oswald, in his jail cell, Ruby was visibly relieved to learn that Oswald had indeed died from his gunshot.[50]

The Reluctant Hit-man

Ruby's activities on Sunday morning provided the Warren Commission with its best indications of unplanned spontaneity in Ruby's killing of Oswald. For a man with a mission that could require his presence in the police basement at any time after 10:00 AM, he certainly was in no rush to get there. Telephone company records show that he received two calls on Sunday morning at his apartment. The first was from a sixty-year-old cleaning lady named Elnora Pitts, who phoned, as she did every Sunday, to make sure that Ruby wanted her to come and clean that day. She told the Warren Commission that Ruby sounded very strange and confused , not like himself at all. The second call came from one of his dancers named Karen Carlin ("Little Lynn"), and it was placed at 10:19 AM. She asked Ruby if he could wire her some money as an advance on her salary, something she had done on occasion in the past. Ruby told her that he would do so.[51]

As he left the apartment, he told George Senator that he was taking Sheba, his favorite dog, to the Carousel. Ruby kept several dogs, which he called his "children," all of which were housed at the club except Sheba, who he liked to refer to as "his wife." It was a twenty minute drive from the apartment in Oak Cliff to the Western Union office, one block from police headquarters. Three television technicians remembered seeing Ruby in the vicinity of the station between 10:30 and 11:00 AM. One of them recalled that Ruby came up to his van and asked, "Has he been brought down yet?"[52] The Western Union records show that Ruby did indeed send a $25 money order to Karen Carlin, as she had requested in her phone call, and that the transaction had taken place at exactly 11:17 AM. From there, leaving Sheba in the car, Ruby walked back to the police station and found a way into the basement, arriving only a couple of minutes before Oswald got off the elevator and walked toward him.

Exactly how Ruby gained access to the basement garage has never been satisfactorily determined. The Warren Commission believed Ruby's story that he walked, unobserved, down the Main Street ramp. But Patrolman Roy E. Vaughn, who was stationed at the top of this ramp, swore that no one got by him. He also passed a polygraph test to that effect. Seven other witnesses corroborated Vaughn's claim that Ruby did not go down the ramp.[53] There is at least one stairway with a street-level door at its entrance that could have been used. The police testified that this door was locked, but that was never proven. Even if locked from the outside, it could have been opened by someone on the inside. There is also testimony from some witnesses that Ruby rode downstairs in an elevator posing as a member of a TV camera crew. At about 11:18, David Timmons and John Tankersly of WBAP Channel 5 in Fort Worth were pushing a large television camera mounted on a dolly off the elevator and into the garage area. Officer W. J. Cutchshaw noticed that a third man was dressed in a suit, unlike the two workers on either side of him, but he was bent well forward, hiding his face from Cutchshaw's view as he helped push the dolly. His story was corroborated by Detective Roy L. Lowery.[54]

Regardless of which method Ruby used, it is difficult to imagine that he managed to enter the well-guarded basement garage at exactly the right time by sheer coincidence and without help.

What Was His Motive?

It is even more difficult to picture Ruby, a crude and violent man since childhood, a man with more regard for his pet *dogs* than for most *people*, sacrificing himself in a "patriotic" or "humane" gesture. We know that the fairy-tale about saving Mrs. Kennedy the ordeal of having to come back to Dallas for a trial was the invention of Ruby's first lawyer, Tom Howard. This was revealed in a note that Ruby passed to one of Howard's replacement lawyers, Joseph Tonahill, during the early stages of his trial. The note read: "Joe, you should know this. Tom Howard told me to say that I shot Oswald so that Caroline and Mrs. Kennedy wouldn't have to come to Dallas to testify. O.K.?"[55]

Since the moment he stunned the television audience by putting a .38 slug into Oswald's abdomen, the haunting question has been, "Why?" Why would a man place himself in the position of committing a murder with no hope of escape from the scene? Let's list and examine the possible answers to that question.

1. He was insane and wanted to make a name for himself at any cost.

2. He thought the public feeling against Kennedy's (alleged) assassin would give him justification, and perhaps even hero stature, for executing the "commie monster."

3. He was ordered by the mob to take Oswald out of the picture or be killed himself.

Possibility number one, that he was insane, was actually the defense chosen by Ruby's primary attorney, Melvin Belli, although his other lawyer, Joe Tonahill, would have preferred to use the "warped state-of-mind" defense described in number two above. Belli's insanity contention was provided support by Dr. Roy Schafer, who analyzed Ruby for three days and found that he suffered, in Dr. Shafer's opinion, from "psycho-motor epilepsy," probably brought about by various blows to the head sustained through his violence-prone life, which could have caused him to be operating in a blackout when he shot Oswald.[56] The jury didn't buy that argument, and sentenced Ruby to death for his act. Which leaves us with possibilities two and three. Given Ruby's personality—he really was in many ways the "screwball" that Warren Commissioner Gerald Ford likes to label him—reason number 2 is certainly not outside the realm of possibility. However, if one considers the sudden dramatic increase in telephone communication between Ruby and his contacts who were known to be mob-connected; if one considers the fact that Ruby was in financial debt to the federal government for about $60,000 in taxes,[57] not to mention what he owed to quite a few people, including some of these same mob-connections; if one considers that, in all likelihood, he had the assistance of one or more of his friends on the police force to gain access to the basement, then reason number three stands out as by far the most plausible.

Ruby himself provided very strong hints that there were others behind his act. Although his attorney would not let him take the stand at his trial, Ruby had quite a bit to say to commissioners Earl Warren and Gerald Ford when they interviewed him in a Dallas jail cell after the trial. Ruby asked several times, practically begged, Chief Justice Warren to take him to Washington because he could not talk freely in Dallas. Here is a partial quote of his testimony to Warren and Ford:

Gentlemen, if you want to hear any further testimony, you will have to get me to Washington soon, because it has something to do with you, Chief Warren...I want to tell the truth and I can't tell it here. I can't tell it here. Does that make sense to you?"

Ruby was obviously in fear for his life, but Warren told him it couldn't be done, he could not take him out of Dallas.[58] There is also a piece of film, uncovered in 1978, of Ruby stating for the camera:

Everything pertaining to what's happened has never come to the surface. The world will never know the true facts of what occurred—my motive... The people who have so much to gain and had such an ulterior motive to put me in the position I am in will never let the true facts be known to the world.[59]

Ruby and Oswald

There has been, it seems to me, an inordinate amount of ink devoted to the question of whether or not Ruby and Oswald knew each other. One might get the impression that the whole question of a conspiracy being involved in JFK's death hinged upon the answer to this particular puzzle. To me, the question has little relevance. It is very possible for Ruby to have been persuaded by those who had a hand in the assassination to eliminate the "fall-guy" without Ruby's ever having seen or heard of Oswald. Conversely, it is also possible that they were close friends and Ruby actually killed him on his own for purely personal reasons (*not very likely in view of the facts discussed herein*). But even though not essential to the case, this subject is intriguing, if only because it adds to the possible "Second Oswald" appearances. The following is a partial list of incidents that indicate that Ruby did indeed know Oswald. Or was it one of his look-alike imposters?

Beverly Oliver, a Dealey Plaza assassination witness and an entertainer at Ben's Colony Club near the Carousel, was married in 1963 to a Dallas gangster named George McGann. She told an investigator for the HSCA that one night about two weeks before the assassination she had gone to visit her friends at the Carousel when she was introduced by Jack Ruby to "Lee Oswald, who has CIA connections."[60]

Walter Weston was a master of ceremonies and comedian at Ruby's club until a few days before the assassination. When questioned by the FBI back in 1963 he had nothing of interest to tell them, but in 1976 he had a fascinating story to tell the *New York Daily News*. He said that he had seen someone he thought was Oswald in the club on at least two occasions prior to November 22, 1963. On the most memorable of these encounters, two weeks before the assassination, "Oswald" had heckled Weston while the comic was at the mike, calling him a "communist" while standing in front of the stage. When he refused to sit back down, Weston jumped off the stage and threw a punch at the heckler, knocking him back into the arms of Jack Ruby. Then, according to Weston, Ruby threw "Oswald" out of the club, telling him, "you SOB, I told you never to come here." Although Weston claims to have recognized this man as Oswald when he saw him on television after the assassination, he says he was afraid to mention it to the authorities and had been advised not to do so by other Carousel employees. Weston also tells of a strange meeting held at the club on November 17, 1963, his last night of employment there. Ruby had been sitting at a front table with six to eight friends from Chicago while Weston was telling jokes on stage. The conversation from the table grew loud enough to annoy Weston so he asked them to "cool it." One of Ruby's guests resented Weston's intrusion and pulled out a gun, just as two uniformed police officers walked in the door. The gun was hastily put away and Ruby assured the officers that everything was all right. After the club closed for the night, Weston says, he went back to retrieve a jacket he had left behind and was stopped at the door by one of the Chicago men who told him, "You can't come in now." Weston sensed that something very secretive was going on inside so he left without his jacket.[61]

A similar meeting was held in late spring of 1963, according to Carousel waitress Ester Ann Marsh in an interview with author Jim Marrs. This gathering was held in a closed meeting room that Marsh was allowed into only long enough to serve drinks. It was attended by Ruby, five men in suits who "were all dark, swarthy men who looked like gangsters out of some movie," and a young man dressed casually and who looked quite out of place among the others. She later recognized this man as Oswald.[62]

Other Carousel employees told of seeing Oswald (or his look-alike) in the club shortly before the assassination. William Crowe Jr., who used the stage name "Bill DeMar" in his magic act, says that about one week prior to the gunshots in Dealey Plaza Oswald had been one of the audience participants in a memory act Crowe was performing. The magician reported this to the Associated Press after Oswald was shot by Ruby, and was then questioned by the FBI. His story was then reported in the *Dallas Morning News*.[63]

Dancers Janet Adams Conforto (Jada) and Kay Coleman (Kathy Kay) and musician Bill Willis all reported seeing Oswald at the club. Coleman claims to have danced with him on one occasion.[64] Non-employees of the club also reported seeing Oswald there. Cabdriver Raymond Cummings told DA Jim Garrison's investigators that he had driven both David Ferrie and Lee Oswald to the Carousel sometime in early 1963.[65]

Madelaine Brown, now commonly known as a mistress of LBJ, sat with some friends at the Carousel in the spring of 1963 when the subject of the attempted shooting of General Edwin Walker came up. Brown recalled that everyone was surprised when Ruby informed them that it was a man named Lee Oswald who had fired that shot at Walker.[66] And finally, General Walker himself has stated to at least one assassination researcher that Ruby and Oswald definitely knew each other.[67]

None of the above described allegations can be proven and there is a very good possibility that at least some of them are the product of an over-active imagination or a desire for historical recognition. On the other hand, with so much smoke it seems unlikely that there would not be at least some fire.

In October of 1966, Jack Ruby, claiming that he had been coerced or duped into his "guilty" plea, was granted a new trial by the Texas Court of Criminal Appeals. Not long after that decision, it was discovered that Ruby had cancer. He told family members that he had been "injected with cancer cells." In less than three months he was dead, the cancer ending his life on January 3, 1967. The autopsy revealed heavy cancer cell concentration in the right lung. It found *no* organic brain damage.[68]

Chapter 8

THE CASE AGAINST OSWALD

The Prosecutor's "Dream"

The Dallas Police, the FBI, the Warren Commission, the House Select Committee on Assassinations and most of the news media have been assuring us for decades that the case against Lee Harvey Oswald was airtight. "Maybe the question of conspiratorial assistance could never quite be laid to rest to everyone's complete satisfaction," they proclaimed, "but Oswald's guilt was beyond question." They had his rifle, the cartridge casings, the whole bullet, the paper bag used to carry his weapon into the building, a palm print on the rifle and more on the boxes in the sniper's nest, and eyewitnesses who saw the assassin firing from the sixth floor window. They had the empty blanket that Marina said the rifle had been wrapped in while it was in the Paine's garage, and fibers from that blanket on the rifle. To further bolster the case that Oswald was the assassin, they had witnesses who identified him as the killer of Officer Tippit, as well as shell casings found at the scene and slugs removed from Tippit's body. The killing of Jefferson Davis Tippit provided further evidence, according to the authorities, that Oswald was in a panic flight after shooting the President of the United States.

It is unfortunate for most of the world, with the exception of the Dallas Police Department the FBI, etc., that Jack Ruby denied us the opportunity to see just how well the above cited evidence would have stood up in court. Oswald's death ensured that the evidence would never be subjected to the adversarial process. There have been several attempts to portray what might have occurred if Oswald had lived to stand trial. Perhaps the two most notable of these have been a made-for-TV movie titled, *The Trial of Lee Harvey Oswald*, aired at least twice on the *Arts & Entertainment* channel, and a book titled *The People v. Lee Harvey Oswald*, by Walter Brown (Carroll & Graf, 1992). In the movie, the prosecutor, played by Vincent Bugliosi, who successfully prosecuted Charles Manson, proves to be too much for the inadequately prepared defense attorney, played by Gerry Spence of Karen Silkwood fame. The jury finds Oswald guilty of the assassination.

In Brown's book, the defense attorney is very well-versed in all the weaknesses of the state's case and exploits them to almost unbelievable perfection. He makes it appear very easy to offset or invalidate every piece of evidence the prosecution presents. In Brown's imaginary trial, Oswald is charged only with the murder of John F. Kennedy, while the charge of killing Tippit is saved for a subsequent trial. By the time the defense finishes demolishing the evidence against Oswald, even the prosecutor is agreeing to drop the charges and to initiate an investigation into the authorities who have manufactured, distorted or destroyed evidence in their efforts to ensure Oswald's conviction. While Brown's book makes it much too easy, it succeeds in emphasizing what kind of a case the authorities really had.

But it does not take a 600 page book to accomplish that goal. Let's pretend that we are back in January of 1964, Jack Ruby was apprehended before he was able to get off a fatal shot, and the state of Texas is preparing to try Oswald for both the murder of Officer J. D. Tippit and the assassination of John F. Kennedy. Consider the following hypothetical dialog between a newly appointed prosecuting attorney and his assistant DA who has studied the evidence and must prepare the prosecutor for the biggest case of his career. Although the dialogue and scene are hypothetical, the descriptions of evidence presented by the ADA are all based on documented facts. I have named the prosecutor "Earl" and the knowledgeable ADA "Harold."

Preparing the Case

"Hi, Harold. How are you? I understand you're going to assist me on the Oswald case," said Earl, laying his briefcase on the conference table and settling back into one of the plush chairs that surrounded it.

"Looks that way, Earl," Harold said, as he took the chair opposite him. "They gave me the job because I've been studying the evidence ever since it happened. It's really fascinating."

"Presidential assassinations always are, aren't they? What I can't figure out is why Henry Wade [Dallas District Attorney] doesn't want to try this one himself."

"I'm not surprised," Harold said. "This case has a lot more to it than meets the eye. There are so many intriguing little aspects that are not common knowledge; you may come to wish that you hadn't been chosen to prosecute this one."

"Are you kidding? This is the chance of a lifetime! How often does a guy get a chance to argue a case of this magnitude and know that he can't lose? This is almost too good to be true!"

"Exactly my point," responded Harold. "Hasn't it occurred to you that the case against Oswald is a little *too* good...a little too pat?"

"So the guy was either stupid or he wanted to get caught. That's nothing new. I've prosecuted a few cases like that. From what I've read and heard, this Oswald is a real screwball. He must have an IQ of about 75. Have you seen his diary? God! My seven-year-old spells better than that!"

"Well, you're right about his spelling, but he may be dyslexic or something. The man can't be all that dumb if he learned to speak and read Russian on his own."

"How do we know he did it on his own? Maybe he had help."

"Quite possible, but according to the FBI and the Marine Corps the only place he could have received that help would have been at the Monterey School in California while he was stationed there just before leaving the Marines. And if that's the case, then it would *really* open up an intriguing can of worms."

"Yes, I see what you're getting at," replied Earl. "Why would the government train him in the Russian language except to use him as an agent of some kind? It makes his early discharge and immediate defection to Russia look like too much of a coincidence, doesn't it?"

"That's not the half of it. Did you know that after renouncing his US citizenship and offering the Russians military secrets, he was not even interrogated when he returned to the States? At least, not on the record."

Earl shrugged. "Well, all that is very interesting but it's irrelevant as far as my job is concerned. I've got the little twerp dead to rights for killing both Kennedy and the cop. Couldn't ask for better evidence than that idiot gave us!"

"Maybe, it depends on how much of it gets thrown out."

"Thrown out?! What the hell do you mean, thrown out?!

"I mean," explained Harold, "that the good old boys on the Dallas Police Force were not all that careful about maintaining the chain-of-possession. In fact, they were appallingly negligent. The defense is going to tear a lot of the evidence to shreds."

"Now wait a minute. Let's take things one at a time and you tell me just what kind of problems they are going to give me. First and foremost, they found a rifle on the sixth floor of Oswald's building, which was unquestionably bought by him. Surely, you are not telling me we have a problem there...are you?"

"Wellll, yes and no. You're absolutely right that we have in our possession a Mannlicher-Carcano rifle purchased by one Alek Hidell, aka Lee Harvey Oswald. But we may have trouble proving that it is actually the one found in the Depository."

"Hey, I know all about the identification blooper that moron of a constable made...calling it a Mauser," Earl sneered. "But I'm confident that I can explain away that error. He corrected himself later and confirmed that we have the right gun. I don't see that as a major problem."

"Don't be too quick to dismiss Deputy Constable Weitzman, Earl. He's no moron, and as a former gun-shop operator and long-time sportsman, he's supposed to know his weapons better than that, especially when it has '6.5mm, MADE IN ITALY' stamped right on the barrel. And, in case you didn't know, Weitzman and Sheriff's Deputy Eugene Mooney found the rifle together and *both* called it a 7.65 Mauser, which any gun-knowledgeable person knows is made in Germany, not Italy. Boone filed his written report with the same 'Mauser' ID in it. It wasn't just a quick, off-hand remark.[1] But that's not your worst problem with the rifle."

"My God! That's bad enough! What do you mean, that's not the worst?"

"I'm afraid the defense is going to have a field day with both the condition of the weapon and the way in which it was handled during the forty-eight hours after it was found."

"You've got my undivided attention. Please explain," Earl said as he shifted uncomfortably in his chair.

"Well, first off, there doesn't seem to be any evidence that this rifle had been recently fired. Further, the absence of any oil traces on the paper bag it's assumed to have been carried in leaves doubt as to whether it was ever really in that bag.[2]

"Then there's the scope," Earl continued. "Not only was it mounted for a left-handed shooter, and as you know, our boy was a 'rightie', it was loose on the mounting, making accuracy impossible."[3]

"So he used the iron sights instead of the scope," Earl scoffed. "That's no big deal."

"The defense will make it a big deal, I'm afraid. Without the scope, that last shot–the one that actually killed the President–becomes an extremely difficult one for a guy who was just a mediocre-to-poor shot while in the Marines. Keep in mind Earl, that the FBI's experts couldn't duplicate Oswald's feat, even using the scope after it was shimmed and sighted in. The gun fired high and to the right at fifteen feet!"[4]

Earl slumped deeper into his chair and let out a long sigh.

"But I still haven't mentioned the *real* problem yet."

"There's more?" Earl asked with a groan.

"Afraid so. As I mentioned earlier, the chain-of-possession rules were violated left and right in this case. Lieutenant Day of the Dallas Police put his mark on the weapon at some point, but no one can verify that he did so when the rifle was found on the sixth floor. Then they turned the rifle over to FBI agent Vincent Drain on the night of the 23rd. Drain took it to Washington for further examination. Not only was this case not within FBI jurisdiction, since this was not a federal case, but Drain did not even have any Dallas officer accompany him and the rifle as it left the state.[5] I'm sure the defense will question how we can be certain that the rifle that was found in the Depository is the same one that returned from Washington."

Earl exhaled with obvious exasperation. "I'm beginning to understand your reservations. No wonder Wade didn't want this case. If the rifle gets disqualified, then the fact that the cartridges and the bullet came from that gun loses a lot of weight."

"Which brings us to our next problem. The chain-of-possession on the cartridges is even more questionable than for the rifle, and as for the whole bullet found on a stretcher at the hospital—well, you can forget about that so-called piece of evidence altogether."

"Why on Earth do you say that?"

"To begin with, one of those three cartridge casings had a dent in the lip that the officers who found it swear was there when they picked it up.[6] It clearly could not have held and fired a bullet in that condition, so what was it doing there in the 'sniper's nest' with the other two? I guess the cops were concerned about that too, because they only put their mark on the two un-dented ones and handled them separately for some unexplained reason.[7] But the prize for mishandled evidence has to go to that amazingly intact bullet."

"What are telling me?, demanded Earl. "That bullet is at least as important to this case as the rifle! If I lose that AND the rifle, I don't have much of a case left."

"Earl, that bullet was found by an orderly named Tomlinson. He turned it over to his supervisor—a man named Wright—who gave it to a Secret Service agent, Johnsen I believe his name was. He passed it on to Secret Service Chief Rowly who turned it over to an FBI agent named Elmer L. Todd. Now, most of the people who handled it, especially the orderly who found it, aren't at all sure that the bullet now in the possession of the FBI is the same one that they handled.[8] Now tell me what the defense will do with *that* story."

"Wow! You weren't kidding about chain-of-possession screw-ups were you? Well, maybe it won't matter that much. There're still plenty of eyewitnesses whose testimony will make him look guilty as hell. What about his co-worker who saw him bring a long paper bag into work that morning? The same type of bag that was later found on the sixth floor near the sniper's nest? That alone would be enough for most juries."

"Ah yes, Mr. Buell Wesley Frazier. Now there is a witness that is guaranteed to give us fits. We need him to connect Oswald with the bag, but if you had read the FBI reports on Mr. Frazier you would not be eager to put him on the stand."

"And why not? What's in those reports?," Earl asked nervously.

"Frazier insists that the bag Oswald brought to work was only twenty-four to twenty-six inches long. That's a foot too short to be the one found on the sixth floor or to have contained the rifle, even when broken down."

"So he was obviously mistaken. Eyewitnesses are notorious for making mistakes in the small details. As long as he saw a bag of the right general size and shape, his testimony is still usable."

"In general I would agree with you, but the way Frazier describes the manner in which Oswald carried the bag as he walked ahead of him in the parking lot, he is very convincing. He passed a lie-detector test on this subject, by the way. Then there is the corroboration supplied by Frazier's sister, who also saw Oswald carrying the bag in a manner that limits its length to just about what Buell describes.[9] I'm telling you, Earl, this guy will do us more harm than good. The problem is, if we *don't* call him, the defense probably will."

"OK, we better give a lot of thought to how we will handle Mr. Frazier. But what about Brennan? He actually saw the assassin fire the last shot from that window and has now identified that person as none other than our boy. I hope you're not going to tell me that *he's* a problem."

"Sorry, but Howard Brennan won't help us much at all. First of all, as you know, he didn't ID Oswald right away. It was several days before he decided that the man he saw was the one in custody.[10] Then there is a little matter of Howard's eyesight. He wears strong glasses as a rule but didn't have them on when he looked up at the window. Then his description of the way the shooter was 'standing' behind the partially opened window as he fired was proven to be impossible.[11] In fact, Brennan's story of where he was sitting on the wall when he looked up at the window, how and when he jumped off the wall to take cover, etc., is full of inconsistencies. Given the fact that he was about 120 feet away, his identification would carry very little weight, even under ideal conditions. No, you can forget about relying on Mr. Brennan. In fact, I wouldn't be surprised if the defense called *him* as a witness."

"Now surely you jest," smirked Earl. "Maybe he isn't the best witness for the prosecution we could ask for, but why would the defense want to put him on the stand?"

"To get him to describe how the assassin slowly and casually withdrew his rifle after the last shot and paused to assess his work before withdrawing from the window.[12] This, coupled with the motorcycle cop's story of how he encountered Oswald in the second floor lunchroom only 90 seconds or so after that last shot comes pretty close to giving our guy an alibi."

"I don't believe this! [Homicide Capt.] Fritz and [DA] Wade led me to believe that this was an iron-clad, open-and-shut case! Now you show me all kinds of holes in it. It's a good thing the evidence is solid in the cop-killing. At least we'll be able to nail his ass on that one, and with any luck, be able to convince the jury that the two murders are connected."

"I hate to keep raining on your parade, Earl, but there are a few holes in that one too. Granted, the eyewitnesses are more plentiful and convincing, but even they are not without problems."

"OK, let's hear it. What kind of problems?"

"Primarily with the way in which the line-ups were conducted. Dallas's finest made sure that Oswald stood out like a sore thumb. Of course, he didn't help himself any by noisily complaining about the way his 'rights were being violated', although I can't say that I blame him. You know, of course, that it was several days before he received any legal representation at all." [In reality, Oswald never did receive any legal assistance.]

"Well, I guess that's the way they do things in these parts, especially when a President and one of their own men get killed. But the jury will be from these parts too, and I doubt they'll be too concerned about the fine points of a cop-killer's civil rights. Even if some of them are so far to the right that they might want to give him a medal for doing JFK, they'll hang him for the cop."

"Unless the defense convinces them that he was framed."

"That's going to be a tough sell in the cop's case when we have the shells found at the scene that came from the revolver taken from Oswald when he was arrested. I know the slugs from Tippit's body couldn't be positively identified as having been fired from that gun, but there's a reason for that. The bullets removed from Tippit's body were slightly undersized for the barrel of Oswald's revolver, preventing the usual creation of clearly identifiable lands and grooves.[13] But the shell casings were a definite match and that should be enough, along with the eyewitness IDs."

"Don't get too excited about those casings, Earl. They present almost as many problems as the rifle cartridges. I'm telling you, this whole thing reeks!"

"You've got to be kidding! What kind of problems? Not chain-of-evidence again?!"

"It's almost the same story as with the rifle. First, somebody refers to them at the scene as automatic shells, not revolver shells.[14] Then there is the problem with the two manufacturers–Winchester and Remington. The numbers don't match. We have three Winchester slugs and one Remington, but we have two of each kind of cartridge cases found at the scene."[15]

"Hell, I can solve that mystery," interrupted Earl. "He fired five shots in all. Three were Winchester bullets and two were Remingtons but one of those missed. One of the three Winchester casings has yet to be found. How's that?"

"It would be a very good explanation if the officers that put their initials on the casings could now find those marks. It seems that the four shells were found by two different witnesses at the scene. Each witness turned over two shells to two different police officers. The officers claim to have marked them at that time with their initials, but later, when one of the officers, name of J. M. Poe, was asked to select from all four the two casings he was given, he picked one of them wrong. Then he couldn't find his marks on either of them.[16] This whole area needs very careful scrutiny before we go to trial."

"Great! Is that all?"

"Not quite. We might have some difficulty even getting Oswald to the crime scene. There's a timing problem."

"Not another timing problem! What is it this time?"

"According to Oswald's housekeeper, Earlene Roberts, he entered the house at exactly 1:00 PM. He left three or four minutes later and then stood out in front for a couple of minutes as if waiting for someone. By the way, a police car had pulled up in front and honked twice as Oswald was grabbing his jacket and his revolver from his room. It was gone by the time he went out. Roberts watched him pause out front for a couple of minutes, then walk away from the house.[17] It is nine tenths of a mile from there to where Tippit was shot. Yet our young friend manages somehow to cover that distance in time to have done the dirty deed and to have one of the witnesses report the crime on the dead cop's radio at 1:16.[18] Now, allowing time for the killer to leave the scene and for the witnesses to react and figure out how to operate the police radio, that puts our best estimate for the time of the Oswald-Tippit encounter at 1:12. You can't walk that far in under 10 minutes, no matter how quick you are. I've tried it. It takes a pretty fast jogging pace to make it, and no one saw a man running anywhere along that route. To make matters worse, we have the Texas Theater concessionaire, Butch Burroughs, stating that he saw Oswald enter the theater only a few minutes after the 1:00 start time of the movie, and come back to buy popcorn a short time later. This is during the time that Tippit was being shot."[19]

"Hmm," thought Earl. "That doesn't sound like something that someone who is on the run from just killing two people would do. Let's hope we can prove that Mr. Burroughs is mistaken."

"As far as eyewitnesses are concerned," Harold continued, "our 'star' is a flake named Helen Markham. She's the only one of the two people who saw the actual shooting who identified Oswald as the killer. Also, the only one who said the assailant was walking *away from*, not toward, Oswald's rooming house. But the problem is she says that when the cop pulled up alongside the assailant, he was walking quite casually along the sidewalk in no particular hurry. She also places the time of the shooting at no later than 1:07, by the way, which would have given Oswald less than five minutes to reach the scene.[20] Just wait till you hear this lady testify! You are in for a real treat!"

"So I've heard," grunted Earl.

"There *was* a guy directly across the street from the patrol car who was the other one that saw the whole thing—Benevides I believe is his name. He's the person who radioed the report in, after another witness who happened along seconds later showed him how to work the radio. Benevides would make a much better witness than Markham, but unfortunately he says he wouldn't be able to identify the shooter." [Benevides was about fifteen feet away from the patrol car on the other side of the street, but when he told the police that he would not be able to identify the killer, they did not bring him to a line-up. Months later, he claimed that he now recognizes Oswald from his photograph as Tippit's murderer.[21]]

"But," replied Earl, "we do have three or four other witnesses who didn't see the actual shooting, but saw the man fleeing the scene with a gun in his hand, and they all picked our boy out of a line-up. I don't care how rigged the line-up was, believe me that's going to be enough for the folks down here. Then the arresting officers are going to tell how he resisted arrest—even tried to shoot one of them. No, Harold. He's not going to get off on the cop-killing, believe me. And if he killed the cop, he must have killed the President as well. Nothing else makes sense.

"I hope the jury agrees with that logic, Earl. But those witnesses you mentioned are disputed by Mr. and Mrs. Frank Wright who say they saw Tippit's killer drive off in a gray coupe and by Acquilla Clemmons who saw *two* men accost the officer."[22]

"Well, you've convinced me that this case is not going to be the snap I thought it was. Here I thought I had a dream case and it turns out to more like a nightmare! It almost makes me wish I was on the other side. They're the ones who are going to have all the fun making fools of our local law-enforcement. There are going to be some pretty red faces in Dallas, and in Washington too, for that matter, before *this* trial is over."

Summary

The above hypothetical dialog provides many, but by no means all, of the obstacles that the prosecution would have had to contend with if Oswald had lived to see his day in court. As Dallas Police Chief Curry was later quoted, "We don't have any proof that Oswald fired that rifle, and never did." The evidence against him is considerably stronger in the case of Tippit. The state had perhaps a fifty-fifty chance of obtaining a conviction there, although the author believes that the most convincing physical evidence, namely, the shell casings, were probably switched to ensure the case would stick.

So we have to ask ourselves, why was so much of the evidence so badly mishandled? Why were the chain-of-evidence rules so blatantly ignored? There are two alternative conclusions—both bad. A. The Dallas Police, the FBI and the Secret Service were grossly incompetent. B. They deliberately mishandled or ignored almost all evidence which would tend to point anywhere other than to the accused.

In addition to the two "mock trials" mentioned at the outset of this chapter, there was one conducted in 1992 by the American Bar Association. This one resulted in a hung jury, with seven voting for conviction and five for acquittal. Of course, in real life it would have only taken one "not guilty" vote to hang the jury.

If I were the defense attorney in Oswald's trial, one question I would be sure to ask the jury in my closing argument would go something like this: If Oswald had planned and carried out the assassination, why would he bother to avoid leaving his prints on the rifle, then leave it and the cartridge casings behind, knowing they could easily be traced to him? And why would he not have his revolver with him, carried inside the bag with the rifle, rather than have to take a bus and a cab back to his rooming house to get it? This "evidence" has all the classic indications of a frame-up

Chapter 9
THE ENIGMA OF DEALEY PLAZA
Through the Looking Glass

The case of the assassination of President John F. Kennedy has been called "a mystery wrapped in a riddle inside an enigma." It is fraught from beginning to end with contradiction and labyrinthine twists and turns that lead to dead ends. It once prompted New Orleans DA Jim Garrison to say that looking deeply into the case of JFK's death was like going through the looking glass into Alice's Wonderland. *Very little* is as it seems! So much of the evidence was suppressed, altered, destroyed, etc. that one can seldom be sure of what can be relied upon in reaching conclusions. Even some of the evidence that does *not* seem to be compromised is often at odds with other evidence.

Of all the puzzling aspects of the case, one of the most frustrating to me is the question of the number, sequence, timing, source and effect of the shots fired in Dealey Plaza on November 22nd, 1963. The official version put forth by the Dallas Police, the FBI and the Warren Commission, that Lee Harvey Oswald, acting alone, fired three shots from his Mannlicher-Carcano rifle and caused all the damage to both Kennedy and Connally, has long been sufficiently discredited that it is no longer believed by the vast majority of the American public, and even less by the rest of the world.

From the very beginning of the so-called investigation, it was concluded that three shots had been fired by Oswald from the easternmost sixth floor window of the TSBD building and from nowhere else. Three cartridge cases had been found beside that window and most of the witnesses said they heard three shots (although several thought there were more than three). In attempting to connect these three shots to the known wounds of President Kennedy and Governor Connally, the FBI (prior to the appointment of the Warren Commission) had concluded that the first shot hit Kennedy in the back, the second shot hit Connally in the back and the third shot hit Kennedy in the head. Then they learned that there had been a small wound in the front of JFK's throat that seemed to the Parkland doctors to have been an entry wound. That fact posed a serious problem for the FBI, which at first asserted that Kennedy must have turned around to wave at someone in the crowd, so that his throat was facing the TSBD at the moment he was hit, at which point JFK was hidden from Abraham Zapruder's viewfinder by the Stemmons Freeway sign.[1] (This momentary obstruction of Zapruder's view was the most troublesome flaw in his film. It made it difficult to pinpoint the exact moment JFK was first struck.) But this theory was disproved by other photographs and movies, which showed that Kennedy faced forward throughout the shooting. Even if this scenario had been viable, it presented the problem of explaining a fourth shot.

Then the Zapruder film presented another problem when it showed that Connally reacted to being struck within one and a half seconds of the point at which Kennedy became visible to a gunman in the sixth floor window as JFK emerged from beneath the foliage of an oak tree (at Zapruder frame 210). Since tests by expert riflemen indicated that it took a *minimum* of 2.3 seconds to fire two semi-aimed shots from Oswald's clumsy bolt-action Mannlicher, the Warren Commission was forced to revise the FBI's scenario or face the unacceptable fact that there had to have been another gunman. Both of these problems were "solved" by the invention of the "single-bullet theory" by commission staffer Arlen Specter. In spite of Connally's (and his wife's) testimony to the contrary, and in spite of the (minimum) one and one half second difference in their reactions to being struck, the commission adopted Specter's theory that the first shot passed through both men. The second shot missed, this theory continued, struck the street and fragmented, sending a piece of lead into the curbing, which in turn flew off and struck the cheek of onlooker James Tague. For weeks, the authorities had tried to ignore the existence of this missed shot, but were finally forced to deal with it. The third shot struck Kennedy in the back of the head and killed him. How did the Warren Commission explain the one and a half second difference in the two men's reaction to being supposedly hit by the first bullet? They simply assumed that Kennedy reacted instantly to being struck while

Connally had a "delayed reaction" to being wounded in three places (chest, wrist and thigh) by that same bullet. They chose to ignore the fact that every doctor questioned on this point expressed the opinion that the type of wounds that Connally suffered would have produced a *more* immediate reaction than might be expected in JFK's case.[2] When he *does* react, it is an obvious physical, involuntary reaction (the cheeks puff out from expended air, the hair flies, the shoulder is driven down).

Let's pause for a moment to see how Governor and Mrs. Connally testified before the Warren Commission on the question of which shot hit which man:

Gov. Connally: Well, in my judgment, it couldn't conceivably have been the first one, because I heard the sound of the shot...It is not conceivable to me that I could have been hit by the first bullet. They talk about the 'one-bullet' theory but as far as I'm concerned there is no 'theory'. There is only my absolute knowledge, and Nellie's too, that one bullet caused the President's first wound, and that an entirely separate shot hit me.

Mrs. Connally: No one will ever convince me otherwise.

Gov. Connally: It's a certainty. I'll never change my mind.

How did the commission cope with the strong conviction of both Governor and Mrs. Connally that he was struck by the second bullet, not the first? The Connallys were probably mistaken, but even if they were right, well then it must have been the first shot that missed and the second that hit both men.

How did the commission explain the fact that the angle through Kennedy's "throat" was upward rather than downward, according to the autopsy photographs of the back wound and the location of the holes in the jacket and shirt? They completely misrepresented the location of the entrance wound, moving it to the "lower neck" instead of the upper back, claiming that the clothing must have been bunched up by the raising of his arm to wave at the crowd. Compare the following: Figure 11, Figure 12, Figure 13 Figure 14, and Figure 6 on page 47 (the *actual* evidence) to the drawing that persuaded the Commission of the feasibility of the single-bullet-theory, upper left in Figure 13. I have inserted a second bullet path to that drawing showing the real entry point and the path the bullet would have taken had it passed through the body, which it did not (lower arrow).

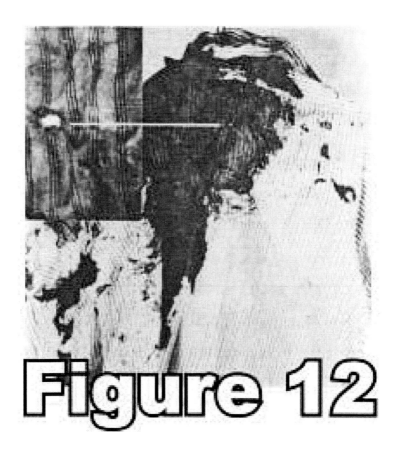

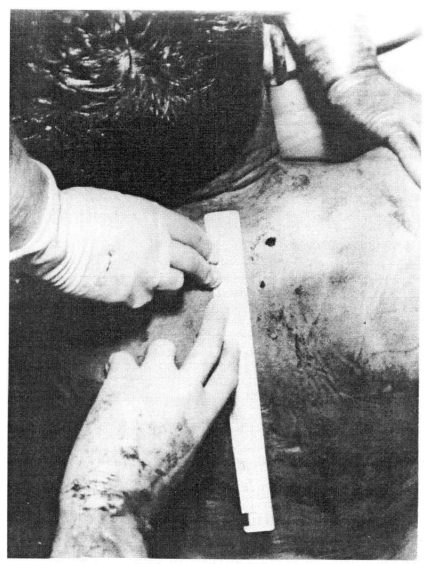

Figure 13

It's Time For the Truth!

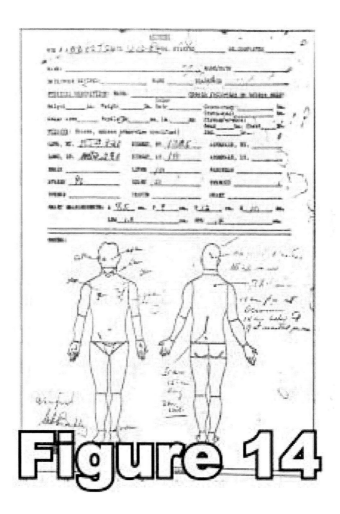

Figure 14

The dot in the upper back indicates the point of entry. Admiral Burkley, the President's personal physician, verified the drawing with his signature. He also issued a death certificate in which he described the location of this wound as being at the level of the third thoracic vertebra,[2] exactly where the Boswell chart indicates

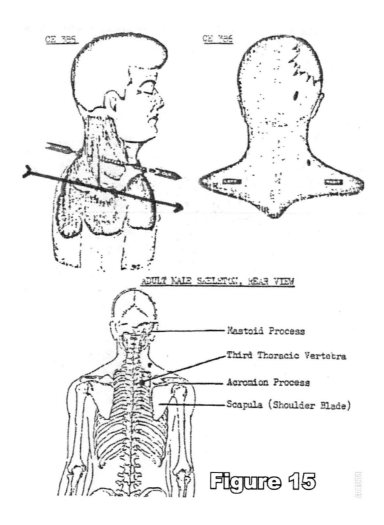

Figure 15

How did the Warren Commission explain the fact that the "exit" wound in the front of JFK's throat was smaller than the entrance in the back? Since this front wound was obliterated by the tracheotomy incision done at Parkland, and the Bethesda surgeons did not even *know* about it until the day after the autopsy was completed,[3] they only had the word of the Parkland doctors as to its size. Humes called Dr. Perry in Dallas Saturday morning to ask if any surgery had been done in Dallas. Perry told him the tracheotomy was done through a very small "puncture wound." This they chose to ignore or discount as "hearsay."

How did they explain the horizontal misalignment (by about 30-35 degrees) of the two men as opposed to the sixth floor window at the moment they concluded the first shot was fired? They simply twisted and turned the stand-ins during their reenactment until they convinced themselves that there was a way to get that line of fire traced back to where "Oswald was firing".

How did they explain the nearly perfect condition of the "stretcher" bullet, commission Exhibit 399, which is supposed to have inflicted all these wounds during its miraculous flight through the two men? It struck no bones in its path through the President, and must have turned during the first half of the journey through Connally's torso. It grazed his rib with its rear end (the only area of the bullet showing any damage). It then continued backwards through his wrist, passing *between* the two large bones rather than striking them head-on, and finally lodged in his thigh, where it later somehow worked its way out and onto the stretcher.

The fact that such bullets when fired through heavy fabric, let alone flesh, blood and bones, suffer more scratches than are found on CE 399, failed to deter its acceptance by the Warren Commission. Neither did the fact that bullets test fired into cotton bales emerged with as much or more distortion than CE 399 (See Figure 16 below. CE 572)

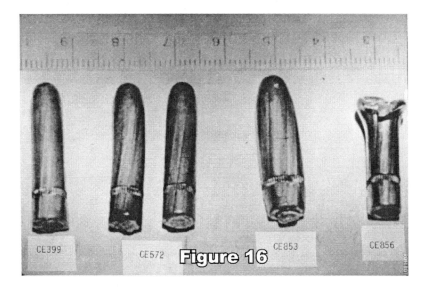

And how have the Warren Commission supporters (the commission itself could simply ignore it, since the public had not been allowed to see the Zapruder film) explained the direction of Kennedy's head snap (back and to the left) upon being struck by the fatal shot? The first attempt to explain this was; "the car must have suddenly accelerated at that moment," but that was easily disproved by several films. Then they said it must have been a neurological spasm of some kind, but not many were willing to accept that explanation as a replacement for the laws of physics. Finally they came up with a very scientific sounding theory that they labeled the "jet effect." According to this new-found phenomenon when a high velocity bullet blasts its way through something like a human skull, the force of the exiting blast causes a reverse reaction on the skull, forcing it in the opposite direction of the bullet. This sounds vaguely plausible, but it would be nice to have some convincing evidence of its validity. So far, the only supporting tests have been performed by physicist Luis Alvarez and urologist Dr. John Lattimer, both of whom are strongly pro-Warren Report and have used simulations that in no way represent the actual event.[4] The jet effect works, as described by Alverez, through the force of the matter being propelled forward out the exit hole, jet-propelling the head in the reverse direction. But in JFK's case, most of the exiting debris was blown backward and to the left, covering the motorcycle policeman riding slightly behind the limo's left rear wheel, obeying Newton's second law of motion, just as his head and body did.

Then, in 2008, a more realistic test of the jet-effect theory was conducted by *The Discovery Channel,* in which an anthropomorphic dummy was constructed to simulate JFK. A live round was fired using Oswald's rifle, at the same distance, angle of elevation and entry point pinpointed by the HSCA. The test was hailed as scientific proof that the shot had to have come from the rear. The problem was that there was *no* backward movement of the dummy's head.

Finally, how did the Warren Commission and the HSCA explain the fact that every one of the Parkland Hospital doctors and nurses described a large "exit" wound in the "back of the head," and every technician who attended the autopsy described the head wound as extending into the "occipital" (back) region of the head? They ignored it! After all, they had photos and X-rays that showed a large exit wound only in the right top and side of the head, and only a small entrance wound in the rear (see Figure 4 on page 45).

Years later, after the legal chain-of-evidence rules had been totally disregarded, some photos and X-rays were finally produced for viewing by a panel of forensic experts (the Clark panel) which "supported" the conclusions of the autopsy and displayed a total absence of any large exit wound in the rear. For years, the government deprived the Parkland doctors of any opportunity to view these exhibits, but they finally did get a chance to see them, thanks to researcher and *High Treason 2* author, Harrison Livingstone, shortly after the House Select Committee filed its report in 1979–*fifteen years* after the assassination! Unanimously (but not publicly) they have expressed serious doubts as to their authenticity.[5]

Inadequate Re-thinking

The Warren Commission's version of the assassination stood as the official story until the HSCA had the Dallas Police tape analyzed and it provided evidence of a shot coming from the very spot the critics had been pointing to for years–the wooden fence atop the grassy knoll. But the existence of *this* proof of conspiracy was not the only problem presented by this tape. It also showed that the first and second (confirmed) shots were only 1.66 seconds apart, just about the interval between JFK's reaction to being hit and Connally's reaction. Moreover, it showed that both of these shots came *earlier* than the Warren Commission had concluded. Did this lead Chairman Robert Blakey and his committee to conclude that there had to be a third shooter? Common sense would seem to dictate this conclusion, and why not admit it, now that the conspiracy door had already been opened. But one co-conspirator was all this group was willing to cope with. They opted for the absurd conclusion that Oswald, using the iron sights instead of the scope, would be able to work the bolt and fire a second, *totally un-aimed* shot in that brief span of time. Aside from the physical improbability of this feat, a reasonable person might ask himself; why would the assassin rush a second un-aimed shot, then wait five seconds before firing the next one? Blakey did try to provide an explanation for this. By reversing the Warren Commission's assumed sequence and labeling shot number one as the bullet that missed, he gives the assassin a reason to try again in rapid order.

Making shot number two the "single bullet" also fits nicely with Governor Connally's testimony of being hit by the second shot. Unfortunately, it *doesn't* fit with the testimony of most of the eyewitnesses, including Nellie Connally, who glanced back at the first sound, that the *first* shot hit JFK.[6] The following witnesses *also* said that they saw the first shot strike his back: Phil Willis, Bill and Gail Newman, Mary Moorman, Emmett Hudson, John Chism, Dave Powers and Ken O'Donnell (to name but a few).

One might think that, given the far-fetched assumption by the HSCA that Oswald could, after all, get off two shots in 1.66 seconds (a feat not even considered possible by the Warren Commission) there would no longer be a need for the much disproved "single-bullet-theory". Why not conclude that the assassin hit Kennedy on the first shot and Connally on the second? Of course, this doesn't allow for a missed shot to explain the Tague hit, or was it simply that old commitments die hard when it comes to this subject? This stubborn adherence to such a disputed theory is even more astounding in view of this committee's admission that JFK's back wound was lower than the Warren Commission portrayed it, which, they also admitted, made the angle connecting this wound with the throat wound slightly *upward* rather than the strong downward trajectory necessary to have been fired from "Oswald's window."[7] *(And then how could it become elevated; even so it raised rather than coming out at a sharp angle that it entered?–*Warren Chief Counsel Lee Rankin, Jan. 27, 1964)

All the arguments about the assumption of Oswald's ability to fire off a second shot and hit his target in less time than it takes to even work the bolt on that rifle become academic in view of the fact that, in the HSCA's version, *both* of the first two (confirmed) shots were fired while the tree obscured the shooter's vision of JFK from "Oswald's" window.[8]

This final, fatal blow to the lone-assassin case is an ironic by-product of the HSCA's answer to the question of which shot struck the President in the head. Was it shot number three (of the four *confirmed* shots on the tape) from the knoll, as the head snap seen in the Zapruder film graphically indicated, or was it shot number four from the rear, which the autopsy evidence seemed to prove? The House Select Committee overlaid the tape's gunshots with the Zapruder film in two possible match-ups. They considered the possibility that shot three (from the knoll) was the one striking the head at Zapruder frame 313. But they rejected that assumption on the basis of the autopsy photo evidence that the head shot came from the rear. They chose to believe that the fourth shot struck the head at 313 and that the knoll shot missed everything. The problem created by that assumption, as mentioned above, is that this moves *both* shots back to a point when the car and its occupants were obscured to any shooter in the famous sixth floor window by the foliage of the oak tree (See Figure 17 below).

Figure 17

Ironically, when the *third* shot (from the knoll) is lined up with Zapruder frame 313, the first two shots are moved ahead to a point where at least Connally is beginning to emerge from beneath the tree at shot number two.

The Committee's preferred scenario also puts the limo and its occupants *even further* out of the alignment that would allow one bullet fired from "Oswald's window" to pass through both men, as well as lengthening Connally's "delayed reaction" another seven tenths of a second to an unbelievable 2.34 seconds. Blakey tries to get around the tree problem by claiming that at shot number two the limo was passing beneath a momentary break in the foliage, providing Oswald a target to shoot at near the end of his 1.66 seconds (see Figure 18 below). This hypothesis may have made some sense if the limo and its occupants had stopped and provided a stationary target and JFK happened to be visible in one of the gaps in the foliage. But moving at 10-12 miles per hour the target would present only fleeting glimpses of only milliseconds. Why would even an expert marksman, which Oswald was not, try such a shot when he would only need to wait a couple of seconds to have a clear target?

One has to be desperately avoiding the very strong indications of other shooters to cling so stubbornly to this unlikely scenario.

Frame 166: view through rifle scope.

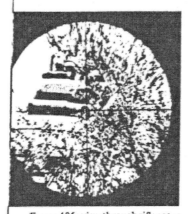
Frame 186: view through rifle scope

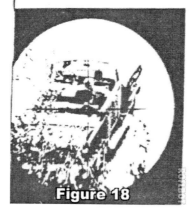
Figure 18

Alternative Theories

Many of the critics of the government's version have put forth their own theories, and most of these have made more sense than the one the authorities would have us believe. But no theory that I have yet heard manages to fit with *all* the evidence. So much of the evidence is controversial and contradictory that one must make choices as to what to accept. In formulating my own hypothesis, I have chosen to rely heavily on the police tape recording analyzed during the HSCA's investigation in 1978, in conjunction with the Zapruder movie film. After the House Select Committee disbanded in late 1979, doubts were cast upon the validity of the conclusions reached about the Dallas Police tape. The National Academy of Sciences found those previously mentioned conflicting sounds on the tape, which they claimed indicated that the sound waves analyzed by Bolt, Beranek & Newman (BBN) could not have been produced during the time of the assassination. However, Blakey and his House Committee members (in spite of their pro-Warren Commission leanings) and many researchers of the case remain convinced that the sounds on the tape are indeed shots being fired at JFK. As the HSCA's report states in its section supporting its conclusions about this tape (pg. 78), "To be sure, those who argue the microphone *was* in Dealey Plaza must explain the sounds that argue it was not. Similarly, those who contend it was *not* in Dealey Plaza must explain the sounds that indicate it was."

It seems to this author that it is far easier to find explanations for the appearance of "conflicting sounds" on the tape than to explain how these acoustical impulses, complete with supersonic shock waves, muzzle blasts and echo patterns, happen to exactly match the "signature" or "acoustical fingerprint" of the test shots fired in Dealey Plaza by the committee, and also coincide perfectly as to timing with the actual shots fired during the assassination. Unfortunately, the original tape is now one of the many missing pieces of crucial evidence.[9] In 2001 a new analysis was conducted by Dr. Donald B. Thomas who published his findings in the *Journal of U.S. Forensic Science Society*. His article, titled *Hear No Evil: The Acoustic Evidence in the Kennedy Assassination*, can be found on-line. It exposes the NAS criticism as faulty and supports BBN. It also brings to light a little known fact, that there was a fifth "acoustic event" on the

Dallas Police tape which matched a test shot from the TSBD. This was rejected as representing a shot purely on the basis that it was only one and two tenths of a second after the second confirmed shot, and therefore could not have been fired from *Oswald's* rifle.[10] The fact that it could have been fired from a *different rifle* apparently did not occur to the committee.

In formulating my scenario I also took into account an independent analysis of the spectrographic test results that were first released to Harold Weisberg in March, 1975, and then to George Evica, author of *And We Are All Mortal*, in November of that year. Evica hired his own spectrographic expert to study the data. Evica's expert reportedly discovered that the lead fragments from the President's head and the lead removed from Governor Connally's wrist were identical. This would indicate that Connally's wrist was struck by a fragment from the President's head shot, not from the "magic" bullet, CE 399. The copper in the jacket of CE 399 showed differences in composition to the copper in one of the fragments found on the floor of the limo, indicating they were *not* the same type of ammunition.[11] Additional analysis by other independent experts should be done to confirm or refute these findings.

This strongly suggests that CE 399 was a "plant." Compare these results with the report of J. Edgar Hoover, in a memo to Lee Rankin in July, 1964, on the results of the spectrographic analysis of bullet 399 and fragments found in the limousine:

...found no significant differences within the sensitivity of the spectrographic method...and *while minor variations in composition were found,* these were not considered sufficient to permit positive differentiation among the larger fragments and thus positively determining from which of the larger fragments any given small lead fragments may have come. [Emphasis added]

If that sounded like double-talk to you, it is because that's exactly what it is. This is a classic example of the word "obfuscation."

In my scenario I have taken into account the testimony of what seem to be the most reliable witnesses at the scene of the shooting. I have also assumed that the other three impulse waves found on the DP tape, but not confirmed as gunshots, are actually shots fired; two from locations other than those that the the HSCA tested and analyzed (the TSBD 6th floor window and the grassy knoll). These two shot indications appear on the tape at the extreme ends of the sequence, one being a fraction of a second before the first confirmed shot, and the other a fraction of a second after the fourth confirmed shot.[12] The HSCA did not accept the two end impulses as shots because they didn't match test shots fired from the two tested locations, but they never fired test shots from any of the neighboring buildings. The third discounted shot *did* match a test shot but was omitted for what seems to be political expediency, in spite of the fact that this impulse matches the very time frame that the Zapruder film and both Mr. and Mrs. Connally's testimony indicate that the Governor was hit. It must have been very difficult for them to accept a *second* shooter at this point in their investigation. A *third* one was more than they could cope with.

To give the reader a clearer understanding of the entire shot sequence on the all-important police tape recording, I offer the following graphic. Bear in mind that Zapruder's camera ran at 18.3 frames per second. All shots in the graphic and the map in Figure 19 below come from behind the President's limousine except shot five. I have also added to the chart the corresponding sequence of the HSCA's placement of the five impulses heard on the tape that matched their test shots (if they had assumed that the shot from the knoll had struck the President at Zapruder frame 312). In their preferred scenario, where he is hit in the head by their last confirmed shot, their first shot would be pushed back to about Z 165, extending Connally's delayed reaction even further.

It's Time For the Truth!

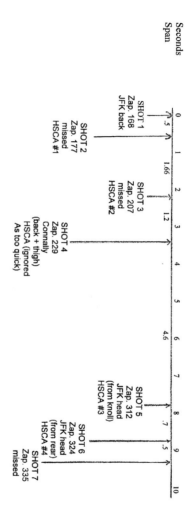

Most ear witnesses said they heard only three shots, but many of these may have been subconsciously influenced by the official story. Several were coerced. Many were confused between echoes and actual shots. Note that there are three *bursts* of gunfire in the sequence, with each burst lasting between .5 and 1.2 seconds. Add echoes and each burst could blend together to sound like a single shot to the untrained ear.

A Personal Analysis

No one has yet been able to devise a scenario that can satisfactorily explain *all* the available evidence, and mine also leaves some mysteries without adequate explanation. But I can offer, I believe, a better accounting of the evidence than the official version or any of the alternatives I have heard up to now. The overview picture of Dealey Plaza in Figure 19 below shows the probable trajectory of the seven shots hypothesized below and should be referred to frequently as you read.

It's Time For the Truth!

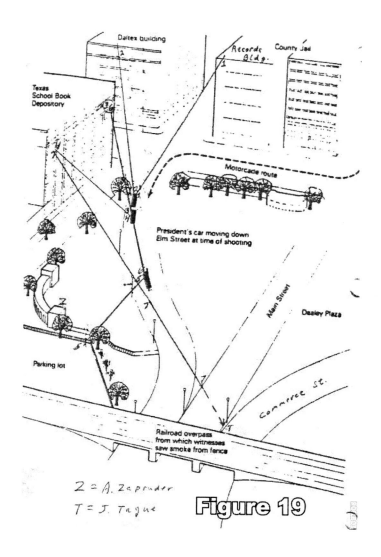

Figure 19

SHOT # 1: Came from somewhere in Dealey Plaza other than the easternmost window on the sixth floor of the TSBD or the grassy knoll. It will require additional test shots and comparative analysis against the first impulse on the tape to determine its source. This shot struck Kennedy in the upper back or shoulder area, not in the back of the neck. The steep downward angle described by FBI agents Sibert and O'Neill, who watched the autopsy doctors probe this wound, and the character of the edges of the fabric around the holes in the clothing, point to the roof of the Records Building on the south-east corner of Elm and Houston as the probable source of this shot. It was fired at a point corresponding to Zapruder frame 168. According to Harold Weisberg in his very informative book *Post Mortem*, the enlarged picture of the hole in the back of JFK's shirt (when correctly oriented) shows the left edge to be the sharper, indicating a left-to-right angle, inconsistent with a shot from the TSBD. The fact that this enlarged inset (see Figure 12 on page 175) was photographed *upside down* by the FBI, making it appear to be consistent with a right-to-left angle, is another in the long line of attempts to falsify and misrepresent the evidence.[13]

Some researchers are convinced that this shot was fired from a manhole on Elm Street or the overpass ahead of the motorcade, and that it struck Kennedy in the front of the throat. I have never been able to accept the throat wound as being the entrance for a bullet, in spite of the assumption that it was by the Parkland doctors. *There was no corresponding exit for it.* It is inconceivable to me that a bullet striking a man in that area of the body would fail to pass straight through and out the back of the neck, torso or head, unless it was a frangible bullet, which would have torn his throat to shreds. It could not have caused the exit wound in the back of the head at this early point in the sequence. Contrary to what many seem to think, Kennedy is *not* clutching his throat in reaction to this shot. His elbows are raised and his fists are clenched and held in front of his face in a reaction to being struck in the back.

I believe that this first bullet only penetrated a couple of inches into his body, just as the autopsy doctors found when they tried to probe it. Perhaps it was impeded by first having to pass through his back brace. I have yet to hear of any discussion of the condition of the back brace or its whereabouts. This bullet probably worked its way out of the body during cardiac massage in Dallas, just as Dr. Humes postulated during the autopsy. It was seen briefly by technicians in Bethesda before it disappeared (see Chapter 2, The Autopsy). It was probably *not* the bullet found on a stretcher at Parkland. That bullet was described by the director of hospital security, O. P. Wright who

It's Time For the Truth! 194

was given the bullet by the orderly who found it, as a *pointed-nose* bullet rather than a round-nose bullet like the one that became CE 399 (see Figure 20 below).[14]

O. P. Wright believes that the stretcher bullet he examined on November 22 looked like the sharp-nosed bullet above. The Commission, however, insists it was blunt-nosed CE 399, below.

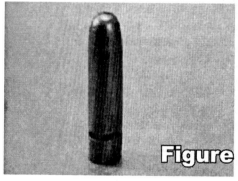

Figure 20

SHOT # 2: Came from the roof of the Dal-Tex building, across Houston Street from the TSBD. This is the first of the *confirmed* shots from the police tape accepted by the HSCA. The mid-point of the Dal-Tex Building's roof is within the same general line of fire to the Presidential limo as the easternmost sixth floor window of the

TSBD (see Figure 19). It was fired one half second after shot 1 at a point corresponding to about Zapruder film frame 177, while the Presidential vehicle was still hidden from the view of the TSBD gunman by the foliage of the large oak tree between him and the street below. Its sound blended with the echoes of shot 1. I believe that this shot somehow missed the limo and its occupants completely and struck the street in front of the limo. It could have been the shot whose fragment struck the curb stone and sent a chip of that curb flying into the face of bystander James Tague.[15] It is admittedly difficult to understand how a member of such an assassination team could be so far off target. This will be discussed in more detail later.

SHOT # 3: Came from the famous sixth floor eastern window of the TSBD, fired by an Oswald double using a rifle with a longer barrel than Oswald's Mannlicher-Carcano, as described by those who saw it protruding from the window.[16] This shot was fired 1.66 seconds after the second shot at about Zapruder frame 208, just as the men in the limo were beginning to emerge from beneath the tree's foliage. This shot also missed, perhaps because of trying to fire through the top part of the tree's foliage. It may have been deflected by a tree branch, just as some of the Warren supporters suggest happened to the first shot in their three-shot scenario.

SHOT # 4: Came from a window on the sixth floor, but at the other (western) end of the TSBD, fired at about Zapruder frame 229, 1.2 seconds after shot three. This is the shot that, although it matched a test shot fired in the re-enactment, was discounted by the HSCA because of its close proximitry to the previous shot. This bullet passed over Kennedy's right shoulder and struck Governor Connally in the right side of his back and passed through his chest. On the way through Connally's body, the bullet grazed the thin part of a rib, leaving at least one fragment of lead behind. It exited from the front of the chest at a steep downward, right-to-left angle and entered the Governor's left thigh.[17] John Connally died in June of 1993. Efforts by the critics to have him disinterred and to have these fragments removed and tested against CE 399 were to no avail.

This shot did *not* cause the wound in his right wrist. It may have been the bullet actually found on one of the stretchers at Parkland Hospital, with CE 399 being switched for it at some point. Since 399 did not fit the description of the bullet found by orderly Tomlinson and given to Mr. Wright, and since the amount of lead removed from and remaining in Connally's body exceeds what is missing from bullet 399, it must be concluded that CE 399 is not the bullet that caused Connally's wounds, much less those of both men. That "pristine" bullet, which so perfectly ties to Oswald's rifle, officially became the one found on the stretcher, despite Wright's description of the found bullet being pointed-nosed. The actual source and history of bullet 399 has never been proven and remains one of the most baffling mysteries in this case. Since the spectrographic tests do not prove that it is tied to any of the wounds, and in fact seem to prove just the opposite, it must have been "introduced" to implicate Oswald.

SHOT # 5: Came from behind the wooden fence at the top of the "grassy knoll". It struck the President in the right temple at Zapruder frame 313, just as Malcolm Kilduff indicated at the Parkland press conference right after the President was pronounced dead (see Fig. 2, page 42). This shot entered at about a 45 degree angle and was deflected slightly by the hardness of the skull and the oblique angle. It blew out a large hole in the upper rear portion of his head, sending Kennedy's head sharply back and to his left, splattering officer Hargis, riding his motorcycle to the left rear of the limousine, with blood and brain tissue, and sending portions of skull bone to the rear. It was one of these skull fragments that Mrs. Kennedy was attempting to retrieve from the back of the vehicle just as Secret Service agent Clint Hill, who had run up from the follow-up car, arrived and climbed aboard the trunk. The head wound seen by the Parkland medical personnel, who desperately tried to save the President's life, led them all to believe that a bullet exited from the rear of the President's head. A bone fragment was later found by a medical student named Billy Harper, whose professor identified it as "occipital bone" before they turned it over to the authorities.[18] The occiput is at the *rear* of the skull. It was found in the grass to the left rear of JFK's position when he was hit. It has been the subject of controversy as to whether it was occipital or parietal (side) skull bone. Like many other pieces of evidence in this case, that skull fragment is now among the missing.

During the latter stages of the autopsy, the skull and scalp at the rear of the head were reconstructed like a jigsaw puzzle for the benefit of those autopsy photos that seem to show this area of the head intact. Since part of the rear scalp was missing,[19] photo retouching was done to conceal the damage.

SHOT # 6: Came from the rifle in the TSBD sixth floor eastern window. It was fired a small fraction of a second after the shot from the grassy knoll. It struck the President's head just above the large exit wound produced by shot 5 (or possibly through it) and fragmented into several pieces. It would not have cancelled out the head snap of shot five because the skull it struck was no longer intact. One of the exiting fragments struck the Governor in the back of the wrist, passed between the two large bones and exited from the front of the wrist, where it was later found on the floor of the limo. Doctor Gregory, who treated Connally's wrist at Parkland, testified to that likelihood. Another fragment struck the inside of the limo's windshield. It was later found on the front seat. The force of this bullet drove a small piece of skull bone down through Kennedy's neck and out his throat, creating the small wound around which so much controversy has swirled as to whether it was an exit or an entrance wound. Although any person knowledgeable about the effects of bullets would conclude that this throat wound could not have been the exit for a 6.5mm bullet, its size does not preclude its being an exit for something smaller than a bullet.

SHOT # 7: Came, like shot # 1, from some undetermined point behind the motorcade not tested by the HSCA, perhaps from the western end of the TSBD like shot #4. It was fired a half-second after shot #6 and apparently missed the limo and its occupants. The extremely close bunching of shots 5, 6 and 7 (all three in less than a second and a half) mesh well with the Warren Commission testimony of Secret Service agent Kellerman. He told Arlen Specter it was "a flurry of shots." When Specter said, "Now in your prior testimony you described a flurry of shells into the car. How many shots did you hear after the first noise which you described as sounding like a firecracker?" Kellerman replied, "Mr. Specter, these shells came in all together." Both he and agent Greer (in the front seat of the limo) had the impression that the shooter was using an automatic weapon or that there were multiple shooters.[20] Note that the authorities chose to accept the testimony of the several (mostly untrained) witnesses who heard only three shots, rather than the detailed description provided by trained Secret Service agents. The fact that the last shot missed everything is not so surprising, since by that time the car was further down Elm St. so the gunman's angle of declination would be considerably less, allowing the bullet to pass closely over JFK's head and still clear the car.

The Great Escape

This scenario, like all its predecessors, does not answer all the questions or mesh with all the known evidence (see list of "Remaining Mysteries" at the end of this chapter). As stated previously, no imaginable scenario can make all the pieces fit perfectly because too many of them contradict each other. But I believe that more of the hard facts in the case are covered by the above portrayal than any I have heard up to this time. It is somewhat similar to that proposed in 1967 by Josiah Thompson in *Six Seconds in Dallas*, but with some important differences. His theory that bullet CE 399 was the one that hit Kennedy in the back and then fell out, does not explain the deformation (flattening) toward the rear of CE 399. His conclusion that Kennedy was hit in the head first by the shot from the rear, and then by the grassy knoll shot, was made at a time when the police tape recording had not yet established the reverse sequence. I have tried to construct a way in which he could still be correct, assuming that the sound of the shots reached the open mike in the reverse order in which the bullets struck home, but the position of the motorcycle and the distances that the sounds and the bullets had to travel don't seem to work into that scenario.

One of the key questions needing to be answered by my hypothesis is the following: What happened to the assassins and their weapons?

How did they escape from the area and leave so little evidence of their presence? In the case of the "grassy knoll gunmen", where evidence of a two-man team was abundant, the answer could be fairly simple. One member of the team, probably the man who posed as the Secret Service agent encountered by Officer Joseph Smith behind the wooden fence just seconds after the shooting, grabbed the expended cartridge case and stashed it and the rifle in the trunk of one of the cars parked behind the fence. The shooter, meanwhile, may have driven off in the car parked near the triple underpass at the edge of the knoll area, which was observed leaving the scene hurriedly by retired policeman Tom Tilson. Tilson gave chase to this suspicious character for a while before giving up and phoning in the license number to the Dallas Police (nothing came of his report).[21] Or the gunman could have hidden in the railroad car parked behind the parking lot. The tallest of the three "tramps" rousted from that car by the Dallas police and taken in for questioning right after the shooting bears a strong resemblance to and may very well have been mob hit man Charles Harrelson, who was serving time for another murder when he died in 2007. These three men were all released shortly after their arrival at the police station. There is a group of photographs showing these well-heeled and well-groomed tramps being led toward the station by two Dallas police officers. For 28 years it was thought that no record of their arrest existed, but in early 1992 the Dallas Police suddenly found and released their arrest sheets. They gave their names as Harold Doyle, age 32, John Gedney, age 38, and Gus Abrams, age 53.[22] Doyle has been located and admits to being the medium height tramp seen in the lead as they proceed to the station. Abrams, the older man bringing up the rear in the march to the station, bears a resemblance to E. Howard Hunt, but most researchers have abandoned that theory because of the age difference at that time. Hunt in later years looked a lot more like Abrams than he did in 1963. The photograph of "Gedney", the tall tramp in the middle of the line who so strongly resembles Charles Harrelson, has been analyzed by photo analysis experts who have compared this tramp photo with those of Harrelson and concluded that they are of the same man with over 95% probability.

The Dal-Tex assassin may well have been mobster Eugene H. Brading, who was also arrested that day as he was leaving the Dal-Tex building. He was mysteriously released shortly afterward with no record of his detainment kept by the police.[23] It has since been learned that Brading had paid a visit to oil magnate H. L. Hunt, a confirmed Kennedy hater, on November 21st, for reasons we can only guess at. We can also only guess at how any Dal-Tex assassin may have hidden the rifle somewhere in the building and retrieved it later, but it would not have been too difficult with all the attention being paid to the building where Oswald worked.

One of the TSBD assassins, in all probability, was the same man who looked enough like Oswald to impersonate him successfully on several occasions and to fool Deputy Roger Craig, who reported that about fifteen or twenty minutes after the shooting he saw a man he thought was Oswald run from the building and get into a Nash station wagon driven by a man who looked Cuban.[24] The biggest difference in this man's appearance from Oswald's was the color of his hair (dirty blond to Oswald's dark brown). This detail also showed up in several of the descriptions of the "second Oswald."

The TSBD conspirators tossed cartridge cases previously fired from Oswald's rifle on the floor where they were sure to be found. Several of the critics have pointed out that one of the three casings was dented at the lip and could not have held a bullet in that condition. It was the kind of dent one would expect to produce by dry-firing the rifle and working the bolt on an empty case.[25]

In addition to the Oswald double, another suspicious looking man was seen leaving the back entrance of the TSBD a few minutes after the shooting by both Richard Carr and James Worrell Jr. This man was dressed like one of two men seen in a sixth floor window just prior to the shooting by witness Caroline Walther. According to Carr, this man got into a Nash Rambler station wagon that fit the description of the one Craig saw "Oswald" get into shortly before.[26] This was probably either the Oswald double's back-up man or another TSBD shooter. Clearly, there was considerable evidence of other possible gunmen in the area, but none of it was given serious consideration by the authorities.

Remaining Mysteries

1. The Early Missed Shots

When the Warren Commission concluded that one of the first two shots "fired by Oswald" missed the entire limousine, they raised the obvious question: How could Oswald, their officially designated assassin, be a good enough marksman to hit his target two out of three tries, something that none of the experts could do with that rifle, even under more favorable conditions, and yet miss not just the man he was aiming at but the entire limo on the other shot? Now that we have such strong evidence that there was a highly trained team of assassins using the standard "triangulation of fire" method to accomplish its goal, we are faced with a similar dilemma. If I am correct in assuming that of the seven indicated shots, two of the first three missed, they came from behind the motorcade at a point when the President's car was not very far from the corner of Houston Street, almost directly in front of the Depository building. It would seem that anyone who had ever fired a rifle at all would be able to at least come close to his target at that range. Something may have distracted or startled the firer of shot # 2. Perhaps he expected to be the leadoff shooter and was startled when he heard the crack of shot # 1 go off somewhere close by, just as he was squeezing the trigger. And, as mentioned earlier, shot # 3 may have been deflected by a tree branch.

2. Kennedy's Throat Wound

The size of the "puncture wound", as it was described by Dr. Perry, who performed a tracheotomy in a vain attempt to keep the President breathing at Parkland Hospital, was smaller than a pencil eraser. It was roughly two thirds the diameter of the entrance wound on JFK's back. It was much too small to have been the exit for the bullet that entered the back, even if the location of the back wound had been high enough to form a downward angle with it, which it wasn't. According to all those who observed this throat wound at Parkland before Dr. Perry disguised its appearance by cutting across it to insert the tracheotomy tube, its size suggested an entrance wound. Many Warren Report critics still believe that it *was* a bullet entrance wound, but no one has offered a believable explanation for what might have become of the bullet if one entered there. The theory put forth by some critics that the back wound was really the exit for this bullet and not an entrance wound at all, requires that all the testimony of the Bethesda doctors about the nature of the back wound, and the FBI's claim that the fibers in the back of the jacket and shirt were pushed inward rather than outward, were falsified. Although there are strong indications that much evidence, particularly the photos and X-rays that were withheld for so long, have indeed been falsified, it is just unrealistic to believe that everything was. If someone at the FBI had reversed the direction of the fibers in the jacket and shirt to change it from "exit" to "entrance", wouldn't they have also made the right hand edge the sharper one to give indication of the proper direction for a bullet from the TSBD (see comments on fibers under SHOT # 1)? Ironically, researcher Harrison Livingstone applied the coup de grace to his own "back exit" theory when, in his book *Killing the Truth*, he quotes the British nurse that he tracked down, Diana Bowron. Nurse Bowron was in the trauma room at Parkland when the President was pronounced dead and was one of those who helped clean up the body before it was placed in the coffin. She was one of very few who saw the back wound. She told Livingstone that there was no doubt in her mind that it was an *entrance* wound.

The evidence recorded and the conclusions reached immediately after the events are apt to be much more reliable than anything produced at a much later date. It is far more plausible that the throat wound was caused by a bone fragment from the head shot that struck from the rear than to accept any of the alternative theories. Even the Warren Commission discussed this idea in their January 27, 1964 meeting.[27] Some critics, notably Josiah Thompson, have used the bone fragment theory to explain why there were no metallic traces found on the shirt hole or necktie nick. But there is a better explanation for that, which was offered by Harold Weisberg. He quotes testimony from the attending doctors that this wound was actually *above* the collar, in the one half inch or so of exposed neck between shirt collar and Adam's Apple, and that the slits in the shirt and nick in the tie were not made by the passage of a bullet (or bone fragment), but by the Parkland medical personnel using scalpels in their haste to remove the President's shirt (see Figure 21 below).[28]

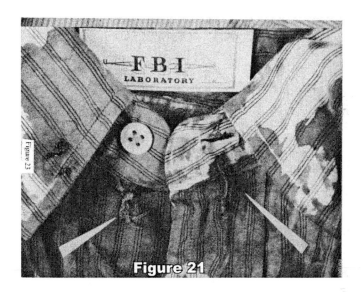

3. The Fatal Head Shot/s

Was it the shot from the sixth floor of the TSBD, or the shot from the grassy knoll, or both that killed the President? Compared to the question of conspiracy or no conspiracy, or the question of Oswald's guilt or innocence, this question is of only academic, technical interest. Yet, it is an intriguing mystery, none-the-less. According to the autopsy doctors, all the medical evidence they saw indicates he was struck only from the rear. Yet, the obvious physical effect of the impact of the bullet seen in the films, and the description of an "exit" wound in the *back* of the head by the Parkland people, would indicate a shot from the right front, or grassy knoll area. Since the police tape has indicated that there *was* such a shot from that precise area, and at the very time the President's head exploded, it is difficult to accept the finding of the HSCA that this shot missed and that only the shot from the TSBD hit its target. With the knoll shot coming just before the TSBD shot, if both bullets struck the head, the one from the rear must have hit during or immediately after the head snap caused by the knoll shot. Seven tenths of a second is not really close enough to being simultaneous to make this scenario easy to embrace. But then, the fact that the blast waves on the tape are seven tenths of a second apart does not necessarily mean that the shots and their impact on the target were spaced by that much. It takes differing lengths of time for both the bullets to travel to their target and for the sound waves to travel to the recording mike, which could shrink that seven-tenths-of-a-second difference. In fact, if the bullet from the rear was traveling at greater than the speed of sound, it would reach its target *before* the sound of the shot reached the microphone, and virtually simultaneous with the shot from in front.

4. The Dallas Police Tape

The previously described conflicting sounds on this tape have caused even some of the Warren Report critics to abandon it as valid evidence. Livingstone has even accused Mary Ferrell and Gary Mack, the researchers who discovered the importance of this tape and turned it in to the House Select Committee, of having introduced it as a "red herring" to deliberately discredit the work of the "real researchers" in their quest for the truth.[29] But the acoustical experts at Bolt, Beranek & Newman, the independent experts BBN employed to check their work (Professor Mark Weiss and assistant Dr. Ernest Aschkenasy) and the staff of the HSCA, including chairman Robert Blakey, remain convinced that the shots on the tape are real. Now further analysis conducted by Dr. Donald B. Thomas has supported their findings.

G. Paul Chambers, author of *Head Shot: the Science Behind the JFK Assassination,* and a research physicist, further analyzed the Dallas Police recording and gave us some convincing statistics. He compared the sounds on the tape with the recording made during the reenactment done in 1978, and did so in several respects, not just in regard to the acoustical fingerprints. He wanted to define the odds against these sounds being caused by random noise (or anything other than shots). He first computed the odds of the tape's sounds following in the same sequence as the test shots which matched microphone placements along Elm Street for the reenactment. This he computed to be one in seven hundred and twenty. When combined with the odds of them appearing in approximately the same estimated speed of the motorcade at that point, the chance of it happening due to random noise greatly decreases. When you then combine those odds with the odds of the sounds being synchronized so closely with the evidence of hits seen in the Zapruder film, the odds against rise to one in sixteen million. When you then combine these odds with the odds of the sounds matching the test shots in acoustical "fingerprint" form, the odds against become eleven billion to one![30] But to convince the doubters of the validity of the recorded impulses, it would take an explanation for those conflicting sounds, one that has not been satisfactorily produced as yet.

5. CE 399

Perhaps the single most perplexing mystery of all is the so-called "magic bullet", commission Exhibit 399. The Warren Commission concluded, in spite of evidence to the contrary, that this was the bullet found by Parkland Hospital orderly Darrell Tomlinson on a stretcher in a corridor sometime during the afternoon of November 22nd. They also concluded, without real proof, that the stretcher on which Tomlinson found his bullet was that on which Governor Connally was transported into the trauma room. But they had great difficulty with both the chain of events that led to Connally's stretcher being in the right location, and the chain-of-possession of the vital piece of evidence allegedly found on it. The bullet was passed from Tomlinson to O. P. Wright, to Secret Service Agent R. Johnsen, to Secret Service Chief J. Rowley, to FBI Special Agent E. L. Todd, none of whom except Todd could subsequently identify it. But the Warren Commission's final conclusion about this bullet, that it had caused *all* the non-fatal wounds to both the President and the Governor, was the most difficult part of this bullet's "history" to swallow. CE 399, until the FBI dug a sliver of copper off the nose and some lead from the base for testing, had not a dent or a scratch except for a squeezed distortion of its roundness at the base. Its length was even less distorted than bullets that the FBI test-fired into cotton tubes, CE 572, and looked nothing like the bullet test fired through a goat carcass, CE 853, or the one fired through the wrist of a cadaver, CE 856 (see Fig. 16 on page 179). The striations (lands and grooves) along 399's length were completely unbroken, even under a microscope, according to FBI ballistics expert, Robert Frazier.[31]

An unfired bullet of this type weighed *an average* of 161 grains while CE 399 weighed 158.6 grains.[32] Since the doctors removed at least three grains of lead from Connally's wrist and left still more in his chest and thigh, there is no way that this bullet could have caused his wounds.

Commander Humes, in response to a question during his Warren Commission testimony as to whether bullet exhibit 399 could have caused the wounds to Governor Connally, said:

...most unlikely. I do not understand how it could have left fragments in either of these locations (chest and wrist)...I can't conceive of where they came from this missile.

Dr. Shaw (Connally's doctor at Parkland hospital in Dallas) in testimony to commission attorney Arlen Specter, author of the "single-bullet theory," said:

I feel that there would be some difficulty in explaining all the wounds as being inflicted by bullet exhibit 399 without causing more in the way of loss of substance to the bullet or deformation of the bullet.

Then we have the as yet unexplained fact that no blood or tissue was found on the bullet that was supposed to have caused wounds to four body parts.[33]

After the initial "investigation", there have been two other revelations that further grind into the ground the fairy tale career attributed to this remarkable bullet by the government. First, the Clark panel reported finding "several metallic fragments, present in this region" (the President's neck area),[34] which would have had to come from CE 399, according to the official story. Second, the above mentioned revelation by FBI ballistics expert, Robert A. Frazier, in his testimony at the trial of Clay Shaw, stated that he had removed lead from the *base* of bullet 399 as well as copper from its nose, further reducing the amount of lead lost in its alleged journey through the two victims. (See Figure 22 bottom. Left photo shows the condition when found.)

Yet, the theories in which this bullet was pre-fired into cotton or water and then planted or substituted for the bullet actually found, for the purpose of incriminating Oswald, leaves one very difficult question unanswered: how did it become slightly flattened at the base?

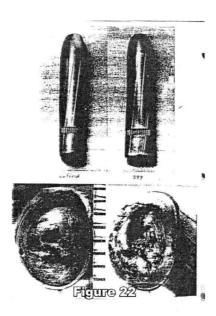

One possibility is that it was fired into a water tank at an angle that deflected its angle upward enough so that it grazed the bottom of the tank rear-first. This of course implies a predetermined plot to incriminate Oswald. If it was indeed the bullet found on the stretcher at Parkland, which is seriously in doubt, it could easily have been planted there by just about anyone, including Jack Ruby, who was seen at Parkland by newsman Seth Kantor between the time the victims arrived and the time the bullet was found. If it is *not* the bullet that Tomlinson found, then it was switched at some later point, and we have yet another serious indication that a conspiracy to frame Oswald extended high into our government.

Chapter 10
CONCLUSIONS
Coming to Grips

This chapter summarizes the major conclusions reached as a result of my decades of studying the assassination of John F. Kennedy. The progression from conclusion # 1 to conclusion # 10 represents an evolution in my thinking over the years as I continued studying the case. I have backed up each conclusion with what I consider the most persuasive evidence upon which it is based, much of which was examined in detail in previous chapters. My outlook on this subject underwent several changes over the years, as more facts came out and different aspects and theories were expounded by the various critics and defenders of the Warren Report. At first I simply believed that the FBI and the Warren Commission had been carelessly mistaken–that in their haste to wrap things up and in their desire to avoid an international crisis they had chosen not to dig too hard, and so they missed the very likely possibility that Oswald had help. Later, it became clear that not only the Warren Commission, but the Dallas Police, the FBI and the CIA had deliberately suppressed and distorted evidence of multiple assassins and a conspiracy. It was also clear that the staff of the Warren Commission, who had done the bulk of the collection and presentation of evidence and the selection of witnesses for the commission, was very biased and selective, avoiding witnesses and evidence like the plague whenever they tended to cast doubt on the already agreed upon verdict that Lee Oswald was solely responsible.

For a long time I felt that the commissioners themselves, particularly Chairman Earl Warren, were simply misled and did not deliberately set out to dupe the American people. Today, it is crystal clear that at least one member of the commission had good reason to conceal the truth. This was Allen Dulles, former director of the CIA, who was forced by Kennedy to resign after the disastrous Bay of Pigs fiasco, sponsored by the agency Dulles headed. Other members, such as Gerald Ford and Earl Warren himself, seemed to feel it was their patriotic duty not to "rock the boat" and risk potentially catastrophic (in their eyes) revelations. Still others, such as Senator Richard Russell and Congressman Hale Boggs, have been openly skeptical of the final findings of the commission on which they served, but, none-the-less, allowed their names to be included in the "unanimous" report. For a few years I believed that LBJ had only used the Warren Commission to cover up the truth to avoid the danger of nuclear war. But now that we know that Hoover was aware that an assassination attempt was being planned (Chicago and Miami tips) it is hard to believe that he would not have shared this information with his close friend Lyndon, who took no steps to prevent the plot from bearing fruit.

My first few conclusions should shock no one at this point. They represent views shared by the vast majority, both in our country and abroad. Some of my other conclusions, however, may seem extreme. But as painful as it may be to contemplate, an objective analysis of the evidence, I feel, makes it difficult to avoid these disturbing inferences.

Each conclusion is accompanied by my personal "estimated probability" of being true. These represent my own subjective degree of conviction, which in many cases has varied from time to time as new facts have come to light. In almost every case, the variation has been in the upward direction.

Conclusion # 1

President Kennedy was killed as a result of a conspiracy*, not by Lee Harvey Oswald acting alone. (Estimated Probability...100%)

Best Evidence:

The evidence pointing to a conspiracy is overwhelming. Without more specific proof even being presented, consider the absurdity of a mediocre rifleman, while in an awkward, cramped position, using a cheap, defective WW2 bolt-action rifle with 20 year old ammunition and a loose, improperly mounted telescopic sight, hitting his moving target two out of three shots in approximately eight seconds. The hypothesis of the official verdict is that Oswald somehow pulled this off when none of the expert marksmen, used by the government in attempts to prove it could be done, were able to accomplish the feat under far less difficult constraints.[1] This was not plausible, even before the most compelling evidence against it is examined. Here is a brief reminder of two of the most obvious pieces of evidence, seen clearly by even a superficial examination of the Zapruder movie.

1. The President and Governor Connally are seen reacting to being struck approximately 1.5 seconds apart: too close together to have been shot by two bullets fired from Oswald's rifle. This forced the Warren Commission to conclude that they were both struck by the same bullet, in spite of massive evidence to the contrary (see Conclusion 2).

2. The President's head is thrown violently backward and to the left by the force of the shot/s that struck his head and killed him. The laws of physics dictate that this reaction is what would be expected from being hit by a bullet fired from the right front of the victim. Oswald is supposed to have been firing from behind the President.

---

* I find it quite disturbing that in the past decade or so the word "conspiracy" has been denigrated to the level of "UFO abduction" or "demonic possession", the implication often being that the user of that word does not have a firm grip on reality, or is paranoid. We should all keep in mind that the word merely means that two or more people have worked together in perpetrating a crime; something that happens many times every day.

Conclusion # 2

Kennedy and Connally were not hit by the same bullet. The "single-bullet theory" is an untenable myth. (Estimated probability...100%)

NOTE: This was a necessary cornerstone to the Warren Commission's conclusion that there was only one assassin, and is therefore dealt with at some length below.

Best Evidence:

1. The wound in Kennedy's back was too low in relation to his throat wound.

a. The holes in his jacket and shirt indicate a back wound lower than the throat wound. The clothing holes are more than five inches below the collar (see Figures. 11 and 12 in chapter nine).

b. The autopsy photos show the back wound to be lower than the throat wound and roughly in the same location as indicated by the clothing (see Figure 13 in chapter nine).

c. The autopsy chart of the body created by Dr. J. Boswell showed this wound to be well below the shoulder line. Boswell later said that he was "careless" and, not realizing that his work would ever be seen, placed the dot signifying the back wound "inaccurately" (see Figure 14 in chapter nine). However, Admiral Burkley, the President's personal physician, verified the drawing with his signature. He also issued a death certificate, pried loose from the National Archives years later by researcher Harold Weisberg, in which he described the location of this wound as being at the level of the third thoracic vertebra,[2] exactly where the Boswell chart indicates. Compare this location with the one in the drawings presented to and used by the Warren Commission (top of Fig. 15) to illustrate how they "assumed" the bullet traversed Kennedy's neck.

d. The angle of decline from the sixth floor window of the Texas School Book Depository was 19-22 degrees at the point on Elm St. where the Warren Commission assumed Kennedy and Connally were hit by the first bullet (Zapruder frame 210). The angle connecting Connally's back and chest wounds was twenty-seven degrees downward.[3] The House Select Committee concluded in

1978, on the basis of the police tape, that they were actually hit almost two seconds *earlier* than the commission concluded (around frame 177), when the angle from the TSBD window to the car was steeper.[4] The description by the autopsy doctors of the entrance wound in JFK's back also indicates a sharp downward angle. The FBI report filed by the attending agents describes it as being *"45-60 degrees downward."*[5] The elliptical shape (7 cm vertical to 4 cm horizontal) is indicative of a bullet entering at a rather steep angle. But, the angle of a line connecting Kennedy's wounds (back and front of throat) was obviously upward. (See Figure 23 below for an exaggerated approximation).

The "lone nut" advocates love to ridicule the critics of the "single bullet theory" by showing that the bullet did not have to take all the zigs and zags indicated in drawings like the one shown below in Figure 23 in order to have passed through both men in a nearly straight line. Indeed, many critics put too much emphasis on this aspect of the problem. I will grant that, had the bullet entered Kennedy's *neck,* the trajectory could have worked, given a slight deflection downward by grazing Connally's rib. But it did *not* enter JFK's neck–it entered his *back* at a point below the so called exit wound, necessitating a path similar to that shown in the drawing. Notice that while sneering at "silly" drawings like this one, they avoid the more difficult problems of the back entry location and the throat exit size, or the delayed reaction of the Governor, or the condition of the bullet.

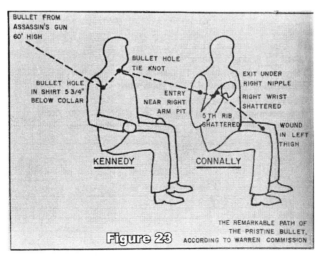

2. The wound in Kennedy's throat was too small.

a. The throat wound was pencil eraser size, about one half to two thirds as big as the entrance wound in the back. Exit wounds are always *larger* than entrance wounds, as demonstrated by the government's own tests using Oswald's rifle.[6]

b. Every doctor and nurse at Parkland Hospital in Dallas who saw this wound assumed it was one of entrance because of its size and smooth edges.[7]

3. The wound in Kennedy's back penetrated no more than two inches. No track through the body could be found.

a. According to remarks by all autopsy doctors during the performance of the autopsy and their testimony to the Warren Commission.[8]

b. According to the testimony of some of the medical assistants who watched efforts to probe through the open chest cavity, to no avail. These include Secret Service agents, FBI agents and medical technicians.[9]

c. According to a report filed by two FBI agents who attended the autopsy.[10]

4. The President's throat wound was probably caused by a bone fragment from the head shot rather than a bullet.

a. The "holes" in the front of the shirt were long slits bearing no resemblance to bullet holes. The slits in the front of his shirt and the nick in the necktie bore no metallic traces unlike the holes in the back of his clothing, nor do they bear any bloodstains. They are also much larger than the wound in the throat and do not match when the two parts of the shirt front are overlapped. They were probably made by the Parkland medical people when they cut off JFK's necktie (see Figure 21 on page 202)[11]

b. Secret Service Agent Kellerman, sitting directly in front of the President, heard him say, "My God, I am hit", immediately after the first shot.[12] It is difficult to imagine him saying anything if a bullet had already torn through his larynx.

5. The alignment of Kennedy and Connally at the time of this shot does not trace back to the TSBD window.

a. They might have been lined up properly at a point further down Elm Street, but when the first two shots were fired the angle of the limo was such that a simultaneous hit would have had to come from a point further to the left of the limo (looking from the rear), such as the Dal-Tex building across Houston St. (see Figure 19).

b. The horizontal angle of a line between the two wounds in JFK (back and throat) was slightly from right to left, starting two inches to the right of the midline of the back. The entrance wound in Governor Connally is well to his right, under his armpit, and traversed his body at a sharper right-to-left angle.

c. Attempts by Warren Commission supporters to show that the two men could have turned or twisted in such a way as to be lined up properly, are disproved by the photographic evidence.

6. The Zapruder film clearly shows Connally un-hit at least one and one half seconds after Kennedy reacts to being hit.

a. In Zapruder frame 230 he can be seen still holding his Stetson hat with the hand whose wrist is supposedly shattered (Figure 24).

b. The timing of shots one and four heard on the Dallas Police tape (3.4 seconds apart) coincides with the reactions seen in the Zapruder film and with Connally's testimony.

7. Governor Connally and his wife are both convinced that the governor was hit by a different shot than the one that hit JFK in the back.

8. The found "stretcher" bullet, CE 399, was in almost perfect condition, with only a minute quantity of lead missing from its base. There was more lead removed from Governor Connally's body than was missing from this bullet, and still more remains in his body that the doctors did not remove. Most of the lead missing from CE 399 was removed by FBI agent Frazier for testing purposes.[13] All the doctors questioned expressed the opinion that this bullet could *not* have caused the wounds to Connally, let alone both men.[14]

9. Even some members of the Warren Commission did not accept the "single-bullet theory,"[15] but were pressured into agreeing to the wording finally compromised upon in the Report:

Although it is not necessary to any essential findings of the commission to determine just which shot hit Governor Connally, there is very persuasive evidence from the experts to indicate that the same bullet which pierced the President's throat also caused Gov. Connally's wounds. However, Governor Connally's testimony and certain other factors have given rise to some difference of opinion as to this probability...

The only alternative to their agreement on that point was to accept the fact that there had to have been more than one assassin—an admission that none was willing to make.

Any one of the first six of the facts outlined above is sufficient by itself to destroy the "single-bullet theory" invented by Arlen Specter. Even as early as 1964 when the evidence in this case was first examined, it was easier to accept the possibility that the "magic bullet" was planted on a stretcher to incriminate Oswald, than to accept the "single-bullet theory" put forth by the Warren Commission.

Conclusion # 3

There were at least four shots fired by at least three gunmen in Dealey Plaza. (Est. probability...100%)

Best Evidence:

1. The Dallas Police tape indicates that there were four confirmed shots (and probably *three* others) with the third of the four coming from the area of the wooden fence at the top of the grassy knoll.

2. The same tape shows that the first two (confirmed) shots, both from the area behind the President, were too close together to have both been fired by Oswald's bolt-action rifle.

3. The movement of JFK's head as shown on the Zapruder film indicates a shot from the right front.

4. Eye and ear witness testimony support both the timing and source of the shots indicated on the tape. Witnesses to the grassy knoll shot include: Lee Bowers, who was in a railroad tower behind the fence atop the knoll; Sam Holland and Ed Hoffman, who were on the overpass with a good view of the area; Jean Hill, Mary Moorman and Beverly Oliver, directly across Elm Street from the knoll.

Conclusion # 4

Lee Harvey Oswald fired *none* of the shots at the presidential motorcade (Estimated probability...98%)

Best Evidence:

1. His whereabouts just before the shooting. Carolyn Arnold, one of the secretaries at the TSBD, claimed that she remembered seeing Oswald in the second floor lunchroom around 12:15 or a little later.[16] This was just 15 minutes before the shooting began and just *ten* minutes before the motorcade was *scheduled* to pass by that point. It was also the same time that other witnesses reported seeing men with rifles in the sixth floor windows.[17]

2. His whereabouts just after the shooting. Within ninety seconds of the last shot (longest of the reenactments performed by the Warren Commission) police officer Marion Baker, accompanied by building superintendent Truly, accosted Oswald in the second floor

lunchroom of the TSBD.[18] Baker was on his way via the stairs up to the roof, which he assumed was the source of at least one of the shots because of the flock of pigeons that had flown from it in response to the loud sounds. Preceded by Truly as they climbed the same stairs that Oswald would have had to descend, Baker caught a glimpse of a man through the glass in a swinging door that led into the lunchroom. At this time Baker was rounding the corner to the next flight of stairs and Truly was already starting up toward the third floor. The angle of the line of sight that Baker had through the door into the vestibule or lunchroom itself would have made it nearly impossible for Baker to see Oswald unless he was passing through the vestibule to enter the lunchroom from the other entrance, from the first floor, not from the staircase (see Figure 25). A close examination of this floor plan reveals just how unlikely it is that Baker could spot Oswald through the window without Truly seeing him from the stairs as he was entering the lunchroom through that door.[19]

It's Time For the Truth!

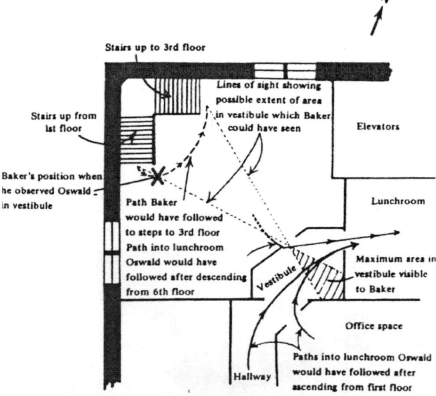

Shown above is a detail of the northwest portion of the second floor. The line of sight from Baker's position at the stairs through the window in the vestibule door shows that he could not have seen a significant portion or the north area of the vestibule. Had Baker continued to the third-floor stairs before looking into the vestibule (i.e., he did not catch a glimpse of Oswals as soon as he arrived on the second floor), his field of view in the vestibule would have moved further south.

Had Oswald entered the vestibule after descending from the sixth floor, he would have followed a path into the lunchroom that would have put him out of Baker's view. The only way Oswald could have been in the area of the vestibule visible to Baker is if he entered through the south door, accessible to him only had he come up from the first floor. To do this, he would have gone the reverse of his "escape route" as illustrated in CE 1118.

Figure 25

Baker confronted Oswald briefly as Oswald was standing in front of a soft drink machine from which he was about to obtain a bottle of Coke. (According to Baker's first report, Oswald already had the Coke in his hand. The report was later edited to exclude that reference.[20]) Obviously, if he had already gotten a Coke out of the vending machine, that adds to the time problem. Oswald told the police that he was having a Coke when confronted by Baker. To have been shooting at the President from the sixth floor window, he would have had to wipe all fingerprints off the rifle (why would Oswald take precious time to try to conceal his connection to the rifle when its purchase could so easily be traced to him?), cross from one corner of the building to the other, wedge the weapon between two stacks of cartons, descend four flights of stairs, and enter the lunchroom through the swinging doors before not only Baker but Truly (who was ahead of Baker on the stairs) reached the second floor landing–all without showing any sign of excitement or exertion. Oswald, not known for his physical fitness, was calm and breathing normally.[21] The Warren Commission's reenactment of this scene succeeded only in proving how unlikely it was to have happened that way.[22] Adding further problems for the Commission's version of events was the testimony of Victoria Adams, who worked on the fourth floor and watched the motorcade from a window with three coworkers. She said that she and Sandra Styles ran to and down the back stairs within seconds of hearing shots to see what had happened. They would have been on the stair case at the same time or just ahead of Oswald and would have seen or heard him if he had descended from the sixth floor as quickly as he would have had to in order to have reached the second floor lunchroom ahead of Baker and Truly. Confirmation of her account was obtained in 2002 by researcher Barry Ernest, who tracked her down after three and a half decades of frustrating search (detailed in his excellent book, *The Girl on the Stairs*.

3. The paraffin test. Paraffin tests were routinely used for many years to establish if a suspect might have fired a gun recently. Today, more sophisticated "gun shot residue" (GSR) tests are used. Firearms leave traces of gunpowder that contain nitrates, which are easily identified. Handguns invariably leave nitrate traces on the

hand that held the weapon. Rifles invariably leave traces on the right cheek of a right-handed shooter. The test on Oswald showed positive for nitrates on *both* hands. This is not proof that he fired a handgun that day, since nitrates can be left by many other substances, such as paint, cigarettes or ink. More significantly, the test on Oswald's face was *negative*; a strong indication that he had *not* fired a rifle recently. Control tests performed in 1964 by Dr. Vincent Guinn, using several men firing the Mannlicher Carcano rifle, produced positive nitrate results.[23]

4. The flawed evidence. The rifle found on the sixth floor of the building where Oswald was working was an Italian World War 2 piece of junk with a loose, improperly mounted scope, mounted for a left-handed shooter (Oswald was right-handed), which fired high and to the right at a range of 15 feet.[24] The rifle does seem to have been ordered by Oswald under the alias of A. Hidell, but there was no evidence that it had even been fired recently, let alone any proof that Oswald fired it at the President. The claim that the shots were easy for a Marine sharpshooter was proven completely false. Oswald had barely qualified as a Marksman (the lowest rifle qualification required to be a Marine) on his last test in the Corps and was considered a "rather poor shot" by his fellow. Marines.[25] Add to this the fact that he had no opportunity to practice since he left the corps.[26] According to Sherman Cooper, one of Oswald's fellow Marines back in 1958-59, in an interview with author Henry Hurt on Jan. 20, 1977: "If I had to pick one man in the whole United States to shoot me, I'd pick Oswald. I saw that man shoot and there's no way he could ever have learned to shoot well enough to do what they accused him of. Take me, I'm one of the best shots around, and I couldn't have done it." This was further borne out by the expert riflemen used by the FBI to attempt to prove this shooting feat possible (two hits on a moving target at those ranges in under six seconds) but proved only that they could *not* duplicate it using this rifle.[27] The brown paper bag that the authorities assumed was used to carry the rifle into the building was connected to Oswald by two highly suspect prints found by the FBI (but not by the police, which is ironically the opposite of the palm print found on the rifle by the police but not the FBI) and by the testimony of Buell W. Frazier, the fellow worker who drove Oswald to work that Friday morning. But Frazier described the bag Oswald brought with

him as too short to have been the bag found on the sixth floor, or to have carried the rifle, even when broken down. Frazier's sister corroborated his estimate that the bag was only two feet long. Also, there were no oil stains or gun-contour creases found on the bag recovered on the 6th floor, therefore no evidence it ever held an oiled rifle.[28] It should also be noted that assembling the broken down Mannlicher required a screwdriver (the screw slots were too small to use a dime) and no screwdriver was found in the TSBD or on Oswald's person.

5. The lack of motive. According to Oswald's long-standing reputation with all who knew him, which was not only accepted but emphasized by the investigating authorities, he was of very left-wing persuasion. This provided a motive for his assumed attempt on the life of General Walker, an extreme right-wing militant and known Kennedy hater, a few months before the assassination.[29] Kennedy had relieved him of command because of his overt ring-wing propagandizing. There is no evidence other than Marina's questionable testimony that it was Oswald who fired at Walker. If that were indeed the case, it hardly makes sense for the same left-winger who wanted to kill the "fascist" Walker to then turn his gun on the very person who people like Walker most wanted to see removed from the scene. On the contrary, everyone close to Oswald, including his wife and closest friends, all claimed to have heard him express admiration for the Kennedys on several occasions; never anything indicating dissatisfaction with the President.

Conclusion # 5

Oswald was not the man who killed Officer Tippit. (Estimated probability...90%)

Best Evidence:

1. Oswald's landlady testified that he entered the house at exactly 1:00 PM that day, grabbed his jacket and his revolver and left a couple of minutes after he arrived (the Warren Report puts his departure at 1:03). Tippit was shot no later than 1:10, according to the witnesses at the scene. The commission's star witness, Helen Markham, one of the two who actually saw the shooting, put it at no later than "six or seven minutes past 1:00."[30] This seems correct

since she was walking to catch a 1:12 PM bus and was on schedule. This means that Oswald would have had to cover, on foot, the nine tenths of a mile between his rooming house and the scene of the shooting in no more than seven minutes (probably less), in order to have been Tippit's killer. Reenactments of Oswald's trip, at a brisk walk, show that it would take over eleven and a half minutes. David Belin, a member of the Warren Commission's staff, walked the route and took twelve minutes. Even this time seems short in view of the fact that it takes 10 minutes to cover nine tenths of a mile at a fast jog.[31]

2. The homicide report filed by the police, and most witnesses to the encounter, said that the killer was walking *west* when he was stopped by Tippit. The only witness who said the assailant was walking east was Helen Markham, a most unreliable witness. The Warren Commission accepted her version.[32] West is *toward*, not *away* from Oswald's rooming house, which means for the assailant to have been Oswald, he would have to go past that area and double back (Figure 26 below).

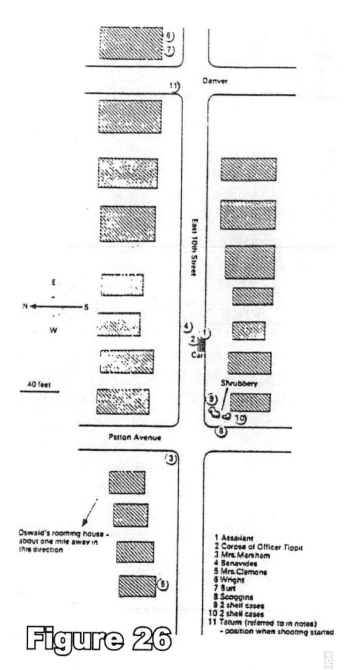

Figure 26

Scene of Officer Tippit shooting

3. The ballistic evidence (bullets and cartridge cases) used to tie the killing to Oswald's revolver were either inconclusive or grossly mishandled by the police, and therefore are not reliable as proof of his guilt. Nor was there any evidence that his gun had even been fired. The slugs from Tippit's body could not be ballistically matched to Oswald's gun. Moreover, there was a mixture of Winchester and Remington bullets and cartridges found at the scene, but the mixture didn't match (3-1 in bullets, 2-2 in shells). When the officer who marked them at the scene was shown them later by the commission, he could no longer find his mark on them![33] The slugs did not contain the usual identifiable lands and grooves because they were .38 Special bullets that had been fired from a standard .38, which has a slightly larger barrel than the Special.

4. The shells found at the scene were from an automatic, according to a police radio transmission made at 1:40 PM. At 1:36 PM a policeman at the scene broadcast a description, obtained from a witness, that the weapon was a ".32 dark-finish automatic."[34] Oswald was carrying a revolver, which does not automatically eject the used casings. No one would deliberately remove and discard revolver casings at the scene unless they wanted to be convicted of the crime.

5. The eyewitnesses who placed Oswald at the scene of the Tippit murder were either unsure in their identification or did so in unfair and prejudicial police lineups. The closest witness to the shooting, Domingo Benevides was not even brought to a line up because he was sure he could not identify the killer.[35] Other eyewitnesses who gave descriptions of a man (or men, in a couple of cases) that were very different from Oswald, were ignored by the authorities. Acquilla Clemons saw two men at the police car who ran off in different directions after the "short heavy man shot the officer." Frank and Mary Wright saw the killer drive off in an old, grey coupe.[36]

Conclusion # 6

Lee Harvey Oswald was an undercover agent for a US intelligence agency. (Estimated probability...90%)

Best Evidence

1. Oswald, who openly flaunted his admiration for Marxism and things Russian throughout his stint in the Marines, was not only *allowed* by the US State Department to defect to the USSR at the height of the Cold War, his way there was expedited.[37] Then, after renouncing his US citizenship and offering classified information to the Soviets,[38] and after marrying a Russian woman whose uncle was part of the Soviet intelligence community,[39] he was assisted financially to return home as soon as he declared he was "disillusioned with Soviet life."[40] All this occurred at a time when US intelligence was sending several bogus malcontents to Russia for the purpose of gathering information for this government. Oswald showed keen interest in one (Robert Webster) who went over and came back within weeks of Oswald himself.[41]

2. After Oswald's return from Russia he was never flagged as a possible threat, in spite of his ostensible history of anti-Americanism. No State Department "lookout cards" were ever issued in his name, although there were ample reasons to issue them. Inquiries into his potentially dangerous leanings were met with assurances from various government officials that he was "all right."[42]

3. People in a position to study government documents not yet available to the public, such as Senator Gary Hart, Senator Richard Schweiker and Pennsylvania prosecutor Richard Sprague, have concluded that Oswald was an agent or double agent for US intelligence. Senator Hart (after his work with the Senate Intelligence Committee) stated: "I don't think you can see the things I have seen and sit on it... Lee Oswald was sophisticated enough to have acted as a double agent." Senator Schweiker (after his work with the Senate Intelligence Committee) stated: "I think that...Oswald was playing out an intelligence role. This gets back to his being a double agent...I personally think he had a special relationship with one of the intelligence agencies. Which one I am not certain. But all the 'fingerprints' I found during my 18 months on the Senate Select Committee on Intelligence point to Oswald as being a product of, and interacting with, the intelligence community."

4. The Minox III camera that was found among Oswald's possessions by the police was an expensive model often used by intelligence agents, rarely by the general public.[43]

5. Oswald's activities in New Orleans in the summer before the assassination, where he frequented the offices of right-winger Guy Banister while otherwise portraying himself publicly as a left-wing pro-Castroite, give all the indications of a double agent or agent provocateur.[44]

Conclusion # 7

Lee Harvey Oswald was framed by a team of anti-Castro activists consisting of Cuban exiles, mobsters and CIA agents and their officers. (Estimated probability...95%)

Best Evidence:

1. Oswald impersonators, at least one of whom bore a startling resemblance to the real Oswald, made several conspicuous appearances of an incriminating nature in and around Dallas and in Mexico City during the period leading up to November 22, 1963.[45] The appearances of imposters or "false Oswalds" began during the latter half of September, 1963, around the very time that Kennedy's plan to visit Dallas in November was publicly announced. There were at least two known men who could have been an Oswald imposter. One was a former Marine buddy of Oswald named Kerry Thornley. Thornley's movements and associates between leaving the Marines and the time of JFK's death closely parallel Oswald's.[46] The other man was John T. Masen, a Dallas gun shop owner and a member of the ultra-right-wing Minutemen. He was arrested in late 1963 for illegally supplying firearms to a group of militant anti-Castro Cuban exiles known as Alpha-66. He was identified as an Oswald impersonator by Treasury agent Frank Ellsworth, who happened to be in Dealey Plaza on Nov. 22, 1963 and who was on the sixth floor of the TSBD when the rifle was found.[47] The Warren Commission investigated several of the Dallas area reports and simply concluded that the individual/s who were reported to have used the name Lee Oswald could not really have been him, because the real one was elsewhere at the time. Instead of pursuing the

question of who this imposter was, they let the matter drop. The appearance of "Oswald" at the Cuban and Soviet embassies in Mexico City was an important element in the Warren Commission's image of Oswald as a leftist malcontent. The House Committee in 1978 was disturbed over the strong indications that the man who represented himself to be Lee Oswald in both embassies was actually an imposter. However, they were never able to obtain the CIA records necessary to prove or disprove who this man was.[48]

2. Oswald's Mannlicher rifle and his pistol were mail ordered at a time when he had barely enough money to survive and in a part of the country where he could have easily purchased guns over the counter and avoided leaving a paper trail. There is no conclusive evidence that Oswald ever fired either weapon or had any great interest in guns.

3. The Dallas police were mysteriously given a description of Oswald within fourteen minutes of the assassination, before anyone could have realized that he was the only missing TSBD employee, if indeed he was, which is doubtful.

4. Of the three or more weapons that the evidence indicates were fired at JFK, only Oswald's rifle was left behind to be found by the police, along with three incriminating cartridge cases that only someone who wanted to be caught would have left behind. If Oswald had wanted to be caught, he would not have resisted arrest and then repeatedly proclaimed his innocence during some 40 hours of police custody. And then there is the almost certainly planted CE 399.

Conclusion # 8

Jack Ruby was acting under orders from the Mafia when he shot Oswald. (Estimated probability...99%)

Best Evidence:

1. Many of Ruby's own comments, especially in his testimony to Earl Warren and Gerry Ford while he was in his jail cell awaiting trial, strongly indicated that there was more to his shooting of Oswald than had been told. He begged to be brought to

Washington where he could talk more freely, and was in obvious fear for his life. His pleas were ignored (see Chapter 7).[49]

2. Ruby's connections to Mob figures, both in the Chicago area before he came to Dallas and in the south since then, are well documented. Although the Warren Commission found "no credible evidence" of these ties in 1964, in spite of all the phone records that proved otherwise, the House Select Committee on Assassinations in 1978 agreed with what the commission's critics had been saying for years about Ruby's connections.[50]

3. Ruby was in serious financial trouble prior to the assassination and was therefore vulnerable to pressure from mobsters.[51] He was a logical choice as the man to silence Oswald because of his many acquaintances in the police department, facilitating his access into the building.[52]

4. At the time of the Oswald transfer through the basement where he was shot to death, security in the building was such that even Ruby could not have gotten in to commit the crime at precisely the right time without the assistance of at least one member of the Dallas Police. Several of these officers had mob ties of their own, according to reliable sources.[53]

Conclusion # 9

A group of extreme right-wing cold-warriors killed JFK. High-ranking elements of the US military and intelligence community planned, organized and approved the assassination. It was then carried out by a team of CIA operatives, Mafia hit-men and anti-Castro Cuban exiles. (Estimated probability...95%)

Best Evidence:

The set-up of Oswald, the planting and alteration of evidence and the stifling of any attempt to perform a really honest investigation are the best indications of what heights the planning of the assassination reached, and how multi-tiered it was.

I have listed below those who the evidence shows to be the most probable participants in the plot, evidence that has been mentioned only briefly in this book, but has been detailed in several of the works of assassination researchers, much of which was not repeated here, lest this book double in length. Readers who are interested should refer to the titles listed in the bibliography and references. Although the suspects listed and their roles are admittedly a product of conjecture and educated guesswork (mine and others'), the basic conclusion is unavoidable as the one that makes the most sense in light of all the evidence available.

Level 1...the hit team. At least five of the following suspects could have been the triggermen or their backups.

Charles V. Harrelson: A hit-man for the Mob, imprisoned for killing another man since the assassination. He admitted, then denied having participated in the shooting of JFK.[54] He was a dead-ringer for one of the three tramps rousted from a freight car minutes after the assassination.

Charles F. Rogers: Alias, Richard Montoya, Rogers was identified by police forensic artist Lois Gibson as the shortest of the three tramps rousted from the RR car. He is the sole suspect in the murder of his parents and is presumed dead.

Lucien Sarti: A member of the French Mafia, named by informant Christian David as one of three Frenchmen hired by Santos Trafficante to kill Kennedy, as revealed to investigator Steve Rivele. He was also named by E. Howard Hunt as one of the shooters, in a death bed confession.[55]

Jean Souetre: Another French Corsican who, according to a CIA report released in 1977, had been expelled from the U.S. at Dallas/Fort Worth two days after the assassination. Souetre was a member of the French Secret Army Organization (OAS) and had been involved in plots on the life of Gen. Charles de Gaulle. There is some doubt as to whether the man deported was really Souetre or another equally dangerous Frenchman named Michael Mertz, who had ties to both the CIA and mob boss Santos Trafficante Jr.[56]

Roscoe White: A Dallas Policeman whose wife and son both claim that he detailed his role in the assassination in a diary before his death.[57]

Jack Lawrence: A former Air Force marksman, working in a Dallas car dealership during the month preceding the assassination. He was detained on Nov. 22 because of suspicious behavior. His car was later found parked in the lot behind the fence atop the grassy knoll. He disappeared after being released for lack of evidence.[58]

Eugene Brading (aka Jim Braden): Another mobster temporarily detained right after the shooting, having been stopped leaving the DalTex Building. He was later released without the police discovering his real identity.[59]

Sauveur Pironti and (first name unknown) Bocognoni: The other two French Mafia hit men named by Christian David to investigator Steve Rivele.[60]

John T. Masen (Oswald look-alike): May have been the man mistaken for Oswald by a Deputy Sheriff, Roger Craig. This man was seen running from the TSBD a few minutes after the assassination. Craig's testimony was disregarded because Oswald was known to be on his way to his rooming house in Oak Cliff at that time. Both Craig and witness Richard R. Carr reported seeing "Oswald" enter a Nash station wagon in front of the TSBD a few minutes after the assassination.[61] This could have been the same man who had impersonated Oswald on several occasions prior to Nov.22nd (see chapter 6).[62]

Level 2...likely members of the support team (provided get-away transport, "safe-houses" and logistic support)

E. Howard Hunt: CIA officer, leader during the Bay of Pigs invasion, staunch anti-Castro activist, future Watergate burglar. He was said by Marita Lorenz (former mistress of Castro) to have met with her, Frank Sturgis and others who drove with her from Miami, Florida to Dallas on 11/21/63 with two cars full of weapons (documented in Mark Lane's *Plausible Denial*).[63] He was not one of the three tramps photographed being led to the police station for questioning, but he was reportedly seen by several witnesses in Dealey Plaza on 11/22/63.

Frank (Sturgis) Fiorini: Another member of the CIA's Bay of Pigs team and future Watergate burglar; one of the men Lorenz says made the trip to Dallas on 11/21/63.[64]

Pedro Diaz Lanz: A pilot who had aided Castro until he announced his Communism. He defected from the Cuban Air Force with Frank Sturgis and joined the anti-Castro forces. Another of those in the Miami-Dallas caravan, according to Marita Lorenz.[65]

Manual Orcarberro Rodriguez: Leader of the Dallas unit of Alpha 66.

Alexander Rorke: CIA contract agent and mercenary.

Orlando Bosch: Cuban exile terrorist and assassin.

Loren Eugene Hall: mercenary with both CIA and Mafia ties.

Antonio Veciana: co-founder and officer of Alpha 66.

Level 3...probable members of the frame-up team (set up Oswald as the patsy).

Guy Banister: Former FBI agent, former New Orleans police officer, private investigator, Cuban exile organizer, anti-Castro activist.[66]

David Ferrie: Adventurer, pilot, anti-Castro activist involved in Bay of Pigs. A close associate of Banister, seen several times with Oswald (or his double) in New Orleans in the summer of 1963.[67]

Sergio Arcacha Smith: Militant Cuban exile closely associated with Guy Banister and David Ferrie.

David Atlee Phillips, alias Maurice Bishop: CIA's Western hemisphere Division Chief in 1963. He probably helped plan the assassination and set up Oswald when he was Chief of the Mexico City unit. May have been the man who supplied photos of a phony "Oswald" entering the Cuban embassy.[68]

Clay Shaw: OSS officer and CIA agent. Was Director of the International Trade Mart in New Orleans. An associate of Banister and Ferrie.[69] The only person ever to be tried for the assassination (by New Orleans DA Jim Garrison in 1969).

Level 4...the cleanup man and possible accessories (eliminated the patsy)

Jack Ruby: Silenced Oswald for the Mob. Low-ranking Mob associate and errand boy. [70]

Dallas Police Assistant Chief Charles Batchelor: In charge of securing the access to the basement against intruders.[71] Probably aided Ruby's access to the police station basement via elevator with a TV crew.

DP Officer William Harrison: Probably tipped Ruby on when Oswald was being brought to the basement. He was on security duty in the basement during Oswald's transfer. Ruby stepped from behind him to shoot Oswald.[72]

DP Officer George Butler: Probably assisted in getting Ruby into the basement. He was assigned to basement security during Oswald's transfer. He was uncharacteristically nervous just before Oswald was brought down. He and Ruby had been close friends for over a decade.[73]

Level 5...the most likely Mob organizers

John Roselli: High-ranking Mob boss based mainly in Las Vegas, Nevada. A close and trusted lieutenant of Sam Giancana. He acted as liaison between the Mob and the CIA in first plotting to assassinate Castro, then JFK.[74]

Robert Maheu: Financial liaison between Howard Hughes, the CIA and major Mafia figures.[75] A former FBI and CIA agent who became Howard Hughes' right-hand man.

Santos Trafficante Jr: Don of the Florida chapter of the Mafia. Along with Marcello and Sam Giancana, was hired by the CIA to try to kill Castro. He had ties to Jack Ruby.[76]

Carlos Marcello: Don of the New Orleans chapter of the Mafia. One of Robert Kennedy's favorite targets. He had been illegally deported by the Attorney General in April of 1961.[77]

Sam Giancana: Don of the Chicago chapter of the Mafia, considered to have been the "boss of bosses." He was Judy Campbell Exner's other lover while she was "seeing" JFK.[78]

Level 6...the probable CIA planners

William Harvey: Senior CIA officer who led the anti-Castro projects after the Bay of Pigs fiasco.[79] One of the principal planners of attempts to assassinate Castro. When those attempts failed, the plan was switched to JFK.

General Edward Lansdale: Long-time CIA operative in the SE Asia theater. He was photographed in Dealey Plaza moments after the shots were fired.[80]

Col. Sheffield Edwards: Security Director for the CIA. He was ordered by Deputy Director Bissell to devise a plan to assassinate Castro. Worked closely with William Harvey.[81]

General Charles Cabell: A Deputy Director of the CIA in charge of the Bay of Pigs invasion. Was fired by JFK because of misinformation he gave the President about the plan and for espousing extreme right-wing views.[82] Probably told his brother Earle, Mayor of Dallas, to change the motorcade route to go through Dealey Plaza instead of straight down Main. May have organized the entire assassination.

Richard Bissell: CIA Deputy Director of Plans fired by JFK after the Bay of Pigs disaster.[83] May have approved and assisted in planning the assassination.

David Morales: JM/WAVE Operations Manager. Close associate of John Roselli and avid JFK hater. He was part of an assassinations program in Vietnam and of several anti-Castro plots.[84]

Cord Meyer: A high-ranking CIA officer who was named by E. Howard Hunt on his death bed as one of the plotters of the JFK murder. His ex-wife Mary, who had been one of JFK's mistresses, was murdered on October 12, 1964.

Earle Cabell: Mayor of Dallas and brother of General Charles Cabell. He was in a position to have changed the motorcade route to go down Elm St. instead of Main. There was no good reason for this revised route, as the Stemmons Freeway was accessible from Main St. after the triple underpass since Elm Street traffic was closed during this period (see Figure 27 below).[85]

Figure 27

This view is looking back toward Dealey Plaza just beyond the triple underpass. The entrance to Stemmons Freeway is barely visible at lower left. Traffic coming down Main Street is normally barred from turning right onto the freeway because of conflict with traffic on Elm (left of photo).. But the low barrier between roads could obviously be ramped over or driven around with all streets blocked off for the motorcade.

Level 7...accessories before and/or after the fact

Allen Dulles: Director of the CIA who was fired by JFK after the Bay of Pigs debacle.[86] Later became a member of the Warren Commission. He must have known about and tacitly approved of the assassination. Shielded the CIA from the Warren Commission.

Lyndon B. Johnson: Became president as a result of Kennedy's murder. A very close friend of Hoover. He very probably knew the assassination was being planned. Then appointed the Warren Commission to thwart any honest investigation.[87]

J. Edgar Hoover: Director of the FBI. He expected to be forced into retirement after JFK was re-elected in 1964. Knew of but did nothing to stop the assassination. Helped to cover it up by ordering his agents to ignore or destroy all evidence not pointing to Oswald.[88]

Regis Kennedy: High-ranking FBI agent based in Dallas. Identified by Beverly Oliver as the man who confiscated and never returned her film of the fatal head shots.[89] Assisted the cover-up by withholding important evidence and distorting testimony.

H.L. Hunt: One of the most powerful members of the right-wing oil cartel. He was flown to Mexico by the FBI an hour after the assassination.[90]

Clint Murchison:...Prominent member of the right-wing oil cartel in Texas. A friend of LBJ. He reportedly met with Hoover and Nixon the evening of November 21.[91]

James Angleton: CIA Director of Counter-intelligence during 1963 and the years following. He consistently helped the CIA withhold evidence in the years following the assassination.[92]

Richard Helms: Deputy Director of Plans for the CIA in 1963. CIA Director from 1966 to 1973. He also helped the CIA withhold information in the years following the assassination.[93]

Gerald Ford: US Congressman and Warren Commission member. He later became president when Nixon resigned. Knew the assassination was the result of a conspiracy and actively worked with the FBI to conceal the truth.[94]

Richard Nixon: Kennedy's opponent in the 1960 presidential election. Was in Dallas on 11/22/63. Probably knew who was behind the assassination. As Eisenhower's Vice President, he had been in charge of the anti-Castro efforts before 1960. The Watergate tapes disclosed Nixon was afraid of what E. H. Hunt could reveal about "The Bay of Pigs thing" during the scandal.[95]

I realize that this conclusion will be the most difficult to accept for most readers. It makes the conspiracy seem too vast to contemplate; too unwieldy to construct and maintain. But remember that each level lists several *probable* suspects, while only two or three were really necessary to accomplish the deed. Level 4 probably had no part in the original plot to kill the President but were "persuaded" to eliminate Oswald. Level 7, in my opinion, played no part in the plot either, but each person mentioned had strong reasons to cover up the truth.

Did the planning for the removal of Kennedy really need to reach such a high level in order to succeed? The most convincing reason to believe that it extended into the highest ranks of our government is the extent and early start of the cover-up that followed the crime and still continues. This cover-up began on the afternoon and evening of November 22nd, when the slain President's body was illegally removed from the jurisdiction of the Texas authorities, and a completely dishonest autopsy was performed on him at Bethesda, Maryland (see Chapter 2).

Almost equally convincing is the fact that those who presented any major threat to expose the facts or raise the consciousness of the American public, such as Mark Lane and Jim Garrison in the 60's and Oliver Stone in 1991, were immediately subjected to the full weight of governmental pressure and discreditation attempts. Why would the authorities be that concerned if they had nothing to hide? Which leads us to ...

Conclusion # 10

The Dallas Police, the Secret Service, the Federal Bureau of Investigation, the Central Intelligence Agency, the Office of Naval

Intelligence, the Warren Commission, the US Congress and the Justice Department have made no real effort to pursue any evidence that led in any direction other than to Oswald, and in fact suppressed, altered and destroyed evidence and distorted or ignored testimony that did not support the "lone assassin" verdict. (Estimated probability...100%)

Best Evidence:

There are enough examples that prove the truth of the above statement to fill several books. Many of them have been previously mentioned in this work, but I have listed below the most damning examples, grouped according to the way in which evidence in this case was handled, or to put it more appropriately, mishandled.

Evidence Known to be Destroyed

Commander Humes' first draft of the autopsy report (see Chapter 2). In his interview with JAMA in 1992, Humes stated that what he burned in his fireplace were his autopsy *notes* because they were tainted by the President's blood. Either way, notes or report, this is a wanton destruction of evidence in the most important murder case in his life.

Many, probably *most*, of the autopsy photos and x-rays of the presidents body were admittedly burned.

FBI agent Hosty's note from Oswald was destoyed.[96]

The presidential limousine was sanitized immediately after the assassination.[97]

Connally's clothing was cleaned before the bullet holes could be analyzed.[98]

Evidence Missing

John Kennedy's brain.[99]

Autopsy slides of the brain.[100]

Autopsy X-rays of the arms, hands, legs and feet.[101]

Autopsy photos of the chest cavity.[102]

A pointed-nose bullet found on the stretcher at Parkland and turned over to the FBI.[103]

The original Dallas Police Department dictabelt tape of the shots fired in Dealey Plaza has disappeared from the National Archives.[104]

The original of the Orville Nix movie, from the files of the HSCA. Nix was filming from the south side of Elm, opposite Zapruder, and captured the knoll area at the moment of the fatal head shot.[105]

Oswald's police interrogation notes (if any).[106]

CIA surveillance photos and voice tapes of the person (supposedly Oswald) who visited the Cuban and Soviet embassies in Mexico City in Sept. of 1963[107]

Much of the contents of Oswald's CIA 201 file. A 201 file is opened by the CIA for persons of interest, including but not limited to agents or prospective agents. For reasons known only to the agency, they opened a file on Oswald before he defected to the USSR.[108]

Oswald's military intelligence file.[109]

The Stemmons Freeway sign, which at least one witness claimed contained a bullet hole, was removed the day after the assassination.[110]

Evidence Altered

Zapruder film frames showing the head impact were doctored to hide damage to the rear of the head, according to photo-analyst Robert Groden.[111] Then two crucial Zapruder frames were switched in the printing of the Warren Report to try to change the head snap from backward to forward.[112]

The President's head wound was enlarged between Parkland and Bethesda. (See Figure 28 below–drawings made by Parkland Hospital Doctor Robert McLelland for Josiah Thompson, author of *Six Seconds in Dallas* (top), and by Bethesda morgue technician Paul O'Connor for David Lifton, author of *Best Evidence* (bottom).[113]

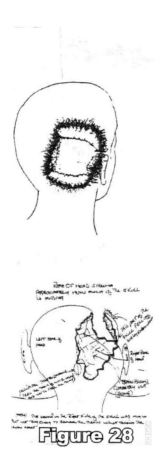

Figure 28

The tracheotomy incision through the small "puncture" wound in the throat was enlarged between Parkland and Bethesda.[114]

The autopsy photos were falsified, particularly, the ones showing no large exit wound in the back of the head (see Figure 4 in chapter 2, page 45).[115]

The autopsy X-rays of the head were falsified. They show bone missing in the facial area (disproved by autopsy photos showing the face completely intact) and show no bone damage to the back or right side of the head, where every doctor at both hospitals says there was a massive defect (see Figure 3 in chapter 2, page 44).[116]

The locations of JFK's wounds were "moved." Of the four known wounds to the President, only the one in the front of the throat did not move substantially from one examination to another. The entrance wound in the back moved from five inches below the collar (upper back), to the shoulder line (lower neck).[117] The entrance wound in the head moved 4 inches from just above the hair line, to the cowlick near the top of the head.[118] See Figure 6 on page 47 for a photograph taken during an FBI re-enactment, showing where the entrance wounds were believed to be at that time. The large exit wound in the head moved from the rear to the top/front of the head.[119]

The enlarged inset photo of JFK's shirt, showing the entrance hole of the back wound, was inverted to reverse the fiber evidence of the angle of entry, changing it from left-to-right to right-to-left, making it consistent with a shot from the TSBD (Figure 12 on page 175)

The damage to the curbstone that was struck by a bullet fragment during the assassination and caused a chip of concrete to scratch the face of bystander James Tague was patched, thus concealing vital evidence as to the composition of the missile that struck it and how it compared with the other bullets and fragments that were found.[120]

Survey drawings made by Chester Breneman and Robert West, showing height and distance figures as they related to the frames of the Zapruder film, were altered. The distance and elevation figures were changed by the Warren Commission or its staff.[121]

The license plate was scratched out on a photo of a car in General Walker's driveway (which was found in Ruth Paine's garage) while the photo was in the possession of the FBI.[122]

Evidence Suppressed

Nearly all the records pertaining to the tragedy in Dallas on November twenty-second, nineteen sixty-three were scheduled to be locked away for at least a half-century, making them unattainable to the public, including legitimate researchers, until the Records Review Board was established in 1999 and (partially) over-rode that edict. In addition, we have the following specific items.

The Zapruder film was not made available to the public for twelve years. Its first viewing by non-government people was at the trial of Clay Shaw in 1969. It was not seen by the general public until 1975 when Geraldo Rivera showed it on *Good Morning America*.[123]

The autopsy photos and x-rays that survived were not shown for several years to the Parkland Hospital (Dallas) medical personnel who treated Kennedy.[124]

The President's back wound was not traced during autopsy at command of high-ranking military officers.[125]

The autopsy doctors and other autopsy room personnel were ordered never to discuss what they saw under threat of court-martial.[126]

The FBI's spectrographic and neutron-activation analysis of the bullets, fragments, clothing holes, etc. were withheld for several years. It was Harold Weisberg's suits to get this data released that helped produce a new Freedom of Information Act. When Weisberg finally succeeded in obtaining some results, after several years of frustrating and persistent effort, it was a mass of raw data with no analysis or final report. The FBI told him they never produced one.[127]

Two tests using "neutron-activation-analysis" were conducted on the fragments to see if they came from the same bullet. The first, done at the request of the Warren Commission, has yet to be fully released. The second, performed for the HSCA by Dr. Vincent Guinn, was done on fragments that, according to Dr. Guinn as he concluded his testimony before the HSCA, were *not* the same fragments as those preserved and recorded in 1963. His much-heralded report that his test of fragments supposedly from Connally's wrist matched lead in 399 was for all practical purposes invalidated by his admission that the fragments he was given to test did not weigh the same as the ones recorded in 1963. If they did indeed come from CE 399 but were not the fragments removed from Connally and recorded by the FBI, then they must be the pieces dug out of the bullet by Special Agent Robert Frazier back in 1963 for the original testing.[128] *And if that is true, then this is one of the most blatant and criminal examples of obstruction of justice in the whole sad affair.*

The page in Oswald's notebook containing FBI agent Hosty's name, phone number and license number was not given to the Warren Commission by the FBI until pressure was applied by the staff. This was one of the rare cases when the commission pressed the FBI.[129]

The existence of Operation Mongoose, a CIA/Mafia plot to kill Castro, was kept from the Warren Commission.[130]

Film of the fatal head shot taken facing the grassy knoll by Beverly Oliver was confiscated right after the assassination by two FBI agents, one of whom she later identified as Regis Kennedy.[131]

Polaroid snapshots taken by Mary Moorman, one of the closest people to the President on the side opposite the grassy knoll at the time of the fatal shot. She snapped a picture just as he was hit. Her photos were confiscated and later returned to her, but two of them had their backgrounds mutilated at crucial points atop the grassy knoll.[132] The most important of the Moorman photos, not confiscated and altered because it was the last one snapped, seems to show two men peering out from behind the wooden fence at the top of the knoll, within feet of the point where BBN's analysis of the Dallas police tape placed the third shot. It has been enlarged, computer enhanced and analyzed by MIT, Itek Corp. and other experts who say that it seems to show the outline of a person.[133] It has been shown in the enhanced form as part of a documentary produced in Europe in 1988 titled *The Men Who Killed Kennedy*. This show was finally aired in the US in June of 1992 on the *Arts and Entertainment* channel's Investigative Reports series. It is one of the few polished programs presenting the conspiracy evidence. It does indeed seem to show a man in uniform firing a rifle at the moment of the fatal shot. (See Figure 29 below)

Figure 29

Testimony Ignored, Discounted or Distorted

FBI and Secret Service records of warnings received about threats to the President during his trips to Chicago and Miami just prior to the Dallas trip.[134]

Governor and Mrs. Connally's statements that he and JFK were hit by different bullets.

Motorcycle officer James Chaney's statement that he saw JFK and Connally get hit by separate bullets. He was riding just to the right of the President's limo.[135]

Carolyn Arnold's account to the FBI that she saw Oswald in the second floor lunchroom at 12:15, 15 minutes before the shots were fired.[136]

Roger Craig's account of a man he thought was Oswald running out of the TSBD and entering a Nash station wagon five minutes after the assassination.[137]

Detective Guy Rose's discovery of a three inch long Minox "spy camera" found in Oswald's Marine sea bag at the Paine residence. The FBI insisted what he found was a "light meter", not a camera, and tried in vain to convince Rose to alter his description of it. However, since it was loaded with film, there is no doubt as to what it really was.[138]

Julia Ann Mercer's account of seeing a man she believed to be Jack Ruby sitting in a pickup truck parked on the curb in front of the grassy knoll a couple of hours before the motorcade arrived. She also saw a man leave the truck and carry a rifle up the hill and go behind the fence. Her statements were altered and when she refused to sign the modified version, her signature was forged.[139]

Sam Holland's account of seeing a puff of smoke come from behind the fence on top of the knoll as the last shot was fired, was grossly distorted.[140]

Ed Hoffman's account of seeing two men behind the wooden fence atop the grassy knoll, one of whom fired a rifle. Hoffman is a deaf mute who said he saw the shooter then pass the rifle to the other man, who was dressed like a railroad worker. This man disassembled the rifle, put it in a tool bag and calmly walked away from the area.[141]

Tom Tilson's account of seeing a man leave the area behind the fence and put something into the back of his car before climbing in and speeding away, seconds after the President's limo sped off to the Parkland Hospital.[142]

Phil Willis' and his daughter's testimony as to the source of the fatal shot (the fence area at the top of the knoll).[1]

Ronald Fischer's description of the hair color of the man he saw in the window of the TSBD, which differed from Oswald's.[144]

Witnesses who were coerced into changing their testimony

Marina Oswald, as to her husband's practice with his rifle and several other topics.

Abraham Zapruder, as to his opinion on the source of the shots.[145]

Parkland Hospital Drs. Malcolm Perry, Charles Carrico and Robert McClelland, as to whether the small wound in the front of JFK's throat "could have been" an exit wound instead of the entrance wound they all believed it was at the time they treated the President.[146]

Kenneth O'Donnell and David Powers, as to the fact they heard shot/s from in front of the motorcade[147]

Critics of the Warren Report Who Have Been Smeared By the Government

District Attorney Jim Garrison, when he opened his own investigation into the murder of JFK.

Oliver Stone, when he planned to produce a movie about the conspiracy to murder JFK, before the movie script was even finished.

Summation of Conclusions

The scope of the cover-up that followed the assassination, and which continues to this day, could not have succeeded to the extent that it has without the cooperation and assistance of very high ranking people in the government. This certainly includes J. Edgar Hoover, who knew that JFK had no intention of waiving his automatic retirement from his FBI directorship, which would have taken place on January 1, 1965, had Kennedy lived and failed to sign a waiver before that date.[148] It also includes Lyndon B. Johnson, who had good reason to believe that he would be dropped from the Democratic ticket in 1964, which would essentially end his political career. Johnson, a very close friend of Hoover, almost certainly knew of the plans to assassinate the President and, like Hoover, said nothing. Then when that assassination made him president, he effectively squelched all impartial efforts at investigation through his appointment of the Warren Commission.

It was a painfully disturbing disillusionment, the process of evolving from the blind acceptance that Oswald alone killed the President, to what I believe now. Back in 1964, I would have thought that anyone who expounded such a hypothesis was "nutty as a fruitcake." So would ninety-five percent of the American public. Maybe a high-level right-wing plot was a little easier to believe for liberals like Harold Weisberg and Mark Lane, who adored Jack Kennedy. Perhaps their natural aversion to the Cold War attitudes of the Right, which Kennedy was veering further and further away from in his last year in office, made the motive for JFK's murder more apparent to them. Liberals had an obvious motivation to seek to blame "right-wingers" for the murder of their idol, and some seemed to take great delight in doing so. However, the Warren Report supporters make a serious mistake when they try to classify all critics of the report as "left-wing ideologues." I have always been a staunch conservative on foreign policy and was once a true believer in the basic integrity of our government. I did not vote for Jack Kennedy and always suspected that he had somehow stolen the election in 1960 through voter fraud in Illinois and Texas, a fact now partially confirmed by the very mobsters who were paid to buy the votes that swung over the state of Illinois.[149] It would have been easy for someone of my political bent to see the murder of Kennedy as a random event and let it go at that. But we have all, liberals and conservatives alike, had our illusions shattered since then, first by the assassinations (three of them in five years), then by Vietnam, Watergate, the Iran-Contra affair and the BCCI scandal. People are not as naive as they used to be. In fact, many now have a hard time believing *anything* that comes out of Washington. Many have yet to be able to take the final step, however, and swallow that difficult pill; the idea that a coup d'état could occur in this country. We pride ourselves on not being a "banana republic." We like to think that in our kind of democracy the voting booth, not the rifle, controls our destiny. But it is a sad fact that on November 22, 1963, we, the people, had that control taken away from us.

The die-hard supporters of the government's version of these assassinations love to use the argument that "conspiracy buffs" arrive at their convictions out of some deep-seated need to find rational explanations for irrational "random" events, so we find it more comforting to "imagine" a plot to kill a president than to accept that someone of high station can be brought down on the whim of one lone madman. This is ludicrous! I, for one, found it much more "comforting" when I believed the government's version of how President Kennedy was killed. Far from being driven by some psychological quirk to see a plot behind every major event, I find it easy to believe completely that John Hinckley, who tried to kill President Reagan, was a "lone nut". I also believe that it is at least ninety percent probable that Arthur Bremer acted alone when he shot George Wallace. So whenever I hear this psychological claptrap, my blood pressure rises, because the reality of political life in America is that immediately after each and every assassination or attempted assassination in this country the "official" word has gone forth before the body was even cold -"No conspiracy involved!"

We had three political assassinations (both Kennedys and Martin Luther King), plus the mysterious death of a celebrity who was romantically linked to both Kennedy brothers (Marilyn Monroe), all within the 1960's. In every one of these cases there was very strong evidence of a conspiracy involved in their death. But in each case, the authorities, before any kind of real investigation was even launched, assured the public that there was no evidence of any plot. Only in America, among the democratic nations of the world, could the authorities hope to pull this off with any degree of acceptance by the public or the press.

The "apologists" have long complained that the "critics" have failed to produce any "new evidence" to support their claim that the official story is wrong. But the reality is that it is the interpretation of the old evidence that is in dispute. Furthermore, new evidence *has* been brought out, such as the analysis of the police tape, but when it is, the Government immediately bends every effort, legal or otherwise, to discredit this evidence rather than admit error in the original findings. The Warren Commission's supporters (who today reside primarily in the Government or the news media) like to refer to people like us as "conspiracy theorists," when they feel like being polite (at other times we are called "conspiracy nuts"). I object even to the more polite term, because it is meant to imply that not only the specific details of who killed JFK, and how, are "theories," but that the fact there even *was* a conspiracy involved in JFK's death is only a theory. This is almost like saying that evolution or gravity is "only a theory." It is no longer merely a theory, it is a fact, attested to by no less an authority than a duly constituted committee of the United States Congress (in spite of all their efforts to avoid reaching that conclusion). The only "theories" left to be proved or disproved are in the identification of the actual participants and in the relatively unimportant details of the shooting itself.

When I read the first two books of Harold Weisberg's *Whitewash* series, back in the early days of my exploration of this subject, I found his accusations of total and intentional cover-up on the part of everyone involved in the investigation of JFK's death to be disturbingly extreme. Even some of the other critics of the official verdict liked to quip that, "Harold doesn't even believe the page numbers on the Report." I later obtained and studied copies of his *Photographic Whitewash*, *Post Mortem*, *Oswald in New Orleans*, *Case Open* and *Never Again!*. Although his writing style may be shrill, repetitive and sometimes difficult to read, it is now obvious that he has been correct all along in his basic assertion: that the FBI never had any intention of conducting an honest investigation of the case and that the Warren Commission and it's staff, apparently in fear of confronting and challenging Hoover, added its own coat of "whitewash" to the whole affair.

There are no less than five possible motives for participating in the cover-up. They are as follows:

1. To hide evidence of personal or group responsibility for the assassination.

2. To hide personal or group malfeasance, incompetence or carelessness, which would result in personal or group embarrassment.

3. To avoid tarnishing the image of our most important governmental agencies.

4. To calm the public and media and avoid a furor that might have led to war.

5. To avoid admitting to having made a hasty and incorrect judgment in so quickly accepting the findings of the Warren Commission.

Regardless of the motive, those who promoted the Big Lie of "no conspiracy" were, and still are, *accessories after the fact* in the murder of our president. The danger of going to war over the assassination has long since past. The only reason to continue the cover-up now is to avoid embarrassment to people who, for the most part, are no longer with us. This is not a good enough motivation to continue the deceit of the American People.

Chapter 11

THE COVER-UP–VILLAINS & HEROES

"...and the Truth Shall Set You Free."

The evidence, only briefly summarized in this work, clearly points toward the fact that there were *two* conspiracies involved in the assassination of President Kennedy. First, there was without doubt the conspiracy to kill him and put the much more conservative (at least in his foreign policy) Lyndon Johnson in the White House. Second, there was the conspiracy to conceal the facts of this killing from the public and to pin the crime on Lee Harvey Oswald, a made-to-order scapegoat.

In my Conclusion # 9 of Chapter 10, I hypothesize a multi-tiered plot to kill JFK that contained at least a score of people. It is my belief that the conspiracy to cover it up was even wider, with at least as many levels. These two conspiracies need not necessarily overlap or intertwine, although common sense dictates that they probably are linked at one or more points in both structures. Nor do the various levels of the cover-up conspiracy have to work closely together, or even have common motives or goals. Everyone in each of these groups did not get together in a massive meeting room and pledge to participate in a grand plot to conceal the truth from the public. It only takes key members of each group to decide, for the various motives described above, to avoid making any waves by bucking the official word, to set the tone for others in that group and allow this kind of distortion of history to work to the degree that it has (which is *far* from perfectly).

These levels started with elements within the Dallas Police and continued on through the US Navy (at the Bethesda autopsy), the Secret Service, the FBI, the CIA, the Warren Commission, the House Select Committee to Investigate Assassinations, the Justice Department, Time/Life, CBS, and most of the rest of the media.

Some variation of this hypothesis has been put forth many times in the past thirty years, and the most common response has been, "What motive could all these people have for concealing the truth."

As itemized in the previous chapter, the particular motive depends on the circumstances of the group in question. It is a tribute to the intelligence of the American public that, in spite of so many prestigious people throwing their weight behind the Big Lie of the lone assassin myth, today the vast majority of the public rejects it. Unfortunately, as Robert Sam Anson pointed out on a Ron Reagan TV panel show many years ago, "...the remaining fifteen percent all seem to work for either the *New York Times* or the government."

What is *not* to the credit of the American People is their willingness, in spite of their knowledge that they have been systematically lied to all these years, to sit back and say, "Oh well, that's the government for you," or, "So what? It's ancient history now." Fortunately, a small handful of courageous souls have been willing to carry on the good fight to uncover the truth from the very beginning, and many continue to do so today. As to the motivation that drives the critical researchers and writers, for the vast majority of them it is simply an intense desire to expose the facts of this historic event to the American People and the world.

Before recognizing those whom I consider to be the "heroes" in the epic battle that has been going on for decades, let us first identify some of those who have, through choice, pressure, ignorance or a warped sense of patriotism, played the role of villain. They fall into several groups, as outlined above.

There is no doubt that several members of the Dallas police force could be included in the "villain" category. Unfortunately, it is difficult, if not impossible, to identify individuals with any certainty. But there are reasons to suspect that Ruby's entrance into the garage at precisely the right time to put a bullet into Oswald was facilitated by Assistant Chief **Charles Batchelor** and Officer **William (Blackie) Harrison**.[1] Whoever was responsible, the cover-up that began with the dummied-up autopsy on Friday really began to take off with Ruby's bullet. With Oswald dead and no trial to worry about, evidence started disappearing like snow in May. Among the first evidence to go up in smoke, both figuratively and literally, was any record of two days worth of interrogation of Oswald. For this appalling gap in the so-called investigation, Homicide Captain **Will Fritz** must shoulder the responsibility. The Captain didn't claim to have burned his notes, a la Dr. Humes. He just didn't bother to make any record of any kind during the most important interrogation of his career.² Nor did he ensure that Oswald had legal counsel during those 48 hours that he was in custody. Even though this took place during pre-Miranda days, it demonstrates an astounding disregard for fundamental legal rights.

A detailed examination of the way the Dallas Police Department handled the tragedy that befell their city on November 22, 1963, reveals an example of law enforcement work that will stand forever as a monument to incompetence. From the moment the shots were fired until their only serious suspect was shot to death in their own building, they did virtually nothing right. The overall responsibility for all this must fall primarily on the head of Chief of Police **Jesse Curry**. In his subsequent book, *JFK Assassination File*, and elsewhere, Curry seems to be objective as to the question of whether Oswald was really the "lone assassin." In fact, he later admitted to an interviewer that he felt their case against Oswald was very weak. But there is no escaping the fact that he allowed his department to focus on one and only one possibility from Friday, the 22nd through Sunday, the 24th of November. He also allowed federal authorities with no jurisdiction to take over his investigation and evidence, tainting the legal value of every piece of evidence they touched and creating both the opportunity for and the distinct possibility of evidence-tampering in the process.³

Representing the US Navy, through their role in the infamous autopsy performed at Bethesda Naval Hospital on the evening of November 22, 1963, were: Captain **John Stover**, commander of the National Naval Medical School, who issued the written order to all who were present in the morgue not to discuss what they saw, under threat of Court Martial;⁴ **Admiral George Burkley**, the President's personal physician, who helped "discourage" the autopsy surgeons from tracing the non-fatal wounds in the back/neck area;⁵ Commander **James Humes**, who was in charge of the autopsy proceedings (or was supposed to be) and did not insist on doing it right. Humes then went along with the back-to-front bullet transit theory that he must have known to be false, altering and destroying autopsy report drafts in the process. I omit the other two autopsy doctors (Boswell and Finck) from the "villain" category simply because they had no authority in the proceedings and were undoubtedly subjected to severe pressure to toe the party line.

The Secret Service's contribution to the cover-up involves its mishandling of the autopsy materials. They may or may not be responsible for the fact that the container holding the President's brain and certain tissue slides is now missing.[6] Most indications seem to point to the President's brother Robert's disposing of these materials for personal reasons. However, Secret Service Chief **Robert Bouck** must bear responsibility for the fact that many of the photos and X-rays taken during the course of the autopsy have disappeared[7] and others have clearly been falsified, perhaps while they were in his custody.

In the case of the FBI, it is fair to say that essentially the entire bureau can be cast as one "super-villain," personified by its legendary Director, **J. Edgar Hoover.** If this sounds like an overstatement, let me point out that to most Americans and to *all* FBI employees, Hoover *was* the FBI. In fact, his agents referred to Hoover as the SOG, for "Seat of Government." Presidents came and went, but Hoover, it seemed, went on forever. If Hoover wanted the evidence in this case "controlled" to ensure the "Oswald did it" verdict, then the personnel involved would move heaven and earth to make it happen. Today, when we have learned of Hoover's ruthlessness and hidden homosexuality, it is difficult to realize that he was once revered as a true American icon, especially by his own agents. There were, of course, a few prominent Special Agents who played key roles in assisting Hoover to attain his goal–people like **J. Gordon Shanklin**, the SAC of the Dallas office of the FBI, **Robert Frazier**, the ballistics expert and **Lyndel Shaneyfelt**, the photographic expert.

On the CIA side, we had a parade of Directors who stonewalled everyone, including the Warren Commission and the House Select Committee, to stymie their investigations, just in case they decided to do any honest and determined examination of the available evidence. The first of these Directors was **Allen Dulles,** who was no longer Director by the time JFK was killed because Kennedy fired him. He knew about Operation Mongoose and its cousins, but as a member of the Warren Commission exerted strong influence over what was and was not revealed to his fellow Commissioners. It is nothing short of amazing how unquestioningly this fox was assigned to help guard the henhouse by LBJ, the man who was the main beneficiary in Kennedy's death.

The second was **John McCone**, who was CIA Director at the time Kennedy was killed and throughout the period of the Warren Commission's efforts. He withheld key information from the Commission, such as the existence of the projects to assassinate Castro, in which his agency worked side by side with the Mafia,[8] and the fact that his agency had a 201 file on Oswald,[9] a strong indication that the CIA had an interest in Oswald since before the assassination.

The third was **Richard Helms**, who was Director of Covert Operations at the time of the assassination and CIA Director during the Nixon administration. Since he was deeply involved in the withholding of vital information from the Warren Commission in his earlier capacity,[10] he was naturally reluctant to expose any embarrassing facts while he was Director.

The fourth was **George Herbert Walker Bush**, who was appointed CIA Director in November of 1975 by President Gerald Ford and presided over the agency during the early days of the House Select Committee's re-investigation of the case. Although the Castro projects had become public knowledge by then, other vital aspects of Oswald's background and activities were still withheld from the Committee by the embarrassed CIA. In particular, the alleged trip by Oswald to Mexico City to obtain a passport to Cuba was never satisfactorily proven one way or the other, thanks to destruction and suppression of evidence by the CIA. After Jimmy Carter replaced Bush as CIA Director with Admiral **Stansfield Turner** in March of 1977, the CIA continued to stonewall the committee in its requests for information.[11]

All of these CIA heads used the "national security" umbrella repeatedly to avoid releasing information that would shed light on just who and what Oswald was.

With respect to the Warren Commission and its staff of lawyers, we had a mix of "bad guys" and "not-so-bad guys." Anyone who "went along" with this farce of an investigation certainly cannot be placed in the "hero" category, but there were some who perhaps should escape being cast as one of the villains.

Those who in no way can escape this label, however, include such notables as **Allen Dulles** (again), **Gerald Ford** and Chief Justice **Earl Warren**, who was, after all, in charge of the whole charade. Ford teamed with **Arlen Specter** in pressuring the rest of the Commission to accept the "single-bullet theory." Later, he co-authored an ironically revealing book, *Portrait of the Assassin*, and remained until his death one of the most outspoken apologists for the Commission on which he served. He steadfastly refused to grant any critic an ounce of respectability.

Earl Warren, for whom one might feel some compassion for having been thrust into this unenviable position by LBJ, must bear the responsibility for failing to force the investigation he chaired to follow all leads, no matter the consequences, as amply demonstrated in Chapter 4. Later he tried to stop publication of Mark Lane's *Rush to Judgment*, the first of the critical books to gain widespread attention.

Of the Commission's staff, upon whom the commissioners leaned far too heavily for the selection of evidence and witnesses and the interpretation of the evidence and testimony, there are several who stand out above the rest as major contributors to the misdirection of this "grand investigation" of the President's murder, which now stands in such ill repute.

J. Lee Rankin, Chief Council to the Commission, and his assistant, - **Norman Redlich** served as a buffer between the hard-working staff of ambitious young lawyers and the seven commissioners. One could picture the Commission's structure as resembling an hour-glass, the commissioners occupying the upper half and the staff the lower half, with Rankin and Redlich in the narrow center. All information, with very few exceptions, had to flow upward (remember, this is information, not sand) through Rankin and Redlich before it could be considered by the commissioners themselves. Since these two men were among the most opposed to the slightest hint of anything not supporting the already widely heralded "lone assassin" story, there was little chance of any dissenting idea, evidence or testimony getting through them.

Among the staff, the prize for the most biased, most persistent and most outspoken proponent of the "Oswald did it" fable has to go to **David Belin**. Belin was teamed with Joseph Ball and given the section of the Report on "The Identification of the Assassin". He later wrote a book defending the Commission's case against Oswald titled, *November 22, 1963: You Are the Jury*, in which he did a decent job of presenting the evidence against Oswald in the Tippit murder, but could not really extend that into a case showing that Oswald killed the President. He often teamed up with Gerald Ford, in the years that followed, to lambaste the critics of their work and to try to shore up the Commission's findings.

Others on the staff who were equally biased and dishonest in their approach to taking testimony, selecting witnesses and interpreting evidence (although not as publicly outspoken as Belin) include **Joseph Ball, Albert Jenner**, and **Wesley Liebeler**. Liebeler was the "Jekyll and Hyde" of the Commission's staff. He granted several very frank interviews with critics such as Jay Epstein and David Lifton, in which he seemed to be quite open-minded as to the introduction of new ideas contradictory to the Warren Report, but he always reverted to the government line. He was also the author of several internal memos to his superiors on the Warren Commission, in which he tried to point out some of the serious weaknesses in the case they were preparing against Oswald. In a memo to the Commission on 9/6/64, he said:

The statements concerning Oswald's practice with the assassination weapon are misleading. They tend to give the impression that he did more practicing than the record suggests that he did. My recollection is that there is only one specific time when he might have practiced. We should be more precise in this area, because the Commission is going to have its work in this area examined very closely.

In spite of Liebeler's seeming objectivity within the confines of the Warren Commission's walls, his questioning of witnesses was among the most one-sided and close-minded of all the staff's interrogations. But the award for "biggest lie" has to go to the former senator from Pennsylvania, (now deceased) **Arlen Specter**. Were it not for his masterpiece of "snake-oil salesmanship" in foisting upon the Commission the "single-bullet theory," now often referred to as the "magic-bullet theory," they might have been forced to admit that there must have been more than one assassin.

It should be mentioned that Specter's partner in the section of the report labeled "The Facts of the Assassination", Francis Adams, left the Commission early to return to private law practice. Perhaps he felt that he could not remain a party to what he could see happening.

Next, we come to a series of Attorneys General, led by **Nicholas Katzenbach**, who was Deputy Attorney General under Robert Kennedy when JFK was killed. He assumed the role of "acting" AG while Robert was in mourning, and became permanent Attorney General when Robert resigned. His attitude toward the investigation of the President's murder was vividly displayed in a memo he sent to Bill Moyers, Kennedy's press assistant, on November 25th, 1963, three days after the assassination and one day after Oswald himself was killed. In this memo, Katzenbach spelled out "the importance of convincing the public that no one except Oswald was involved in the President's death."[12]

The next Attorney General was **Ramsey Clark**. His major contribution to the cause of "official truth" came when he appointed a panel of four "forensic experts" to examine the autopsy evidence in early 1968 and issue a report supporting the Warren Commission. He then held back the results of this super-secret examination for eleven months, until it could achieve the maximum effect on Jim Garrison's efforts to prosecute Clay Shaw as one of the conspirators in JFK's death. Otherwise, Garrison might have succeeded in his subpoena to obtain the autopsy materials for his investigation.[13]

Following Clark in the Attorney General's office were **John Mitchell** and **Richard Kleindienst**, those "stalwart defenders of law and order" under Richard Nixon. Before running afoul of the law themselves over the Watergate cover-up, both made sure that the Justice Department would continue to be the guardian of all those dangerous files and potentially embarrassing evidence, protecting them from the prying eyes of those "morbid, radical conspiracy nuts" seeking to shoot more holes into the official story.[14]

After the assassination, the Kennedy family had placed a five year restriction on examination of the autopsy materials by anyone, regardless of credentials. After this period had elapsed, several qualified experts were seeking the necessary special permission to examine the photos and X-rays, which had been left to the discretion of the family's representative, **Burke Marshall**. The first "qualified expert" was granted this privilege over eight years after the assassination, in January of 1972. He was Dr. **John Lattimer** (of "jet-effect" fame), whose area of expertise was in the field of urology.[15] Since Dr. Lattimer's field had not the slightest connection to the cause of Kennedy's death, it would seem that the decision to select him for this honor was based on other than his qualifications as a "forensic expert." Could it be that he was chosen because of his steadfast and outspoken support for the findings of the Warren Commission, both before and after his examination of this evidence?

Several judges also played leading roles in helping to at least slow the advance of truth in this historic case. Two are worthy of "honorable mention." Judge **John Pratt** presided over Harold Weisberg's Freedom of Information Act (FOIA) suits to win the release of the FBI's tests (spectrographic and neutron activation) on the bullets and fragments. He systematically and repeatedly cooperated with the FBI and the Energy Research and Development Administration (formerly a branch of the Atomic Energy Commission), which performed the neutron activation tests. As a result of Judge Pratt's complicity, it took Weisberg *years* and a change in the FOIA law before he was able to pry loose *anything*, and then all he got was nearly indecipherable raw data with no summaries of that data's meaning.[16]

Judge **Edward Haggerty** presided over the trial of Clay Shaw. Garrison didn't have much of a case to begin with, once David Ferrie died, but Judge Haggerty put the finishing touch on it when he ruled as "inadmissible" the most convincing piece of evidence that Shaw used the alias "Bertrand." This evidence came from the fact that the police officer who booked Shaw upon his arrest in Garrison's conspiracy charge, Officer Aloysius Habighorst, had filled in the area of the arrest sheet that calls for the arrestee's aliases, if any, with the name "Clay Bertrand." Habighorst was ready to testify that this name was provided to him by Shaw during the booking procedure. But because the officer did not advise Shaw of his right to remain silent, Judge Haggerty ruled against admission of the arrest sheet and refused to allow Habighorst's testimony.[17] Clay (or Clem) Bertrand was the man who asked New Orleans attorney Dean Andrews on November 23rd, 1963, to go to Dallas to provide Oswald the legal assistance he was desperately seeking, according to Andrews. Bertrand was also connected to Oswald, Dave Ferrie, Guy Bannister and the CIA.[18] By failing to prove that Shaw was Bertrand, Garrison had no case at all.

When **G. Robert Blakey** took the reins of the House Select Committee to Investigate Assassinations in 1978, he almost succeeded in turning it into a carbon copy of the Warren Commission. Even though the acoustical evidence on the police tape forced him to revise his opinion and accept the basic fact of a conspiracy, he steadfastly clung to the "single-bullet theory" and the conclusion that all shots that struck JFK came from Oswald's rifle, fired by Oswald.[19] His committee blew a golden opportunity to get to the real truth behind the President's death. Later, Blakey teamed with Richard Billings to write a book titled, *The Plot to Kill the President*, in which they tried to convince the reader that the Mob, and *only* the Mob had sponsored Oswald's action. Organized crime, it seemed, provided a convenient alternate scapegoat, especially since there were so many indications of their involvement in the crime. For a good analysis of the flaws in this reasoning, see Carl Oglesby's piece, *Is the Mafia Theory a Valid Alternative?*, which appears in his anthology, *The JFK Assassination: The Facts & the Theories* (also published as an afterword in Garrison's *On the Trail of the Assassins*).

When it comes to the news media, accessories to the cover-up abound. It is difficult to say which of them have been knowingly helping to promulgate the government's Big Lie, and which are merely deluding themselves into believing that the original investigation really gave us the truth. The two names that stand out above all the rest, both because of their stature in their field and because of their constant and steadfast devotion to the official word, are **Walter Cronkite and Dan Rather** of CBS.

Rather deserves special mention for his stellar performance when he took to the television airways on the day after the assassination to proudly proclaim that he had been allowed to view the Zapruder film (when practically no one else had) and that it showed the fatal head shot "thrusting the President's head forward!"[20] Dan must have figured that this home movie would never see the light of day to make such an outrageously false statement on nationwide television.

Cronkite lost his fatherly credibility and became one of the "villains" to the conspiracy proponents when he hosted, back in 1967, a classic whitewash, the four-part series in which CBS pulled out all the stops and threw honesty to the winds in its effort to defend the Warren Report. I wrote a lengthy letter at the time in which I took them to task in no uncertain terms, pointing out many of the errors and biased arguments presented in that series. The reply I received from CBS was astonishing. It pretended that I had actually praised the program and thanked me for my "complimentary remarks and constructive criticism."

Cronkite added insult to injury when he lent his prestigious voice to PBS's 1988 NOVA episode titled, *Who Shot Kennedy*, another Warren Report booster even less honest than the CBS series. Perhaps one of the reasons why CBS has been so biased toward the Warren Commission is the fact that, during that time, the Administrative Assistant to the head of CBS News was none other than Ellen McCloy, the daughter of John McCloy, who was one of the most anti-conspiracy members of the Warren Commission.[21] The other two major networks, NBC and ABC, have not been quite as blatant as CBS in their attempts to discredit the critics and prop up the Warren Report. However, they have been far from impartial in their coverage of the controversy.

As to the printed media, most have consistently followed the lead of the *New York Times,* the *Washington Post* and *Time Magazine* in their stubborn refusal to grant credibility to those who dare to stand up and say, "the emperor is without clothes."[22] Certain individual journalists have been in the forefront of the assault on anything and anyone who dared to question the government's version of truth. People like **George Lardner Jr**. of the *Washington Post,* **Anthony Lewis** and **Tom Wicker** of the *New York Times,* and **Alexander Cockburn** of *The Nation* have consistently distorted and misstated the facts in their frenetic attempts to discredit the critics. These reporters were among the earliest to jump aboard the Warren Report bandwagon back in 1964, praising it to the skies even before it was printed and well before anyone had a chance to fully read it. Having made that naive commitment, they are now unable to admit their role as sycophants for the government. I have often wondered to what extent they are really convinced that the official version is accurate, and how many are simply supporting that version because they sincerely believe it is better for the mental health of the country if the public accepts and history records this version of events.

Whatever their motives, these supposed guardians of our fundamental right to an impartial presentation of the news have repeatedly labeled as "lunatics" or "imbeciles" those who dared to express the belief that JFK was the victim of a conspiracy. Let me point out that there are quite a few well known and reputable people being lumped into that highly insulting category by these government mouthpieces. In addition to the "heroes" I will mention shortly, there are senators, congressmen, movie stars, former CIA employees, former FBI employees, college professors, and even a few from the news profession, who have expressed just such a belief.

One notable exception to this pervasive tendency of prominent newsmen to pan Warren Report critics, and Oliver Stone's *JFK* in particular, is Thomas Oliphant of the *Boston Globe*. When nearly all the others were competing with each other to see who could write the most devastating critique of Stone and his "shameless distortion of history," Oliphant had the courage to buck the trend and state in print that he agrees with Stone's assessment of his film as "a myth in the classical sense...an allegory that points to an inner truth." Oliphant went on to say that, "as such, it is credible; it is honest."[23] It is most unfortunate but not surprising, given their track record, that there were so few in the news media who could look past the film's admitted flaws and artistic liberties to evaluate the important basic message it was presenting in such convincing fashion.

Last but by no means least in the parade of "villains" are the US Presidents–all of them, from **Lyndon Johnson** to **Bill Clinton** (I will exclude George W. Bush and Barack Obama from this group because they had too many more important issues to worry about to even consider a case this cold). Any one of them could have insisted on a new and completely honest investigation of the assassinations of both Kennedy brothers. None have expressed any interest in doing so. **Jimmy Carter** had the best opportunity, when Congress, without encouragement from him, decided to restudy the JFK and King assassinations in 1978. But he failed to use his influence as president to ensure that a really fair and complete job was done. Then, when the Committee was forced by the evidence on the police tape to issue a report finally admitting that both King and Kennedy had "probably" been killed as a result of conspiracies, and made several recommendations to the Justice Department for looking deeper into certain aspects, Carter, and **Ronald Reagan** who soon followed, allowed Justice to sit back and ignore these recommendations.

During the eight years of the Reagan administration and three years of the first Bush administration, it was as if the JFK controversy never existed. It lay in a dormant state until Stone's movie came along in December of 1991 and revived it. Between the movie itself and all the hoopla in the press, which tried so desperately to discredit it, public interest and demand for the release of the files reached an all-time high. It is ironic that this came at a time when we had a former Director of the CIA, who was a high-ranking officer of that agency at the time of the Kennedy assassination, in the White House. George Bush Sr. has denied ever working for the CIA before he was appointed its director, but the evidence indicates otherwise. It is too much of a "coincidence" that the Bay of Pigs invasion was code named *Zapata* and the two ships that landed the exile invaders had been renamed *Barbara* and *Houston*, at a time when George Bush was running a Houston based oil company named *Zapata Off Shore Co.* and was married to a Barbara. Then there was a memo from FBI director Hoover to the State Department dated November 29, 1963 (one week after the assassination) stating that Captain William Edwards of the Defense Intelligence Agency had briefed "Mr. George Bush of the Central Intelligence Agency" about the reaction of Miami's Cuban exile community to the assassination. Hoover pointed out that there had been another George Bush working for the CIA at that time, but investigation showed that the other Bush was a lower level researcher who would not have received such a briefing.[24] As President, George Bush Sr. has said on many occasions that he has yet to see or hear any reason to disbelieve the Warren Report. He was in no rush to sign into law the Assassination Records Review bill to release the files on the case, which was passed by both houses of Congress several weeks before he finally did sign it, seven days before he was defeated in his bid for re-election.

Bill Clinton seemed to hold out some hope for action when, during his campaign for the presidency, he agreed with Vice-Presidential candidate Al Gore's stated opinion that "there was a conspiracy involved in the assassination of JFK." However, Clinton allowed over fifteen months to pass before appointing the review panel necessary to carry out the file-review bill signed into law by Bush. On the thirtieth anniversary of the assassination Clinton added insult to injury when he changed his viewpoint and came out in favor of the "lone-assassin" conclusion.

****

Now let's take a look at who some of the "heroes" have been in the ongoing battle to uncover the truth about John Kennedy's murder. They come from a wide range of occupations and from both sides of the political fence; contrary to what their opponents would have us believe (..."they're all left-wing crackpots!"). None of them have halos glowing over their heads. They are all human beings with faults and weaknesses like everyone else. Some have indeed profited to some extent from their examination of the case, but profit is not the prime motive that drives these people. In most cases, it is a sincere desire to pry the lid off the covered truth of how and why JFK was killed that is the compelling force that makes them willing to do what they do, in spite of the vilification that has been heaped upon them. They tend to bicker a lot with each other, and some critics may not agree with the inclusion of some of my choices for the label of "hero," but I believe that each one has made an important contribution to the cause of truth.

First and foremost is "the father of the assassination researchers," the late **Harold Weisberg**. Prior to 11/22/63, he had been an investigative reporter and a Senate investigator. He devoted most of his life since then to obtaining and analyzing suppressed information on the JFK case and writing prolifically to expose the cover-up. A major improvement in the law governing a citizen's access to information was one important by-product of Weisberg's tireless efforts to force a stubborn government to provide relevant data from the many phases of the various investigations. When no publisher cared (or dared) to print his explosive early revelations, he set up his own publishing business and printed and distributed his books himself. Weisberg came to be recognized, even by his arch-rival the FBI, as the world's leading authority on the assassination of President Kennedy. He probably published more previously suppressed documents related to the case than all the other researchers combined. Ironically, Weisberg's penchant for criticizing the other critics, nearly as often as he does the government, often prompts the Warren apologists to quote him in support of their attacks on those who dare to question officialdom, and prompted Weisberg to refer to himself as "the man in the middle."

Weisberg's lawyer over the many years of battle with the various government agencies was **James Lesar**, who assisted Weisberg in his efforts to uncover the truth, virtually without fee. Lesar and **Bernard Fensterwald Jr.**, another lawyer and long-time Warren Report critic, founded the Washington-based *Assassination Archive and Research Center* (AARC), an organization dedicated to the collection, analysis and storage of assassination-related materials. It was the AARC that provided some of the photographic illustrations contained herein.

My next hero, the flamboyant and outspoken attorney, **Mark Lane**, has made a lot of enemies, not all of them on the Warren Commission's side of the issue. But there is no denying Lane's contribution to the awakening of the public to the many flaws in the Warren Report. His early work, the best-selling *Rush to Judgment*, was the first book I read on the subject and it opened a lot of people's eyes besides mine. As the legal representative of Oswald's mother, Marguerite Oswald, during the Commission's "investigation," Lane was the only critic to testify before that august body. Of course, his questions and protestations were ignored by the Commission. Lane also has done some excellent work in the area of the King assassination (his book on that case is titled, *Code Name Zorro*). His outspokenness and high visibility over the years since 1963 made him the early number one target of the government's Warren Report supporters.

Sylvia Meagher made two major contributions to the pursuit of truth. First, she compiled the first and only subject index to the

Warren Report and its twenty-six volumes of testimony and exhibits, which has greatly facilitated the work of all researchers on this case. Second, her well documented book, *Accessories after the fact: The Warren Commission, The Authorities and The Report*, is generally considered to be one of the finest on the JFK case. No one could read this book and come away with their image of the FBI intact.

Penn Jones, Jr. was the editor and publisher of a small town Texas newspaper called the *Midlothian Mirror* since before the assassination occurred. He was among the first to see the fallacy of the official story and he began publishing articles in his paper calling for the truth to be brought forth. He concentrated in particular on the series of strange and suspicious deaths of JFK or Tippit witnesses and suspects and wrote a series of books on the subject titled *Forgive My Grief*, volumes I-IV.

Next is **Josiah Thompson**, a philosophy professor at Haverford University, whose *Six Seconds in Dallas* offers convincing evidence that Kennedy was struck in the head from the front. His detailed analysis of the backward head snap, so vividly captured by the Zapruder film, made it impossible for the Warren supporters to explain it away with any credibility.

Then there is **David Lifton**, a physics professor from Cornell University, whose *Best Evidence* was an excellent analysis of the discrepancies, contradictions and skullduggery involved in the Bethesda autopsy. It is Lifton's belief that JFK's body was worked on, probably at Walter Reed, before it ever reached the morgue at Bethesda, at which time bullets were removed and wounds altered to eliminate evidence of a shot from the front. Whether Lifton's theory is accurate or not, his further exposure of what went on in Bethesda that Friday evening was a valuable addition to the critical literature.

One of the founders and leaders of the *Assassination Information Bureau* in Washington, DC, was **Carl Oglesby**. He contributed to the anti-Warren crusade for many years, through his writings and talk-show appearances. He compiled some of his own writings along with some of the most interesting pieces written by others, into a collection titled, *The JFK Assassination: The Facts and the Theories*.

The next wave of literary contributors included **Anthony Summers**, with *Conspiracy* (1980 and 1989) and by **Jim Marrs**, with *Crossfire* (1989, one of the two books upon which Stone's movie *JFK* was based). Both of these works provide a very comprehensive overview of the entire subject for the reader who has never entered this labyrinth before.

Robert Groden is a photographic expert who has done a great deal of work in analyzing the Zapruder film. He was used as a consultant by the House Select Committee during its re-investigation in 1978-79. Groden managed to obtain a good copy of the Zapruder film and some of the autopsy photos and X-rays during his work for the HSCA. He enhanced the Zapruder movie from its original 8mm form into a 35mm version, which he then used in lectures to students on college campuses all over the country. Largely thanks to him, hundreds of "bootleg" copies of this film were made available to interested students of the case, including this writer. Groden teamed up with author **Harrison Livingstone** to produce the book *High Treason*, in which they published some of the autopsy films. Their book lays the blame for Kennedy's death squarely on the shoulders of high-ranking elements within our own government. Groden uses his photographic expertise to point out subtle indications of "touching up" on some of the autopsy pictures. Livingstone subsequently produced *High Treason 2*, in which he publishes more of the autopsy photos and X-rays and presents convincing evidence that at least some of these have been faked to conceal damage to the back of the head, hiding proof of a shot coming from the front.

Gary Mack, a relative late-comer to the case, became interested when he discovered, back in the mid-seventies, that the shots fired in Dealey Plaza on 11/22/63 may have been accidentally recorded by a police microphone. It was his pursuit of this possibility that led researcher Mary Ferrell to make her now-famous contribution to the HSCA's investigation that so dramatically altered its results.

Mary Ferrell was a tireless researcher from Dallas who, while not one of the literary luminaries, made one of the most significant contributions to the advancement of truth. Among her large treasure trove of JFK assassination artifacts was a copy of the Dallas Police dictabelt that Gary Mack convinced her might contain the sounds of gunfire in Dealey Plaza. When she turned this copy over to the House Select Committee in 1978, it prompted them to have it analyzed.[25] Thanks to her action, at least one arm of the US government was finally forced to admit the existence of a conspiracy.

Professor **Jerry D. Rose** of the *State University of New York* in Fredonia is the editor and publisher of a bi-monthly journal named *The Fourth Decade* (formerly, *The Third Decade*). This journal published a wide variety of articles and letters from people interested in the JFK case from both sides of the fence (although Rose is definitely on the side of the WR critics). It was an excellent vehicle for those with a serious interest in the case to keep up to date and to exchange points of view. In July of 1995 his publication printed an excerpt from this manuscript titled *Some Thoughts on the Cover-up*.

Not all of the heroes in this case are authors or researchers. There were many witnesses who have shown remarkable courage in speaking out by describing what they saw, even though it contradicted the official story line. Perhaps the most important of these are the medical people; doctors and nurses at Parkland Hospital in Dallas, who tried in vain to save Kennedy's life when he was so abruptly brought there within five minutes of the shooting. They were all put in the very difficult position of suddenly being handed the bullet-torn body of the President of the United States and given the impossible task of trying to save his life. Later, they were placed in an even *more* difficult position when the autopsy report contained findings that were in direct conflict with what they observed when they examined the President's wounds. None of the doctors saw the wound in the upper back because they never turned him over, and interestingly, none of them observed the small "entrance wound" in the back of his head either. But several saw the neat, tiny "puncture" wound in the front of the throat, and all who did see it assumed it was an entrance wound of a small caliber bullet.[26]

Every medical person who entered the trauma room while Kennedy was there described a large, "blasted out" wound in the back of his head. Unfortunately, up to now, only two of the doctors who were there have been willing to defy the official line and risk harming their careers. The first to speak his mind, right from the beginning, was

Dr. **Robert McClelland**, who has never backed away from his description and location of the large head wound. From his detailed description to such researchers as Josiah Thompson and David Lifton, this wound was more in the back and considerably smaller than the top-of-head exit wound described in the autopsy report.[27]

After twenty-eight years of silence on the subject, Dr. McClelland was joined by Dr. **Charles Crenshaw**, whose small paperback book, *Conspiracy of Silence*, explains why he kept quiet all these years and why others are still refusing to speak out. He confirms what McClelland has consistently said about the nature of the head wound.

Unfortunately, Crenshaw did not help his credibility when he went beyond stating his long held belief that Kennedy was shot from the front. He claimed that he received a call from President Johnson while he and other doctors were working to save Oswald's life on Sunday, November 24th. According to Crenshaw, Johnson wanted him to try to extract a death-bed confession from Oswald. This story was strongly doubted by the "establishment", not because Johnson was above making such a phone call, but because it is unlikely he would speak with Dr. Crenshaw, who was not the senior doctor working on Oswald at the time. But Crenshaw says that LBJ did not ask for anyone by name, he just happened to be the one who picked up the phone. His story is corroborated by Drs. Phillip Williams and Robert McClelland, according to Harrison Livingstone.[28]

It is my fondest hope, that one day Dr. Malcolm Perry or Dr. Charles Carrico, or one of the other good and reputable people who worked over the President at Parkland, will reach a point in their career where they will be willing to step forth and tell it like it really was, providing the corroboration that McClelland and Crenshaw now lack.

There have also been medical "heroes" who emerged from the autopsy room in Bethesda, Maryland. **Floyd Riebe**, the medical photographer; **Jerrol Custer**, an X-ray technician; **Paul O'Connor**, a lab assistant; **James Jenkins**, Dr. Boswell's assistant; all have stated to several of the researchers that they observed a large wound, devoid of scalp, in the *back* of Kennedy's head. When shown the "official" photos and X-rays that display the back of the head intact (except for the roaming small entrance hole), they all labeled this evidence as forgeries! In fact, Riebe, Custer and O'Connor attended a press conference in late May, 1992, in which they disputed the claims of the three autopsy doctors and their very partial and unscientific JAMA presentation, and tried to tell the world that the films were fakes. Unfortunately, the media refused to take them seriously.[29]

There is one other medical personage who was not in any way involved in the aftermath of the assassination but who nevertheless has been a standout in the quest for truth. I refer to Dr. **Cyril Wecht**, one of this nation's most renowned forensic pathologists. He has consistently stood up against the majority of those in his field who persisted in toeing the official government line. He has made numerous TV appearances to point out the obvious flaws in the "single-bullet theory."

One of the more recent contributors to truth is a prominent member of the *Assassinations Records Review Board*, **Douglas Horne** (mentioned in Chapter 3). Besides helping to release many of the long-suppressed files on the JFK case he has pointed out several serious problems with the medical testimony and evidence.

Several of the witnesses in Dealey Plaza that fateful day who were standing closest to the limousine when Kennedy was hit by the fatal shot/s have been brave enough to tell exactly what they saw and heard, and *not one* supports the conclusions of the Warren Commission.

Standing at the curb on the north side of Elm Street, just in front of the grassy knoll, were **Bill Newman** and his wife and young son. They all "hit the deck" when the fatal shot seemed to have struck the President "just above the right ear." Newman has gone on record with several interviewers, describing a shot "whistling over his shoulder" from directly behind him, indicating the area behind the picket fence at the top of the knoll.[30]

On the other side of Elm, directly across from the Newmans, were **Beverly Oliver** (the "babushka lady"), **Jean Hill** and **Mary Moorman**. They can be plainly seen in the Zapruder film just before the fatal shot/s hit. Oliver worked at that time in a club near

Jack Ruby's Carousel Club and knew Ruby well. She refused to be identified or interviewed for several years, but now says, not only that the head shot came from behind the fence on the knoll, but that Ruby and Oswald knew each other (she had seen them at the same table at Ruby's club.[31])

Moorman is the woman whose Polaroid camera recorded one of the most important pictures taken that day. It may show, in the background, the grassy knoll assassin firing the fatal shot (see Figure 29 on page 241). She says she saw the flash of the muzzle, then saw and smelled gunpowder.

Jean Hill, the girl in the red raincoat, has been a guest on several shows covering the conspiracy to kill JFK. She has never wavered from her description of the fatal shot coming from the right front of the limo, in spite of numerous death threats. She is the subject of the book, *JFK: The Last Dissenting Witness*, by Bill Sloan. Although Hill and Newman were questioned and provided depositions to the Warren Commission's *staff*, none of these witnesses were ever called before the Commission itself to give their testimony.[32]

A little further back up Elm St., pointing his camera in the direction of Abraham Zapruder as he took snapshots of the motorcade, were - **Philip Willis** and his family. They described hearing shots from the direction of the TSBD but insist, like the people mentioned above, that the head shot came from the right front.[33]

Arnold Rowland and his wife were standing across Houston St. where they had an excellent view of the front of the TSBD. Rowland tried to tell the FBI about seeing *two* men armed with rifles (whom he assumed to be Secret Service) in the windows at the opposite ends of the sixth floor when he looked up a couple of minutes before the motorcade arrived. His story was totally disregarded.[34]

Last but by no means least on my list of heroes is the dauntless **Oliver Stone**, who's *JFK* may one day be proven to be one of the most influential films ever made. Not many directors would have had the intestinal fortitude to buck the system and proceed with the production of this very controversial motion picture, once the full weight of the establishment was brought to bear to destroy his reputation as a film director and as a man. The resurgence of interest in the assassination, created by Stone's movie, resulted in the release of *many* of the suppressed files. If the rest of the withheld files are ever released, and if that release ultimately leads to the revelation of what really took place in Dealey Plaza (even if not who actually pulled the triggers), then Stone's epic will certainly deserve the lion's share of the credit for breaking one of the biggest, if not t*he* biggest story in US history!

There are many other researchers who have contributed to the pursuit of truth in this case and who deserve to be recognized. Most of them have worked more behind the scenes than those whose names I mention here, so their contributions are largely unsung. I omit their names only because it would be impossible to ensure including them all. You know who you are and I salute you.

The reader may have noticed by now that one name is conspicuously absent from either of my lists–the name of **Jim Garrison**. This is because there are reasons for including him on *both* lists, and it is debatable which label he deserves the most. In one sense, Garrison was a "hero" for using the Shaw trial as a vehicle for bringing many things about the case to the light of day. His showing of the Zapruder film was a breakthrough, and his questioning of key witnesses, such as autopsy doctor Pierre Finck, provided new exposure to some of the long-suppressed facts of the case.

On the other hand, his repeated, self-serving boasts, during the trial preparation stage, that he would "solve the assassination" for the American People, followed by his pitifully weak case against the man he was prosecuting, made him a laughing stock. The most tragic thing about it was that *his* failure rubbed off onto *all* the critics of the Warren Report. Because of Garrison's utter failure in the Shaw case, talk of a conspiracy in Kennedy's murder, for years, became the stuff of tabloids, held in the same esteem as stories of UFO abductions. Today, opinion is still divided among the "critical community" as to whether Garrison (who died in 1992 at the age of seventy) was a "hero" or a "villain." His penchant for downplaying, if not denying, the obvious role of organized crime in the assassination, while focusing exclusively on the CIA and the Cuban exiles caused many researchers to suspect Garrison's motives. But I am not one of those who think that he was a government "plant," put up to the fiasco of the Shaw trial for the express purpose of discrediting all "conspiracy buffs." He was steadfast over the years in his support of the critics of the government's version of the assassination, and continued until he died to promote the theory that JFK was killed by a plot whose roots were in the US Government. To this author, anyone who was that close to the truth can't be all bad.

Chapter 12
KEEPING THE LID ON
Dead Men Tell No Tales

A question frequently heard from sincere and thoughtful people during the years since Jack Kennedy was killed is: "How could a conspiracy of the magnitude and scope that I am hypothesizing be kept quiet all these years? Surely someone who was involved in such a conspiracy would have spilled the beans by now."

My answer to that is simple. A few *have* spoken out and many others have tried or threatened to and were soon dead. There has been a clear pattern of murder and intimidation of those who might have shed light on the questions surrounding the events in Dallas on 11/22/63. The victims have come from a wide range of backgrounds; from strippers to police officers to mafia dons to high ranking CIA and FBI officials, and possibly even a Warren Commission member and a presidential candidate. Only a plot sponsored from the highest level could have hoped to carry off and perpetuate this type of cover-up. But in spite of its initial success, it has been unraveling for many years. The proof of this fact is the proliferation of books on the subject, many with something new to offer in the way of evidence or insight.

Several of the books critical of the official findings have provided lengthy lists of the many people who were somehow involved in the events surrounding JFK's death, or the investigation of it, and who have since prematurely died. Most of these lists have included people who died of natural causes, along with those whose deaths were suspicious. I have provided a condensed composite of these lists below, in which the obviously innocent or marginally relevant deaths have been omitted. I have, however, included a few whose deaths were *ruled* "natural" or "accidental" that many researchers on this subject find highly suspect. The names are listed in chronological order of their deaths.

*—Lee Harvey Oswald 11/24/63 Shot to death

Accused of killing President Kennedy and Dallas Policeman J. D. Tippit

*—Gary Underhill 5/64 Gunshot (suicide?)

CIA operative who said the Agency was involved in the assassination.[1]

*—Hugh Ward 5/64 Plane crash

Worked with Guy Banister and David Ferrie in New Orleans.[2]

*—Guy Banister 6/64 Heart attack?

New Orleans private detective, former FBI and CIA agent, anti-Castro activist. Oswald worked out of his office while performing as a pro-Castro spokesman.[3]

*—Mary Meyer 10/64 Murdered

A mistress of JFK whose diary was confiscated by the CIA after her death.[4]

*—Maurice Gatlin 5/65 Fatal fall

Pilot who worked for Guy Banister.[5]

*—Rose Cherami 9/65 Hit and run

Former dancer in Ruby's club who was thrown from a car a few days before the assassination and told doctors who treated her that JFK was going to be killed in Dallas.[6]

*—Dorothy Kilgallen 11/65 Drug overdose

Famous syndicated columnist. Was last person to interview Ruby before he died. Claimed to be ready after the interview to "blow the lid off the JFK assassination." A couple of days later she was dead.[7]

*—Lee Bowers 8/66 Car crash

Was in the railroad watchtower behind the grassy knoll on 11/22/63. Saw men behind the fence moments before the shooting. Saw "flash of light or puff of smoke" when shots were fired.[8]

*—William Pitzer 10/66 Gunshot (suicide?)

Took movies of the entire autopsy of JFK. His own autopsy report was never released to his family, who are convinced he was murdered to keep him quiet (no powder burns or muzzle marks on body) His movies have disappeared.[9]

*—James Worrell Jr. 11/66 Auto accident

Saw a man fleeing from the rear of the TSBD building a few minutes after the shooting.[10]

*—Jack Ruby 1/67 Fast acting cancer (injected?)[11]

Mob-connected nightclub owner who shot Oswald in the basement of the Dallas police station.

*—Harold Russell 2/67 Killed by policeman.

Saw Tippit's killer flee the scene.[12]

*—David Ferrie 2/67 Apparent suicide

Anti-Castro activist who worked with Guy Banister in New Orleans. Was Oswald's instructor during his Civil Air Patrol days.[13] Jim Garrison considered him the key to unraveling the conspiracy to kill JFK. Died just before he would have been arrested in connection with the crime.[14]

*—Eladio del Valle 2/67 Murdered (gun/axe)

Associate of David Ferrie being sought by Garrison.[15]

*—Robert Kennedy 6/68 Shot to death

President's brother and candidate for president himself in 1968. Had threatened to reopen the investigation of JFK's death if he became president.[16] Was assassinated on the night he all but clinched the Democratic nomination. His death also leaves many traces of conspiracy.[17]

*—Philip Geraci 8/68 Electrocuted

He told of a connection between Clay Shaw and Oswald.[18]

*—E.R. ("Buddy") Walthers 1/69 Shot to death

Dep. Sheriff who found a bullet in the grass near Elm St.[19]

*—Rev. Clyde Johnson 7/69 Shot to death

Was supposed to testify about a Shaw/Oswald connection in the Shaw trial, but was beaten up the day before he was scheduled.[20]

*—Salvatore Granello 12/70 Murdered

Mobster involved in Castro assassination plots.[21]

*—George McGann 10/70 Murdered

Mobster connected to Ruby. His wife, Beverly Oliver ("the babushka lady"), took movies of the assassination.[22] He was killed in the home of Ronny Weeden, an associate of Charles Harrelson, a convicted killer who may have been the knoll gunman.[23]

*—James Plumeri 09/71 Murdered

Mobster involved in Castro assassination plots.[24]

*—Hale Boggs 7/72 Lost while flying over Alaska.

US Rep. from Louisiana. One of the members of the Warren Commission who had expressed doubts about its findings.[25]

*—Dorothy Hunt 12/72 Killed in plane crash in Chicago. (Sabotage was suspected.)[26]

Wife of E. Howard Hunt. She was used as hush-money courier during the Watergate break-in aftermath.[27]

*—Richard Cain 12/73 Murdered

Multi-lingual lieutenant of Sam Giancana who had been a Chicago cop and had worked with anti-Castro Cubans.[28]

*—Joseph Milteer 2/74 Died unexpectedly after improving from injuries suffered from a stove explosion. Right-wing militant who on 11/9/63 described to an FBI informant how JFK was going to be hit from an office building in a southern city.[29]

*—Clay Shaw 8/74 Cause undetermined[30]

The man Garrison could not prove was tied to the CIA, Ferrie and Oswald, but whom former CIA agent Marchetti later confirmed to be CIA.[31]

*—David Yaras 01/74 Murdered

Mobster associate of both Jimmy Hoffa and Jack Ruby.[32]

*—John Martino Summer/75 Heart attack?

A mobster with close ties to Santos Trafficante. Participated as a CIA contract agent in a failed attempt to prove there were still missiles in Cuba in the summer of 1963. Later claimed anti-Castro Cubans killed JFK.[33]

*—Sam Giancana 6/75 Murdered[34]

Major Mob figure who had worked with the CIA on "operation Mongoose", the Mob/CIA plan to kill Castro. The other man (besides JFK) in Judy Campbell Exner's life.[35]

*—James Riddle Hoffa 7/75 Missing and presumed dead

Teamsters union leader and Mob boss aligned with Sam Giancana, Santos Trafficante and Carlos Marcello. Bitter enemy of Bobby Kennedy.[36]

*—Rolando Masferrer 10/75 Blown up in his car

Former Batista henchman. Knew Jack Ruby, Loren Hall, Carlos Bringuier and other anti-Castro Cubans. His brother may have been the "Angelo" who visited Silvia Odio.[36]

*—John Roselli 7/76 Murdered[38]

Major Mob figure who worked alongside Giancana in the CIA/MOB projects. Told Jack Anderson, shortly before he was killed, that the "Mongoose team" killed JFK.[39]

*—William Pawley 1/77 Shot (suicide?)

Former Brazilian ambassador. Connected to anti-Castro activists.[40]

*—George DeMohrenschildt 3/77 Shot (suicide?)

Long-time CIA man and world traveler who befriended the Oswalds after their return from Russia. He and his wife Jeanne knew Oswald as well as anyone at the time of the assassination. Died just as he was located to testify before the HSCA. Left behind an unfinished manuscript in which he described Lee Oswald as an unwitting patsy in the plot to kill JFK.[41]

*—Charles Nicoletti 3/77 Murdered

One of Sam Giancana's top lieutenants and, according to Sam's younger brother Chuck, one of the Dealey Plaza gunmen. Was killed the same day that DeMohrenschildt died.[42]

*—Lou Staples 5/77 Shot (suicide?)

Dallas talk show host who said he was about to break the JFK case.[43]

*—William C. Sullivan 11/77 Shot ("hunting accident")[44]

Number three man under Hoover as head of FBI's Domestic Intelligence Division at time of JFK's death. He knew of the FBI's cover-up of the assassination evidence and of Oswald's intelligence ties.[45]

*—David S. Morales 5/78 Heart attack? (age 52)

The ultimate Cold-warrior, would-be Castro assassinator, Kennedy hater and JM/WAVE Operations Chief.[46] His closest friends did not believe his death was due to natural causes.[47]

There are several others whose names would be on this list but for some extraordinarily good luck. There were attempts on their lives but they survived. Roger Craig, the Deputy Sheriff reported that he saw a man he thought was Oswald leave the TSBD a few minutes after the shooting.[48] Craig survived several attacks, but some years later committed suicide. Richard Carr, also saw a man leave the TSBD building and enter the same Nash Rambler that Craig said the Oswald double got into, who was dressed like the man Caroline Walther saw in the sixth floor window. Three attempts were made on his life (car bomb, gunman, and stabbing) but he survived them all.[49] Warren Reynolds, saw the slayer of Tippit leave the scene and would not identify the killer as Oswald until after he (Reynolds) was shot in the head and survived.[50] Antonio Veciana, the co-founder of Alpha 66 and the man who connected CIA officer "Maurice Bishop" to Lee Oswald prior to the assassination. He was struck in the head by a ricocheting bullet during an attempt on his life in July of 1979.[51]

An oft-quoted actuarial computed by the *London Sunday Times*, put the odds against a *much shorter* list of eighteen material witnesses involved in the assassination dying as they did in the first three years after the events of 11/22/63 at one hundred thousand trillion to one. *The Times* later admitted to have computed incorrectly and that the correct odds were much lower.[52] But you could lop off several zeros from the above number and the odds would still be astronomical. Be that as it may, could anyone peruse such a list as that offered above and not conclude that the JFK assassination was an unhealthy subject to know too much about?

The *most* suspicious deaths are: Lee Oswald and Jack Ruby, for the obvious reason of silencing them; Sam Giancana, John Roselli and George DeMohrenschildt, who died just as they were about to testify before the House Select Committee on Assassinations; Dorothy Kilgallen, who threatened to break open the case; William Pitzer, who knew too much about the nature of JFK's wounds, and Robert Kennedy, who had told confidants that if he became president he would reopen the case of his brother's death.

The supporters of the official lone-nut history try to explain all these deaths as being nothing but coincidence. We see many coincidences every day of our lives. But when you see a recurring pattern like the one that is obvious within the list shown above, one has to ask, when does a series of coincidences start to defy the laws of probability?

In addition to the above names, there are several people whose deaths, although not obviously suspicious, nevertheless make it more difficult to get to the full truth of the assassination of President Kennedy. In this category are such important names as Lyndon Johnson, J. Edgar Hoover, Earl Warren, Allen Dulles, Gerald Ford, David Atlee Phillips, Richard Helms, Richard Bissell, E. Howard Hunt, Earle Cabell and General Charles Cabell. There are, however, still a few people left alive (at the time of this writing) who could provide a lot of relevant information if they chose to speak out (or could be compelled to).

Why would anyone who loves his country accuse its government and its agencies of the terrible things that I accuse them of in this book? The answer is quite simple: we once had a tremendous pride in being citizens of the greatest country on earth and, although that pride has not been destroyed, it has been badly tarnished by what has been happening in America since 11/22/63. The image of our country has greatly suffered, in the eyes of its own people as well as the rest of the world; because of Iraq, because of Iran-Contra, because of Watergate, because of Vietnam, but perhaps most of all, because of the assassination of John F. Kennedy and our utter failure to bring his killers to justice. As far as this particular citizen is concerned, the only way we can ever hope to remove, or at least reduce, the tarnish from that image is to face the truth, reveal the facts (as much as possible at this late date), follow relentlessly whatever leads still exist, and prosecute those who can be identified and are still alive. This includes those who have been guilty of the crime of *obstruction of justice* through their role in the cover-up, as well as those who played a part in the conspiracy to assassinate the President.

Although the murder of John F. Kennedy has been referred to many times as "the crime of the century," there is an even greater crime than the murder of President Kennedy that needs to be addressed, no matter how belatedly. The *real* crime of the century is no longer the murder of our 35th president–it is the immense lie and cover-up that has continued now for several decades, and which has allowed the guilty parties, without fear of prosecution, to change the course of history.

EPILOG
Case Closed?

Human beings have one unfortunate psychological trait that inhibits our ability to get to the truth behind a controversial question. We have a built-in tendency, once we have formed an opinion, to stick with it and defend it regardless of all evidence against it. This has never been more apparent than in the case of the assassination of President Kennedy. Those, including this author, who have been convinced that the Warren Commission and other government agencies got it wrong and that we still have not learned the real story of the murder in Dealey Plaza, are just as susceptible to this trait as those who cling to the belief that the official history is correct. It seems that the JFK assassination has joined politics and religion as topics to be approached with great care among friends.

The best way to combat this mental trap, I believe, is to try to reach conclusions only through an open-minded evaluation of the evidence. When the evidence is fraught with apparent contradictions, one must weigh all the evidence on one side versus all the evidence on the other side, including motives and abilities, before forming an opinion. In chapters 1 and 8 of this work I have presented the evidence indicating that Lee Harvey Oswald was the assassin of JFK (or at least one of them) and the killer of Police Officer J. D. Tippit (or at least one of them). I have also shown the weaknesses and flaws in that evidence while showing a multitude of evidence of other shooters, and that Oswald was probably *not* one of them. I have also presented a plethora of evidence of a determined and on-going attempt to suppress any indication of conspiracy. Yet, there is a sizable minority in this country that persists in clinging to the government's "lone-nut" conclusion in spite of so much evidence to the contrary. Some of the arguments that the Warren Commission supporters continue to cling to include: "…someone would have talked by now…" – *they have, many times (see previous chapter);* "…those honorable men would not have taken part in any such cover-up…" *–depends on their motivation*; "…the news media would love to expose a conspiracy if there was really any proof of one…"—*not if their professional reputation depended on sticking to a long-held* *commitment;* "...the problems pointed out by the critics have all been explained scientifically..."—*but these "scientific" explanations do not stand up under closer scrutiny. In many cases the arguments presented by the supporters of the Warren Commission are made through faith without regard to the preponderance of evidence.*

Since the controversy surrounding the assassination of President Kennedy began in 1964, many attempts have been made, both by supporters and by critics of the official "Oswald did it alone" conclusion, to explain one or more of the many frustrating mysteries that have defied a fully, mutually acceptable explanation. Anyone who researches this case, even to a minor degree, will find all kinds of banter, blurbs and outright BS coming from both sides of the controversy, especially on the internet. The author grants that some of the claims and theories put forth by the Commission's detractors have been easily disproved and some have been downright bizarre. The Warren Report supporters seem to believe that this just shows that *all* criticisms of the official findings are unworthy of consideration; again, faith instead of logic.

A friend of mine, who is still a believer in the official story of the assassination, recently asked me what it would take to convince me that the Warren Commission was basically correct in their conclusion that Oswald did it and did it alone. His question had me stumped for a moment. I finally told him that his question was like asking me what it would take to convince me that the creationists have it right; that evolution is a hoax, the story in Genesis is literally true and the Earth is really only about six thousand years old.

Those who have been committed for years to one side or the other of the controversy surrounding the death of President Kennedy will probably never be convinced that they have it wrong, no matter how many more documents are released or how many facts are uncovered or how many theories expounded. Critics and defenders of the official "lone-gunman" story will continue to try to debunk the arguments of the other side. But the Warren Report defenders have a rather daunting disadvantage in this fight. Each side may continue to disprove arguments or shaky "facts" presented by the other, but it only takes one piece of solid evidence of a second gunman that cannot be convincingly disputed for the critics to win the day and for that 75-80 percent of the public, who believe that the truth is yet to be learned, to know that their convictions are justified. Once you are convinced that the evidence proves that there had to be more than one shooter and, therefore, a conspiracy, then the concerted and perpetual efforts on the part of every agency, commission or committee involved in the "investigation" to persuade us otherwise, coupled with the systematic destruction, distortion and suppression of files and evidence, can be construed as nothing other than a blatant and obvious cover-up of mammoth proportions.

Posner's Sham

In August, 1993, as scores of eager researchers swamped the National Archives with requests to examine the thousands of newly released pages of documents pertaining to the assassination of President Kennedy, a new book on the subject was announced with a great deal of fanfare. A young lawyer-turned-author named Gerald Posner had produced the first serious defense of the official findings to appear in several years. *Case Closed* purported to prove that the Warren Commission, in spite of a few minor errors of detail, was correct in its basic conclusions that Lee Harvey Oswald was the assassin of President Kennedy and that he acted alone. Not surprisingly, Posner's book was greeted with undisguised glee by the major media, who hailed this "brilliant and exhaustive restudy of the case" as the final and definitive word on the subject. Foremost of these, *US News & World Report* published lengthy excerpts in its September 6 issue and praised Posner's work to the heavens. Then ABC's *20/20* featured an interview with the author, which provided him with a virtually unchallenged opportunity to plug his views (and his book) to a nation-wide audience.

Posner's book addressed in some depth many of the points made by the critics over the years, and in particular, the testimony or comments made by several witnesses that conflict with the official findings. He is the first of the government supporters to at least make a show of facing these points head-on rather than ignoring or denigrating them. However, in doing so he brands as liars, usually on flimsy or irrelevant evidence, many people whose backgrounds provide no real support for that assessment. In the process, he repeatedly distorts testimony in his efforts to make his point. He also claims as his own, "discoveries" that are actually only theories previously brought out by others. Worst of all, he pretends and implies that the computer enhancement and analysis that plays a major role in his "proof that Oswald did it" was done by the firm named *Failure Analysis* exclusively for him. The truth is that *Failure Analysis* did this work for the *American Bar Association* in connection with a mock trial of Oswald that they held in 1992. As mentioned in chapter 8, that trial resulted in a hung jury, with seven voting Oswald guilty and five voting him innocent (it would only have taken *one* "innocent" vote to hang a real jury). The work done by *Failure Analysis* produced arguments for both the prosecution *and* the defense. But Posner chose to give us only the parts done for the prosecution and never even mentioned that there was another side presented.

It would take yet another book to adequately refute all the inaccuracies, distortions, misstatements, omissions and outright slander contained in Posner's book. In fact, after publication of *Case Closed*, another book was published that did exactly that. Harold Weisberg's *Case Open* (Carroll & Graf, 1994) is a hastily put together condensation of a much larger collection of evidence by Weisberg in which he refutes almost everything Posner claims. But it does not require another book to destroy a few of the key points upon which Posner bases his "proof" of no conspiracy. Let's look at a few of his less-than-honest attempts to "close" the case.

Single-bullet theory

It is amazing that after all the juggling that has been done with the timing of the shots fired in Dealey Plaza that day, there has been no defender of the "lone-gunman" verdict who has devised a scenario that allows for Kennedy and Connally to have been struck by separate bullets. Posner continues the efforts to support the insupportable; that one bullet (from Oswald's rifle) passed through both Kennedy and Connally, causing seven wounds in all before falling out of the Governor's thigh and turning up on a stretcher to become Warren Commission Exhibit 399. The basis of Posner's new wrinkle to this old argument is FA's analysis of the Zapruder movie film that he claims indicates that the first shot was fired earlier than the Commission assumed and missed everything because it was deflected by a branch of the oak tree (a hypothesis that was first put forth by the CBS four-part series back in 1967). All the eyewitness testimony and photographic evidence that the first shot did *not* miss but struck the President in the back is, of course, ignored.[1]

Then, Posner's theory contends, the second shot struck both men at Z224, as indicated by the fact that Connally's "lapel flies up" at that point. But this so-called proof of a bullet strike is pretty hard to accept when one sees where the actual exit hole in Connally's jacket was located (see Figure 30 below).

Photo provided by Robert Groden

Figure 30

By moving the point of this bullet's impact forward, somewhat later than the Warren Commission assumed and *much* later than the HSCA concluded, Posner manages to reduce Connally's "delayed reaction" time and make the theory sound a bit more plausible, at least in that one respect.[2] But, as we have seen, several factors covered in detail in chapter 10 of this book disprove the single-bullet theory, one of which is the size of the wound in the President's throat. In spite of the fact that most of the Parkland doctors have not yet found the courage to publicly dispute the official autopsy findings, their description of this wound on 11/22/63 and at several times thereafter shows it to be clean, round, and only 3-5mm wide, not the 5-8mm claimed by Posner on page 306 of his book. As previously pointed out, it was smaller, not larger, than the 4 X 7mm hole in the back.[3] All tests done so far attempting to prove that a Mannlicher-Carcano bullet could produce an exit hole that resembled that in JFK's throat have only proved the opposite; that exit holes are invariably larger, not smaller than their corresponding entrances. This is not to say that the throat wound could not be the exit of something smaller, such as a fragment of either lead or skull, but certainly not that of a whole 6.5 Caliber bullet.

The small size of the throat wound was "explained" in an article by Warren Commission supporter John McAdams, part of his on-going internet forum titled *The Kennedy Assassination (1995 to the Present)*. His argument is that the size of this "exit wound" was limited by being constricted by the dress shirt JFK was wearing. He goes into a lengthy thesis on experiments done on through-and-through bullets that were inhibited in some way as they exited, which prevents the usual explosive effect on the flesh, and therefore can reduce the size of the wound and give it the appearance of an entrance wound.[4] Thus, McAdams hopes to throw some doubt on the critics' claim that JFK's throat wound was too small to be a bullet exit.

The problem is that the constriction argument doesn't apply in this case if one accepts the testimony of the Dallas doctors and nurses who saw the wound before the clothing was cut off. They described that wound as being *between the Adams Apple and the top of the collar*.[5]

Another of McAdams' refutations concerns the location of the wound in JFK's back. He talks extensively about the placement of the dot on the autopsy face sheet that was meant to indicate the location of this wound. When the furor against the single-bullet-theory reached a point where it could no longer be ignored, the autopsy doctors explained that this dot was not meant to be precise and was done in haste. The actual wound, they claimed, "was higher than depicted." McAdams wonders in his blurb why the critics continue to insist on a low back wound on the strength of an imprecise drawing. What McAdams doesn't mention is that the autopsy photo clearly shows the wound in the back to be exactly where it is depicted on the face sheet, and the pictures of the bullet holes in the shirt and jacket show they coincide exactly with both (all of these are depicted in chapter 9). Many supporters of the Warren Commission's findings have tried to explain the low entrance hole in the president's jacket by claiming it was bunched up" at the moment of impact. This not only ignores the location of the wound in JFK's back as seen in the autopsy photo, it is disproved by several photos taken in Dealey Plaza that show no such bunching just prior to the shots. It also ignores the location of the hole in the president's shirt, which corresponds exactly with the jacket hole. Do they really think that a tucked-in dress shirt could have been "bunched up" also?

Getting back to Posner, one of his grossest distortions of evidence was in his declaration that the entry wound in Connally's back was "1.25 inches long–the exact length of the bullet–indicating the bullet was tumbling end over end" (as a result of having first transited the President's body). Dr. Robert Shaw, who treated Connally's wounds in Parkland Hospital, did first report this wound to be "about 3 centimeters (1.17 inches) at its widest point," but he later corrected himself in his testimony before the Warren Commission when he set its size at only 1.5 centimeters (slightly over 1/2 inch) at its widest dimension.[6] This contradiction can be resolved by merely comparing the two conflicting measurements against the size of the hole in the Governor's clothing (1/4 X 5/8 inch).[7] This proves that the doctor's *revised* measurement was the accurate one and that Posner's statement is both wrong and misleading. The slightly elliptical shape of the entrance hole is created by the rather sharp downward angle of the bullet as it struck. What no one seems to ask is; why would a bullet, as it exits JFK's throat, leave a round hole 1/5 inch in diameter, then four feet further on in its flight create a hole 5/8 of an inch long? That's an awfully quick yaw! Ironically, Posner's claim that the entrance hole in Connally's back was *1.25 inches* in length makes this discrepancy even more ridiculous.

Then we have the magic bullet itself. Posner offers us an explanation for its amazingly intact condition that is neither new nor acceptable. Posner instructs us that by the time this bullet had passed through the torsos of both men, only glancing against a rib in the process, it had lost most of its speed. Therefore, when it smashed Governor Connally's wrist bone, it was traveling slowly enough as it entered the wrist backwards to avoid damaging itself (except for a slight squeeze at the base). Posner claims that he has seen a test performed on a velocity-reduced bullet that emerged, after being fired into the wrist of a cadaver, in better condition than CE 399. There have been several tests conducted over the years using this type of ammunition against blocks of material set up to simulate the two torsos, wrist and thigh (minus bones). It is interesting that in *none* of these simulations has a test bullet been proudly displayed as having emerged as cleanly as 399. I challenge Mr. Posner (or anyone else) to produce one *verifiable* bullet fired in an *accurately simulated* test that comes close to the condition of CE 399.

During the House Select Committee on Assassinations hearings in 1978, Larry Sturdivan presented the committee with a lengthy and detailed" explanation" for how it was possible for CE 399 to have done all the damage to both Kennedy and Connally and still emerged in such good condition. He presented a theory he called *Diminished Velocity*.[8] This is the same theory repeated by Gerald Posner in *Case Closed*. To most laymen, this theory doesn't pass the logic test on its face, but if you need further proof of its invalidity I refer the reader to a very detailed, step-by-step analysis showing where and how this theory used incorrect velocities, slanted in the theory's favor at every phase of the bullet's flight. This scholarly refutation, written by John Hunt, can be found by Googling *Breakability:CE-399*.

The Acoustic Evidence

I wish that Dr. James Barger, formerly of *Bolt, Beranek and Newman*, or Professor Mark Weiss and Dr. Ernest Aschkenasy, who confirmed Barger's findings, could somehow demand that further tests be conducted on the tape they examined in 1978. Their expert and detailed analysis of the Dallas Police tape led the House Select Committee on Assassinations to conclude in 1978 that there had been a shot fired from the grassy knoll and, therefore, a conspiracy. BBN was chosen for this task because they were at the top of their field of acoustics interpretation. Their work was independently refined and confirmed by Professor Weiss and Dr. Aschkenasy, who verified the existence of the shot from the grassy knoll to at least a ninety-five percent degree of certainty.[9]

But Mr. Posner, with help from a Dallas Sheriff who played the tape on *20/20* and could not hear any shots on it, has declared this evidence "false". Again, he is not the first to do so. Several years ago the National Academy of Sciences, as mentioned earlier in this book, pointed out the presence of conflicting sounds on the tape that seemed to indicate that it could not have been recorded at the time the shots were fired in Dealey Plaza. But no one has yet offered an explanation as to what else could have caused these impulses, which so closely match those of shots test fired in the plaza. Only further test shots, measured against the sounds on the original tape, testing that could have and should have been done by the NAS, can resolve the questions surrounding this recording.

Oswald's Guilt

In the *US News* article reviewing Posner's book, there is an inset sub-titled *THE LUNCHROOM DEBATE*. It discusses the question of whether or not Oswald was seen in the second floor lunchroom at 12:15, fifteen minutes *before* the shooting, by Secretary Carolyn Arnold. But the more important lunchroom issue is only sketchily mentioned. Scarcely more than a minute *after* the last shot was fired, Oswald was confronted by Officer M. Baker in that lunchroom as Baker was rushing up the stairs, preceded by building super Roy Truly. According to Posner, Oswald had "dropped the rifle into an opening between several large boxes" as he rushed to get out of the building after shooting the President. What Posner avoids is the fact that the assassin had to take the time to wipe the weapon completely free of fingerprints and then stash it painstakingly between and under several cartons in a position that would require several seconds to accomplish. Later, Posner says that after the confrontation with Baker, "Oswald went to the soda machine and purchased a Coke as he decided how to depart the depository." He fails to mention that in the first, unedited version of the report filed by Officer Baker, Oswald already had the Coke in his hand when confronted by Baker.[10] These details may seem trivial unless you understand the difficulty the authorities had in re-enacting the movements of Baker and Oswald in such a way as to show that Oswald could have succeeded in descending from the 6th floor sniper's nest to the lunchroom before Baker reached that point (*and* before Truly, who was ahead of Baker on the stairs).

Elsewhere in his book, Posner distorts the testimony of B. W. Frazier, who drove Oswald to work that day, and Frazier's sister, Linnie Mae Randle, who have repeatedly stated that the "long, bulky package" Lee carried was not long enough to have carried the disassembled rifle. Posner claims (pg. 224) that Randle described this package as being carried by Oswald with "one end tucked under his arm and the other end not quite touching the ground." This is one of Posner's many gross distortions of testimony. Randle actually testified that she saw Oswald approach the car that morning carrying the package so that one end almost touched the ground but was held by the other hand near the top, not "tucked under his arm."[11] Frazier, meanwhile, described the way Oswald carried the package as he walked from the car toward the depository as being cupped in his right hand under one end with the other end tucked under his armpit.[12] This cannot be done with anything three feet long (the disassembled rifle was just under thirty-five inches and the bag found in the depository was thirty-eight inches long). Both Randle and Frazier repeatedly insisted, despite relentless grilling by the Warren Commission staff, that the package they saw with Oswald was only 24-27 inches in length. What Posner has done is combine elements of Frazier's and Randle's descriptions to make it sound as though the bag they saw Oswald carrying was much longer than they described it and, therefore, compatible with the length of the rifle and the bag found in the TSBD.

One of the most ironic statements ever made on television was made by Gerald Posner during his *20/20* interview when he stated that, "Most people who have written conspiracy books started with their conclusions already done. They knew it was a conspiracy in their heart and they went around to prove that case." This is one of the best examples of "the pot calling the kettle black" in history! If the Dallas Police, the FBI, the Warren Commission and the news medial had not predetermined the case against the man they had in custody and who was so conveniently silenced, we would not still be seeking answers to so many questions decades later.

Of all the many flaws in Mr. Posner's book, perhaps the most obvious one can be found right in the title itself. *Case Closed* is a clear-cut combination of extreme chutzpah and wishful thinking! *US News & World Report* admitted (Oct. 11, 1993 issue) that response from readers to the Posner excerpts was running 8 to 1 against! Even most "no-conspiracy" advocates will admit that this case will probably never be closed, although when admitting it, they blame the "fanatic stubbornness of the conspiracy theorists" instead of the government's failure to make a convincing case.

Mailer's Tale

In May of 1995, one of America's most prominent writers, Norman Mailer, brought forth his latest epic, *Oswald's Tale: An American Mystery*. Unlike Posner in *Case Closed*, Mailer's purpose is not to convince the reader that Oswald was the one and only assassin. Rather, he *starts* from that assumption and tries to explain WHY Oswald did it. With his cohort and interview expert, Larry Schiller, Mailer explores in great depth Oswald's early life, and his activities in the USSR and in the U.S. after his return from the Soviet Union. He quotes copiously from the Warren Report, from Priscilla McMillan Johnson's book, *Marina and Lee*, and from personal interviews with Marina Oswald and many others.

While Mailer's work is interesting and adds something to our knowledge of this very mysterious young man, it raises many of the questions that researchers have been asking for years without providing much in the way of answers. While there are far fewer factual errors here than in Posner's book, Mailer repeats some of

Posner's mistakes (although he points out others). For example, on page 515, Mailer states: "There is a famous photograph Lee took of General Edwin Walker's backyard that shows a parked car with a hole in the print large enough to obliterate the license plate. Posner points out: 'A photo of evidence taken from Oswald's flat after the assassination shows a hole was in the print at that time'." Both Posner and Mailer are wrong on this point. Not only did Marina Oswald testify to the Warren Commission that this hole was *not* in the photo at the time it was collected by the Dallas Police, her testimony was proven to be true in this instance when Chief Jesse Curry published a photo of several pieces of evidence the police had collected on page 113 (top) of his 1969 book *JFK Assassination File*. In Curry's photo can be seen, among several other items, a view of the Walker backyard photo that, although the car is partially obscured, shows no hole in the license plate area. Since this is a fact well known to serious researchers of this case, one can only conclude that both Posner and Mailer are trying to conceal the fact that this mutilation of evidence took place while the photo was in the possession of the FBI or one of the other authorities.

Mailer admittedly makes some valid points as to Oswald's often contradictory personality, but he falls far short of providing convincing evidence of Oswald's guilt. In fact, there are times when Mailer seems almost to be arguing the case that Oswald was an agent provocateur, working for some branch of the US intelligence community. On page 484 Mailer asks, "Was Oswald being groomed to become some sort of provocateur for left-wing organizations?" A page earlier Mailer asserts, "Suddenly he [Oswald] was able to pay off the rest of his debt [to the US government for the money to get home from Russia], ten times as much [as he had paid previously]– $396.00!–in the interval from December 11, 1962, to January 29, 1963–that is, in seven weeks."

Later, on page 487, Mailer adds, "There is nothing he does in January that would prove he is some kind of petty provocateur-in-training, and if not for his sudden ability to pay off the State Department, one could even be comfortable with the notion that everything he does is on his own; but still, there is that mysterious money, never accounted for, and now he goes on a spree of purchasing left-wing pamphlets and magazine subscriptions as if to establish a radical name for himself on a few lists."

Another interesting excerpt, from page 437 where Mailer is discussing the Oswald-DeMohrenschildt relationship, Mailer quotes DeMohrenschildt as saying:

Lee's English was perfect, refined, rather literary, deprived of any Southern accent. He sounded like a very educated American of indeterminate background....I taught Russian at all levels in a large university and I never saw such proficiency in the best senior students who constantly listened to Russian tapes and spoke to Russian friends.

Yet Mailer finds no incongruity between the above description and the statements of the Russian embassy personnel in Mexico City whom he quotes in a later chapter, (pages 637-638) to whit:

Pavel Yatskov, who was the first to arrive at his desk that Saturday morning, was relieved when Kostikov joined him inasmuch as the stranger [supposedly Oswald] who had just come in for an interview was speaking in English—which Yatskov barely understood. Pavel interrupted his monologue and said, since their visitor had been in the Soviet Union, lived and worked there, that he could probably explain himself in Russian and looked at him disapprovingly. Without answering, 'Oswald' switched over to *broken Russian*, in which the rest of the conversation was conducted.

Other accounts of this encounter also indicate that the man who presented himself at the embassy as Oswald "spoke very poor Russian." Does this sound like the real Lee Harvey Oswald?

Mailer seems throughout the book to address many of the concerns of the Warren Report critics, often admitting that there are legitimate and puzzling questions remaining to be answered, only to glide on past them to the inexorable conclusion that he was, after all, THE ASSASSIN. In a no-less-than-astounding chapter on Jack Ruby, Mailer actually paints a most convincing picture of Ruby as an "amateur hit-man" for the Mob, providing some interesting insights, if not satisfactory answers, to Ruby's strange behavior over that fateful weekend. According to Mailer's reasoning, even though Oswald acted alone and without encouragement, the Mob had good reasons to want him silenced and used Ruby to accomplish it. Mailer offers two hypotheses as to why the Mob would order the hit on Oswald. One is that they had issued the order to kill Kennedy, and because of the levels of insulation between those who assigned the contract and the actual gunmen, had no way of knowing that a "lone nut" had beaten them to it. The other theory goes; the Mob (specifically, Marcello and/or Trafficante) knew that Oswald was not one of theirs but wanted Hoffa to think that he was and that they had JFK killed for his (Hoffa's) sake, so they had to silence Oswald to preserve this deception (pgs. 742-744). One has to give Mailer credit for the most imaginative and dichotomous views of the JFK assassination devised to date.

Perhaps the most interesting feature of Mailer's book is found near its end where he finally explores the physical evidence. Conceding that a good lawyer could have gotten Oswald off ("if the trial were moved outside the Dallas area"), Mailer points out the difficulty in accepting the "magic bullet," the misaligned scope that had to be shimmed and adjusted before the rifle was even capable of hitting a stationary target, and the questionable marksmanship of Lee Harvey Oswald. In an attempt to downplay Oswald's inability, as reported by the Russians interviewed by Mailer and Schiller, to hit a rabbit with a shotgun at ten feet (pg. 777), Mailer points to Oswald's great variation in several areas between his best and worst performances. Mailer tries to suggest that a rifle marksman's performance may vary in the same way as a basketball player's ability to shoot the ball through the hoop. This is a false analogy! The mechanics of anatomy involved in shooting a basketball are far more complex and instinctive than is involved in firing a rifle, and subject to much more variation in performance. An experienced rifleman seldom has a really "bad day," and certainly never one as bad as those described by Oswald's Russian and Marine Corp. acquaintances. To assume that this shooter, who was mediocre at best, was able to rise to the occasion on what would have to have been the most nerve-wracking day of his life, to accomplish what experts could not duplicate, simply indicates the extent of the author's prejudice. Mailer then seeks to leave himself an escape hatch by admitting that he is even now only seventy-five percent convinced of Oswald's lone guilt (pg. 778).

Even when conceding that the acoustic evidence and other indications prevent him from discarding the possibility that there was a shot from the knoll, Mailer repeats the old argument that the existence of such a shot would not prove conspiracy, but could have been merely another, unrelated gunman. Seriously?

Perhaps the most cogent statement Mailer makes in this book is to be found on page 779 where he argues that no serious conspirators would have employed Mr. Oswald as one of their shooters, given his unreliability and instability. I could not agree more! That is precisely why, once one is convinced that the evidence demonstrates a carefully orchestrated plot, one has to have serious doubts that Oswald was part of it, other than in his (probably unwitting) role as patsy.

A third pro-Warren Commission book that must be mentioned here appeared in 2007 written by the distinguished prosecuting attorney and author, Vincent Bugliosi, who won a conviction against Charles Manson and his "family" in the Sharon Tate murder case. This was a mammoth tome titled, *Reclaiming History: The Assassination of President John F. Kennedy.* With a total page count of nearly 2800 (including Endnotes and Source Notes) it just about tripled the size of the 888 page Warren Report. After seeing the way Mr. Bugliosi handled the evidence as prosecutor in the mock trial of Oswald mentioned earlier in Chapter 8 (The Case against Oswald), I knew what to expect from this long-time WC supporter. I couldn't force myself to spend my time plowing through and rebutting another coat of whitewash of this magnitude. I knew others would do it for me and for all those who are still fighting to pry loose the truth in this case. For those who want to read such a rebuttal, I recommend Googling Dr. David W. Mantic's excellent article titled, *Reclaiming History: A Not Entirely Positive Review,* where you will find a thought-provoking comparison between the scientist's and the lawyer's way of viewing and evaluating evidence, especially forensic evidence.

In October of 2012 Bill O'Reilly, assisted by Mark Dugard, came out with a follow-up to his best-selling *Killing Lincoln,* titled *Killing Kennedy.* Most of the book was devoted to interesting vignettes of Kennedy's trials, tribulations, sexual dalliances, failures and successes while in office. But when it addressed the assassination it was chock full of opinion, impressions, etc., containing very few facts and no text-specific source references. Mr. O'Reilly's sole connection to the case seems to be an inconsequential acquaintance with George DeMohrenschildt, Oswald's mysterious friend after his return from Russia.

He tries to paint an image of Oswald as a very good shot when he wanted to take it seriously, which he apparently *didn't* when he got those "Maggie's drawers" while on the shooting range in the marines. Yet he describes Oswald taking an easy shot at the sitting General Walker and missing. I guess he didn't take that attempt seriously either.

O'Reilly also claims that Oswald rode the bus carrying his rifle to a practice location on several occasions, in direct contradiction to the evidence and testimony of those who knew him, including his wife.

Here are just a few of the many *factual* errors Mr. O'Reilly made in his account of the events surrounding the assassination.

1. He states (assumes) that Oswald saw the map of the motorcade route in the *Dallas Morning News,* so he knew the President would "pass almost directly below the window of the depository." But, as mentioned earlier in this book, that map showed it continuing straight down Main Street, not making the very unwise turns onto Elm, thereby staying a fairly safe distance from that building.

2. He has Oswald up on the sixth floor moving boxes into position to make his sniper's nest while most other employees were using their lunch break to await the motorcade. But Secretary Carolyn Arnold swears she saw Oswald eating his lunch in the second floor lunchroom at that time, which O'Reilly does not address.

3. He tells of Aaron Arnold and his wife seeing a man standing behind the sixth floor window, as do Ronald Fischer and Robert Edwards six minutes later. This was sixteen and ten minutes before the arrival of the motorcade, respectively. But this coincides with Carolyn Arnold's sighting of Oswald in the lunchroom..

4. He has Oswald *standing up* behind the window to take his shots, when it is common knowledge among those who have studied the case at all that the window was open only a few inches from the bottom, so a shooter would have to have been kneeling or to have shot *through* the glass.

5. O'Reilly goes on to describe how Oswald "dropped his rifle as he rushed to make his escape." Has he not seen the photos of where the rifle was found, wedged out of sight between stacks of book cartons.

6. He describes how the bullet that went into JFK's head exited from "the front of his skull." Figure 1 of this book shows otherwise.

Errors of this nature are a dead giveaway that Mr. O'Reilly has been very selective in his information sources. In fact, the main sources he cites at the end of his book are; The Warren Report, Manchester's *"Death of a President"* and Bugliosi's *Reclaiming History*, all of which support the official line. All of his sources, one-sided as they are, refer in general terms to an entire chapter with no superscripted reference numbers in the text tying the statement to the reference.

With virtually no intimate knowledge of the case, he preaches the official line that Oswald did it and did it because he was "crazy." It's a shame that being a celebrity gives one the opportunity to write on a subject the writer knows so little about.

Summation

Let's take one more look at a list of just a few of the improbabilities the Warren Report apologists are asking us to believe.

1. That a poor-to-mediocre rifleman with little, if any, current practice was able to perform a feat of marksmanship that experts could not duplicate, and that he did so with a defective weapon that couldn't shoot straight.

2. That Oswald could wipe the fingerprints off the rifle and hide it, and still make it from the sixth floor window to the lunchroom in less time than reconstructions would indicate.

3. That a bullet could leave lead fragments behind in the President's neck and the Governor's chest, wrist and thigh, which *all* came from the base of the bullet and which amounted to more lead than was missing from that base.

4. That the sound impulses on the police tape recording can somehow match so precisely: (a) in form, the test shots fired in Dealey Plaza; (b) in timing, the shots fired during the assassination; and still be declared to be "invalid evidence".

5. That the overwhelming majority of eye- and ear-witnesses who saw and heard things differently from the official story are simply mistaken or lying.

A complete list of "improbabilities" would stretch into the dozens.

But even more disturbing is the list of claims by the Warren Commission supporters which seem beyond "improbable" and which have yet to be provided any rational explanation. We are all waiting for those supporters to answer the following questions.

1. How is it possible for a bullet to enter a man's upper back at a downward angle and exit from the Adams Apple area, producing an exit wound that is smaller than the entrance wound?

2. How is it possible for a bullet striking the head from behind thrust that head backward?

3. How is it possible for a bullet to pass through a man's torso, crack a rib and go on to shatter a wrist bone and emerge with no more than a slightly squeezed base?

4. How is it possible for every doctor who worked over the President at Parkland Hospital in Dallas to observe a large exit wound in the back of the skull, and yet have that wound disappear at the autopsy at Bethesda?

What is *most* disturbing to this writer is the unwillingness of those such as Gerald Posner, who defend the basic findings of the government in this case, to admit that their version depends on *all* these very unlikely events having taken place. Instead of attempting to deal fairly and honestly with these problems, they cast aspersions on those who cannot accept their illogical explanations.

Warren Report critic, Harold Weisberg, in his book *Photographic Whitewash*, put it as well as anyone can as to why we should still care about seeing the truth finally brought forth on this subject:

If the government can manufacture, suppress and lie when a president is cut down and get away with it, what cannot follow? Of what is it not capable, regardless of motive?

In the years since I started putting this book together a few documentaries have aired on TV, usually on *The History Channel, A&E* or PBS, addressing the case of the JFK assassination. In almost every broadcast another attempt is made to convince the viewing public that the conspiracy buffs are all wrong and that Oswald really did it and did it alone. But in every such program there are at least two glaring problems.

First, they always address only one or two of the multitude of questions raised repeatedly by the critics over the years. Second, in examining their selected problem area, they focus on only one aspect of the controversy and ignore all the others that would greatly weaken their argument.

One such program focused primarily on the police dictabelt recording that the HSCA found contained the sounds of at least four shots fired during the assassination. The program claimed that it has been shown that the motorcycle with the open microphone could not have been in the right spot on Houston Street for the analysis done by *Bolt, Beranek and Newman* to be accurate and authentic, therefore rendering this evidence invalid. But no attempt was made to explain how it could be that the shock waves and echo patterns that were scientifically matched against the test shots fired from the sixth floor window and from the fence atop the knoll could otherwise have appeared on the tape.

Other programs have tried to show that a single bullet could indeed have passed through both Kennedy and Connally without all the zigzagging claimed to have been necessary by the critics. But they don't even address the entrance/exit locations problems, or the wound size problem, or Connally's reaction problem, or the lack of damage to bullet 399, or the inability of the autopsy doctors to probe a path through JFK's back.

On November 22, 2009, *The Discovery Channel* ran three hour-long documentaries on various aspects of the assassination. Two were heavily slanted toward the official verdict, while the other, oddly and inconsistently, argued that the Mob was behind "Oswald's" action. All three were heavily flawed, in spite of elaborate and costly reconstructions. For example, the staging of test shots from the grassy knoll, attempting to prove that a shot from there would have exited the left side of the head and struck Mrs. Kennedy, portrayed the shooter firing directly from the right side of JFK. But all evidence, pointed out by the critics for decades, indicates that the shot came from the right *front*, at an angle that would cause the large exit wound at the back of the head seen by the Parkland doctors, and leaving Mrs. Kennedy unscathed.

What can we do now?

Since the publication of Gerald Posner's book in 1993, the subject of the JFK assassination has once again faded into the background. Is he right? Is the case really closed? It seems to be as far as the media is concerned. But I don't believe that it will ever be closed as far as the American public is concerned...not as long as all the questions raised in this book and the many that have gone before it remain unanswered. The problem is that no one seems to know what to do about it or have the power to do it if they did. This is a crime that occurred several decades ago and the trail has grown quite cold. It may not be possible to ascertain who the real killers were at this point in time. But even as we approach the fiftieth anniversary of President Kennedy's murder there are those who are still interested enough in finding the truth to continue examining the evidence and finding flaws in the government's case. One such person is Professor Cliff Spiegelman of Texas A&M University, who as recently as the summer of 2008 produced a study that cast doubt on the findings of the FBI's bullet fragment analysis done in 1976, which concluded that all the fragments from JFK's and Governor Connally's body came from the same bullet. And then there is the previously mentioned analysis of the acoustical evidence done by Dr.

Donald B. Thomas of Dallas, which further substantiates the work done by BBN for the HSCA in the nineteen seventies showing at least four shots fired in Dealey Plaza.

There is still much that could be done if the government could be pressured by public demand into making the effort. If a new investigation were to be conducted by a team composed of experts who sincerely wanted to find the facts, rather than cover them up, we could still learn a great deal. Such a team would have to be headed by someone who has absolutely no reason to want to protect any agency of the government or any individual–someone who has long suspected that we have not been told the truth about the assassination. Power on such an investigative team should be distributed among three or four co-chairmen to ensure that no one man could be compromised, breached, bought off or otherwise persuaded to shade things either way.

This investigation should explore two crimes, not just one. It should attempt, of course, to find out who was behind the killing of the President, but it should expend at least as much effort in finding out who is guilty of obstruction of justice through such crimes as the destruction and falsification of autopsy photos and X-rays, the switching of ballistic evidence, the destruction of vital evidence like the President's brain, tissue slides and dictabelt tapes, the alteration or destruction of movie film, etc. Like the HSCA, which was divided into two teams of investigators, (one devoted to the JFK case and one to the MLK case) this new investigative body should be divided into separate teams devoted to the two major questions listed above. The cover-up team would examine the motives of those who have exerted so much time and effort to prop up the government's version of the crime. Perhaps a good place to begin in this regard would be with Mr. Posner. Was there more to his gross misrepresentations of evidence and testimony than merely a desire to make a name for himself, or was there some powerful force supporting and encouraging his efforts? Was it merely a coincidence that his book, the first in many years to support the Warren Commission's findings, was published just a few months after Oliver Stone's movie caused the opening of most of the files?

Why did both President Clinton and Vice-President Gore reverse themselves, once in office, on the question of conspiracy in the JFK case? What or who has changed their attitude? Why has every administration felt obligated to maintain the official story and continue to cover for evidence-tampering that occurred during the Johnson and Nixon administrations? What possible national security concern could justify the continued censorship or outright withholding of documents pertaining to Lee Harvey Oswald and the JFK assassination by both the CIA and the FBI so long after the event? It is long past time for the American People to demand that we be told the truth about the death of our president and the flawed investigations of that death.

It is not too late, even now, to learn a great deal, *if* a truly impartial and serious effort is made. It would almost certainly mean that we would have to face some unpleasant facts about our government and its agencies, but it is difficult to conceive of any revelation that would traumatize us worse than almost fifty years of cover-up already has. Here are some specific things that a new investigative committee should and could do.

1. Subject the autopsy photos and X-Rays to a thorough and impartial analysis to determine the reasons for their lack of consistency with each other and with the known condition of JFK's head and body.

2. Make a concerted effort to locate the President's brain, or at least determine the reason for its disappearance. If found, examine it to determine the number and type/s of metal fragments left in it and, if possible, the path of all missiles that struck it.

3. Override the objections of the Connally family and disinter Governor Connally's body to remove the remaining bullet fragments. Then subject these fragments to the best possible tests to determine if they match the metallic composition of CE 399.

4. Re-examine the fragments analyzed in 1978 by the HSCA's Dr. Vincent Guinn, and weigh the results of that testing against the previous NAA and spectrographic tests. Find out why Dr. Guinn stated that the fragments he tested were not the same as those tested by the FBI for the Warren Commission. Was there a switch, and if so, who is responsible?

5. Have a reliable, non-governmental acoustics firm conduct further tests on the Dallas Police tape recording to settle the shots question. This should include test-firing from other locations in Dealey Plaza (besides the TSBD window and the fence atop the knoll) to see if matches can be found for the other wave-forms on the tape.

6. Question all doctors and assisting staff about other missiles found during the autopsy. Exactly what was turned over to FBI agents Sibert and O'Neill who reported receipt of a "missile recovered during the autopsy."

7.. Question these same people to resolve the conflicts over how the body arrived and what it arrived in.

8.. Question Parkland Hospital doctors Malcolm Perry, Charles Carrico, and all other medical personnel who saw the condition of the President's head that day. Demand that they state for the record their opinions as to the nature of the wounds and how they coincide (or don't) with the autopsy photos and X-rays and with the official autopsy report.

9. Make a concerted effort to identify the person or persons who posed as Oswald on the numerous occasions leading up to the assassination, focusing major effort on the three visitors of Silvia Odio, and on Mexico City.

10. Determine from the still withheld files whether Oswald had any connections to any intelligence agencies, which ones and in what roles.

This is only a sampling of the areas a new investigation could and should explore. There is no way to predict where the threads will lead, once new revelations begin to be uncovered. But one fact is certain; the case is not, and must never be considered "closed" until all the facts that can be uncovered are brought forth and we get as many of the answers to our questions as can be provided at this late point in time. Achieving this goal will not be easy or cheap.

Try as they have and will continue to, critics of the official story are not going to be able to answer these questions by themselves. Nor is the government going to conduct the kind of investigation that is necessary on its own volition. It is going to take some serious arm-twisting before any investigation along the lines outlined above is undertaken.

But, as *Legacy of Secrecy* author Lamar Waldron points out on page 763 of his 2008 book, the CIA is still refusing to release over a million records pertaining to the JFK case until at least 2017, in spite of the Assassinations Records Collection Act's intentions.

President Kennedy himself tried to warn us about the increasing tendency of the power elite to use the national security shield to hide all sorts of embarrassing mistakes. In a speech he gave at the Waldorf-Astoria in New York on April 27, 1961, shortly after the Bay-of-Pigs fiasco, he made the following prophetic remarks:

Even today, there is little value in insuring the survival of our nation if our traditions do not survive with it. And there is very grave danger that an announced need for increased security will be seized upon by those anxious to expand its meaning to the very limits of official censorship and concealment. *That* I do not intend to permit to the extent that it's in my control. And no official of my Administration, whether his rank is high or low, civilian or military, should interpret my words here tonight as an excuse to *censor the news, to stifle dissent, to cover up our mistakes or to withhold from the press and the public the facts they deserve to know*. (emphasis added)

If the fiftieth anniversary of this historic event does not create enough interest to prompt a new look at the case, the murder of our thirty-fifth president will fade into history, not only unpunished but unresolved. Tragically, it looks like the perpetrators of both the assassination and the cover-up have gotten away with it. For this we can thank the deception skills of several of our governmental agencies, the stubborn pride of the mainline media, and the apathy of most Americans.

If you, the reader, have been angered enough by what you have just read, I implore you to write to your senators and representatives and strongly request that they work toward implementing at least some of the methods listed above and whatever can be done to finally bring the truth to American People. They certainly aren't going to do it on their own initiative.

The End

NOTE: If you enjoyed the logic and writing style in this book, you might also want to check out my other book, titled, *The Dawn of a New Age of Reason: Religion in the Twenty-first Century*. It is available through Amazon.

It's Time For the Truth!

BIBLIOGRAPHY
***

The President's Commission on the Assassination of President Kennedy. *The Warren Report and the 26 volumes of testimony/exhibits*. Government Printing Office, 1964

Anson, Robert Sam. *They've Killed the President*. Bantam Books Inc., New York, NY 1975

Belin, David. *November 22, 1963: You Are the Jury*. Quadrangle/The New York Times Book Co., New York, NY 1973

Benson, Michael. *Who's Who in the JFK Assassination*. Citidel Press, New York, NY 1993

Blakey, Robert/Billings, Richard. *The Plot to Kill the President*. Times Books, Division of Quadrangle/The New York Times Book Co., Inc., New York, NY 1981

Brown, Walt. *The People v. Lee Harvey Oswald*. Carroll & Graf Publishers, Inc., New York, NY 1992

Calder, Michael. *JFK vs. CIA*. West LA Publishers, Los Angeles, CA 1998

Chambers, G. Paul. *Head Shot: The Science Behind the JFK Assassination*. Prometheus Books, Amherst, NY 2010

Crenshaw, Dr. Charles. *JFK: Conspiracy of Silence*. Signet, Division of Penguin Books USA, Inc., New York, NY 1992

Curry, Jesse. *JFK Assassination File*. American Poster and Printing Co., Inc., Dallas, TX 1969

Davis, John. *Mafia Kingfish: Carlos Marcello and the Assassination of John F. Kennedy*. McGraw-Hill Publishing Co., New York, NY 1989

DiEugenio, James. *Destiny Betrayed* . Skyhorse Publishing, New York, NY 1992

Douglass, James. *JFK and the Unspeakable,* Orbis Books, Maryknoll,NY 2008

Epstein, Edward J. *Inquest*. The Viking Press, New York, NY 1966

Epstein, Edward J. *Legend.* (1978) References are from the paperback edition of *The Assassination Chronicles* (trilogy containing *Inquest, Counterplot and Legend*), Carroll & Graf, New York, NY 1992

Ernest, Barry. *The Girl on the Stairs The Search For a Missing Witness to the JFK Assassinaton.* Pelican Publishing Co. Gretna Louisiana 2013

Evica, George M. *And We Are All Mortal.* University of Hartford Press, W. Hartford, CT 1978

Fensterwald, Bernard Jr./Committee to Investigate Assassinations. - *Coincidence or Conspiracy?* Zebra Books, Division of Kensington Publishing Corp., New York, NY 1977

Fonzi, Gaeton. *The Last Investigation.* Thunder's Mouth Press, New York, NY 1993

Ford, Gerald/Stiles, John. *Portrait of the Assassin.* Simon and Schuster, New York, NY 1965

Garrison, Jim. *On the Trail of the Assassins.* Warner Books, Inc., New York, NY 1988

Giancana, Sam & Chuck. *Double Cross.* Warner Books Inc., New York, NY 1992

Groden, Robert J./Livingstone, Harrison. *High Treason.* The Berkley Publishing Group, New York, NY 1989

Groden, Robert J. *The Killing of a President.* Viking Studio Books, New York, NY 1993

Hancock, Larry, *Someone Would Have Talked.* JFK Lancer Productions and Publications, Southlake, TX 2006

Hinkle, Warren/Turner, William. *Deadly Secrets: The CIA-Mafia War Against Castro and the Assassination of JFK.* Thunder's Mouth Press, New York, NY 1993

Hurt, Henry. *Reasonable Doubt.* Henry Holt and Co., Inc., New York, NY 1985

Kantor, Seth. *The Ruby Cover-up.* Zebra Books, Division of Kensington Publishing Corp., New York, NY 1978, 1992

Kurtz, Michael. *Crime of the Century.* University of Tenn. Press, Knoxville, TN 1982

La Fontaine, Ray & Mary. *Oswald Talked.* Pelican Publishing, Gretna, LA 1996

Lane, Mark. *Rush to Judgment.* Holt, Rinehart & Winston, New York, NY 1966

Lane, Mark/Freed, Donald. *Executive Action.* Dell Publishing Co., Inc., New York, NY 1973

Lane, Mark. *Plausible Denial.* Thunder's Mouth Press, New York, NY 1991

Law, William M. *In The Eye of History* JFK Lancer Productions & Publications, Southlake, TX

Lifton, David. *Best Evidence.* Macmillan Publishing Co., Inc., New York, NY 1980

Livingstone, Harrison. *HighTreason 2.* Carroll & Graf Publishers, Inc., New York, NY 1992

Livingstone, Harrison. *Killing The Truth.* Carroll & Graf, New York, NY 1993

Mailer, Norman. *Oswald's Tale: An American Mystery.* Random House, New York, NY 1995

Manchester, William. *The Death of a President.* Harper & Row, New York 1967

Marchetti, Victor/Marks, John. *The CIA and the Cult of Intelligence.* Dell Publishing Co., Inc., New York, NY 1974

Marrs, Jim. *Crossfire, The Plot That Killed Kennedy.* Carroll & Graf Publishers, Inc., New York, NY 1989

McDonald, Hugh. *Appointment in Dallas.* The Hugh McDonald Publishing Corp., New York, NY 1976

Meagher, Sylvia. *Accessories after the fact.* Vintage Books, Div. of Random House, New York, NY 1967

Melanson, Philip. *The Robert F. Kennedy Assassination.* Shapolsky Publishers, Inc., New York, NY 1991

Model, F. Peter/Groden, Robert. *JFK: The Case for Conspiracy.* Manor Books, Inc., New York, NY 1977

Morrow, Robert. *Betrayal.* Henry Regrery Co., Chicago, IL 1976

Newman, John M. *JFK and Vietnam.* Warner Books, New York, NY 1992

North, Mark. *Act of Treason.* Carroll & Graf Publishers, Inc., New York, NY 1991

O'Reilly, Bill and Mark Dugard *Killing Kennedy* Henry Holy and Company, 2012

O'Toole, George. *The Assassination Tapes.* Penthouse Press Ltd., New York, NY 1975

Oglesby, Carl. *The JFK Assassination: The Facts & the Theories.* Signet, Division of Penguin Books USA, Inc., New York, NY 1992

Popkin, Richard. *The Second Oswald.* Avon Books, Division of The Hearst Corp, New York, NY 1966

Posner, Gerald. *Case Closed.* Randon House, New York, NY 1993

Roffman, Howard. *Presumed Guilty.* A. S. Barnes and Co., Inc., Cranbury, NJ 1976

Russell, Dick. *The Man Who Knew Too Much.* Carroll & Graf Publishers, Inc., New York, NY 1992

Scheim, David. Scheim-*Contract on America.* Shapolski Publishers, Inc., New York, NY 1988

Sloan, Bill. *JFK: Breaking the Silence.* Taylor Publishing Co., Dallas, TX 1993

Sloan, Bill. JFK: *The Last Dissenting Witness,* Pelican Publishing, LA, 2008.

Smith, Matthew. *Conspiracy: The Plot to Stop the Kennedys.* Citadel Press, Kensington Publishing Corp., 850 Third Ave., New York, NY 2005

Stone, Oliver/Sklar, Zachary. *JFK: The Book of the Film.* Applause Books, New York, NY 1992

Summers, Anthony. *Conspiracy.* (1980, Europe), Paragon House, New York, NY 1989,US. (references are from the 1991 updated paperback edition)

Thompson, Josiah. *Six Seconds in Dallas*. Bernard Geis Associates, New York, NY 1967

US House of Representatives, Ninety-Fifth Congress. *Report of the Select Committee on Assassinations*. U.S. Government Printing Office, Washington, DC 1979

Ventura, Jesse. *They Killed Our President*. Skyhorse Publishing, New York, NY 2013

Waldron, Lamar & Hartman, Thom. *Legacy of Secrecy*. Counterpoint Berkeley 2008

Weisberg, Harold. Weisberg-*Whitewash*. Dell Publishing Co., Inc., New York, NY 1966

Weisberg, Harold. *Whitewash II*. Dell Publishing Co., Inc., New York, NY 1967

Weisberg, Harold. *Photographic Whitewash*. Harold Weisberg, Publisher, Route 12, Old Receiver Rd., Frederick, MD 1967, 1976

Weisberg, Harold. *Whitewash IV*. Harold Weisberg, Publisher, Route 12, Old Receiver Rd.,Frederick, MD 1974

Weisberg, Harold. *Oswald in New Orleans*. Harold Weisberg, Publisher, Route 12, Old Receiver Rd., Frederick, MD 1967

Weisberg, Harold. *Post Mortem*. Harold Weisberg, Publisher, Route 12, Old Receiver Rd.,Frederick, MD 1969, 1971 1975

Weisberg, Harold. *Case Open*. Carroll & Graf, New York, NY 1994

Weisberg, Harold. *Never Again!*. Mary Ferrel Foundation Press, Ipswich, MA 2007

Zelizer, Barbie. *Covering the Body*. The University of Chicago Press, Chicago, IL 1992

It's Time For the Truth!

SOURCES

The following abbreviations will be used to designate the governmental sources:
WR,p: Warren Report, page p; WHv,p: Warren Hearings (26 volumes of testimony and exhibits), volume v, page p; CEn: Commission Exhibit # n; CDn,p: Commission Document # n, page p; HSCR,p: House Select Committee on Assassinations Report, page p; HSCHv,p: House Select Committee Hearings, volume v, page p.

Introduction
1. Humes burns autopsy draft: –WH2,373; –WH17,48; –Lane-*Rush to Judgment*,385; –Meagher-*Accessories After the Fact*,137; –Weisberg-*Post Mortem*,524; –Waldron-*Legacy of Secrecy*,181
2. Police tape analysis: –HSCR,65-81
3. HSC recommendations to Justice: –HSCR,480-483
4. Media on Oliver Stone: –Stone-*JFK: The Book of the Film*
5. Luces on Castro/Oswald: –HSCH10,83; –Summers-*Conspiracy*,420-422; –Kurtz-*Crime of the Century*,219; –Groden/Livingstone-*High Treason*,191-192; –Russell-*The Man Who Knew Too Much*,403; –Fonzi-*The Last Investigation*,52-59; Waldron-*Legacy of Secrecy*,164,220
6. Zapruder film suppressed: –Garrison-*On the Trail of the Assassins*,279-280; –Thompson-*Six Seconds in Dallas*,14,15

Chapter 1 - November 22, 1963: The Basic Facts
1. Texas political turmoil: –Curry-*JFK Assassination File*,4;
2. Prevalence of the radical right: –Summers-*Conspiracy*,1-2;4
3. Adlai Stevenson incident: –Curry-*JFK Assassination File*,3; –Sam Anson-*They've Killed the President*,17
4. Anti JFK ad and handbill: –.Curry-*JFK Assassination File*,19-20
5. Tape by FBI of Miami plot: –Meagher-*Accessories After the Fact*,89; –Summers-*Conspiracy*,404-405; –Marrs-*Crossfire*,265-266; –Waldron-*Legacy of Secrecy*,77-78
6. Motorcade leaves Love Field: –Curry-*JFK Assassination File*,26
7. Motorcade route map: –Curry-*JFK Assassination File*,11; –Garrison-*On the Trail of the Assassins*,117-118,375
8. Dealey Plaza name origin: –Marrs-*Crossfire*,10
9. Limo nearly stopped: –Meagher-*Accessories After the Fact*,3-5
10. Motorcycle officer splattered: –WH6,294; –Lane-*Rush to Judgment*,57; –Curry-*JFK Assassination File*,30; –Marrs-*Crossfire*,73-74.

11. Jackie on back of the limo: –Summers-*Conspiracy*,13-14; –Hurt-*Reasonable Doubt*,128; –Marrs-*Crossfire*,13

12. Dr. Perry does trach over wound: –Curry-*JFK Assassination File*,34; –Meagher-*Accessories After the Fact*,144-146; –Lifton-*Best Evidence*,56

13. "Shot in right temple". (Kilduff): –Meagher-*Accessories After the Fact*,162; –Lifton-*Best Evidence*,330,589; –Livingstone-*High_Treason_2*,290

14. Dr. Perry refers to throat wound: –WH6,11,14; –Meagher-*Accessories After the Fact*,150-156; –Kurtz-*Crime of the Century*,70-72; –Lifton-*Best Evidence*,55,62

15. Head entrance wound not seen: –WH6; –Lane-*Rush to Judgment*,57-59; –Meagher-*Accessories After the Fact*,162; –Lifton-*Best Evidence*,8,39

16. Body forcibly seized: –Summers-*Conspiracy*,8; –Lifton-*Best Evidence*,389-390; –Crenshaw-*Conspiracy of Silence*,118-120

17. Body wrapped in a sheet: –Lifton-*Best Evidence*,595,600,674; –Livingstone-*High_Treason_2*,105

18. "Stretcher bullet" found: –Lane-*Rush to Judgment*,79-80; –Thompson-*Six Seconds in Dallas*,175-176; –Kurtz-*Crime of the Century*,11; –Groden/Livingstone-*High Treason*,66

19. Crowd converges on the knoll: –Lane-*Rush to Judgment*,41-42; –Thompson-*Six Seconds in Dallas*,100

20. "Secret Service" behind fence: –Meagher-*Accessories After the Fact*,26; –Thompson-*Six Seconds in Dallas*,24-25; –Summers-*Conspiracy*,29,50-51

21. Casings found near window: –WR,84; –Curry-*JFK Assassination File*,53; –Thompson-*Six Seconds in Dallas*,141-146; –Kurtz-*Crime of the Century*,50-53

22. Rifle between stacks of cartons: –WR,84; –Curry-*JFK Assassination File*,53-54; –Sam Anson-*They've Killed the President*,31; –Roffman-*Presumed Guilty*,212-213,216

23. Description of suspect: –Lane-*Rush to Judgment*,81-87; –Curry-*JFK Assassination File*,48-49

24. Witnesses to Tippit shooting: –WR166 69;WH6,447; –Lane-*Rush to Judgment*,176-189; –Meagher-*Accessories After the Fact*,255-259; –Summers-*Conspiracy*,86-94

25. Police notified of shooting: –WH23,857;WH6,448;WH24,202; –Lane-*Rush to Judgment*,171-173; –Sam Anson-*They've Killed the President*,36; –Summers-*Conspiracy*,92

26. Description revised: –Lane-*Rush to Judgment*,180,188; –Curry-*JFK Assassination File*,67

27. Automatic shells found: –CE1974,78; –Meagher-*Accessories After the Fact*,273; –Curry-*JFK Assassination File*,68; –Summers-*Conspiracy*,89-90; –Marrs-*Crossfire*,342-345

28. Tip on Texas Theater: –Curry-*JFK Assassination File*,68; –Sam Anson-*They've Killed the President*,36-37; –Marrs-*Crossfire*,350

29. Oswald is pointed out: –Meagher-*Accessories After the Fact*,259; –Sam Anson-*They've Killed the President*,38; –Marrs-*Crossfire*,351

30. Oswald's alias: –WCR,118 22;312-314; –Summers-*Conspiracy*,56; –Curry-*JFK Assassination File*,98;

31. Oswald's arraignments: –Curry-*JFK Assassination File*,78-80

32. "I'm just a patsy": –Newsreels of Oswald's questioning by reporters in the halls.

33. Questionable line ups: –Lane-*Rush to Judgment*,190-193; –Weisberg-*Whitewash*,150-157; –Kurtz-*Crime of the Century*,128-129

34. Brennan fails to ID Oswald: –WH3,148; –Lane-*Rush to Judgment*,396; –Weisberg-*Whitewash*,90; –Kurtz-*Crime of the Century*,43

35. Autorities get warning calls: –WR,209; –Meagher-*Accessories After the Fact*,398,401; –Kantor-*The Ruby Cover-up*,120; –Weisberg-*Whitewash II*,57-62

36. Ruby kills Oswald in DP basement: –Kantor-*The Ruby Cover-up*,143-150

37. Grammer recognizes Ruby's voice: –Taped interview with Jack Anderson; –Hurt-*Reasonable Doubt*,407-408

38. AG Carr starts Texas inquiry: –Kantor-*The Ruby Cover-up*,158-160

39. Impeach Earl Warren" billboards: –Kantor-*The Ruby Cover-up*,106,110

40. Marina in "protective custody.": –Lane-Rush to Judgment,310; –Weisberg-*Whitewash* II,25-26

41. Marina changes her testimony: –Lane-*Rush to Judgment*,307 16; –Weisberg-*Whitewash II*,25,47; –Meagher-*Accessories After the Fact*,238-241; –Sam Anson-*They've Killed the President*,59-60

Chapter 2 - The Autopsy

1. Body forcibly removed from Dallas: –Lifton-*Best Evidence*,389-390; –Summers-*Conspiracy*,8; –Marrs-*Crossfire*,363; –Crenshaw-*Conspiracy of Silence*,102-104
2. The choice of autopsy doctors: –Summers-*Conspiracy*,8; –Thompson-*Six Seconds in Dallas*, appendix D,278-280; –Weisberg-*Post Mortem*,146;
3. Finck ordered more X rays: –WH2,364; –Weisberg-*Post Mortem*,152,163
4. X rays of extremities missing: –Weisberg-*Post Mortem*,162-163
5. "Brass" controlled proceedings: –Lifton-*Best Evidence*,611-612; –Garrison-*On the Trail of the Assassins*,288-292; –Livingstone-*High_Treason_2*,242,261; –Marrs-*Crossfire*,368-369
6. Failure to dissect "neck" wound: –Lifton-*Best Evidence*,101-106; –Meagher-*Accessories After the Fact*,145-149; –Kurtz-*Crime of the Century*,18
7. Humes talks to Perry on 11/23/63: –Weisberg-*Post Mortem*,72,150; –Lifton-*Best Evidence*,160-161; –Kurtz-*Crime of the Century*,72
8. Custer/Jenkins on found bullet: –Law-*In the Eye of History*,132-133; –Livingstone-*High_Treason_2*,206-210,216; –Livingstone-*Killing the Truth*,170,677;
9. Adm. Osborne on found bullet: –.Lifton-*Best Evidence*,646-647; –Livingstone-*High_Treason_2*,210
10. FBI receipt for a "missle": –Lifton-*Best Evidence*,648-651; –Weisberg-*Post Mortem*,266
11. Air Force One to Walter Reed: –Lifton-*Best Evidence*,681;
12. FBI report, "surgery of head": –Weisberg-*Post Mortem*,72; –Lifton-*Best Evidence*,172; –Livingstone-*High_Treason_2*,234
13. Brain stem already severed: –Lifton-*Best Evidence*,454-464; –Livingstone-*High_Treason_2*,2Z6,233-234,239,241,287,293-295; –Law-*In The Eye of History*,80-81
14. No craniotomy needed: –.Kurtz-*Crime of the Century*,17; –Livingstone-*High_Treason_2*,233-234,239
15. Brain weight: –WR,228; –Waldron-*In the Eye of History*,46
16. Body bag, cheap casket: –Law-*In the Eye of History*,9,35,36,69; –Lifton-*Best Evidence*,579,595,598-600,609,637; –Livingstone-*High_Treason_2*,146,165,268,270,274
17. J. Custer saw Jackie arrive: –Lifton-*Best Evidence*,620-621; –Livingstone-*High_Treason_2*,125-126,222-223

18. AF Major's body outside morgue: –Lifton-*Best Evidence*,231-232; –Livingstone-*High_Treason_2*,132,230-232;
19. Autopsy evidence burned: –Livingstone-*High_Treason_2*,245,322; –Livingstone-*Killing the Truth*,277
20. Safe broken into by agent Blahut: –Summers-*Conspiracy*,12; –Groden/Livingstone-*High Treason*,37,107,385
21. JFK's brain now missing: –*New York Times*, 8/27/72; –Summers-*Conspiracy*,10; –Kurtz-*Crime of the Century*,100; –Garrison-*On the Trail of the Assassins*,286; –Waldron-*Legacy of Secrecy*,334
22. Entrance wound in right temple: –Lifton-*Best Evidence*,143-45,330-331; –Law-*In the Eye of History*,17,22,73,134-135
23. Head entrance wound relocated: –HSCR,43;HSCH7,254; –Kurtz-*Crime of the Century*,163,175; –Summers-*Conspiracy*,11; –Groden/Livingstone-*High Treason*,34
24 Parkland doctors on head wound: –Lifton-*Best Evidence*,309-311; –Thompson-*Six Seconds in Dallas*,106-108; –Livingstone-*High_Treason_2*,324-325; –Summers-*Conspiracy*,479-480
25. Head reconstruction: –Livingstone-*HighTreason 2*,257; –Law-*In the Eye of History*,275
26. Drs. Humes and Boswell in JAMA: –Livingstone-*Killing the Truth*,622-641; –*Journal of the American Medical Association*,5/19/92
27. Medical community responds: –Livingstone-*Killing the Truth*, Appendix G; –Subsequent issues of JAMA, reprinted in *The Fourth Decade*;
28. Spinal cord: –Livingstone-*High_Treason_2*,152
29. Gag order on autopsy personnel: –Marrs-*Crossfire*,369; –Lifton-*Best Evidence*,607-608,610, 619,639; –Law-*In the Eye of History*,47,129,138-139

Chapter 3- The Non-investigation
1. Arrest of Eugene Brading: –WH24,202;WH25,626; –Marrs-*Crossfire*,337-339; –Summers-*Conspiracy*,452-454; –Groden/Livingstone-*High Treason*,121,185,319
2. C. V. Harrelson: one of "tramps"?: –Marrs-*Crossfire*,333-336; –Groden/Livingstone-*High Treason*,142; –Livingstone-*High_Treason_2*,77
3. TSBD not sealed immediately: –Weisberg-*Whitewash*,77,96

4. Rifle found was a 7.65 Mauser: –WH3,291 95;WH26,599; – WH24,228,829; –Lane-*Rush to Judgment*,114-120; –Evica-*And We Are All Mortal*,15-36; –Hurt-*Reasonable Doubt*,102-106
5. Chain of evidence on rifle, etc: –Lane-*Rush to Judgment*,198-199; – Brown-*The People vs. Lee Harvey Oswald*, passim
6. No interrogation notes taken: –WR,180; –Weisberg-*Whitewash*,141-142; –Lane-*Rush to Judgment*,370
7. Source of LHO's description: –WR,144; –Summers-*Conspiracy*,52; –Lane-*Rush to Judgment*,81-99
8. Early pronouncement of LHO guilt: –Roffman-*Presumed Guilty*,74-76; – WH24,751,754,764,772,787,788,823
9. Hoover's fear and hatred: –*Act of Treason*,passim
10. Warren's meeting with LBJ: --Manchester-*Death of a President*,630
11. Senator R. Russell's footnote: –Weisberg-*Whitewash IV*,21; – Groden/Livingstone-*High Treason*,67; –Hancock-*Someone Would Have Talked*,298
12. Warren Commission attendance and testimony percentages; – Epstein-*Inquest*,107-109; –Kurtz-*Crime of the Century*,155
13. Orville Nix movie: –Thompson-*Six Seconds in Dallas*,223-225; – Sam Anson-*They've Killed the President*,145-148; –Marrs-*Crossfire*,35; – Groden/Livingstone-*High Treason*,224-225; –Livingstone-*Killing the Truth*,336
14. Hoffman's view behind the fence: –Marrs-*Crossfire*,81-86; – .Groden/Livingstone-*High Treason*,462-463
15. Sibert & O'Neill's autopsy report: –Weisberg-*Post Mortem*,531-536; –Lifton-*Best Evidence*,101-107
16. Most witnesses not heard by the WC: –Epstein-*Inquest*,211; – Lane-*Rush to Judgment*,387
17. Garrison/Long conversation: –Garrison-*On the Trail of the Assassins*,13-14; –Waldron-*Legacy of Secrecy*,370
18. Clark panel finds fragments: –Weisberg-*Post Mortem*,199,592; – Roffman-*Presumed Guilty*,121-122; –Kurtz-*Crime of the Century*,73
19. Timing of Clark panel report: –Weisberg-*Post Mortem*,133-142,574; –Roffman-*Presumed Guilty*,115
20. HSCA leadership fight Fonzi: –*The Last Investigation*,178-194; – Blakey/Billings-*The Plot to Kill the President*,62-68;
21. CIA withholds from HSC: –Summers-*Conspiracy*,519-520; – Waldron-*Legacy of Secrecy*,744-745

Chapter 4 - Forks in the Road
1. Weisberg obtains transcripts: –Weisberg-*Post Mortem*,485-487; –Weisberg-*Whitewash IV*,5-21; –North-*Act of Treason*,507-509, 514-516
2. Ford's synopsis of the 1/27/64. executive session: –Ford-*Portrait of the Assassin*,24; –Weisberg-*Whitewash IV*,130
3. Ford's absence: –Weisberg-*Whitewash IV*,35

Chapter 5 - Cuba: Rosetta Stone to the Assassination
1. Intent to withdraw from Vietnam: –National Security Action 263 Marrs-*Crossfire*,306-308; –Summers-*Conspiracy*,396; –Stone-*JFK: The Book of the Film*,531-532
2. Trafficante Jr. in Cuban prison: –Waldron-*Legacy of Secrecy*,242; –Kantor-*The Ruby Cover-up*,40,254-259; –. Blakey/Billings-*The Plot to Kill the President*,292-293; –. Hancock -*Someone Would Have Talked*,188
3. Nixon behind invasion of Cuba: –Morrow-*Betrayal*,10i; –Evica-*And We Are All Mortal*,245; –Summers-*Conspiracy*,224; –Marrs-*Crossfire*,139,269; –Groden/Livingstone-*High Treason*,191
4. E. Howard Hunt: –Sam Anson-*They've Killed the President*,256,269, 286-289; –Evica-*And We Are All Mortal*,132,138,198-200,271; –Summers-*Conspiracy*,224-225,233-234,319,498; –Russell-*The Man Who Knew Too Much*,473-477
5. Frank Sturgis (ne Fiorini): –Lane-*Plausible Denial*,288-290; –Evica-*And We Are All Mortal*,138,198-200; –Summers-*Conspiracy*,319,498,627; –Waldron-*Legacy of Secrecy*,714-715
6. JFK cancels air cover: –Marrs-*Crossfire*,140-141; –Groden/Livingstone-*High Treason*,310-315
7. Threat to dismantle the CIA: –Summers-*Conspiracy*,226; –Marchetti-*The CIA and the Cult of Intelligence*,31
8. Tracy Barnes: –Evica-*And We Are All Mortal*,59,245; –Russell-*The Man Who Knew Too Much*,180,217,407-410; –Hancock-*Someone Would Have Talked*,422-426
9. Richard Helms: –Summers-*Conspiracy*,131-132,322; –Blakey/Billings-*The Plot to Kill the President*,55-61; –Russell-*The Man Who Knew Too Much*, 236,381-382; –Waldron-*Legacy of Secrecy*,141-142,144-145,298-300
10. William Harvey: –Summers-*Conspiracy*,137,226-227,240,528-531; –Blakey/Billings-*The Plot to Kill the President*,54-56; –Russell-*The Man

Who Knew Too Much,235,245,247,381; –Waldron-*Legacy of Secrecy*,65,206-207

11. Desmond Fitzgerald: –Summers-*Conspiracy*,322,400-401,497-498; –Blakey/Billings-*The Plot to Kill the President*,151; –Russell-*The Man Who Knew Too Much*,146-149,290-292

Waldron-*Legacy of Secrecy*,299; –Hancock-*Someone Would Have Talked*,339-340

12. General Edward Lansdale: –Evica-*And We Are All Mortal*,257; –Blakey/Billings-*The Plot to Kill the President*,56, 59-60; –Russell-*The Man Who Knew Too Much*,244-246; –Hancock-*Someone Would Have Talked*,336

13. Colonel Sheffield Edwards: –Evica-*And We Are All Mortal*,256-257; –Blakey/Billings-*The Plot to Kill the President*,53-59; –Groden/Livingstone-*High Treason*,311,313; –Russell-*The Man Who Knew Too Much*,381-382; –Waldron-*Legacy of Secrecy*,376

14. Successes of ZR/RIFLE: –Summers-*Conspiracy*,137; –Blakey/Billings-*The Plot to Kill the President*,54-56; –Garrison-*On the Trail of the Assassins*,342; –Marrs-*Crossfire*,205-207; –Russell-*The Man Who Knew Too Much*,381

15. MKULTRA: –Groden/Livingstone-*High Treason*,401; –Marrs-*Crossfire*,184-186; –Russell-*The Man Who Knew Too Much*,380-384; Waldron-*Legacy of Secrecy*,141-142

16. JM/WAVE/David Morales: –Evica-*And We Are All Mortal*,117,121; –Summers-*Conspiracy*,228; –Russell-*The Man Who Knew Too Much*,261,389; –Waldron-*Legacy of Secrecy*,37,245; –Hancock-*Someone Would Have Talked*,121-134

17. Operation Mongoose: –Evica-*And We Are All Mortal*,257; –Blakey/Billings-*The Plot to Kill the President*,55-56; –Russell-*The Man Who Knew Too Much*,244-245;

18. Rorke/Lorenz attempt on Castro: –Evica-*And We Are All Mortal*,201-204,246

19. Roselli-Harvey connection: –Evica-*And We Are All Mortal*,102,256, 258,262; –. . Blakey/Billings-*The Plot to Kill the President*,58-61; –Russell-*The Man Who Knew Too Much*,381; –Groden/Livingstone-*High Treason*,312; –Waldron-*Legacy of Secrecy*,65

20. Maheu-Hughes connection: –Waldron-*Legacy of Secrecy*,345; –Evica-*And We Are All Mortal*,102,208,212,256; –Groden/Livingstone-*High Treason*,312

21. Roselli's death: –Evica-*And We Are All Mortal*,191; – Groden/Livingstone-*High Treason*,141; –Waldron-*Legacy of Secrecy*,739
22. Richard Cain: –Evica-*And We Are All Mortal*,188,249; – Giancana-*Double Cross*,298-299,334-335; –Waldron-*Legacy of Secrecy*,61,75,193,309
23. David A. Phillips (M. Bishop): –Marrs-*Crossfire*,149-150; –Evica-*And We Are All Mortal*,120-121; –Summers-*Conspiracy*,149-150,504-519; –Hurt-*Reasonable Doubt*,331-337; –Russell-*The Man Who Knew Too Much*,419-422; –Fonzi-*The Last Investigation*,262,263,394-396,408; –Waldron-*Legacy of Secrecy*,30
24. Antonio Veciana/Alpha 66: –Summers-*Conspiracy,3*25; –Hurt-*Reasonable Doubt*,327-337; –Marrs-*Crossfire*,149-150; –Russell-*The Man Who Knew Too Much*,295-298; –Waldron-*Legacy of Secrecy*,30,63,87
25. Veciana's testimony on LHO: –Summers-*Conspiracy*,328-330; – Hurt-*Reasonable Doubt*,328; –Russell-*The Man Who Knew Too Much*,417-418; –Waldron-*Legacy of Secrecy*,30
26. Manuel Artime: –Evica-*And We Are All Mortal*,122,269,284; – Russell-*The Man Who Knew Too Much*,291-292; –Summers-*Conspiracy,3*22,418; –Waldron-*Legacy of Secrecy*,27-29
27. deVarona/Prio Socarras: –Summers-*Conspiracy,2*40; –Marrs-*Crossfire*,153; –Waldron-*Legacy of Secrecy*,103,452,706
28. Sergio Arcacha Smith: –Weisberg-*Oswald in New Orleans*,334-348; –Russell-*The Man Who Knew Too Much*,293,395; –Summers-*Conspiracy*,297-299,338; –Hurt-*Reasonable Doubt*,337
29. Jose Aleman Sr: –Evica-*And We Are All Mortal*,288,309-311
30. Jose Aleman Jr. quotation: –Evica-*And We Are All Mortal*,221; – Summers-*Conspiracy*,254-255; –Scheim-*Contract on America*,59,60; – Russell-*The Man Who Knew Too Much*,516; –Waldron-*Legacy of Secrecy*,59
31. Guy Banister: –Weisberg-*Oswald in New Orleans*,327-333; – Summers-*Conspiracy*,290-298; –Hurt-*Reasonable Doubt*,226-227,291-293; –Russell-*The Man Who Knew Too Much*,395-396
32. 544 Camp St. on leaflets: –Summers-*Conspiracy*,286-288; –Marrs-*Crossfire*,148; –Russell-*The Man Who Knew Too Much*,394
33. Ferrie/FBI/Garrison: –Marrs-*Crossfire*,494-496; –Blakey/Billings-*The Plot to Kill the President*,46-48; –Hurt-*Reasonable Doubt*,261-289; – Garrison-*On the Trail of the Assassins*,6-7,10-11; –Waldron-*Legacy of Secrecy*,252-254

34. Ferrie/Marcello: –Blakey/Billings-*The Plot to Kill the President*,46; –Summers-*Conspiracy*,490; –Hurt-*Reasonable Doubt*,283-285; –Russell-*The Man Who Knew Too Much*,293; –Waldron-*Legacy of Secrecy*,103

35. Norman Rothman: –Evica-*And We Are All Mortal*,197,200,204-205; –Summers-*Conspiracy*,437-438; –Waldron-*Legacy of Secrecy*,452; –Hancock-*Someone Would Have Talked*,187-188

36. Rolando Cubela (AMLASH): –Evica-*And We Are All Mortal*,284-291; –Hurt-*Reasonable Doubt*,340-345; –Summers-*Conspiracy*,321-324,400-402; –Fonzi-*The Last Investigation*,329; –Waldron-*Legacy of Secrecy*,19,35,97-98,203

37. John Martino: –Fonzi-*The Last Investigation*,323-324; –Waldron-*Legacy of Secrecy*,55,63,68-69; –Hancock-*Someone Would Have Talked*,passim

38. Morales' dying brag: –Fonzi-*The Last Investigation*,389-390; –Hancock-*Someone Would Have Talked*,136-137

39. Rolando Masferrer: –Evica-*And We Are All Mortal*,143,252; –Summers-*Conspiracy*,231; –Russell-*The Man Who Knew Too Much*,262-263; –Waldron-*Legacy of Secrecy*,29-30

40. Orlando Bosch: –Evica-*And We Are All Mortal*,143,267,271; –Blakey/Billings-*The Plot to Kill the President*,175

41. Manuel Rodriguez: –Sam Anson-*They've Killed the President*,270-271; –Evica-*And We Are All Mortal*,101-104; –Russell-*The Man Who Knew Too Much*,541-542

42. Pedro Diaz Lanz: –Evica-*And We Are All Mortal*,198-199,320; –Lane-*Plausible Denial*,300

43. Loren Hall/J. E. Hoover: –Sam Anson-*They've Killed the President*,195-198; –Evica-*And We Are All Mortal*,198-199; –Blakey/Billings-*The Plot to Kill the President*,174-175; –Summers-*Conspiracy*,390-393

44. Hall's "disinformation.": –Evica-*And We Are All Mortal*,278-280; –Russell-*The Man Who Knew Too Much*,480-482

45. G. P. Hemming/Morita Lorenz: –Lane-*Plausible Denial*,300; –Blakey/Billings-*The Plot to Kill the President*,175

46. Charles Nicolletti: –Livingstone-*High_Treason_2*,468; –Waldron-*Legacy of Secrecy*,71,106

47. JFK's false hopes to exiles: –Sam Anson-*They've Killed the President*,269-270; –Blakey/Billings-*The Plot to Kill the President*,159-160; –Summers-*Conspiracy*,229-234

48. JFK's promise to N. Khrushchev: –Summers-*Conspiracy*,230; – Groden/Livingstone-*High Treason*,410

Chapter 6 - Who Was Lee Harvey Oswald?

1. Biographical data: –WR, Appendix 10I
2. Reading preferences: –WH19,319; –Waldron-*Legend/Assassination Chronicles*,350; –Summers-*Conspiracy*,113
3. Oswald's enlistment: –WR,607,681; –Sam Anson-*They've Killed the President*,156; –Waldron-*Legend/Assassination Chronicles*,350; –Summers-*Conspiracy*113; –Marrs-*Crossfire*,101
4. Atsugi was CIA base: –.WR,683;WCH8,298; –Sam Anson-*They've Killed the President*,156-157; –Marrs-*Crossfire*,103-104; –. . Summers-*Conspiracy*,114-116
5. Oswald's "secret" access: –.Summers-*Conspiracy,127*
6. The Queen Bee nightclub: –Marrs-*Crossfire*,107; –.Waldron-*Legend/Assassination Chronicles*,360-361,369-370; –Russell-*The Man Who Knew Too Much*,145 46
7. Court martials: –.WR,683; –Summers-*Conspiracy*,116; –Marrs-*Crossfire*,106
8. Early "hardship" discharge: –WR,689;WH19,736-737; –Waldron-*Legend/Assassination Chronicles*,377-378; –Summers-*Conspiracy*,119; –Marrs-*Crossfire*,111
9. Marina thinks Lee is Russian: –Summers-*Conspiracy*,157; –Waldron-*Legend/Assassination Chronicles*,419; –Marrs-*Crossfire*,125
10. Oswald's reading material: –*The Man Who Knew Too Much*,143; –Secret Service Report, 11/23/63
11. Russian language test: –WR,685;WH8,307;WH24,662; –Waldron-*Legend/Assassination Chronicles*,373; –Summers-*Conspiracy*,123-125; –Groden/Livingstone-*High Treason*,162
12. Monterey School of the Army: –.WC Exec. Session of 1/27/64; –Weisberg-*Whitewash IV*,101
13. Trip to Russia: –.WR,690; –Sam Anson-*They've Killed the President*,159-160; –Waldron-*Legend/Assassination Chronicles*,378-381; –Summers-*Conspiracy*,119-120; –Marrs-*Crossfire*,118
14. Embassy statement: –WR,260-261,748;CE917; –Waldron-*Legend/Assassination Chronicles*,381-383; –Summers-*Conspiracy*,120; –Marrs-*Crossfire*,119

15. "The Russians did it" theory: –Marrs-*Crossfire*,130-134; –Waldron-*Legend/Assassination Chronicles*,295,339; –Summers-*Conspiracy*,164-173; –Russell-*The Man Who Knew Too Much*,199,213-214,465-466

16. Loan for return trip: –WR,770; –Waldron-*Legend/Assassination Chronicles*,434; –Summers-*Conspiracy*,185; –Marrs-*Crossfire*,127

17. Route to Holland: –Summers-*Conspiracy*,185-186; –Marrs-*Crossfire*,127

18. Landing in U.S: –.WR,635; –Sam Anson-*They've Killed the President*,172; –Waldron-*Legend/Assassination Chronicles*,438-439; –Summers-*Conspiracy*,187

19. No action taken: –WR,434-435; –Sam Anson-*They've Killed the President*,173; –Summers-*Conspiracy*,189; –Hurt-*Reasonable Doubt*,217-218

20. DeMohrenschildt's suicide: –HSCR,217; –Waldron-*Legend/Assassination Chronicles*,555-557; –Summers-*Conspiracy*,192-201,206-212; –Groden/Livingstone-*High Treason*,130-131,145; –Marrs-*Crossfire*,285-287,564-565; –Livingstone-*High_Treason_2*,457; –Fonzi-*The Last Investigation*,192,742

21. Oswald at JCS in Dallas: –Summers-*Conspiracy*,200-201; –Waldron-*Legend/Assassination Chronicles*,472-474
 Hurt-*Reasonable Doubt*,219-222; –Russell-*The Man Who Knew Too Much*,269-270

22. Walker bullet:...Summers-*Conspiracy*,208; –Waldron-*Legacy of Secrecy*,264

23. Backyard photos ruled authentic: –.HSCR,55; –Summers-*Conspiracy*,64-69; –Groden/Livingstone-*High Treason*,172,200
 Waldron-*Legacy of Secrecy*,264

24. The Hunter of Fascists: –Summers-*Conspiracy*,211; –Waldron-*Legend/Assassination Chronicles*,489,560-561,647

25. Delphine Roberts' statements: –HSCR,145; –Summers-*Conspiracy*,293-297; –Hurt-*Reasonable Doubt*,291-292; –Groden/Livingstone-*High Treason*,289; –Garrison-*On the Trail of the Assassins*,48

26. Oswald offers help to exiles: –WH10,33-34;WH14,240; –Sam Anson-*They've Killed the President*,249-250; –Summers-*Conspiracy*,271-272; –Hurt-*Reasonable Doubt*,293; –Marrs-*Crossfire*,146; –Waldron-*Legacy of Secrecy*,260

27. Bringuier scuffle/arrest/FBI: –WR,382;WH4,432-433;WH11,358; –Sam Anson-*They've Killed the President*,249; –Summers-*Conspiracy*,271-277; –Hurt-*Reasonable Doubt*,293; –Marrs-*Crossfire*,146

28. FPCC leaflets, radio debate: –WH11,171,358;WH10,42; –Summers-*Conspiracy*,268-273, Marrs-*Crossfire*,146-147

29. Oswald at W. B. Reily Co: –WR,403; –Hurt-*Reasonable Doubt*,291; –Marrs-*Crossfire*,145; –Russell-*The Man Who Knew Too Much*,348

30. Alba's testimony: –Summers-*Conspiracy*,282-284; –Hurt-*Reasonable Doubt*,296

31. Oswald being manipulated?: –Garrison-*On the Trail of the Assassins*,80-81; –Russell-*The Man Who Knew Too Much*,404-405,671-677

32. False Oswald sightings: –WR318; –Lane-*Rush to Judgment*,334; –Popkin-*The Second Oswald*,63-94; –Summers-*Conspiracy*,375-393; –Marrs-*Crossfire*,545

33. CIA pictures of "Oswald": –WR,669 74; –Garrison-*On the Trail of the Assassins*,74; –Summers-*Conspiracy*,348-362; –Marrs-*Crossfire*,193-195; –Waldron-*Legacy of Secrecy*,213

34. CIA tape recording of "Oswald": –Summers-*Conspiracy*,359-360; –Marrs-*Crossfire*,195-196

35. "Leon's" statements per S. Odio: –.WH11,372;HSCH10,24; –Sam Anson-*They've Killed the President*,194-196; –Summers-*Conspiracy*,388; –Waldron-*Legacy of Secrecy*,178; –Hancock -*Someone Would Have Talked*,20-22

36. "Leon" Oswald: –Russell-*The Man Who Knew Too Much*,443-444

37. John T. Masen: –Evica-*And We Are All Mortal*,98-102; –Stone-*JFK: The Book of the Film*,166; –Russell-*The Man Who Knew Too Much*,541-545; –Hancock -*Someone Would Have Talked*,207-209

38. Hosty note: –Groden/Livingstone-*High Treason*,125; –Summers-*Conspiracy*,370-373; –Fonzi-*The Last Investigation*,256

39. Height variances: –.Sam Anson-*They've Killed the President*,208-210; –Garrison-*On the Trail of the Assassins*,65; –Marrs-*Crossfire*,549

40. LHO talks, acts differently: –Marrs-*Crossfire*,549

41. Hoover's memo on birth certif: –.Sam Anson-*They've Killed the President*,200; –Summers-*Conspiracy*,384; –Marrs-*Crossfire*,123,539

42. Frazier on paper bag: –Lane-*Rush to Judgment*,144-145; –Meagher-*Accessories After the Fact*,56

43. Oswald in lunchroom at 12:15: –Summers-*Conspiracy*,77-78; – Hurt-*Reasonable Doubt*,90-91; –Marrs-*Crossfire*,49-50
44. Oswald exits TSBD: –Roffman-*Presumed Guilty*,222-223; –Marrs-*Crossfire*,51-52
45. Oswald's morticians' statement: –.Marrs-*Crossfire*,551-553;
46. Burial vault broken: –Marrs-*Crossfire*,551-553
47. Sam Anson quote: –.Sam Anson-*They've Killed the President*,189-190
48. Robert Webster et al: –Russell-*The Man Who Knew Too Much*, xxv3 Waldron-*Legacy of Secrecy*, 381

Chapter 7. Jack Ruby. Screwball or Mob Pawn?
1. Ruby's alleged motive: –WR,349 50; –Sam Anson-*They've Killed the President*,220; –Blakey/Billings-*The Plot to Kill the President*,279-280; –Hurt-*Reasonable Doubt*,171
2. Ruby's mother is committed: –WR,691; –Sam Anson-*They've Killed the President*,230; –Kantor-*The Ruby Cover-up*,193; –Blakey/Billings-*The Plot to Kill the President*,282
3. Ruby sent to foster home: – WR,690; –Sam Anson-*They've Killed the President*,230; –Kantor-*The Ruby Cover-up*,193; –Blakey/Billings-*The Plot to Kill the President*,283; –Marrs-*Crossfire*,381
4. Capone's errand boy: –CE1288; –Sam Anson-*They've Killed the President*,230; –Kantor-*The Ruby Cover-up*,195; –Blakey/Billings-*The Plot to Kill the President*,283; –Marrs-*Crossfire*,381-382
5. Ruby's early employment: – Kantor-*The Ruby Cover-up*,195-198; –Sam Anson-*They've Killed the President*,232; –Blakey/Billings-*The Plot to Kill the President*,283-284
6. Ruby in California: –Sam Anson-*They've Killed the President*,232 Blakey/Billings-*The Plot to Kill the President*,284;
7. The Leon Cooke shooting: –Kantor-*The Ruby Cover-up*,198-199; –Sam Anson-*They've Killed the President*,232-233; –Blakey/Billings-*The Plot to Kill the President*,284-285;
8. Dorfman replaces Martin: –Kantor-*The Ruby Cover-up*,200; –Sam Anson-*They've Killed the President*,233-234; –Blakey/Billings-*The Plot to Kill the President*,284-285; –Marrs-*Crossfire*,383
9. The name change: –.Kantor-*The Ruby Cover-up*,203; –Sam Anson-*They've Killed the President*,234; –Marrs-*Crossfire*,384

10. Ruby goes to Dallas: –Kantor-*The Ruby Cover-up*,203-204; –Sam Anson-*They've Killed the President*,234; –Blakey/Billings-*The Plot to Kill the President*,285-286; –Marrs-*Crossfire*,384-385
11. Informant's story: –Blakey/Billings-*The Plot to Kill the President*,287
12. Ruby's Mob friends in 1947: –Marrs-*Crossfire*,385; –Sam Anson-*They've Killed the President*,234; –Blakey/Billings-*The Plot to Kill the President*,286;
13. Sheriff Guthrie's story: –Meagher-*Accessories After the Fact*,423-424; –Sam Anson-*They've Killed the President*,234-235; –Kantor-*The Ruby Cover-up*,205-209; –Blakey/Billings-*The Plot to Kill the President*,285-286;
14. Butler/Newman story: –Meagher-*Accessories After the Fact*,424; –Sam Anson-*They've Killed the President*,235; –Marrs-*Crossfire*,385
15. Recordings missing: –Kantor-*The Ruby Cover-up*,209; –Blakey/Billings-*The Plot to Kill the President*,285
16. Jones frequents Ruby's club: –Marrs-*Crossfire*,386; –Blakey/Billings-*The Plot to Kill the President*,286; –Hurt-*Reasonable Doubt*,173;
17. Ruby/Bonds relationship: –Kantor-*The Ruby Cover-up*,211-212; –Hurt-*Reasonable Doubt*,174
18. Ruby/Paul relationship: –.Kantor-*The Ruby Cover-up*,212-213; –Hurt-*Reasonable Doubt*,174
19. Ruby's failures and depression: –.Kantor-*The Ruby Cover-up*,213-214
20. Ruby as an FBI informant: –Sam Anson-*They've Killed the President*,237; –Model/Groden-*JFK: The Case for Conspiracy*,254
21. The jeep sale: –Sam Anson-*They've Killed the President*,239-240; –Model/Groden-*JFK: The Case for Conspiracy*,242-243; –Blakey/Billings-*The Plot to Kill the President*,295; –Marrs-*Crossfire*,395 96
22. Gun running with Rothman/Davis: – Marrs-*Crossfire*,391-392; –Kantor-*The Ruby Cover-up*,42-46, 264-265; –Hurt-*Reasonable Doubt*,400-405; –
23. N. P. Rich working for Ruby: –Lane-*Rush to Judgment*,288-289; –Model/Groden-*JFK: The Case for Conspiracy*,251
24. Meetings with the Colonel: –WH14,350; –Lane-*Rush to Judgment*,287-297; –Sam Anson-*They've Killed the President*,240-241; –Model/Groden-*JFK: The Case for Conspiracy*,251-253

25. Ruby's concern with New Orleans: –Hurt-*Reasonable Doubt*,180-181; –Blakey/Billings-*The Plot to Kill the President*,303; –Summers-*Conspiracy*,449-450

26. Mob control of strip clubs: –Blakey/Billings-*The Plot to Kill the President*,289-290

27. Joe Campisi: –Marrs-*Crossfire*,387; –Blakey/Billings-*The Plot to Kill the President*,313-314; –Waldron-*Legacy of Secrecy*,52

28. Joe Civello: –Marrs-*Crossfire*,388; –Blakey/Billings-*The Plot to Kill the President*,236,258,291,314; –Waldron-*Legacy of Secrecy*,104

29. Louis McWillie: –Marrs-*Crossfire*,389; –Evica-*And We Are All Mortal*,148,167,168,200,204-205; –Kantor-*The Ruby Cover-up*,40,250-255; –Blakey/Billings-*The Plot to Kill the President*,38,82,293-302,308; –Waldron-*Legacy of Secrecy*,49

30. Lennie Patrick: –Sam Anson-*They've Killed the President*,231; –Model/Groden-*JFK: The Case for Conspiracy*,236; –Kantor-*The Ruby Cover-up*,57-60, 75-76; –Marrs-*Crossfire*,388; –Blakey/Billings-*The Plot to Kill the President*,287-288,304-305

31. Dave Yaras: –Sam Anson-*They've Killed the President*,231-232; –Model/Groden-*JFK: The Case for Conspiracy*,236; –Kantor-*The Ruby Cover-up*,74-75; –Blakey/Billings-*The Plot to Kill the President*,287-288,304-305

32. Barney Baker: –Sam Anson-*They've Killed the President*,228; –Kantor-*The Ruby Cover-up*,52-53, 72-77; –Marrs-*Crossfire*,387; –Blakey-*The Plot to Kill the President*,304-305

33. Roselli et al: –Marrs-*Crossfire*,387-388; –Waldron-*Legacy of Secrecy*,......

34. Ruby's brutality: –Sam Anson-*They've Killed the President*,236-237; –Kantor-*The Ruby Cover-up*,216. Blakey/Billings-*The Plot to Kill the President*,292;

35. Ruby's arrest record: –Kantor-*The Ruby Cover-up*,215; –Marrs-*Crossfire*,391

36. Ruby's police friends: –Kantor-*The Ruby Cover-up*,117

37. Harrison shields Ruby .. Kantor-*The Ruby Cover-up*,144-145

38. Ruby's tipster?: –Kantor-*The Ruby Cover-up*,137-138

39. Butler acting very nervous: –WH15,593-595; –Kantor-*The Ruby Cover-up*,136; –Meagher-*Accessories After the Fact*,425; –Sam Anson-*They've Killed the President*,236

40. Ruby at 12:30, 11/22/63: –Sam Anson-*They've Killed the President*,220; –Model/Groden-*JFK: The Case for Conspiracy*,232-233; –Kantor-*The Ruby Cover-up*,84-86; –Hurt-*Reasonable Doubt*,84-86

41. Ruby at Parkland Hospital: –WH15,79 81,388-396; –Meagher-*Accessories After the Fact*,394-397; –Sam Anson-*They've Killed the President*,220; –Kurtz-*Crime of the Century*,12; –Kantor-*The Ruby Cover-up*,88-89. Blakey/Billings-*The Plot to Kill the President*,315;

42. Ruby at police headquarters: –Meagher-*Accessories After the Fact*,428-429; –Sam Anson-*They've Killed the President*,221; –Kantor-*The Ruby Cover-up*,96-99
Blakey/Billings-*The Plot to Kill the President*,317; –Hurt-*Reasonable Doubt*,185

43. Ruby at first press conference: –.Kantor-*The Ruby Cover-up*,99-101
Sam Anson-*They've Killed the President*,221; –Blakey/Billings-*The Plot to Kill the President*,317-318;

44. Ruby corrects DA Wade: –Kantor-*The Ruby Cover-up*,101; –Sam Anson-*They've Killed the President*,221; –Hurt-*Reasonable Doubt*,186

45. Ruby meets Olsen/Coleman: –Kantor-*The Ruby Cover-up*,103

46. Ruby, Senator, Crafard at sign: –Kantor-*The Ruby Cover-up*,108-110

47. Ruby inquires about transfer: –WH15,491; –Meagher-*Accessories After the Fact*,404; –Sam Anson-*They've Killed the President*,222; –Kantor-*The Ruby Cover-up*,114; –Blakey/Billings-*The Plot to Kill the President*,319

48. Ruby back at the station: –Kantor-*The Ruby Cover-up*,114-116
Blakey/Billings-*The Plot to Kill the President*,319;

49. Warning phone calls: –Weisberg-*Whitewash*,172-174; –Weisberg-*Whitewash* II,57-62; –Meagher-*Accessories After the Fact*,398-401; –Kantor-*The Ruby Cover-up*,120; –Hurt-*Reasonable Doubt*,407-408

50. Ruby's reaction to LHO's death: –Taped interview with Jack Anderson

51. Sunday AM calls to Ruby: –Kantor-*The Ruby Cover-up*,123-124; –Blakey/Billings-*The Plot to Kill the President*,320; –Waldron-*Legacy of Secrecy*,235-236

52. Ruby outside station at 11 AM: –Blakey/Billings-*The Plot to Kill the President*,320

53. Ruby's access via ramp: –Kantor-*The Ruby Cover-up*,140; –Meagher-*Accessories After the Fact*,404-419; –Blakey/Billings-*The Plot to Kill the President*,321

54. On elevator with TV crew: –Kantor-*The Ruby Cover-up*,144

55. Ruby's note to Tonahill: –Kantor-*The Ruby Cover-up*,130
Sam Anson-*They've Killed the President*,229; –Blakey/Billings-*The Plot to Kill the President*,333;

56. Ruby's insanity defense: –Kantor-*The Ruby Cover-up*,228-229; –Meagher-*Accessories After the Fact*,392; –Sam Anson-*They've Killed the President*,224; –Blakey/Billings-*The Plot to Kill the President*,331-332

57. Ruby's financial situation: –Hurt-*Reasonable Doubt*,181
Blakey/Billings-*The Plot to Kill the President*,307;

58. Ruby asks to go to DC: –WH5,194; –Lane-*Rush to Judgment*,243-245; –Blakey/Billings-*The Plot to Kill the President*,335-336; –Summers-*Conspiracy*,431-432; –Hurt-*Reasonable Doubt*,188-189; –Waldron-*Legacy of Secrecy*,309

59. Taped interview: –Hurt-*Reasonable Doubt*,189

60. Beverly Oliver: –Kantor-*The Ruby Cover-up*,393-394; –Marrs-*Crossfire*,36-37

61. Wally Weston: –Marrs-*Crossfire*,406-407

62. Ester Ann Marsh: –ibid.,408-409

63. William Crowe Jr: –ibid.,404

64. Janet Adams Conforto: –ibid.,406

65. Raymond Cummings.ibid: –,404

66. Madelaine Brown: –ibid.

67. General Walker: –ibid.,403

68. Ruby's death: –Marrs-*Crossfire*,429-433; –Sam Anson-*They've Killed the President*,245; –Blakey/Billings-*The Plot to Kill the President*,338; –Waldron-*Legacy of Secrecy*,387

Chapter 8 - The Case Against Oswald

1. The "Mauser" ID: —See Note 4 in chap. 3
2. No oil on paper package; —Meagher-*Accessories After the Fact*,62-63
3. Scope was useless: —WH3,443-444; —Meagher-*Accessories After the Fact*,106-110; —Waldron-*Legacy of Secrecy*,194
4. FBI experts' test results: —WH3,402-406; —Hurt-*Reasonable Doubt*,100-01
5. Rifle's chain-of-possession: —Hurt-*Reasonable Doubt*,107-109; —Brown-*The People v. Lee Harvey Oswald*,326-327
6. Dented cartridge case: —See Note 21 in chapter I
7. Casings handled separately: —Thompson-*Six Seconds in Dallas*,142-143; —Brown-*People V. Lee Harvey Oswald*,199-200
8. C399 chain-of-possession: —Thompson-*Six Seconds in Dallas*,156; —Brown-*People V. Lee Harvey Oswald*,253-254
9. Frazier/Randle on bag length: —See Note 28 in chap. 10.
10. Brennan's ID of Oswald: —See Note 34 in chap. I
11. Brennan saw shooter "standing,": —WH3,144; —Lane-*Rush to Judgment*,83-85
12. Brennan sees slow withdrawal: —WH3,144; —Lane-*Rush to Judgment*,85; —Hurt-*Reasonable Doubt*,89
13. Tippit slugs unmatchable: —See Note 33 in chap. 10.
14. Shell casings called "automatic": —See Note 27 in chap. I
15. Non-pairing of casings and slugs: —.See Note 33 in chap. 10.
16. Poe can't ID shells: —WH3,68-69;WH24,415; —Lane-*Rush to Judgment*,197-198; —Hurt-*Reasonable Doubt*,153-154
17. Oswald leaves room at 1:03: —.WH6,438-40; —Belin-*Nov. 22, 1963: You Are the Jury*,418-419–Hurt-*Reasonable Doubt*,139-140
18. Shooting reported at 1:16: —See Note 25 in chap. 1
19. .Burroughs sees Oswald in theater: —.Marrs- *Crossfire, 352-353*
20. Markham says Tippit shot at 1:07: —See Note 30 in chap. 10.
21. Benevides/Bowley use radio: —Lane-*Rush to Judgment*,178,179; —Hurt-*Reasonable Doubt*,141
22. Wright and Clemmons: —Lane-*Rush to Judgment*,193-194; —Summers-*Conspiracy*,90-91; —Hurt-*Reasonable Doubt*,148-149

Chapter 9 - The Enigma of Dealey Plaza

1. JFK behind sign at Zap. 210: –Meagher-*Accessories After the Fact*,28-29; –Evica-*And We Are All Mortal*,71; –Summers-*Conspiracy*,13; –Marrs-*Crossfire*,66
2. Drs. say Connally would react sooner: –WCH4,115-16; –Meagher-*Accessories After the Fact*,30; –Lifton-*Best Evidence*,73
3. Humes learns of throat wound: –WCH6,16,WCH3,380; –Meagher-*Accessories After the Fact*,144-146; –Weisberg-*Post Mortem*,150; –Lifton-*Best Evidence*,81-82; –Marrs-*Crossfire*,372
4. Head-shot simulation: –Livingstone-*High_Treason_2*,372
5. Dallas Drs. say X-rays false: –Livingstone-*High_Treason_2*, 286-287,313-339
6. First shot struck the President: –Lane-*Rush to Judgment*,72-73; –Thompson-*Six Seconds in Dallas*,34-38
7. HSCA finds wounds' angle upward: –HSCH7,175; –Kurtz-*Crime of the Century*,173
8. Tree obscures view until Z210: –WR105; –Meagher-*Accessories After the Fact*,28; –Weisberg-*Post Mortem*,90,108,383; –Evica-*And We Are All Mortal*,68
9. Police tape's validity: –HSCR,67-78;Groden/Livingstone-*High Treason*, 240-261; –Summers-*Conspiracy*,474-476; –Blakey/Billings-*The Plot to Kill the President*,91-107
10. Thomas's analysis: –Smith-*The Plot to Stop the Kennedys*,70; –Science & Justice (the journal of Britain's Forensic Science Society,Vol. 41,21-32
11. CE 399 not like fragments: –Evica-*And We Are All Mortal*,75-84
12. Six "blasts" on police tape: –HSCR,68-71; –Groden/Livingstone-*High Treason*,242-246
13. Shirt hole picture upside down: –Weisberg-*Post Mortem*,331
14. Stretcher bullet "pointed": –Groden/Livingstone-*High Treason*,235; –Thompson-*Six Seconds in Dallas*,175; –Hurt-*Reasonable Doubt*,70; –Livingstone-*HighTreason 2*,209-210.
15. The first miss: –WH7,508-09;WH6,238; –Popkin-*The Second Oswald*,99; –. . Meagher-*Accessories After the Fact*,31-32
16. TSBD rifle not a Mannlicher?: –WH5,560;WH7,108;WH24,228; –WH3,295;WH14,507-509; –Lane-*Rush to Judgment*,114-120; –Evica-*And We Are All Mortal*, first 5 chapters; –Hurt-*Reasonable Doubt*,102-103

17. Fragments left in Connally's body: –WH6,111;WH2,376; –Meagher-*Accessories After the Fact*,169-170; –Weisberg-*Post Mortem*,83; –Livingstone-*High_Treason_2*,312

18. The Harper skull fragment: –Weisberg-*Post Mortem*,80,81; –Thompson-*Six Seconds in Dallas*,101,108; –Summers-*Conspiracy*,32

19. Part of JFK's scalp gone: –Groden/Livingstone-*High Treason*,39-40,458-460
 Thompson-*Six Seconds in Dallas*,113;

20. SS men describe "flurry": –WCH2,76,78,79; –Thompson-*Six Seconds in Dallas*,96-97; –Summers-*Conspiracy*,19,21; –Livingstone-*High_Treason_2*,71

21. Tilson's chase of a suspect: –Summers-*Conspiracy*,51-52

22. Tramps "identified": –Livingstone-*High_Treason_2*,570,609-610

23. Brading detained, released: –Hurt-*Reasonable Doubt*,123-124; –Scheim-*Contract on America*,45-47; –Groden/Livingstone-*High Treason*,121,185,305

24. Roger Craig sees a "getaway": –Lane-*Rush to Judgment*,173-174; –Hurt-*Reasonable Doubt*,124-125; –Groden/Livingstone-*High Treason*,132; –Law/Hancock -*Someone Would Have Talked*,394

25. One of cartridges dented: –Thompson-*Six Seconds in Dallas*,143-145

26. Carr sees "backup man" escape: –Hurt-*Reasonable Doubt*,119; –Groden/Livingstone-*High Treason*,139-140

27. Fragment caused throat wound: –Thompson-*Six Seconds in Dallas*

28. Shirt holes were "cuts": –Weisberg-*Post Mortem*,332,598; –Hurt-*Reasonable Doubt*,60

29. Livingstone on the DP tape: –Livingstone-*Killing the Truth*,356,382

30. Chambers on police tape odds: –*Head Shot: the Science Behind the JFK Assassination*,142-143

31. Frazier on 399 striations: –WH3,430-431

32. Weight of bullets: –WH3,430; –Thompson-*Six Seconds in Dallas*,151

33. No blood or tissue on CE 399: –WH3,429; –Weisberg-*Whitewash*,292-293; –Weisberg-*Post Mortem*,95; –Lifton-*Best Evidence*,88,212

34. Clark panel finds more lead: –See note 17 in chapter 3

Chapter 10 – Conclusions

1. Rifle experts fail test: –WH3,444-446; –Weisberg-*Whitewash*,69; –Lane-*Rush to Judgment*,125-129; –Meagher-*Accessories After the Fact*,107-109
2. Dr. Burkley's death certificate: –Weisberg-*Post Mortem*,304,308-309; –Kurtz-*Crime of the Century*,69-70; –Groden/Livingstone-*High Treason*,98
3. Bullet angle through Connally: –Lane-*Rush to Judgment*,74-75; –Meagher-*Accessories After the Fact*,32; –Kurtz-*Crime of the Century*,82; –Groden/Livingstone-*High Treason*,265
4. HSCA placement of shot #1: –HSCR,79-81
5. JFK's back wound angle: –Lane-*Rush to Judgment*,74-75; –Meagher-*Accessories After the Fact*,32-33; –Weisberg-*Post Mortem*,225,535; –Groden/Livingstone-*High Treason*,94,265
6. Size of the throat wound: –WH17,29; –Thompson-*Six Seconds in Dallas*,51-52; –Weisberg-*Post Mortem*,508; –Kurtz-*Crime of the Century*,70,74; –Groden/Livingstone-*High Treason*,95,262-263
7. Parkland Drs. say, "entrance": –Lane-*Rush to Judgment*,47,51-54; –Meagher-*Accessories After the Fact*,150-154; –Thompson-*Six Seconds in Dallas*,51-52; –Kurtz-*Crime of the Century*,70-72; –Lifton-*Best Evidence*,56-58
8. Autopsy Drs. on back wound: –Lifton-*Best Evidence*,159; –Meagher-*Accessories After the Fact*,144-145; –Thompson-*Six Seconds in Dallas*,43-44; –Hurt-*Reasonable Doubt*,39-40; –Groden/Livingstone-*High Treason*,94-95
9. Witnesses to probe attempts: –Lifton-*Best Evidence*,612-613; –Hurt-*Reasonable Doubt*,39-40; –Livingstone-*High_Treason_2*,161-163
10. FBI report on back wound: –Thompson-*Six Seconds in Dallas*,43; –Weisberg-*Post Mortem*,535
11. No metallic traces on shirt: –Thompson-*Six Seconds in Dallas*,52; –Weisberg-*Post Mortem*,204,358,598; –Kurtz-*Crime of the Century*,75
12. Kellerman hears JFK speak: –WH2,73;WH18,724; –Thompson-*Six Seconds in Dallas*,39; –Sam Anson-*They've Killed the President*,82
13. Fragments from Connally: –Thompson-*Six Seconds in Dallas*,147-150; –Weisberg-*Post Mortem*,506; –Sam Anson-*They've Killed the President*,81
14. Drs. on bullet CE 399: –Lane-*Rush to Judgment*,77; –Thompson-*Six Seconds in Dallas*,148-150; –Sam Anson-*They've Killed the President*,81; –Groden/Livingstone-*High Treason*,64-65

15. Commissioners dissent on 399: –Epstein-*Inquest*,148-149; –Sam Anson-*They've Killed the President*,52; –Groden/Livingstone-*High Treason*,67

16. C. Arnold sees LHO in lunchroom: –Marrs-*Crossfire*,49; –Thompson-*Six Seconds in Dallas*,234-235; –Roffman-*Presumed Guilty*,184-186; –Hurt-*Reasonable Doubt*,90-91; –Summers-*Conspiracy*,77-78; –Hancock -*Someone Would Have Talked*,71-71

17. Two men seen on sixth floor: –Lane-*Rush to Judgment*,397; –Thompson-*Six Seconds in Dallas*,235-240; –Roffman-*Presumed Guilty*,189; –Summers-*Conspiracy*,42-43; –Hurt-*Reasonable Doubt*,91-93; –Marrs-*Crossfire*,20-21,50

18. Officer Baker encounters LHO: –WH3,221-25,250-252; –Meagher-*Accessories After the Fact*,70-72; –Belin-*Nov. 22, 1963: You Are the Jury*,258-265

19. Vestibule window problem: –Weisberg-*Whitewash*,87; –Roffman-*Presumed Guilty*,217-218

20. Coke or no Coke?: –Weisberg-*Whitewash* 2,77-79; –Meagher-*Accessories After the Fact*,74; –Summers-*Conspiracy*,80; –Marrs-*Crossfire*,51

21. LHO's appearance at encounter: –Weisberg-*Whitewash*,88; –Meagher-*Accessories After the Fact*,71; –Roffman-*Presumed Guilty*,222; –Summers-*Conspiracy*,80

22 Baker-Oswald re-enactment: –WH3,228-54; –Roffman-*Presumed Guilty*,201-224; –Summers-*Conspiracy*,80-81; –Weisberg-Case Open,117-124

23. Paraffin test results: –WR,560; –Lane-*Rush to Judgment*,148-151; –Meagher-*Accessories After the Fact*,171; –Weisberg-*Post Mortem*,437-438,446; –Groden/Livingstone-*High Treason*,175; –North-*Act of Treason*,409-410

24. Rifle problems: –CE549;WH3,406-07;WH17,245; –CE2560;WH15,799; –Brown-*The People v. Lee Harvey Oswald*,624-625

25. LHO's "marksmanship": –Lane-*Rush to Judgment*,123-124; –Roffman-*Presumed Guilty*,229-234; –Hurt-*Reasonable Doubt*,99-100

26. Lack of practice opportunity: –Meagher-*Accessories After the Fact*,131-133; –Roffman-*Presumed Guilty*,231-247

27. Experts' test results: –Meagher-*Accessories After the Fact*,107-109; –Hurt-*Reasonable Doubt*,100-101

28. The brown paper bag: –Lane-*Rush to Judgment*,142-147; –Meagher-*Accessories After the Fact*,55-57; –Roffman-*Presumed Guilty*,162-166
29. Gen E. Walker's hatred for JFK: –Summers-*Conspiracy*,205-206; –Meagher-*Accessories After the Fact*,128-131; –North-*Act of Treason*,247,253, 331-332,371
30. Fixing time of Tippit's death: –Lane-*Rush to Judgment*,187-188; –Kurtz-*Crime of the Century*,1341-36; –Hurt-*Reasonable Doubt*,144; –Marrs-*Crossfire*,348
31. Oswald-to-Tippit re-enactment: –Kurtz-*Crime of the Century*,134; –TV special hosted by James Earl Jones in 1992
32. Tippit's killer was going west: –Curry-*JFK Assassination File*,84; –Lane-*Rush to Judgment*,191; –Summers-*Conspiracy*,94; –Hurt-*Reasonable Doubt*,149-150
33. Problems with physical evidence: –WR,559,560; –Lane-*Rush to Judgment*,196-200; –Meagher-*Accessories After the Fact*,280-282; –Summers-*Conspiracy*,88-89; –Hurt-*Reasonable Doubt*,143; –Marrs-*Crossfire*,343
34. Murder weapon an automatic: –Curry-*JFK Assassination File*,68; –Summers-*Conspiracy*,89
35. Eyewitness ID of Oswald: –Lane-*Rush to Judgment*,176-195; –Meagher-*Accessories After the Fact*,255-257; –Hurt-*Reasonable Doubt*,145-147; –Marrs-*Crossfire*,340-342
36. Some witnesses saw 2 assailants: –Lane-*Rush to Judgment*,193-194; –Summers-*Conspiracy*,90-91; –Hurt-*Reasonable Doubt*,148-149; –Marrs-*Crossfire*,342
37. Passage to the USSR expedited: –Sam Anson-*They've Killed the President*,160; –Summers-*Conspiracy*,119-120; –Marrs-*Crossfire*,118
38. Oswald offers classified info: –Sam Anson-*They've Killed the President*,161; –Waldron-*Legend/Assassination Chronicles*,383;
39. Marina's uncle's background: –.Sam Anson-*They've Killed the President*,59,165; –Waldron-*Legend/Assassination Chronicles*,417-418
40. Loan for passage back home: –WR,770; –Sam Anson-*They've Killed the President*,169; –Waldron-*Legend/Assassination Chronicles*,432-433; –Summers-*Conspiracy*,185; –Marrs-*Crossfire*,127
41. Other "defectors" sent to spy: –Summers-*Conspiracy*,147-151; –Marrs-*Crossfire*,116-117
42. Oswald is "all right"; –Weisberg-*Oswald in New Orleans*,31; –Summers-*Conspiracy*,104,179,189; –Marrs-*Crossfire*,189-90

43. The Minox 3 camera: –.Summers-*Conspiracy*,202; –Marrs-*Crossfire*,190-91
44. Oswald's activities in New Orleans: –Summers-*Conspiracy*,262-315; –Marrs-*Crossfire*,145-149
 Weisberg-*Oswald in New Orleans*,passim
45. False Oswald appearances: –See Note 32 for chapter 6
46. Kerry Thornley's movements: –Garrison-*On the Trail of the Assassins*,81-87
47. J. T. Masen, Oswald double: –See Note 37 in chapter 6
48. False Oswald in Mexico City: –See Notes 33 & 34 in chapter 6
49. Ruby pleads to be moved: –See Note 58 in chapter 7
50. Ruby's Mafia connections: –See Notes 26-33 in chapter 7
51. Ruby's financial problems: –See Note 57 in chapter 7
52. Ruby's police connections: –See Notes 36-39 in chapter 7
53. Some officers had mob ties: –Kantor-*The Ruby Cover-up*,30-31,
54. Charles Harrelson: –Hurt-*Reasonable Doubt*,349; –Marrs-*Crossfire*,333-337; –Livingstone-*High_Treason_2*,77; –Giancana-*Double Cross*,334; –A&E's *The Men Who Killed Kennedy*, June of 1992
55. Lucien Sarti: –.Summers-*Conspiracy*,523-527; –Marrs-*Crossfire*,208-209; –A&E's *The Men Who Killed Kennedy*, June of 1992
56. Jean Souetre: –Summers-*Conspiracy*,622; –Hurt-*Reasonable Doubt*,414-419
 Marrs-*Crossfire*,207-208; –Russell-*The Man Who Knew Too Much*,557-564; –Waldron-*Legacy of Secrecy*,69-70,108,230-231; –Hancock-*Someone Would Have Talked*,455-456
57. Roscoe White: –Double Cross,335; –Livingstone-*High_Treason_2*,463-469
58. Jack Lawrence: –Hurt-*Reasonable Doubt*,126-127; –Marrs-*Crossfire*,339-340; –Giancana-*Double Cross*,334
59. Eugene Brading alias Jim Braden: –Summers-*Conspiracy*,452-453; –Evica-*And We All Are Mortal*,165-167; –Hurt-*Reasonable Doubt*,123-124; –Groden/Livingstone-*High Treason*,318-319; –Marrs-*Crossfire*,337-339
60. Pironti & Bocognoni: –Marrs-*Crossfire*,209
61. "Oswald's" escape: –Lane-*Rush to Judgment*,173-174; –Hurt-*Reasonable Doubt*,119-121; –Marrs-*Crossfire*,328-332
62. John T. Masen: –See Note 37 in chapter 6

63. E. Howard Hunt: —See Note 4 in chapter 5; —Sam Anson-*They've Killed the President*,288-289; —Lane-*Plausible Denial*,130-131,152-156,182-188,296-299, 321-22

64. Frank (Sturgis) Fiorini: —See Note 5 in chapter 5; —Groden/Livingstone-*High Treason*,347-349; —Lane-*Plausible Denial*,294-297

65. Pedro Diaz Lanz: —See Note 42 in chapter 5

66. Guy Banister: —See Note 31 in chapter 5

67. David Ferrie: —See Note 33 & 34 in chapter 5

68. David Atlee Phillips alias Maurice Bishop: —See Note 23 in chapter 5

69. Clay Shaw alias Clem Bertrand: —Russell-*The Man Who Knew Too Much*,444; —Garrison-*On the Trail of the Assassins*,100-104

70. Jack Ruby, mob hitman: —Kantor-*The Ruby Cover-up*,409-410; —Summers-*Conspiracy*,446-451,471; —Scheim-*Contract on America*,255-269,. Groden/Livingstone-*High Treason*,380,413,. Sam Anson-*They've Killed the President*,243-245;

71. Assistant Chief Batchelor: —Groden/Livingstone-*High Treason*,188,236-237;

72. William Harrison: —Kantor-*The Ruby Cover-up*,137-138,144-145,283-284; —Summers-*Conspiracy*,465-466;

73. George Butler: —Sam Anson-*They've Killed the President*,236; —Kantor-*The Ruby Cover-up*,136-137; —Summers-*Conspiracy*,467; —Groden/Livingstone-*High Treason*,188

74. John Roselli: —.Sam Anson-*They've Killed the President*,298-299; —Evica-*And We Are All Mortal*,207-217,259-265; —Summers-*Conspiracy*,238-239,495-496,412-413,527-528; —Groden/Livingstone-*High Treason*,154,312,378-380; —Waldron-*Legacy of Secrecy*,40-61,65,98

75. Robert Maheau: —Sam Anson-*They've Killed the President*,299; —Evica-*And We Are All Mortal*,207-215,237-243; —Summers-*Conspiracy*,238,496,594; —Groden/Livingstone-*High Treason*,154,312,378-379,412-413; —Waldron-*Legacy of Secrecy*,705-706

76. Santos Trafficante Jr: —Evica-*And We Are All Mortal*,276-91; —Summers-*Conspiracy*,239-240,254-255,499-500; —Hurt-*Reasonable Doubt*,178-179; —Scheim-*Contract on America*,51-60; —Waldron-*Legacy of Secrecy*,42-46

77. Carlos Marcello: –Summers-*Conspiracy*,256-261,308-313,500-504; –Hurt-*Reasonable Doubt*,183,185,284-286; –Scheim-*Contract on America*,54-65,231-235; –Davis-*Mafia Kingfish*,passim; –Waldron-*Legacy of Secrecy*,42-44

78. Sam Giancana: –.Evica-*And We Are All Mortal*,249-252; –Summers-*Conspiracy*,238-240,248-51,494-495,527-528; –Marrs-*Crossfire*,175-179; –Giancana-*Double Cross*,334-335

79. William Harvey: –Evica-*And We Are All Mortal*,255-259; –Summers-*Conspiracy*,137,226,470-471,528-531; –Groden/Livingstone-*High Treason*,312-313; –Russell-*The Man Who Knew Too Much*,245-247

80. Gen. E. Lansdale: –Evica-*And We Are All Mortal*,255-257; –Russell-*The Man Who Knew Too Much*,244-246

81. Col. S. Edwards: –Evica-*And We Are All Mortal*,208-210,248-249; Fensterwald-*Coincidence or Conspiracy*,81-82,156-158,166-168; –Groden/Livingstone-*High Treason*,311-313

82. Gen. Charles Cabell: –.Garrison-*On the Trail of the Assassins*,119-121,204; –Groden/Livingstone-*High Treason*,154,306,311-315

83. Richard Bissell: –Evica-*And We Are All Mortal*,208-210; –Groden/Livingstone-*High Treason*,311,410,439

84. David Morales: –Fonzi-*The Last Investigation*,366-373; –Waldron-*Legacy of Secrecy*,37-39

85. Earl Cabell: –Garrison-*On the Trail of the Assassins*,118,375; –Groden/Livingstone-*High Treason*,154

86. Allen Dulles: –.Groden/Livingstone-*High Treason*,311,433-435; –Lane-*Plausible Denial*,164-165

87. Lyndon Johnson: –Marrs-*Crossfire*,223-26,239-40,289,295-298; –Groden/Livingstone-*High Treason*,234-235,282,290,309,416,433; –North-*Act of Treason*,51-54; –Waldron-*Legacy of Secrecy*,225-230,244-246

88. J. Edgar Hoover: –(same as above)

89. Regis Kennedy: –Summers-*Conspiracy*,496-497; –Marrs-*Crossfire*,36; –Groden/Livingstone-*High Treason*,121,420

90. H.L Hunt: –Groden/Livingstone-*High Treason*,305; –Russell-*The Man Who Knew Too Much*,521-522,586-594,606-607

91. Clint Murchison: –Groden/Livingstone-*High Treason*,237,281-282,305; –Russell-*The Man Who Knew Too Much*,520-524

92. James Angleton: –Evica-*And We Are All Mortal*,325; –Groden/Livingstone-*High Treason*,333; –Lane-*Plausible Denial*,164-166; –Russell-*The Man Who Knew Too Much*,460-462,475-477,614; –Waldron-*Legacy of Secrecy*,208-210

93. Richard Helms: –*They've Killed the President*,122,346; –Evica-*And We Are All Mortal*,158; –Kantor-*The Ruby Cover-up*,186,188-189,308-309; –Groden/Livingstone-*High Treason*,107,186,189; –Lane-*Plausible Denial*,57-58; –Russell-*The Man Who Knew Too Much*,459,475,494,497,614; –Waldron-*Legacy of Secrecy*,201-206,212-215

94. Gerald Ford: –Evica-*And We Are All Mortal*,48-50; –Hurt-*Reasonable Doubt*,32-33; –Groden/Livingstone-*High Treason*,5,268-269,330; –Lane-*Plausible Denial*,43,374; –Russell-*The Man Who Knew Too Much*,709

95. Richard Nixon: –Marrs-*Crossfire*,271-274; –Sam Anson-*They've Killed the President*,275, 287-288,295; –Evica-*And We Are All Mortal*,234-235,316; –Summers-*Conspiracy*,132-133,522-523; –Groden/Livingstone-*High Treason*,191-192,283,332-333; –Lane-*Plausible Denial*,110-111; –Russell-*The Man Who Knew Too Much*,690,709

96. Hosty's note: –WR,195; –Sam Anson-*They've Killed the President*,185; –Waldron-*Legend/Assassination Chronicles*,530,655; –Marrs-*Crossfire*,239; –Groden/Livingstone-*High Treason*,125,185,308

97. Limo cleaned, rebuilt: –Hurt-*Reasonable Doubt*,84; –Marrs-*Crossfire*,239; –Groden/Livingstone-*High Treason*,86-87

98. Connally's clothing laundered: –Groden/Livingstone-*High Treason*,119; –Thompson-*Six Seconds in Dallas*,14,131,171-72

99. JFK's brain missing: –Kurtz-*Crime of the Century*,100; –Hurt-*Reasonable Doubt*,53-57; –Livingstone-*High_Treason_2*,557

100. Slides Missing: –Weisberg-*Post Mortem*,358-59; –Kurtz-*Crime of the Century*,100; –Hurt-*Reasonable Doubt*,57; –Marrs-*Crossfire*,377; –Groden/Livingstone-*High Treason*,119; –Livingstone-*High_Treason_2*,557

101. X-rays missing: –WH2,364; –Weisberg-*Post Mortem*,162-163, 215; –Kurtz-*Crime of the Century*,87; –Marrs-*Crossfire*,377; –Groden/Livingstone-*High_Treason_2*,209

102. Chest cavity photos: –Hurt-*Reasonable Doubt*,55-57; –Groden/Livingstone-*High Treason*,119; –Livingstone-*High_Treason_2*,212,321

103. Pointed-nose bullet: —See Note 15 for chapter 9
104. Original dictabelt: —Groden/Livingstone-*High Treason*,123
105. Original Nix movie film: —See Note 12 for chapter 3
106. Interrogation records missing: —Meagher-*Accessories After the Fact*,223; —Groden/Livingstone-*High Treason*,188
107. Mexico City photos & tapes: —Summers-*Conspiracy*,522-523; —Groden/Livingstone-*High Treason*,121; —Russell-*The Man Who Knew Too Much*,462-463; —Waldron-*Legacy of Secrecy*,213-214
108. Contents of Oswald's 201 file: —Summers-*Conspiracy*,133-139; —Marrs-*Crossfire*,191-192; —Groden/Livingstone-*High Treason*,107
109. Oswald's military intel. file: —Hurt-*Reasonable Doubt*,237-239; —Groden/Livingstone-*High Treason*,162
110. Stemmons Freeway sign: —Meagher-*Accessories After the Fact*,33; —Groden/Livingstone-*High Treason*,121
111. Zapruder frames doctored: —Marrs-*Crossfire*,69; —Livingstone-*High_Treason_2*,363-366
112. Zapruder frames switched: —Sam Anson-*They've Killed the President*,84; —Hurt-*Reasonable Doubt*,129; —Marrs-*Crossfire*,67; —Groden/Livingstone-*High Treason*,117
113. Head wound enlarged: —Lifton-*Best Evidence*,308-320; —Groden/Livingstone-*High Treason*,37
114. Tracheostomy incision enlarged: —Lifton-*Best Evidence*,271-278; —Marrs-*Crossfire*,372
115. Autopsy photos falsified: —Marrs-*Crossfire*,377-378; —Groden/Livingstone-*High Treason*,37-40; —Livingstone-*High_Treason_2*,317-321,339
116. Head X-rays falsified: —Livingstone-*High_Treason_2*,210-211,213,363
117. Back wound relocated: —Hurt-*Reasonable Doubt*,53-54; —Livingstone-*High_Treason_2*,160-164
118. Head entrance wound relocated: —Summers-*Conspiracy*,11; —Hurt-*Reasonable Doubt*,50-53; —Groden/Livingstone-*High Treason*,34,37; —Livingstone-*High_Treason_2*,157-158,339
119. Head exit wound relocated: —Groden/Livingstone-*High Treason*,37; —Livingstone-*High_Treason_2*,152-157
120. Curbstone patched: —Hurt-*Reasonable Doubt*,130
121. Survey drawings altered: —Marrs-*Crossfire*,454-457
122. Walker photo mutilated: —Marrs-*Crossfire*,259; —Groden/Livingstone-*High Treason*,212

123. Zapruder movie suppressed: —Sam Anson-*They've Killed the President*,84; —Hurt-*Reasonable Doubt*,128
124. Autopsy photos, X-rays suppressed: —Marrs-*Crossfire*,378; —Livingstone-*High_Treason_2*,107,286
125. Brass prevents probe of back: —See Note 5 for chapter 2I
126. Autopsy personnel gagged: —See Note 25 for chapter 2
127. Bullet/fragment test results: —Weisberg-*Post Mortem*,403-466; —Sam Anson-*They've Killed the President*,90-92; —Hurt-*Reasonable Doubt*,135-138
128. HSCA test done on wrong fragments: —Kurtz-*Crime of the Century*,181-182; —Hurt-*Reasonable Doubt*,82,86; —Marrs-*Crossfire*,447-448; —Groden/Livingstone-*High Treason*,69,73-74,118; —Livingstone-*Killing the Truth*,62
129. Page of Oswald's address book: —HSCR,186,244; —Meagher-*Accessories After the Fact*,211; —Sam Anson-*They've Killed the President*,183; —Hurt-*Reasonable Doubt*,251
130. Castro plots hidden from WC: —Summers-*Conspiracy*,132; —Blakey/Billings-*The Plot to Kill the President*,52-53; —Waldron-*Legacy of Secrecy*,301-303
131. Beverly Oliver's film stolen: —Marrs-*Crossfire*,36; —Groden/Livingstone-*High Treason*,121-122
132. Moorman photos suppressed: —Marrs-*Crossfire*,38; —Groden/Livingstone-*High Treason*,123
133. Moorman's "badgeman" photo: —Marrs-*Crossfire*,79-81; —Groden/Livingstone-*High Treason*,123,462
134. Chicago and Miami warnings: —Waldron-*Legacy of Secrecy*,193; —Groden/Livingstone-*High Treason*,13-14,158-159; —Hancock -*Someone Would Have Talked*,242-245
135. Chaney sees separate shots: —WH2,43-45;WH3,266;WH4,161; —Weisberg-*Never Again*,395
136. C. Arnold's sighting of Oswald: —Meagher-*Accessories After the Fact*,225; —Marrs-*Crossfire*,49; —Groden/Livingstone-*High Treason*,174-175
137 Craig's report of seeing "LHO": —Marrs-*Crossfire*,329-331; —Sam Anson-*They've Killed the President*,217; —Hurt-*Reasonable Doubt*,120-121; —Groden/Livingstone-*High Treason*,132
138. Oswald's "spy" camera: —Marrs-*Crossfire*,190-191; —Groden/Livingstone-*High Treason*,125

139. Julia Ann Mercer's story: –WCH7,352; –Meagher-*Accessories After the Fact*,21; –Hurt-*Reasonable Doubt*,114-116; –Marrs-*Crossfire*,18-19; –Groden/Livingstone-*High Treason*,135

140. Holland's puff of smoke: –Marrs-*Crossfire*,56-59,320-321; –Meagher-*Accessories After the Fact*,19; –Sam Anson-*They've Killed the President*,27-28

141. Ed Hoffman's story: –TV Documentary, *The Men Who Killed Kennedy;* –Marrs-*Crossfire*,81-86; –Groden/Livingstone-*High Treason*,462,463

142. Tom Tilson's story: –TV Movie, *The Trial of Lee Harvey Oswald;* –Marrs-*Crossfire*,325-327

143. The Willis's testimony: –TV Documentary, *The Men Who Killed Kennedy;* –Marrs-*Crossfire*,24-25; –Groden/Livingstone-*High Treason*,454

144. R. Fischer's description: –Thompson-*Six Seconds in Dallas*,190; –Kurtz-*Crime of the Century*,120; –Marrs-*Crossfire*,23

145. Zapruder's opinion on shots: –WCH7,572,576; –Lane-*Rush to Judgment*,41; –Meagher-*Accessories After the Fact*,459; –Lifton-*Best Evidence*,18,21; –Summers-*Conspiracy*,27; –Marrs-*Crossfire*,65-66

146. Parkland Drs. on throat wound: –See Note #7, this chapter

147. Powers and O'Donnell: –Waldron-*Legacy of Secrecy*,307

148. Hoover's motive for cover-up: –Waldron-*Legacy of Secrecy*,228-230; –North-*Act of Treason*,160,163,169,171,199,243-244

149. Vote fraud in 60 election: –Giancana-*Double Cross*,286-288,289-290

Chapter 11 - The Cover-up: Villains & Heroes

1. Batchelor, Harrison help Ruby: –Kantor-*The Ruby Cover-up*,281-284,410; –Groden/Livingstone-*High Treason*,188

2. Fritz takes no notes: –WR,180; –Meagher-*Accessories After the Fact*,223; –Groden/Livingstone-*High Treason*,188

3. FBI given evidence: –Kurtz-*Crime of the Century*,152

4. Stover's court martial threat: –See note 29 in Chapter 2

5. Burkeley prevents neck probe: –Garrison-*On the Trail of the Assassins*,289-290; –Livingstone-*High_Treason_2*,242,260-261,293

6. Brain, slides missing: –See Notes 99,100 in chapter 10

7. Photos and X-rays missing: –See Note 101 in chapter 10

8. McCone withholds information: –Hurt-*Reasonable Doubt*,335; –Summers-*Conspiracy*,531-532

9. Oswald's '201' file: —Hurt-*Reasonable Doubt*,246-247; —Groden/Livingstone-*High Treason*,121

10. Helms withholds information: —Blakey/Billings-*The Plot to Kill the President*,79; —Groden/Livingstone-*High Treason*,312,315,377; —Lane-*Plausible Denial*,57-58; —Waldron-*Legacy of Secrecy*,201-204

11. CIA/Bush withhold information: —.Blakey/Billings-*The Plot to Kill the President*,148-150

12. Katzenbach memo to Moyers: —Kurtz-*Crime of the Century*,24; —Groden/Livingstone-*High Treason*,257; —Waldron-*Legacy of Secrecy*,241

13. Timing of Clark Panel report: —See Note 18 in chapter 3

14. Mitchell/Kleindienst stonewall: —Roffman-*Presumed Guilty*,105-106; —Weisberg-*Post Mortem*,217-218,286,349,611-612

15. Lattimer examines X-rays: —Weisberg-*Post Mortem*,386-388

16. Judge Pratt presides over FOIA: —Weisberg-*Post Mortem*,413-416,424-430

17. Haggerty rules against Shaw alias: — Hurt-*Reasonable Doubt*,275-276; —Garrison-*On the Trail of the Assassins*,283

18. Bertrand (Shaw) connections: —Garrison-*On the Trail of the Assassins*,91-100

19. Blakey's conclusions: —HSCR,169-179; —Blakey/Billings-*The Plot to Kill the President*,106-107

20. Dan Rather's big lie: —Sam Anson-*They've Killed the President*,132; —Summers-*Conspiracy*,31; —Groden/Livingstone-*High Treason*,117-118; —Waldron-*Legacy of Secrecy*,235

21. Ellen McCloy/CBS News: —*JFK: The Book of the Film*,493-494

22. NY Times leads the way: —Meagher-*Access. After the Fact*,458-459

23. Oliphant praises *JFK*: —*JFK: The Book of the Film*,282-283

24. Bush in CIA in the 1961-63 period: —Lane-*Plausible Denial*,330-333, 371-378;
Russell-*The Man Who Knew Too Much*,709-710

25. Mary Ferrell's tape: —Blakey/Billings-*The Plot to Kill the President*,91-93

26. Parkland Drs. saw "entrance": —See Note 7 in chapter 10

27. Dr. McClelland's comments: —Thompson-*Six Seconds in Dallas*,107-108; —Lifton-*Best Evidence*,316,322-323

28. Dr. Crenshaw corroborated: —Livingstone-*Killing the Truth*,103

29. Bethesda aides say "forgery": — Livingstone-*Killing the Truth*,169; —Livingstone-*High_Treason_2*,288,308, 319,325-326

30. The Newmen's description: –Thompson-*Six Seconds in Dallas*,103-105; –Hurt-*Reasonable Doubt*,118
31. Oliver on Ruby-Oswald: –Groden/Livingstone-*High Treason*,122,292
32. Grassy knoll witnesses not heard: –See chapter 3
33. Willis' testimony: –See Note 143, chapter 10
34. Rowland's testimony: –Thompson-*Six Seconds in Dallas*,180,235; –Roffman-*Presumed Guilty*,186-187; –Garrison-*On the Trail of the Assassins*,106-107

Chapter 12 - Keeping the Lid On

1. Gary Underhill: –Marrs-*Crossfire*,559; –Groden/Livingstone-*High Treason*,143-144; –Hancock -*Someone Would Have Talked*,497
2. Hugh Ward: –Marrs-*Crossfire*,559; –Groden/Livingstone-*High Treason*,144,288
3. Guy Banister: –Marrs-*Crossfire*,559; –Groden/Livingstone-*High Treason*,144,288
4. Mary Meyer; –Marrs-*Crossfire*,559; –Russell-*The Man Who Knew Too Much*,460-462
5. Maurice Gatlin: –Marrs-*Crossfire*,559; –Groden/Livingstone-*High Treason*,145
6. Rose Cherami: –Marrs-*Crossfire*,559; –Groden/Livingstone-*High Treason*,141; –Waldron-*Legacy of Secrecy*,259
7. Dorothy Kilgallen: –Marrs-*Crossfire*,559; –Groden/Livingstone-*High Treason*,138; –Waldron-*Legacy of Secrecy*,369
8. Lee Bowers: –Meagher-*Accessories After the Fact*,299; –Thompson-*Six Seconds in Dallas*,115-119; –Marrs-*Crossfire*,560; – Groden/Livingstone-*High Treason*,134-135
9. William Pitzer: – Marrs-*Crossfire*,560; –Groden/Livingstone-*High Treason*,143; –Law-*In the Eye of History*,xvi
10. James Worrell Jr: –Meagher-*Accessories After the Fact*,299; –Sam Anson-*They've Killed the President*,67; –Marrs-*Crossfire*,560
11. Jack Ruby: –Meagher-*Accessories After the Fact*,452-453; –Marrs-*Crossfire*,561; –Groden/Livingstone-*High Treason*,142
12. Harold Russell: –Meagher-*Accessories After the Fact*,299; –Sam Anson-*They've Killed the President*,67; –Marrs-*Crossfire*,561
13. Ferrie knew Oswald: – Waldron-*Legacy of Secrecy*,84-86; – Garrison-*On the Trail of the Assassins*,10,50,122-123

14. Ferrie's death: –Meagher-*Accessories After the Fact*,299; –Marrs-*Crossfire*,561; –Garrison-*On the Trail of the Assassins*,162-165; – Groden/Livingstone-*High Treason*,136
15. Eladio del Valle: –Marrs-*Crossfire*,561; –Groden/Livingstone-*High Treason*,136; –Waldron-*Legacy of Secrecy*,396-397
16. RFK planning to reopen case: –Scheim-*Contract on America*,287; – Davis-*Mafia Kingfish*,345; –Waldron-*Legacy of Secrecy*,291
17. Robert Kennedy's death: –Livingstone-*High_Treason_2*,383-390; –Melanson-*The Robert F. Kennedy Assassination*,passim; –Waldron-*Legacy of Secrecy*,630-645
18. Philip Geraci: –Marrs-*Crossfire*,561
19. E. R. Walthers: –Marrs-*Crossfire*,561
20. Rev. C. Johnson: –Marrs-*Crossfire*,562
21. Salvatore Granello: –Marrs-*Crossfire*,562
22. G. McGann's wife Beverly Oliver: –Groden/Livingstone-*High Treason*,142
23. McGann's death/associates: –Marrs-*Crossfire*,562; – Groden/Livingstone-*High Treason*,142
24. James Plumeri: –Marrs-*Crossfire*,562
25. Hale Boggs: –Marrs-*Crossfire*,562; –Groden/Livingstone-*High Treason*,134; –Livingstone-*High_Treason_2*,408
26. Hunt's plane sabotaged?: –Livingstone-*High_Treason_2*,423-433
27. Dorothy Hunt: –Groden/Livingstone-*High Treason*,324-325; – Livingstone-*High_Treason_2*,408-409
28. Richard Cain: –Double Cross,350-351; –Waldron-*Legacy of Secrecy*,728
20. Joseph Milteer: –Marrs-*Crossfire*,562; –Waldron-*Legacy of Secrecy*, 729
30. Clay Shaw's death: –Marrs-*Crossfire*,563; –Groden/Livingstone-*High Treason*,144-145
31. Was Shaw CIA?: –Groden/Livingstone-*High Treason*,144; – Waldron-*Legacy of Secrecy*,524
32. David Yaras: –Marrs-*Crossfire*,563
33. John Martino: –Groden/Livingstone-*High Treason*,145
34. Sam Giancana: –Evica-*And We Are All Mortal*,251-252; –Marrs-*Crossfire*,563-564; –Groden/Livingstone-*High Treason*,141; –Waldron-*Legacy of Secrecy*,734
35. Giancana-Exner-JFK ties: –Summers-*Conspiracy*,248-249; –Marrs-*Crossfire*,176-178

36. Jimmy Hoffa: –Summers-*Conspiracy*,493; –Waldron-*Legacy of Secrecy*,734
37. Rolando Masferrer: –Evica-*And We Are All Mortal*,267,315,322 Livingstone-*High_Treason_2*,412; –Russell-*The Man Who Knew Too Much*,511-512; –Waldron-*Legacy of Secrecy*,735
38. John Roselli: –Evica-*And We Are All Mortal*,191-193; –Marrs-*Crossfire*,563; –Groden/Livingstone-*High Treason*,141; –Waldron-*Legacy of Secrecy*,739
39. Revelations to Jack Anderson: –Waldron-*Legacy of Secrecy*,704; –Sam Anson-*They've Killed the President*,257-258; –Russell-*The Man Who Knew Too Much*,422
40. William Pawley: – Marrs-*Crossfire*,565; –Groden/Livingstone-*High Treason*,145
41. George DeMohrenschildt: –See Note 20 in chapter 6
42. Charles Nicoletti: –Summers-*Conspiracy*,494; –Marrs-*Crossfire*,564; –Waldron-*Legacy of Secrecy*,742
43. Lou Staples: –Marrs-*Crossfire*,565
44. William Sullivan's "accident": –Evica-*And We Are All Mortal*,326; –Summers-*Conspiracy*,497; –Marrs-*Crossfire*,5645-65; – Groden/Livingstone-*High Treason*,145; –Livingstone-*High_Treason_2*,414-416
45. Sullivan's knowledge of Oswald: –Summers-*Conspiracy*,497
46. David S. Morales: –Fonzi-*The Last Investigation*,371
47. Morales' death suspicious: –Fonzi-*The Last Investigation*,387
48. Roger Craig shooting: –Lane-*Rush to Judgment*,173-174; –Marrs-*Crossfire*,328-332; –Groden/Livingstone-*High Treason*,144
49. Richard Carr: –Hurt-*Reasonable Doubt*,119-120;
50. Warren Reynolds: –Meagher-*Accessories After the Fact*,293; – Summers-*Conspiracy*,557
51. Antonio Veciana: –Groden/Livingstone-*High Treason*,144; – Russell-*The Man Who Knew Too Much*,422
52. London Times actuarial: –Sam Anson-*They've Killed the President*,67; –Hurt-*Reasonable Doubt*,412-413; –Groden/Livingstone-*High Treason*,128-129

EPILOG

1. The first shot did not miss: —See Note 6 in chapter 9; —Lane-*Rush to Judgment*,72-73
2. Connally's delayed reaction: —See Note 2 in chapter 9
3. Size of throat wound: —See Note 6 in chapter 10
4. McAdams' theories: —To learn more about McAdams' false claims Google McAdams JFK throat wound claims.
5. Throat wound above collar: —WH3,355,362; WH6,58,59; —Weisberg-*Post Mortem*,332-398; —Hurt-*Reasonable Doubt*,60
6. Size of Connally's back wound: —WH6,85,WH4,104; —Meagher-*Accessories After the Fact*,166; —Kurtz-*Crime of the Century*,176; —Groden/Livingstone-*High Treason*,65
7. Size of clothing holes: —Meagher-*Accessories After the Fact*,166; —Groden/Livingstone-*High Treason*,65
8. Sturdivan's theory: —HSCH1,383-4276
9. BBN's analysis of the tape: —See Note 9 in chap. 9
10. Oswald with Coke: —See Note 20 in chap. 10
11. Randle on bag length: —WH,7,248; —Weisberg-*Whitewash*,53; —Meagher-*Accessories After the Fact*,57
12. Frazier on bag length: —Lane-*Rush to Judgment*,144-145; —Meagher-*Accessories After the Fact*,56

Index

20/20 (ABC News) 283,289,291
Abrams, Gus (see Tramps) 198
Accessories After the Fact
   (Meagher) 264
Acoustical evidence
   (see Dallas Police, tape recording)
Act of Treason (North) 56
Adams, Francis 256
Adams, Janet (Jada) 143,156
Adams, Victoria 220
AGVA (see American Guild
   of Variety Artists
Air Force Major's body 40
Air Force One 38
Air Force Two 39
Alba, Adrian 125
Aleman, Jose Jr. 105
Aleman, Jose Sr. 105
Alexander, William 76,81,91
Alpha 66 99,104,109,128,224,229
Alvarez, Luis 180
Ambulance/s 39,51
American Bar Association 170,284
American Broadcasting Co. (ABC) 259
American Guild of Variety Artists 144
AM/LASH (see Cubela, Rolando)
Anderson, Jack 103
Andrews Air Force Base 39
Andrews, Dean 64,258
And We Are All Mortal (Evica) 187
Angleton, James 233
Anson, Robert Sam 135,250
Arcacha-Smith, Sergio 99,105
Archives (see National Archives)
Arnold, Carolyn 60,132,215,241,289, 296

ARTICHOKE 102
Artime, Manuel 105,108
Aschkenasy, Dr. E. 203,289
Assassination Archives &
   Research Center (AARC)
   70,263
Assassination Information
   Bureau 264
Assassination Records
   Collection Act (ARCA)
   16,42,261,304
Assassination Records
   Review Board (ARRB)
   16,48,70-71,268
Atsugi Air Force Base
   110,115,118
Atomic Energy Commission
   (see Energy Research &
   Development Admin.)
Autopsy (of JFK) 10,27,33-
   52,234,264,274-275,303
   aides/technicians 180,
      192,211 (see also:
      Custer, Jerrol;
      Jenkins, James;
      O'Connor, Paul;
      Riebe, Floyd
   charts/drawings 177,
      178,209,287
   draft report destroyed
      10,41,235,250-251
   personnel "gagged"
      51-52,239
   photos 15-16,40-44,47,
      50-51, 65,70,180-181,
      183,196,201,209,235,

Index

237-238,252,256-257, 265,267-268,287,301-303
Slides 41,235,252,301
X-rays 15-16,34,40-44,50-51, 65,180-181,201,235,237-238,252,256-257,265, 267-268,301-303
Babushka Lady (see Oliver, Beverly)
Back brace 192
Bag (brown paper) 24,164-165,219,290-291
Baker, Barney 145
Baker, Officer Marion 132-133,215-218, 289-290
Baker, Virgie 61
Ball, Joseph 58,255
Banister, Guy 64,66,106-107,120,124-126,229,258,274-275
Barber, Steve 12
Barger, Dr. James 289
Barker, Bernard 105
Barnes, Tracy 101
Batchelor, Charles 230,250
Batista, Augustin 98
Batista, Fulgencio 98,108-109,144,277
Bay of Pigs 7,99-101,103-104,110, 134,207,229-232,261
Belin, David 58,63,97,220,255
Belli, Melvin 155
Benavides, Domingo 25,169,222
Bertrand, Clem (see Shaw, Clay)
Best Evidence (Lifton) 38,48,236,264
Bethesda Naval Hospital (see Autopsy)
Betrayal (Morrow) 101
Betzner, Hugh Jr. 61
Billings, Richard 258
Bishop, Maurice (see Phillips, David A.)
Bissell, Richard 100-101,231
Blahut, Regis 40-41
Blakey, Robert 60,68-69,181,185-186, 203,258
Bocognoni, (first name unknown) 228
Body bag 39-40,51

Boggs, Hale 38,58,79-81,83-86, 89-90,92, 208,276
Bolden, Abraham 20
Bolt, Beranic & Newman 11, 186,203,289,299
Bonds, Joe (see Locurto, Joe)
Bosch, Orlando 99,108-109,229
Boston Globe 260
Boswell, Dr. J. T. 33,36,39,50, 52,71,209,303
Bourk, Robert 41,252
Bowers, Lee 215,274
Bowley, T. F. 25
Bowron, Diana 201
Braden, Jim (AKA)
Brading, Eugene 53-54, 198-199,228
Brain (see Kennedy, John F.)
Breakability CE-399 (Hunt) 288
Brehm, Charles 61
Breneman, Chester 238
Brennan, Howard 25,28,54-55, 165-166
Brigade 2506 100,110
Bringuier, Carlos 106-109,125, 277
Brown, Madelaine 157
Brown, Maggie 61
Brown, Walt 159
Bugliosi, Vincent 159,295,297
Bullet/s (see also, Commission Exhibit 399) 12,36-37,50, 51,61, 192-193,222,235,286
Bundy, McGeorge 56
Burkeley, Adm. George 34,36, 60,209,251,203,289,299
Burroughs, Butch 168
Bush, George H.W. 16,253,261
Butler, George 140,147,230
Cabell, Gen. Charles 101,231
Cabell, Earle 231,279
Cain, Richard 104,276
Campisi, Joseph 144

Index

Capone, Al 103
Caracci, Frank 145
Carlin, Karen 151-152
Carousel Club 141-142,146,148,150, 155-157,268
Carr, Richard 199,228,278
Carr Waggoner 29,75-76
Carrico, Dr. Charles 243,267,303
Carter, Jimmy 260-261
Cartridges
   from rifle 8,24,54,164,199
   from Tippit case 8-9,26,54,167,222
Case Closed (Posner) 149,283,288,291
Case Open (Weisberg) 246.284
Casings (see Cartridges)
Casket 23,37,39-40,50
Castorr, Col. Robert L. 143
Castro, Fidel 7,11,13,32,56,68,98-111,124-125,135,144,146,229-232,239,253,276-277
CBS (see Columbia Broadcasting System)
Central Intelligence Agency (CIA) 11,16,32,44,64,68-69,76,82,84-86, 98-111,115,120-121,127,207,224-236,239,252-253,258,261,270, 274,276-278,302,304
Chambers, G. Paul 203-204
Chaney, Officer James 59,241
Cherami, Rose 274
Chicago Daily News 139
Chicago plot to kill JFK 208,241
Chism, John 61,182
Chism, Mary 61,
Christian Democratic Movement 99
Church Committee (see Senate Select Committee on Intell. Activities) 32
Church, Sen. Frank 32
Civello, Joseph 146
Clark Panel 45,64-65,180-181,205
Clark, Ramsey 34,44,64-65,256
Clemons, Aquilla 25,169,222
Clinton, Bill 16,260-262,301-302

Clothing damage
   Kennedy's 173-175,192,210, 212,238,287
   Connally's 235,286-287
Cockburn, Alexander 259
Code Name Zorro (Lane) 263
Coleman, Kay Helen 148-149,156
Columbia Broadcasting System 13, 22,249,258-259
Commission Exhibit 399 12,24,37,, 65,148,164,179,187,195,197,204-206,215,225,285,288,298-302
Conforto, Janet (see Adams, Janet)
Connally, Governor John 10,19,21, 58,65,172-173,179,181,187,194, 204-205,213-214,241,285-286,302
Connally, Nellie 173,182,214,241
Conspiracy (Summers) 126,265
Conspiracy of Silence (Crenshaw) 267
Cooke, Leon 138
Cooper, Senator John 58,82-84
Cooper, Sherman 219
Crafard, Larry 150
Craig, Roger 128,199,228,242,278
Crenshaw, Dr. Charles 51,267
Cronkite, Walter 258-259
Crossfire (Marrs) 265
Crouch, Mark 40,42
Crowe, William Jr. 156
Crusade to Free Cuba 125
Cuba 13,97-101,142-144
Cuban embassy 69,229
Cuban exiles 98-100,104-110,124-125,224,226
Cuban missile crisis 7,110-111
Cuban Revolutionary Council 106, 125
Cuban Student Directorate 99
Cubela, Rolando 101,108
Cummings, Raymond 156
Curbstone 21,62,172,194,238
Curry, Jesse 20,55,146,150-151, 170,251,292

Index

Custer, Jerrol 36,40-41,71,267
Cutchshaw, W. J. 154
Dallas Morning News 19,21,148,156, 296
Dallas Police 8,19,53,146-147,162, 170,198,207,225-226,234,249-251
   handling of evidence 163-167
   interrogation of Oswald (see Oswald, interrogation of)
   lineups 9,28,166
   relationship to Ruby 146-147
   tape recording of shots 11-12,68, 181,186-188,191,193,197,203-204, 210-211,214-215,235,265-266,289, 294-295,298-301,303
Dallas Times Herald 149-150
Dal-Tex Building 21,53,193-194,198-199, 213,228
David, Christian 227
David, Dennis 39-40
Davis, Thomas III 142
Day, J. C. 163
Dealey Plaza 171-206
Death Certificate (JFK's) 210
Death of a President (Manchester) 297
Decker, William 20
del Valle, Eladio 275
DeMar, Bill (see Crowe, William Jr.)
DeMohrenschildt, George 120-121, 129,277-279,293,296
de Varona, Antonio 105
Discovery Channel 300
Documents (see files)
Donaldson, Ann 61
Dorfman, Paul 138
Double Cross (Giancanna) 97
Downing, Thomas 67
Doyle, Harold (see also, Tramps) 198
Drain, Vincent 163
Dreyfus, Captain Alfred 62-63
Dulles, Allen 11,32,56,58-59,75-79,82, 85-86,90-91,99-101,207,232,252,254

Eberhardt, A. M. 148-149
Eddowes, Michael 118,133
Edwards, Col. Sheffield 101,231
Eisenhower, Dwight D. 99
Ekdahl, Edwin 113
Ellsworth, Frank 224
Energy Research & Development Administration 56,257
Epstein, Edward J. 9-10,59,121,255
Evica, George 187
Evidence
   chain-of 26,42,54,162-164,167, 170,180,204
   destruction of 15,127,129,235
   missing 34,41,187,196,235,252
   suppression of 14-15,50,69-70, 238-241,253,263
   tampered with 44-49,236-238,264
Executive Action (the movie) 13
Executive Action Program (see ZR/RIFLE)
Exner, Judith Campbell 231,277
Eyewitnesses (see Witnesses)
Failure Analysis 284-285
Fair-Play-for-Cuba Committee 106, 124-125,149
Federal Bureau of Investigation (FBI) 8,27-29,35,37-38,42,46,56-58,61, 69,73,75-84,87-92,103-104,110, 125-129,132,138,141-142,163, 170-172,191-192,201,204-207, 210-212,219,233-235,238-243, 257,263-264,269,278,292,302
Fence (atop grassy knoll) 24,54,60, 181,195,198,215,228,240-242,268 269,274,299,303
Fensterwald, Bernard Jr. 263
Ferrell, Mary 203,265-266
Ferrie, David 64-66,106-107,124,156, 229,258,274-275
Files (government records) 15-16, 37,69-71,73,134,269,302-303

Index

Finck, Dr. Pierre 33-35,50,270,303
Fiorini, Frank (see Sturgis, Frank)
Fischer, Ronald 242
Fitzgerald, Desmond 101
Folsom, Lt. Colonel A. G. 116
Fonzi, Gaeton 68,104,121
Ford, Gerald 56,58,74,93,154,207-208,225,233,253-255
Forgive My Grief (Jones) 264
Fox, James K. 40,42-43
Fragments
　Bullet 37,61,65,187,196,205,239,298,300,302
　Skull 195-196,212
Frazier, Buell W. 129-132,164-165,219,290
Frazier, Robert A. 205,214,252
Free Cuba Committee 149
Freedom of Information Act (FOIA) 42,239,257
French Corsican Mafia 102,227
Friends of Democratic Cuba 99
Fritz, Capt. Will 54-55,149,151,166,250-251
Gag-order on Bethesda people (see Autopsy)
Galaxy Magazine 12
Garrison, Jim 14,31,34,64-67,106-107,110,135,156,171,229,234,255,257-258,270-271,275-276
Gatlin, Maurice 274
Gawler's Funeral Home 48
Gedney, John (see also, Tramps) 198
Geraci, Philip 275
Giancana, Chuck 97,278
Giancana, Samuel Jr. 97,103-104,145,230-231,276-279
Gonzalez, Henry 67-68
Gore, Al 262,301-302
Grammer, Billy 28-29,151
Granello, Salvatore 276
Grant, Eva 139-140,148
Grassy knoll 12,54,60,68,181,183,195,198,202-203,215,240,274,289
Greer, William 21,197
Gregory, Charles 196
Griffen, Burt 58
Groden, Robert 43,236,265
Gruber, Al 147
Guevara, Che 98
Guinn, Vincent 218,239,302
Guthrie, Steve 139-140,147
Habighorst, Aloysius 257-258
Haggerty, Edward 257-258
Hall, Loren 108-110,142,229,277
Hargis, Bobby 22,195
Harper, Billy 195
Harrelson, Charles 53,198,227,276
Harrison, William (Blacky) 29,146-147,230,250
Hart, Senator Gary 223
Harvey, William 101-104,231
Head Shot (Chambers) 203-204
Helms, Richard 101-102,233,253
Hidell, Alek (see Oswald alias)
High Treason (Groden, Livingstone) 265
High Treason 2 (Livingstone) 181,265
Hill, Clinton 22,195
Hill, Jean 61,215,268-269
Hoffa, James R. 105,138,145,277,294
Hoffman, Ed 60,215,242
Holland, Sam 215,242
Hoover, J. Edgar 55-58,73,77-79,81-83,86-91,109,131,187-188,208,233,243,252,261,278
Home, Douglas 48,70,268
Hosty, James 79,129,235,239
House Select Committee on Assassinations (HSCA) 11-12,32,40,43,50,60,67-70,104-105,122-123,127-128,144,146-147,155,180-182,186,188,193,196,202-203,210-211,225-226,234,239,245,249,253,258,260-261,265-266,279,286,288-289,299

Index

Houston Post 76,79,84-85
Howard, Tom 153
Hubert, Leon 58
Hudkins, Alonzo 76-79,84-85,87,91
Hudson, Emmett 182
Hughes, Howard 103,230
Humes, Comander James 10,33-39, 50,69,71,178,192,205,251,30
   destroys autopsy draft 10,41, 235,250-251
Hunt, Dorothy 276
Hunt, E. Howard 100-101,103, 105,108,198,227-228,233
Hunt, Haroldson L. 199,233
Hunt, John 288
Hurt, Henry 219
Inquest (Epstein) 9,59,121
Insurrectional Movement for the Recovery of the Revolution (MIRR) 99
Itek Corporation 7,60,240
Jada (see Adams, Janet)
Jaggers-Chiles-Stovall 121
Jaworski, Leon 76
Jenkins, James 36,39-41,267
Jenkins, Walter 56
Jenner, Albert 58,255
Jet-effect theory 180,257,303
JFK (the movie) 13-14,16,49,97,102, 106,130-131,135,260,265,269-270
JFK: Conspiracy of Silence (Crenshaw) 51
JFK and Vietnam (Newman) 135
JFK Assassination File (Curry) 251, 292
JFK: The Last Dissenting Witness (Sloan) 269
JM/WAVE 102,108,111,231,278
John Birch Society 19,29,150
Johnsen, Richard 164 ,204
Johnson, Rev. Clyde 275-276
Johnson, Lyndon B. 19,23,29,56,61 102,208,233,243,249,253,260,267

Johnson, Priscilla McMillan 291
Jones, Paul Roland 139-141,147
Jones, Penn Jr. 264
Journal of the American Medical Association (JAMA) 49-50,71,235,268
Journal of U.S. Forensic Science Society 187
Junta of the Government of Cuba in Exile (JURE) 99,127
Justice Department (see United States Dept. of Justice
Kantor, Seth 140,146,148,206
Katzenbach, Nicholas 56,78,86,256
Kay, Kathy (see Coleman, Kay)
Kellerman, Roy 196-197,212
Kennedy, Jacqueline 21-22,40,153, 195,300
Kennedy, John F.
   Addison's disease 34
   and Cuba 97-111
   and missile crisis 7,110-111
   autopsy of (see Autopsy)
   brain of 22,39,41,48,50,70,235 252,301-302
   clothing damage 173,192,210,238
   death certificate of 210
   wounds of (see Wounds)
Kennedy, Regis 233,240
Kennedy, Robert 11,31,41,55,78,83-87,97,101-102,105,230,245,252,256, 275,277,279
Khruschev Killed Kennedy (Eddowes) 118,133
Khruschev, Nikita 7-8,56,110,134
Kildruff, Malcolm 23,41,195
Kilgallen, Dorothy 274,279
Killing the Truth (Livingstone) 201
King, Martin Luther 11,31-32,67, 245,263
Klein's Sporting Goods 121
Ku Klux Klan 19
Labriola, Paul 138
Lamumba, Patrice 102

Index

Lane, Mark 9-10,61,228,234,254,263
Lansdale, Gen. Edward 101-102,231
Lansky, Jake 144-145
Lansky, Meyer 105,108,144
Lanz, Pedro Diaz 109-110,229
Lardner, George Jr. 69,259
Lattimer, Dr. John 180,257
Law, William 36,40-41
Lawrence, Jack 228
Legacy of Secrecy (Waldron) 136,304
Legend (Epstein) 121
Lesar, James 263
Lewis, Anthony 259
Liebeler, Wesley 58,63,128,255
LIFE Magazine 14,22,66,122
Lifton, David 37-40,48,236,255,264
Limousine (President's) 21-22,61,183-184,196,235
Lineups (see Dallas Police)
Little Lynn (see Carlin, Karen)
Livingstone, Harrison 36,181,201, 203,265
Locurto, Joseph 141
Long, Senator Russell 64
London Sunday Times 278-279
Lorenz, Morita 103,110,228-229
Lorenzo, Aurelio 61
Love Field (Dallas airport) 20,23,33
Lowery, Roy L 152
Luce, Claire Booth & Henry 13
Luciano, Charles ("Lucky") 105
Lunchroom (in TSBD) 60,132-133, 166,215-218,241,296
Mabra, W. W. 61
Mack, Gary 203,265
Mafia (see Organized Crime)
Magic Bullet (see Commission Exhibit 399)
Maheu, Robert 103,230
Mailer, Norman 291-295
Mannlicher-Carcano (see Rifle)
Mantic, David 295
Marcello, Carlos 32,69,106,108,114, 143,145,230,277,294
Marchetti, Victor 276
Marina and Lee (Johnson) 291
Markham, Helen 25-26,168,220
Marrs, Jim 156,265
Marsh, Ester Ann 156
Marshall, Burke 42,257
Martin, Jack 138
Martino, John 108,277
Masen, John T. 109,128,224,228
Masferrer, Rolando 108,277
McAdams, John 286-287
McClelland, Dr. Robert 51,236,243, 267
McCloy, Ellen 259
McCloy, John 58,83-84,86-91,259
McCone, John 101,253
McCoy, Perry 28
McDonald, M. N. 26
McGann, George 155,276
McKeown, Robert 142
McWillie, Louis 144
Meagher, Sylvia 263-264
Media (see News Media)
Mercer, Julia Ann 242
Mertz, Michael 227
Meyer, Cord 234
Meyer, Mary 274
Miami, Florida (plot to kill JFK) 19-20,241
Microphone (DP motorcycle) 11,186, 197,203,265,299
Midlothian Mirror 264
Miller, Murry ("Dusty") 145
Millican, A. J. 61
Milteer, Joseph 19-20,276
Minox camera 224,242
Minutemen 19,109,128,224
Missile crisis (see Cuban missile crisis)
Mitchell, John 256
MKULTRA 101-102,115
Mob, The (see Organized crime)
Mongoose 101-102,239,252,277

Index

Monroe, Marilyn 245
Monterey School of Languages 117, 161
Montoya, Richard (see Rogers, Charles
Mooney, Eugene 162
Moore, Elmer 76
Moorman, Mary 61,182,215,240,268
Morales, David 102,108,111,231,278
Morgue (see Autopsy)
Morrow, Robert 101
Morticians 48-49
Motive
   For the assassination 17,97-111
   For the cover-up 246
Motorcade 8,20
Motorcade route 20,231,296
Moyers, Bill 256
Muchmore, Marie 61
Murchison, Clint 233
Murret, Charles ("Dutz") 114,125
Nagell, Richard C. 128
Nation, The 76,83,89,259
National Academy of Sciences (NAS) 12,186,289
National Archives 16,37,42,235
National-Security-Action-Memo-263 97
Navy (see U. S. Navy)
Neutron Activation Analysis (NAA) 61, 239,257,302
Never Again! (Weisberg) 246
Newman, John M. 135
Newman, Mort 140
Newman, William & Gail 59,182,268
New Orleans 64
News media 31,64-66,71,258,268
New York Daily News 155
New York Times 13,77,250,259
Nicoletti, Charles 110,277-278
Nitrate tests 218
Nitti, Frank 103
Nix, Orville 60,236
Nixon, Richard 19,99,233
North, Mark 56

Nosenko, Yuri 119
November 22, 1963: You Are the Jury (Belin) 255
O'Connor, Paul 39-40,236,267
O'Donnell, Kenneth 182,243
O'Neill, Francis 38,60,191-192,303
O'Reilly, Bill 295-296
Oak tree 172,182-184,194
Odio, Sylvia 109,127,277,303
Odum, Bardwell 131
Oglesby, Carl 258,264
Office of Naval Intel. (ONI) 234
Oldman, Gary 130-13
Oliphant, Thomas 260
Oliver, Beverly 61,155,215,233,240, 268-269,276
Olsen, Harry 148-149
On The Trail of the Assassins (Garrison) 258
Operation-40 109
Organized Crime 32,68-69,97-98, 101,103-104,107-109,144-147, 155,224,293-294
Osborne, Adm. David 37
Oswald in New Orleans (Weisberg) 246
246
Oswald's Tail: An American Mystery (Mailer) 291
Oswald, Lee Harvey
   201 file 236,253
   alias of 27,121,162,219
   and Jack Ruby 155-156,269
   arraignment of 2
   arrest of 26
   as FBI informant 73-92
   as Intelligence operative 104,117, 222-224,278,292,303
   as Marxist 114,121,124-125,223
   as "patsy" 111,134-135,229-230
   as sharpshooter 116,219,294,296
   as Tippit's killer 25,97
   attitude toward JFK 30,134,220

Index

autopsy of 33
backyard photos of 122-124
biographical data of 113-114
death of 8,28-30,274 ,279
description of 25-26,54-55,225
diary of 119
embalming/burial of 133
exhumation of 133
height variations of 129-130
impersonation of 104,126-131,133-134,155,194.199,224
in Dallas 121-124
in Fort Worth 120-121
in Japan 110,115-116
in Marine Corps 114-117
in Mexico City 69,126-127,129,225,229,236,293,303
in New Orleans 106,113-114,124-126
in Russia 27,56,101,116-120,129-131,223,291
in TSBD 132-133,215-218,289-290
interrogation of 26-27,5
rifle practice 30,219,243,255,296
transfer of 28-29,147,150-153,230
Oswald, "Leon" 109,127
Oswald, Marguerite 30,113,263
Oswald, Marina 27,30,119-120,122-123,131,133,220,243,292
Oswald, Robert 113
Paine, Ruth & Michael 27,121,131
Parade route (see Motorcade route)
Paraffin tests (see Nitrate tests)
Parking lot (behind TSBD) 53-54,60,132,165,198
Parkland Hospital 10,29,41,51,148,178
Parkland Hospital medical staff 10,22-23,70,180-181,195,201-202,212,236,238,243,266,286,298
Patrick, Lennie 138,145

Paul, Ralph 141
Pawley, William 13-14,277
Pecora, Nofio 145
Perrin, Nancy (see Rich, Nancy)
Perrin, Robert 142-144
Perry, Dr. Malcolm 22-23,35-36,178,200-201,243,267,303
Phillips, David Atlee 104,108,229,278
Photographic Whitewash (Weisberg) 246,299
Pic, John 113,130
Picket fence (see Fence)
Pironti, Sauveur 228
Pistol (see Revolver)
Pitts, Elnora 151
Pitzer, William 275,279
Plausible Denial (Lane) 228
Plumeri, James 276
Poe, J. M. 167
Police (see Dallas Police)
Popkin, Richard 126
Porter, Marina (see Oswald Marina)
Portrait of the Assassin (Ford) 92,254
Posner, Gerald 151,283-291,298-301
Post Mortem (Weisberg) 73,192,246
Powers , David 182,243
Powers, Francis Gary 85-86,118
Pratt, John 257
President's Commission on the Assassination of John F. Kennedy (see Warren Commission)
(Press (see News media)
Prio, Carlos (see Socarras, Carlos Prio)
Prouty, Fletcher 102
Quigley, John 125
Ragen, James 145
Raikin, Spas 120
Randle, Linnie Mae 131
Rankin, J. Lee 37-38,58,63,74-92,116-117,182,187,254,290
Rather, Dan 22,258-259

Index

Ray, James Earl 31
Ray, Manuel 99
Reagan, Ronald 261
Reclaiming History (Bugliosi) 295,297
Reclaiming History: A Not Entirely Positive Review (Mantic) 295
Records Building 192
Redlich, Norman 58,254
Re-enactments 178,203-204,215,218, 220-221,238
Reily Coffee Co. 125
Review Panel (see Assassination Records Collection Act)
Revolutionary Democratic Front (FRD) 105
Revolver 8-9,26-27,121-122, 222,225
Reynolds, Warren 278
Rich, Nancy Perrin 142-143
Riebe, Floyd 39-40,71,267
Rifle (Oswald's) 8,27,162-163,172, 218-219
   accuracy/quality of 163
   discovery of 24,54,162
   misidentification of 162
   ordering of 121-122,225
   seen in window 194,196
Rivelle, Steve 227
Roberts, Delphine 124
Roberts, Erlene 168
Rodriguez, Manuel Orcarberro 109, 229
Rogers, Charles F. 227
Rorke, Alexander 103,229
Rose, Dr. Earl 23
Rose, Guy 242
Rose, Jerry 266
Roselli, John 103,108,110,145, 230-231,277,279
Ross, Barney 137
Rothman, Norman "Roughhouse" 107-108,142
Rowland, Arnold 60,269

Rowley, James 164
Rubenstein, Jacob (see Ruby, Jack)
Ruby, Earl 133-138
Ruby, Eva (see Grant, Eva)
Ruby, Hyman 136-137,149
Ruby, Jack 8,28-30,75,83,88-89, 98,137-225-157,206,226,230,268-269,274-277,279,293
Ruby, Sam 138-139
Rush to Judgment (Lane) 9,61,254,263
Russell, Harold 275
Russell, Richard (author) 128,135-136
Russell, Senator Richard 56,58-59,75-79,82-85,88-91,208
Russian embassy 293
Sarti, Lucian 227
Schafer, Roy 153
Schweiker, Richard 104,223
Scoggins, William .25
Scope (telescopic sight) 163,181,218-219
Secret Service 20,22-24,27,40,42, 76-77,88,164,170,196-197,212, 234,241,249,252
Senate Select Committee on Intelligence Activities 11,68,103,223
Senator, George 150
Shaneyfelt, Lyndel 252
Shaw, Clay 31,34,64-66,229,238, 256-258,270,275-276
Shaw, Dr. Robert 205,287
Shenklin, J. Gorden 252
Shots
   effect of 21-22,66,172,180, 195-196,202-203,209,212,215
   number of 12,25,62,68,171-172, 190,196-197
   recording of (see Dallas Police, tape recording)
   source of 8,12,22-24,27,41,51,60, 66,181,183,188,191-194,202, 209,215,238,242-243,2665,267-269,289,300

Index

timing of 181-184,187-189,194, 196,202-203,209,214,284-285, 298
Sibert, James 38,60,191-192,303
Siegel, "Bugsy" 147
Sight (on Oswald's rifle, see scope)
Similas, Norman 60
Single-bullet theory 35,38,50,57-58, 172,182,205,210-214,256,258,268, 284-286
Sirhan, Sirhan 31
Sitzman, Marilyn 21
Six Seconds in Dallas (Thompson) 197, 236,264
Skull (see Fragments)
Sloan, Bill 269
Smith, Joseph 24,198
Smith, Sergio Arcacha 99,106,229
Smith, L. C. 61
Socarras, Carlos Prio 99,105
Somersett, William 19-20
Somoza, Anastasio 105
Sorrells, Forest 55
Souetre, Jean 227
Southeast Asia (see Vietnam)
Soviet embassy (see Russian embassy)
Soviet Union 8,27,29,30,56,85,98,115, 118-121,126,136,223,291,293
Specter, Arlen 37,58,172,196-197, 205,254-255
Spectrographic tests (on bullets) 61, 187-188,195,239,257,302
Spence, Gerry 160
Spiegelman, Cliff 300
Spinal cord (JFK's) 51
Sprague, Richard 67-68,223
Staples, Lou 278
Stemmons Freeway sign 61,172,236
Stevenson, Adlai 19
Stiles, John 92
Stockade fence (see Fence)
Stokes, Louis 68
Stone, Oliver 13-14,16,49,97,102, 106,130-131,135,234,260-261,265, 269-270,300
Storey, Robert 76
Stover, Captain J. H. 37,251
Stretcher bullet (see Commission Exhibit 399)
Sturdivan, Larry 288
Sturgis, Frank 100-101,103,105, 108-110,228-229
Sullivan, William 278
Summers, Anthony 124,126,132,265
Sweatt, Allen 76-81,91
Tague, James 21,172,194,238
Tankersly, John 152
Tannenbaum, Harold 143
Tape recording of shots (see Dallas Police)
Telescopic sight (see Scope)
Testimony ignored, distorted, suppressed 173,196-197,241-243
Texas School Book Depository (TSBD) 8,21,24,28,54,60,128, 171,187-188,91-192,194,196, 199,201-202,210-213,215-219, 224,228,269,275,278 ,289-290, 296-297
Texas Theater 8,26,133,167
The Fourth Decade 266
The JFK Assassination: The Facts & the Theories (Oglesby) 258,264
The Last Investigation (Fonzi) 68
The Man Who Knew Too Much (Russell) 128,135-136
The Men Who Killed Kennedy (A&E) 240
The Oswald File (see *Khrushchev Killed Kennedy*)
The People v. Lee Harvey Oswald (Brown) 159
The Plot to Kill the President (Blakey/ Billings) 258
The Ruby Cover-up (Kantor) 142
The Second Oswald (Popkin) 126

Index

The Trial of Lee Harvey Oswald (A&E) 159
They've Killed the President (Sam Anson) 135
Thompson, Josiah 197,201,236,264
Thomas, Dr. Donaid B. 187,203, 300-301
Thornley, Kerry 116,224
Tice, Wilma 148
Tilson, Tom 198,242
Time Magazine 259
Time/Life 13,22,249
Timmons, David 152
Tippit, Jefferson D. 8-9,25-28,97, 121, 160,166-170,220-222,255,275, 278
Todd, E. L. 204
Tomlinson, Darrell 23-24,164,195, 204,206
Tonahill, Joseph 155
Tracheotomy 22-23,35,178,237
Trafficante, Santos Jr. 32,69,98-99, 104, 106,108-110,144,146-147,227, 230,277,294
Tramps 53,198,227-228
Trujillo, Rafael 102
Truly, Roy 25,132-133,215-216, 289-290
Turner, Stansfield 253
U-2 spy plane 115,118,121
Underhill, Gary 274
United States Department of Justice 12,32,50,69,78,83,146,234,249,256, 261
United States Navy 33,42,249
US News & World Report 283,289, 291
USA Today 71
USSR (see Soviet Union)
Vaughn, Roy 152
Veciana, Antonio 99,104,229,278
Vietnam 97,135
Wade, Henry 55,75-78,80,146,149, 161,164,166

Waldo, Thayer 147
Waldron, Lamar 136,304
Walker, Gen. Edwin 122-123,134, 157,220,296
  photo of auto mutilated 122,238, 292
Wallace, George 245
Walter Reed Army Hospital 33,38-39,264
Ward, Hugh 274
Walther, Carolyn 60,199,278
Walthers, E. R. 275
Warren Commission 8,9,11-12,15, 29-32,38,50,56-59,63, 68-69, 92 ,97, 122 ,127-128,137,139,142,144,146-148,151-152,172-173,178-181, 196-197,200-201,204-205,207-210, 214,218,224-225,232,234,238-239, 243,249,252-256,259,268,276,281-283,286-287,298,302
  executive sessions of 73-92,116
  primary purpose of 56-58,80
  staff 9,37,58,63,207,220,269
Warren, Earl 8,29,56,58,61,71,74, 76-81,83-92,152,156,207-208,225-226,254
Warren Report 8-11,13,31,37,59,61-63,70,207,220,236,244,255,259-264,282-283,293,295,297
Washington Post 13,69,259
Watergate 17,31,71,100,105,228, 233,244,256,276,280
Webster, Robert 136,223
Wecht, Cyril 268
Weeden, Ronny 276
Weinberg, James 138
Weisberg, Harold 54,59,73,187,192, 201,209,239,246,257,262,284,299
Weiss, Mark 11,203,289
Weitzman, Seymour 54,162
West, Robert 61,238
Western Union (Ruby telegram) 152
Weston, Walter 142,155-156
White, Roscoe 227

Index

Whitewash (Weisberg) 246
Whitewash IV (Weisberg) 73
Who Shot Kennedy (NOVA) 259
Wicker, Tom 259
Wiener, Irwin 145
Willens, Howard 78
Williams, Dr. Phillip 267
Willis, Bill 156
Willis, Phil, 182,242,269
Wilner, Jack 139-140
Witnesses 8-9,15,25-26,28,41,54,59-61,93,152,155,159,164, 215,241-243,268-269,298
  deaths of 264,273-280
Wooden fence (see Fence)
Woodward, Mary 61
Worrell, James Jr. 199,275
Wounds
  Connally's 23,37,50.179,187, 194-196,205,212-213,285-288
  Kennedy's
    back 34-35-38,50,58,60,65, 173-178,182,191-192,210-213,237-238,287,298,300
    throat 23,35-38,47,50-51,65, 172,178,182,192,200-201,209, 210-213,237,243,286,288,298
    head 23,38-39,41,44-51,180-181, 195,202,215,236,238,258,265, 267,2 97-298
  Tague's 21,172,182,194,238
Wright, Mr. & Mrs. Frank 25,169, 222
Wright, O. P. 24,164,192-193,195, 204
X-rays (see Autopsy)
Yaras, David 145,276
Yarborough, Sen. Ralph 19
Yatskov, Pavel 293
Zapruder, Abraham 21-22,172,243
Zapruder film 12,14,22,30,47,50,66, 172,180,182-183,186,188,192,194-195,209-210,213-214,236,238,258, 264,265,270,285
ZR/RIFLE 101
Zuckerman, Ben 138,145

It's Time For the Truth!

ACKNOWLEDGMENTS

I would like to thank all those who assisted me in one way or another in producing this book.

Laura Shinn who designed the front and back covers and enhanced several of the illustrations.

The late John Davis, author of *Mafia Kingfish*, who read my manuscript, called it "definitely publishable," and told me to keep trying.

Jim Marrs, author of *Crossfire*, who read my manuscript and told me it was both very readable and "right on the money."

Pamela Painter, who edited one of the early drafts and taught me how a book should be structured.

Debra Conway, of JFK Lancer, who supplied some of the research materials from her vast array of JFK documents and photos.

Then there are those who read drafts at various stages and provided feedback in the way of typographical corrections, suggested additions or deletions, ideas to improve the overall structure of the text, and just plain encouragement to keep fighting the good fight. For privacy reasons, I will include only their first names but they know to whom I refer.

Sam, Steve (MD.), Mike, Gary, Lucille, Rick, and Steve, thank you for taking the time to read my work, even when you may not have started with a high level of interest in the topic:

It's Time For the Truth!

Charles Hurlburt is an eighty-one-year-old former software engineer. He lives in Westborough Massachusetts with his wife of thirty-seven years, Ruth (nee Hebert). He plays tennis a couple of times a week and is an avid puzzle solver. He has pursued the answers to the puzzle of the assassination of President Kennedy since 1966. His background and qualifications for writing on this subject are defined in the Introduction.

It's Time For the Truth!